An ARTHURIAN READER

A selection of lost classics from Arthurian literature.

THE MOST ANCIENT AND FAMOVS HISTORY OF THE RENOWNED *PRINCE* ARTHVR

King of *Britaine,*

The firſt Part.

Wherein is declared his Life and Death, *with all his glorious Battailes againſt the* Saxons, Saracens *and* Pagans, which (for the honour of his Country) he moſt wor- thily achieued.

As alſo, all the Noble Acts, and Heroicke Deeds of his Valiant KNIGHTS of the ROVND TABLE.

Newly refined, and publiſhed for the delight, and profit of the READER.

LONDON,

Printed by *William Stansby,*

for *Iacob Bloome,* 1634.

An ARTHURIAN READER

Selections from Arthurian Legend, Scholarship and Story

Selected and edited by
John Matthews

The Aquarian Press
An Imprint of HarperCollins*Publishers*

The Aquarian Press
An Imprint of HarperCollins*Publishers*
77-85 Fulham Palace Road,
Hammersmith, London W6 8JB

First published by The Aquarian Press 1988
This paperback edition 1991
3 5 7 9 10 8 6 4 2

A catalogue record for this book
is available from the British Library

ISBN 0 85030 909 3

Typeset by MJL Limited,
Hitchin, Hertfordshire

Printed and bound in Great Britain by
Mackays of Chatham PLC, Kent

Dedication

For Kathleen Raine,
Guardian of the Perennial Wisdom

Acknowledgements

To Caitlín, as always, for typing, collating and all those other little jobs I was too lazy to do.
To August Closs for permission to reprint the essay by Hannah Closs.
To all the friends and colleagues who sent me rare and out of the way books and occasionally scoured the bookshops of the land for others.
To Simon Franklin for faith in the idea.
To Emrys for letting me get on now and then.

Contents

Introduction

Over a period of some 20 years researching the Matter of Britain in all its aspects, a large amount of fascinating material has come my way. Much of its remains little known beyond the specialist fields of Arthurian and Celtic scholarship, or else has been forgotten or ignored through the passage of time, which has sometimes made it seem to be superseded by more up to date scholarly work.

In many cases however, the researches of such early writers as Jessie Weston, A.E. Waite or W.S. Glennie are far from being made redundant by more recent trends and fashions in scholarship. Their theories have sometimes remained unchallenged or neglected for many years, and part of the object of the present collection is to bring them once again into public circulation, where they can be dusted off, examined and discussed by a new generation of Arthurians.

The other purpose behind the editing of such a collection is to offer the interested reader a cross-section through the intricate and sometimes daunting world of the Arthurian Mythos. To be faced, as I was when I first began to investigate Arthur back in the 1960s, with a subject so vast that current bibliographies list over 12,000 titles, ranging from the highly specialized to the popular, can be a prospect guaranteed to unsettle the most avid reader. Where, after all, does one begin?

In the selection of material which follows, I have tried to give as broad a slice of the cake as possible. Here are speculations both scholarly and esoteric, well set about with footnotes or containing some astonishing undocumented flights of fancy. Both belong in the total spectrum of the mythos. Here also is the most recent dimension of all, the new story-tellers and poets who have helped keep alive the ancient traditions by retelling the famous tales or adding to the already vast heritage their own insights, dreams and visions.

Together with *The Grail Seeker's Companion* (Aquarian Press, 1987) it is hoped to form a basis for further study among those who hold the Inner History of these islands to be of the greatest importance.

The Matter of Britain is a theme of incredible richness, and here is only a small sample of the wealth that lies in store for those who wish to seek further. A list for further reading can be found at the back of this volume to aid such seekers in their quest 'beyond the blue Septentrions'. May their own work bear fruit in the years to come.

John Matthews
London, September 1987

PART ONE: THE MATTER OF BRITAIN

Chapter 1.

The Finding of Merlin

by Harold Massingham

Perhaps the most perennial character amongst those who people the Arthurian world is Merlin. As Arthur's councillor he is a cunning statesman, while to all who oppose the young king he is a wily and implacable enemy. As a mage he is a wise and miraculous purveyor of wonders, and as a prophet he guides the destinies of those who cross his path. Yet his origins are mysterious, the source of his power seemingly unknowable, and his ending, like that of Arthur, is obscure.

Harold Massingham, a respected antiquarian who wrote one of the best early accounts of Prehistoric Man, as well as numerous books on the history of the countryside, wrote his witty and penetrating book *Fe, Fi, Fo, Fum* in 1926. Though he set out primarily to discuss the early legends of the giants who were said to have inhabited this country in the distant past, Massingham's researches lead him inevitably to Merlin, whom he saw as a precursor of the earliest settlers in this land. In so doing he said some very interesting and original things about the old mage.

Nowadays, Massingham's historical theories are considered dated, modern computer archaeology having overtaken him; yet many of his insights are still of value, and his account of Merlin shows that his understanding of the mythos of this country was more than just scholarly. Just how much this was so we can judge from the following quotation, also from *Fe, Fi, Fo, Fum*:

'I cannot sufficiently express my gratitude to the great sorcerer whom I have hunted through Fairyland ... until at last, taking pity on ... the winded huntsman, he came to meet me, magnanimously delivered himself and revealed at last the magical secret of his identity ... He told me the way into Fairyland through the stone chambers of the mound, of how to read romance as history and history as romance ... and many other things worth the telling ... but when I turned to him at the end of his narrative ... [he] had disappeared through the chamber of the mound whereon we were seated and gone back to Fairyland...'

Few commentators can have had so unusual an induction into the mythos. Whether or not we accept Massingham's theories of Merlin's origin, we cannot help but be fascinated by its author's unique approach.

THE BUILDING OF STONEHENGE

One of the stories in the Mabinogion relates how King Lludd (who gave his name to Ludgate Hill) overcame two dragons that fought one another

and turned England upside down.[1] He stupified them with mead,
shut them up in a magic cauldron, and buried them in a cist on Snowdon at a place called Dinas Emrys between Beddgelert and Capel Curig.
Five centuries later, Vortigern took refuge in Snowdon and began to
build a tower at Dinas Emrys itself. But whatever he built in the day-
time always fell down in the night. The wizards that he consulted
informed him that his tower would never stand unless he could find
a child without a father and sprinkle the tower with his blood. So Vortigern despatched his messengers into all parts of the kingdom and at
length they found Merlin who was a child without a father. Him Vortigern made ready to sacrifice, but the boy caused the foundations of
the tower to be dug, and there they found the red and white dragons
sleeping. The two dragons (the mead having worked off) immediately
began to fight one another, and then Merlin proceeded to deliver his
celebrated 'prophecies' to Vortigern concerning the defeat of the Britons by the Saxons.

This is the story told by Nennius[2] who wrote between the 8th and
the 10th centuries, but the Chronicle of Geoffrey of Monmouth (*Histories of the Kings of Britain,* written in the 12th century) gives a fuller
account of the same story. According to him, Merlin was found at Carmarthen owing to a youth named Dalbutius tanting him with his
bastardy.

> 'At that word the messengers lifted up their faces, and looking narrowly
> at Merlin, asked the bystanders who he might be. They told him that none
> knew his father but that his mother was the daughter of the king of Deme-
> tia, and that she lived along with the nuns in St Peter's church in that
> same city.'

Accordingly, his mother was fetched to Vortigern and revealed the secret
of her son's parentage, a secret I shall keep to myself until the proper
place for disclosing it. The rest of the narrative is as in Nennius, except
that more space is devoted to the confounding of the official wizards,
and that the dragons are described as sleeping in two hollow stones.
Giraldus Cambrensis also gives Dinas Emrys as the scene of Merlin's
prophecies to Vortigern.

Another of the Merlin stories in Geoffrey of Monmouth makes him
the engineer of Stonehenge. 'After giving it all the attention I can,' writes
Prof. Rhys,[3] 'I have come to the conclusion that we cannot do better
than follow the story of Geoffrey which makes Stonehenge the work
of Merlin.' This time Merlin is associated not with King Vortigern but
Aurelius. After his victory over the Saxons, Aurelius rebuilt the churches
that had been destroyed by them. He was also moved to set up a very
different type of building to commemorate the dead. Whereupon he
summoned Merlin, and Merlin counselled him to fetch 'the Dance of
the Giants that is in Killaraus, a mountain in Ireland'.

Figure 1: 'Merlin and Nimue' by Dora Curtis.

> 'For a structure of stones is there that none of this age could raise save
> his wit were strong enough to carry his art. For the stones be big, nor
> is there stone anywhere of more virtue, and so they be set up round this
> plot in a circle, even as they be now there set up, here shall they stand
> for ever.'

Aurelius makes merry over this proposal and Merlin answers him:

> 'Laugh not so lightly, King . . . For in these stones is a mystery and a
> healing virtue against many ailments. Giants of old did carry them from
> the furthest ends of Africa, did set them up in Ireland what time they
> did inhabit therein. . . '

So the Britons took an army, set sail and came to Mt Killaraus. But
though they were able to defeat the defenders of the circle, neither their
wit nor their stength availed 'to fetch down the Dance'. 'And when
they were all weary and spent, Merlin burst out on laughing and put
together his own engines,' and laid them down 'so lightly as none would
believe.' So the stones were fetched over the water—those self-same blue-
stones which the mineralogists of today say were brought not from
Ireland but from the Prescelly Mountains of Pembrokeshire—to make
the circles of Stonehenge before the setting up of the great trilithons.

One could hardly find a clearer example of an attempt to put a meaning to, to make a story out of, to rationalize, a mighty temple of the
men of old that had come down without a definite history, but with
shreds of tradition, to a people whose ways were not their ways. Aurelius,
following his victory, rebuilds the churches devastated by the Saxons,
and as a memorial of the same event sets up a temple of the heathen
upon the counsel of an enchanter whose birth is not as other men's,
who knows these stones possess mysterious virtue, and who fetches
them from a distance as in actuality we know that they were fetched.
The archaic civilization has become attached to the wars between the
Celts and the Saxons like an old beam used in the construction of a
new building. How easy to distinguish that beam from the rest of the
ceiling to which it is neither essential nor appropriate!

THE LIVING DEATH OF MERLIN

The quest of Merlin now takes us to the fourth book of the *Morte d'Arthur*, where the distinguished necromancer falls into a dotage upon
one of the damosels of the Lake, hight Nimue. She was one of those
by no means unfamiliar damsels who prefer a commonplace young hero
to a spell-binder of the intellectual calibre of Merlin. Also she was
afeared of him 'because he was a devil's son and she could not beskift
him by no means'. So to rid herself of his solicitations she induced him
to enter a dolmen in Cornwall 'wrought by enchantment' and there
to a *living death* she left him for ever.

From Cornwall to Marlborough will we go, as the Ancient Mariners

went before us. Five miles from Mount Silbury, and like it, on the banks
of the Kennett, there is a huge chalk pyramid in the grounds of Marlborough College. The Roman road which diverts its course to avoid
Silbury pays the same compliment to Merlin's Barrow. The name of
Marlborough originated in Merlin's Barrow according to Walter of
Coventry (1070), to Domesday Book, to Camden's translation of Neck-
ham's couplet in 'De laudibus divinæ sapientiæ' (1586).

> 'Great Merlin's Grave
> The name to Marlborough in Saxon gave.'

The earliest arms of Marlborough were 'a castle argent upon a field
sable' with the legend round the shield, 'Ubi nunc sapientis ossa Merlini?' The sceptical reader when he expects me to arrive at the apocalyptic finale of placing the *ossa Merlini*[4] beneath the Marlborough
mound, forgets that he has already been buried in Cornwall. There is
also a tomb of Merlin in Brittaany in the forest of Brécelande, and yet
another in the Isle of Sein where he was both born and immortally imprisoned. Pomponius Mela says of the Isle that it once had an oracle with
attendant priestesses who could cure diseases and raise storms. They
at once remind us of the Donegal witches and their sacred stones that
possessed the same powers—the Donegal witches who lived in earth-
works and were of gigantic stature. I need hardly say that there are
megaliths in the Isle of Sein. Merlin, be it remembered, was a greater
magician than Arthur who was buried in twenty different places. A
scepticism may quite legitimately demur at the derivation of Marlborough from Merlin's barrow, but it entirely fails to explain why tombs
which we know to have been raised by the megalith-builders should
have been honoured as the sepulchre of that supreme enchanter's
immortal remains.

THE POWERS OF MERLIN

Where now do we stand with Merlin? Wherever, like the Vice in the
old Comedie, he makes his totally irrelevant appearance upon the Celtic stage, he is dressed from head to foot in the old-fashioned clothes
of the megalithic period. He is decidedly *démodé*. Be begins as a destined victim of human sacrifice because he is a son without a father,
a garbled reminiscence of the old solar cult and its foundation sacrifices.
He is on such familiar terms with dragons that he can smell them out
from beneath the earth, and he knows all about their water-powers.
Not merely is he linked up with stone circles, but he is the architect
of Stonehenge, the unique temple of 'Bronze Age' Britain, whose magical and medicinal stones his expert knowledge of engineering causes
to be fetched from another country, whether that country be Ireland
or Wales. Again, he is a well of information about giants who origi-

nally brought the megalith-habit from Africa. Lastly, he is buried either under an earthen pyramid near the capital of archaic England (Avebury) or under a stone dolmen in the country where the long and round barrow men sought gold and copper and tin for their bronze.[5] He is buried but he dies not die, and the glorious immortality of the miner-mariners and the giant kings has degenerated into a living death.

Always he is credited with supernatural endowments: if his was no natural birth, so his were more than mortal faculties. The complex of magico-mythical beliefs embalmed in folk-memory and handed down, as I have so constantly insisted, from the towering reputation attaching to the archaic civilization, and the search for magical 'givers of life', are focused into his own proper person. Yet though he drifts into the chronicles of a later age, like a derelict galleon into an anchored fleet of comparatively modern warships, his abilities as an Arch-Medicine Man are neither random nor generalized. They are architectural, draconian, and calendrical, for, as Spenser and Geoffrey testify, he was one having authority over the sun and the moon, the night and the day, while other legends call him the Ruler of Heaven. In other words, he was a calendar maker, the earliest native embodiment of Old Moore's Almanac, and as such was following in the steps of Osiris of the lunar calendar and the later Pharoahs of the solar dynasties. His main preoccupations were with stone-working, agriculture (through irrigation and the watery empire of the dragon), and the heavenly bodies; and these elements are a triangular formula for the archaic civilization. Metallurgy is lacking, but that is the only flaw in his character. I admit it is a serious one.

Observe, too, his psychological discontinuity with the other actors in the romances and chronicles. He has no stake in the stories; cut him out and they make a distinct gain in homogeneity. He is a waif, an alien, a man born out of his time and among punier men than he, a Rip van Winkle who wakes into a new world after a sleep of hundreds of years, still trailing clouds of faded glory and escorted by dreams of the past. He is a king's daughter's son, but without aristocratic, much less princely rank. He is not even a salaried court-magician, but a king's councillor without a portfolio. In the grand style and with a wealth of symbolism drawn from his specialized draconian lore, he makes rapt prophesies about events that have already occurred. Evidently, he has journeyed so far upon his Time-Machine that his line of communications is broken, and he halts the car when he has passed the stage of phenomena concerning the coming of which he delivers so impressive an oration. Could there be testimony more manifest of the journey itself? Is it not plain that he is old wine poured into a new bottle, and that he belongs to a lineage, a society, an era more ancient than that of Iron?

The other figures in the old stories have at least a quasi-historical, a semi-realistic being, but Merlin comes from the clouds and passes across the scene still muffled in their cloak. It is now my business to try and show that he was just as historical as they were. A real man walked and breathed under the enchanted cloak, and it is by unclasping it ourselves that we shall discover who that man was. We have got him back into an older civilization than the Celtic; the next step is the part he played in it.

THE STROLLING MAGICIANS OF THE EAST

Since by now the reader must be thoroughly acclimatized to an atmosphere of magic, he will bear a sudden transportation to the Pacific. In Mr W. J. Perry's *The Children of the Sun*,[6] we are given example after example of the Islanders' traditions, first as to the transportation of sacred stones in the founding of one settlement after another; next as to the perfectly definite association of these stones with wonderful strangers who came from the sky-world, founded their lines of chiefs and priests, and taught them all their arts and crafts; and lastly as to the magical powers possessed by these 'culture-heroes'. The founders of Ponapé in the Carolines, which are full of megalithic monuments, came from Yap on stones that swam in the water.[7] These stones were inhabited by spirits (i.e. the deified ancestors of the Chiefs of Ponapé), who originally dropped down from the sky and turned into stones; and the gods could not be approached except through the medium of these stones, which were only to be found in certain places. If they were lacking from them, so was the cult of the gods. The stones possessed medicinal properties and other magical powers. So in Melanesia, sacred stones were petrified sky-beings. Opoa in Raiatea was the Avebury-cum-Silbury of Polynesia, the most sacred *maræ* or Pyramid-temple in all the Polynesian group. Thence stones were taken to other islands, where other *maræ* were set up. Throughout Polynesia, in fact, the sacred stones were 'derived from pre-existing settlements'. Lastly, in Indonesia, the founders of new villages took stones with them from their original homes, and thus from island to island preserved the continuity of specific culture and religious observance.

Thus sky-beings, the distribution of settlements, and magical properties are inseparable from the wanderings of sacred stones, and it is a fact worthy the attention of the theorists as to the spontaneous and independent origins of cultures that these stones invariably settled down in the neighbourhood of pearl and pearl-shell beds, gold mines, and other metalliferous regions. The sower from the sky-world went forth to sow, but he did not drop his stones by the wayside; and it is by his calculated movements, the uniformity of his actions, and the clues left upon his trail that we can decipher whence he came, whither he went, and what was the object of his travels.

The magical strangers in the Pacific were, in fact, the pioneers of civili-

zation in the East; and from their unparagoned achievements and the
magical beliefs and practices diffused by them arose the folk-tales and
traditions of their supernatural powers. Thus, the Phillippine Islanders
relate how the ancestors of their chiefs possessed special powers over
nature; they could transport themselves from one place to another
before you could say the Tinguian equivalent for Jack Robinson, they
could create men out of betel-nuts, control the weather and the heavenly
bodies, wither people they did not like, and were in various other
respects most accomplished graduates in the *literæ humaniores* of sorcery and enchantment. These magicians formed, indeed, an Interna-
tional Board of Thaumaturgy, for in Egypt, India, Polynesia, and North
America, they were endowed with almost exactly identical powers. They:

> 'by words could call out of the sky
> Both Sunne and Moone. . .
> Huge hostes of men they could alone dismay.
> And hostes of men of meanest things could frame.'

Their functions were creative (they animated stones into men), architectural, draconian (they are very frequently associated with 'water-
monsters'), and calendrical. They were mainly concerned with stone-
working, agriculture, and the heavenly bodies, and through them all
with 'givers of life'. In one labour-saving word, they were the Merlins
of the East; and we can after all heal the flaw in Merlin's character,
since through stones, dragons, and his own life-giving powers, he was,
though indirectly, a spright of metallurgy.

But who were the strolling magicians? The answer is a life-giving one
in itself: they were sons without a father, Lasaeo, the stranger-lord of
the Celebean Toradja, Lumawig of the Philippine Bontoc, Oro of Raiatea,
Tane of the Maories, Tangaroa of Mangaia, Sa Tagaloa of Samoa, Zamna
of Yucatan, Dravidian Karna.[8] These and many others with less mel-
lifluous names were sons without a father, because their male parent
was the Sun. They were the ancestor-gods of the peoples whose ruling
houses they founded, the stone-heroes, the metal-hunters, the seekers
after the gift of life, the Children of the Sun, the sowers that sowed
the seeds of civilization on stony ground, the makers of rain and sunshine like the kings of Egypt, the masters of magic, the kings with their
cultural merchandise, the Ancient Mariners of the Pacific whose oars
broke the silence of the furthest seas. It might be urged that in burning out the mythical prowess from these heroes, one had reduced them
to ashes. But surely in measuring them down to reality, we have height-
ened their romance. Pure myth is tedious because it is too far removed
from human experience and gods are a poor substitute for men.

A last leaving of England before we sum up. Alfred Nutt in the *Revue
Celtique*[9] has shown that the Irish magician, Aengus, was yet another
of these boys without a father, and if we turn back to Prof. Rhys, we

shall find him insisting upon the resemblances between the Mac Oc (Aengus) and the Merlin legends. Now the Man Oc was not only associated with stones but with the Fir-Bolg, the pre-Celtic colonists of Ireland. One of the feats of Merlin was to go to sea in a magic house of glass, and he is known in the Triads as the 'Divine and Immortal One of the Stronghold of the Sea'. The Fir-Bolg were kings of a kingdom under the sea.

Prof. Rhys, again, calls the Mac Oc 'the representative of the Aryan Zeus in his *original* character of god of the sun'. The stories of him, he adds, 'belonged originally to Irish mythology before any Celts had settled in Ireland.' I have emphasized the word 'original' because it is very important to distinguish the Irish representative of Merlin from the Goidelic heroes. They were connected with the sun in a *new* character, which has very little to do with the sun at all, or Merlin-Mac Oc in *his* original character. It is evident we are getting warm. Or turn to the traditions of Brugh na Boinne of which the megalithic tumuli of New Grange and Dowth form a part. It was called the 'House of Aengus' who was the 'Presiding Fairy of the Boyne'. Celtic Finn says after the death of Diarmid, 'Let us leave this tulach for fear that Aengus and the Tuatha De Danann might catch us.' Aengus is also said to have the power of sending a soul into the dead Diarmid so that he had become a supernatural being when the Celtic heroes ruled the land. We read, again, in the Leabhar na h-Uidhri, a non-ecclesiastical MS. of the 11th century[10] that the nobles and kings of the Tuatha and the Fir-Bolg were buried at Brugh, which was likewise the cemetery of the kings of Tara. Discredit these legends? Well, Minos himself was a legend before he became historical.

THE MAGIC BIRTH OF MERLIN

And now what has Geoffrey of Monmouth to say about the illegitimacy of Merlin? When his mother, the King's daughter, was brought from her nunnery before Vortigern, he enquired of her:

> '"Who was the father of the lad?" "One thing only I know," replied the lady, "that one appeared unto me in the shape of a right comely youth, and embracing me full straitly in his arms did kiss me, and after that he had abided with me some little time did suddenly vanish away so that nought more did I see of him." Amazed at her words the king commanded that Maugantius should be called unto him, and when he had heard the story, he said unto Vortigern: "In the books of our wise men and in many histories I have found that many men have been born into the world in this wise. For . . . certain spirits there be betwixt the moon and the earth, the which we do call incubus demons. These have a nature that doth partake both of men and angels, and whensoever they will they do take upon them the shape of men, and do hold converse with mortal women."'

Merlin in short was one of the Children of the Sun.[11] To understand the full purport of this derivation, I would ask the reader to [understand] that the rise of the Children of the Sun to power followed upon the inspiration of the priests of Heliopolis in propounding the theory that the Pharoahs were gathered to their father Rê after death. The new idea was that the Pharoah was born of Rê, the Sun God, by a virgin of royal birth, and the dissemination of this idea corresponded with a profound political revolution. Henceforth the kings of the ancient East were the Sons of the Sun. Hercules and other of the Argonauts were of this lineage, and the evidence suggests that it was their descendants who introduced the full sun-cult to Western Europe. The reason why I have sought the Pacific for parallels to Merlin is because there is no evidence of any carriage of civilization antecedent to them and no confusion in consequence between the 'Neolithic' and the Bronze Ages.

The evidence appears to me to be clear that Merlin[12] was one of the divine kings of Britain probably of the second or Bronze Age megalithic period, that his memory survived into the Bronze and Iron Ages of the Celts, and was finally crystallized in the monkish chronicles. But, absorbing as the interest of him in these records is, we have not yet exhausted it. It is remarkable how faithfully they reproduce the details of the Sun-paternity myths. Though it appears only a minor incident, the nunnery portion of the narrative is one of the surest clues of identification. The story of Danæ in her tower visited by the sun-god in a shower of gold is an obvious parallel; the Incas of Peru shut up their daughters in convents right up to the arrival of Pizarro; and analogies from other parts of the world are abundant.

But there is one very significant difference between the Oriental and the English accounts of the parentage of the Children of the Sun. The father of Merlin is no longer the sun-god but an incubus demon, a supernatural being of a status between men and angels. A clearer case of degeneration could hardly be found, and the incubus demon is plainly another version of the giants who. . .were degenerate gods. 'There were giants in the earth in those days: and also after that when the sons of God came in unto the daughters of men and they bare children unto them; the same became mighty men, which were of old, men of renown.' Lastly, we can link up these inferences with the fact that when the Celts began to move westward, the sun-god, as among other warrior nomads, had disappeared and been amalgamated with his lineal descendant, the war-god. The heathen Celts possessed innumerable relics of solar ritual in their religion, but they were not authentic sunworshippers.

The one remaining difficulty seems to me to be, Where did Merlin come from? If he was the builder of Stonehenge, then his ancestors (and possibly he himself) were the ancestors of the House of Atreus, who were buried in the shaft-graves of Mycenæ. For, as I have discussed in another book (Downland Man), there is strong evidence for making Mycenæ the parent of the early Bronze Age in Britain, while the

Stonehenge Trilithons exactly resemble the Lion-gate of Mycenæ. He
was at any rate the first king of Britain of whom we have any record.
In the First Triad we read that Britain's first name was Clas Myrdin
or Merlin's Close. Thus can we restore a son to his father and a king
to his kingdom.

[1] The red and white dragons symbolizing the wars between the Britons and the
Saxons. These, as I have pointed out, are the colours of Upper and Lower Egypt.
[2] *Six Old English Chronicles*, edited by J. A. Giles (1848).
[3] *Lectures on the Origin and Growth of Religion as Illustrated by Celtic Heathendom* (1892).
[4] Compare the stories of the relics of Buddha and Osiris also found in different
places and made the goals of pilgrimages.
[5] See my *Downland Man* (1926) for fuller details of this statement.
[6] Methuen, 1923.
[7] One of the stories in the Mabinogion is of a huge sarcophagus, which ten yoke of
oxen could not move from its place. It was conveyed across the sea at the bidding of
a Saint, and reached the opposite shore without crew, pilot, or captain.
[8] 'The son of the Sun by a royal maiden', *Mahabharata*.
[9] 'Les Derniers Travaux Allemandee sur la Legend du Saint Graal' *Revue Celtique*
XII (1891).
[10] See *New Grange* (1924), by George Coffey, the Keeper of Antiquities in the Dub-
lin Museum.
[11] The Birth of St Brendan: 'Now the mother of Brendan saw a vision before he was
born. It seemed to her that her bosom was full of pure gold [like Danæ's] and that
her paps shone like snow. When she told this to Bishop Erc, he said that a wondrous
birth would be born to her, who would be full of the grace of the Holy Spirit, meaning
Brendan.' St Brendan was, in fact, Bran, who made the voyage to the Isles of the Blest,
from which were excluded all but the Children of the Sun. The quotation is from Revd
C. Plummer's *Lives of the Irish Saints*, and is given in Mr Perry's *Origin of Magic and
Religion* (Methuen, 1923), page 91.
[12] Doctor Gaster in a paper published in *Folk-Lore*, Vol. XVI, has cited numerous
oriental parallels to the story of the tower and the boy without a father.

Chapter 2.
Merlin and Grisandole

Stories about Merlin which lie outside the scope of the Arthurian world are few, yet there are clear indications that his adventures in the time of Arthur are only the latest in a life whose beginning is not always easy to account for. In particular the stories mention several forays abroad during and after the period of Arthur's coming of age. The present story comes from this period, and tells an amusing story which shows Merlin extending his sway beyond the realm of Britain. It comes from a vast and prolix text known as The English Merlin which is a very early translation of the old French text which became part of the Vulgate Cycle, a vast collection compiled in the 13th Century by Cistercian clerics. I have chosen not to modernize the spelling or punctuation since this detracts considerably from the charm and character of the story; however glosses of unusual or difficult words will be found in the footnotes to help the reader unaccustomed to Mediaeval English. Reading the text aloud can also make more impenetrable passages intelligible. My own retelling of this story, as Merlin himself might have told it, can be found in The Second Book of Merlin edited by R. J. Stewart (Blandford Press, 1988).

❦❧

As soone as Merlin was departed from Arthur, he wente in to the forestes of Rome that were thikke and depe, and in that tyme Julyus Cesar was Emperour; but it was not that Julyus Cesar that the deed knyght slough in his pavilion of Perce. But it was that Julius that Gawein, the newev of kynge Arthur, slough in bateile vnder Logres at the grete disconfiture that after was be-twene hym and the kynge Arthur that hym diffied, and what the cause was that Merlin wente that wey, it is reson it be declared. This is throuthe that this Julyus Cezar hadde a wif that was of grete bewte, and she hadde with hir xij[1] yonge men araied in gise of wymen, with whom she lay at alle tymes that the Emperour was oute of hir companye, ffor she was the most lecherouse woman of all Rome; and for the dredde that theire beerdes sholde growe she lete a-noynte her chynnes with certeyn oynementes made for the nones, and thei wre clothed in longe traylinge robes, and theire heer longe waxen, in gise of maydenes and tressed at theire bakkes, that alle that hem saugh wende wele thei were wymen; and longe thei endured with the Empress vn-knowen.

In this tyme that the Emperesse ledde this lif, it fill that a mayden com to the Emperours court that was the doughter of a prince, and

the name of this prince was matan, Duke of Almayne; this mayden
com in semblannce of a squyer, and this matan the Duke Frolle hadde
disherited and driven out of his londe, and she com to serue[2] the
Emperour, ffor she wiste not where her fader ne moder were be comen,
and she was moche and semly, and well shapen and demened hir well
in all maners that a man ought, saf only eny vylonye, and neuer was
she knowen but for a man by no semblante, and so a-boode with the
Emperour, and was of grete prowesse, and peyned tendirly to serue well
the Emperour and plesed hym so well that she was lorde and gouer-
nour of hym and his housolde; and the Emperour hir loved so well
that he made hir knyght atte a feeste of seint John with other yonge
squyers, wher-of were mo than CC,[3] and after made hir stiward of all
his londe. Than the newe knyghtes reised a quyntayne in the mede of
Noiron, and be-gonne the bourdinge[4] grete and huge, and many ther
were that dide right wele, but noon so well as dide Grisandoll, for so
she lete hir be cleped; but in bapteme her name was Anable. This bourdinge endured all day on ende till euesonge that thei departed, and
Grisandols bar a-wey the pris a-monge alle other, and whan the
Emperour saugh Grisandoll of so grete prowesse, he made hym stiward
of all his londe and comaunder a-bove alle that ther weren, and Grisandols was well beloved of riche and pore.

  And vpon a nyght after it fill that the Emperour lay in his chamber
with the Emperesse; and whan he was a-slepe he hadde a vision that
hym thought he saugh a sowe in his court that was right grete be-fore
his paleys, and he hadde neuer seyn noon so grete ne so huge, and
she hadde so grete bristelis on her bakke that it trayled on the grounde
a fadome large, and hadde vpon hir heed a cercle that semed of fyn
golde, and whan the Emperour a-vised hym wele hym thought that
he hadde seyn hir other tymes, and that he hadde hir norisshed vp;
but he durste not sey of trouthe that she were hys, and while he
entended to a-vise hym on this thinge he saugh come oute of his chamber xij lyonsewes,[5] and com in to the courte to the sowe, and assailed
hir oon after a-nother, whan the Emperour saugh this merveile he asked
his Barouns what sholde he do with this sowe by whom these lyonsewes hadde thus leyn, and thei seide she was not worthi to be conuer-
saunt a-monge peple, ne that no man sholde ete nothinge that of hir
come, and Iuged[6] hir to be brente,[7] and also the lyonsewes to-geder;
and than a-wooke the Emperour sore affraied and pensif of this a-vision.
Ne neuer to man ne to wif wolde he it telle, for he was full of grete
wisdom. On the morowe as soone as he myght se the day, he a-roos
and yede to the mynster to here messe, and whan he was come a-gein
he fonde the barouns assembled, and hadde herde messe at the mynster and the mete was all redy; and whan thei hadde waisshen thei satte
to mete, and were well serued. Than fill that the Emperour fill in to
a grete stodye, wher-fore all the courte was pensif and stille, and ther

was noon that durste sey a worde for sore thei dredde for to wrathe the Emperour. But now we moste turne a litill to Merlin that was come in to the foreste of Romayne to certefie these thinges and these a-visiouns.

While that the Emperour satte at his mete a-monge his Barouns thus pensif, Merlin come in to the entre of Rome and caste an enchauntement merveilouse, ffor he be-com an herte the gretteste and the moste merveilouse that eny man hadde seyn, and hadde oon of his feet be-fore white, and hadde v braunches in the top, the grettest that euer hadde be seyn, and than he ran thourgh Rome so faste as all the worlde hadde hym chaced, and whan the peple saugh hym so renne, and saugh how it was an herte the noyse a-roos, and the cry on alle partyes, and ronne after grete and small with staves and axes, and other wepen, and chaced hym thourgh the town, and he com to the maister gate of the paleys where-as the Emperour satte at his mete, and whan thei that serued herde the noyse of the peple, thei ronne to the wyndowes to herkene what it myght be, and a-noon thei saugh come rennynge the herte and all the peple after; and whan the herte com to the maister paleys he drof in at the yate sodeynly, and than he ran thourgh the tables a bandon and tombled mete and drynke all on an hepe, and be-gan ther-in a grete trouble of pottis and disshes; and whan the herte hadde longe turned ther-ynne he com be-fore the Emperour, and kneled and seide, 'Julius Cezar, Emperour of Rome, wheron thinkest thow, lete be thi stodyinge for it a-vaileth nought, ffor neuer of thyne a-vision shalt thow not knowe the trouthe be-fore that man that is sauage the certefie, and for nought as it that thow stodyest ther-on eny more.'

Than the herte hym dressed and saugh the yate of the paleyse cloos, and he caste his enchauntement that alle the dores and yates of the paleise opened so rudely that thei fly alle in peces, and the herte lept oute and fledde thourgh the town, and the chace be-gan a-gein after hym longe till that he com oute in to the playn feeldes; and than he dide vanysshe that noon sey where he be-com, and than thei returned a-gein, and whan the Emperour wiste the herte was ascaped he was wroth and lete crye thourgh the londe that who that myght brynge the sauage man or the herte sholde haue his feire doughter to wif, and half his reame, yef that he were gentill of birthe, and after his deth haue all; and lepe to horse many a vailaunt knyght and squyer of pris, and serched and sought thourgh many contrees, but all was for nought, ffor neuer cowde thei heere no tidinges of that thei sought, and whan thei myght no more do thei returned a-gein. But euer Grisandols serched thourgh the forestes, oon hour foreward, another bakke that so endured viij[8] dayes full; and on a day as Grisandol was a-light vnder an oke for to praye oure lorde to helpe and to spede for to fynde that he sought, and as he was in is prayours the herte that hadde ben at Rome com be-fore hym and seide, 'Auenble,[9] thow chacest folye, ffor thow maist not spede of thy queste in no maner, but I shall telle the what thow shalt do. Purchese flessh newe and salt, and mylke and hony, and hoot breed newe bake, and bringe with the foure felowes, and a boy to turne the spite till it be I-nough rosted, and com in to this foreste by the moste vn-couthe weyes that thow canste fynde, and sette a table by the fier, and the breed, and the mylke, and the hony vpon the table, and hide the and thi companye a litile thens, and doute the nought that the sauage man will come.'

Than ran the herte a-grete walope thourgh the foreste, and Grisandol lept to horse and thought well on that the herte hadde seide and thought in his corage that it was somme spirituell thinge that by hir right name hadde hir cleped,[10] and thought well that of this thinge sholde come some merveile; and Grisandol rode forth to a town nygh the foreste vij myle, and toke ther that was myster, and com in to the foreste ther as he hadde spoke with the herte as soone as he myght, and roode in to the deepe of the foreste, where-as he fonde a grett oke full of leves, and the place semed delitable, and he a-light and sette theire horse fer thens, and made a grete fier, and sette the flesshe to roste, and the smoke and the sauour spredde thourgh the foreste, that oon myght fele the sauour right fer; and than sette the table be the fier, and whan all was redy thei hidde hem in a bussh.

And Merlin that all this knewe and that made all this to be don couertly that he were not knowen drough that wey that he were not knowen with a grete staffe in his nekke smytinge grete strokes from oke to oke, and was blakke and rough for rympled and longe berde, and bar-foote, and clothed in a rough pilche;[11] and so he com to the fier, ther as the flessh was rosted, and whan the boy saugh hym come he was so a-ferde that he fledde nygh oute of his witte; and he this com to the fier and be-gan to chacche and frote a-boute the fier, and saugh the mete and than loked all a-boute hym and be-gan to rore lowde as a man wood oute of mynde, and than be-heilde, and saugh the cloth spredde and soche mete ther-on as ye haue herde, and after he be-heilde towarde the fier, and saugh the flesshe that the knaue hadde rosted that was tho I-nough, and raced of it with his hondes madly, and rente it a-sonder in peces, and wette it in mylke, and after in the hony, and ete as a wood man that nought ther lefte of the flessh; and than he eete of the hoot breed and hony that he was full and swollen grete, and somwhat was it colde, and he lay down by the fier and slepte; and whan Grisandol saugh he was on slepe she and hir felowes com as softely as thei myght, and stale a-wey his staffe, and than thei bounde hym with a cheyne of Iren streytely a-boute the flankes, and than delyuered hym to oon of the companye by the tother ende of the cheyne; and whan he was so well bounde he a-wooke and lept vp lightly, and made semblaunt to take his staff as a wilde man, and Grisandolus griped hym in his armes right sore and hilde hym stille, and whan he saugh hym so bounde and taken, he hilde hym as shamefaste and mate; and than the horse were brought forth and he was sette vpon oon of hem, and bounden to the sadell with two bondes, and a man sette be-hynde hym that was bounde to hym and enbraced hym by the myddill, and so thei rode forth her wey, and the sauage man loked on Grisandolus that rode by hym, and be-gan to laugh right harde, and whan Grisandolus saugh hym laughe he approched ner and rode side by side, and a-queynted with hym the beste that he myght, and enquered and asked many thinges, but he ne wolde nought ansuere, and Grisandol asked why he lough, but he wolde not telle. Saf that he seide, 'Creature formed of nature chaunged in to other forme fro hens-forth be-gilynge alle thinges venimouse as se[r]pent, holde thi pees, for nought will I telle the till that I com be-fore the Emperoure.'

With that the sauage man hilde his pees and spake no more, and rode forth to-geder, and Grisandolus of this that he hadde seide spake to his companye, and thei seide that he was wiser than he shewed, and that som grete merveile sholde falle in the londe. Thus thei ride spekynge of many thinges till thei passede be-fore an abbey, and saugh be-fore the yate moche pore peple a-bidinge almesse, and than the sauage man lowgh[12] right lowde; and than Grisandol com toward hym and swetly praide hym to telle wherfore he lough, and he loked proudly on trauerse, and seide, 'Ymage repaired and disnatured fro kynde, holde thy pees, ne enquere no mo thinges for nought will I telle the but be-fore the Emperour;' and whan Grisandolus this vndirstode, he lete hym be at that tyme and no more thinge hym asked, and here-of spake thei in many maners.

Thus thei ride forth all day till nyght, and on the morowe till the hour of prime, and fill that thei passed by-fore a chapell where a preste was toward masse, and fonde a knyght and a squyer heringe the seruyse; and whan Grisandolus saugh this, thei a-light alle the companye, and entred in to here the masse, and whan the knyght that was in the chapell saugh the man bounde with chaynes he hadde merveile what it myght be, and while the knyght be-heilde the man that was sauage, the squyer that was in an angle be-hynde the chapel dore come a-gein his lorde, and lifte yp his hande and yaf[13] hym soche a flap that alle thei in the chapell myght it here, and than returned thider as he com fro all shamefaste of that he hadde don, and whan he was come in to his place he ne rofte no-thinge, for the shame lasted no lenger; but while he was in returnynge, and whan the sauage man saugh this, he be-gan to laugh right harde, and the knyght that was so smyten was so a-baisshed that he wiste not what to sey but suffred; and Grisandolus and the other companye merveiled sore what it myght be. A-noon after the squyer com a-gein to his lorde, and yaf hym soche a-nother stroke as he dide be-fore, and wente a-gein in to his place, and the sauage man hym be-hilde and be-gan to laughe right harde, and yef the knyght be-fore were a-baisshed, he was than moche more, and the squyer that hadde hym smyten returned sorowfull and pensif to the place that he com fro, and hilde hym-self foule disceyved of that he hadde don, and whan he was in his place he rought neuer, and Grisandolus, and the companye mer-veiled right sore, and herden oute the seruise be leyser,[14] and in the mene while that thei thoughten vpon these thinges that thei hadde seyn, the squyer com the thridde tyme and smote his lorde sorer than he hadde don be-fore, and ther-at lowgh the wilde man sore, and be that was the masse at an ende, and than Grisandolus and alle wente oute of the chapell, and the squyer that hadde smyten his lorde com after and asked Grisandolus what man it was that thei hadde so bounde, and thei seide that thei were with Julius Cezar, Emperour of Rome, and ledde to hym that sauage man that thei hadde founded in the fore-ste, for to certefie of a vision that was shewed hym slepinge. 'But, sir,' seide Grisandolus, 'tell me wherefore hath this squyer yow smyten thre tymes, and ye ne spake no words a-gein, haue ye soche a custome,' and the knyght ansuerde that he sholde it wite in tyme comynge.

Than the knyght cleped his squyer and asked hym be-fore Grisando-lus wherefore he hadde hym smyten, and he was shamefaste, and seide he wiste neuer, but so it fill in his corage, and the knyght hym asked yef he hadde now eny talent hym for to smyte, and the squyer seide he hadde leuer be deed, 'but that,' quod he, 'it fill in my mynde that I myght not kepe me ther-fro,' and Grisandolus lough of the merveile. Than seide the knyght that he wolde go to court with hem for to here what the sauave man wolde sey, and with that thei rode forth on her wey, and Grisandolus by the sauage mannes side, and whan thei hadde a-while riden, he asked the wilde man wherfore he lough so thre tymes whan the squyer smote hir lorde, and he loked on hir a trauerse, and seide, 'Ymage repeyred, semblaunce of creature wherby men ben slayn and diffouled, rasour trenchaunt, ffountayne coraunt, that neuer is full of no springes holde thy pees, and nothinge of me enquere, but be-fore the Emperour, for nought will I telle the,' and whan that Grisan-dolus vndirstode the fell wordes that he spake, he was all a-baisshed and pensef, and durste not no more enquere, and rode forth till thei come to Rome, and whan thei entred in to the town, and the peple hem parceyved thei wente all a-geins hym for to se the man that was sauage, and the noyse was grete of the peple that folowed, and be-hilde his facion as longe as thei myght, and so thei conveyed hym to the paleise, and whan the Emperour herde the tidinges he com hem a-geins,

and mette with hem comynge vpon the greces, and than com Grisandolus be-fore the Emperour, and seide, 'Sir, haue here the man that
is sauage that I to yow here yelde, and kepe ye hym fro hens-forth for
moche peyne haue I hadde with hym,' and the Emperour seide he wolde
hem well guerdon,[15] and the man sholde be well kepte, and than he
sente to seche a smyth to bynde hym in chaynes and feteres, and the
sauage man badde hym ther-of not to entermete, 'ffor wite it right well,'
quod he, 'I will not go with-oute youre leve,' and the Emperour hym
asked how he ther-of sholde be sure, and he seide he wolde hym asur
by his cristyndome. Quod the Emperour, 'Art thow than cristin?' and
he seide, 'Ye with-oute faile,' 'How were thow than baptized,' seide the
Emperour, 'whan thow art so wilde.'

'That shall I telle yow,' quod he, 'This is the trouthe that my moder
on a day com from the market of a town, and it was late whan she
entred in to the foreste of Brocheland,[16] and wente oute her way so fer
that the same nyght be-hoved hir to lye in the foreste, and whan she
saugh she was so a-lone be hir-self she was a-feerde and lay down vnder
an oke and fill a-slepe, and than come a sauage man oute of the foreste and by hir lay, be-cause she was sool by hir-self. Durste she not
hym diffende, ffor a woman a-loone is feerfull, and that nyght was I
be-geten on my moder, and whan she was repeired hom, she was full
pensif longe tyme, till that she knewe verily that she was with childe,
and bar me so till I was born in to this worlde and was baptised in
a fonte, and dide me norishe till I was grete, and as soone as I cowde
lyve with-outen hir,[17] I wente in to the grete forestes for by the nature
of my fader be-houeth me thider to repeire, and for that he was sauage
I am thus wilde. Now haue ye herde what I am.'

'So god me helpe,' seide the Emperour, 'neuer for me shalt thow be
putte in feteres ne in Irenes seth thow wilt me graunte that thow will
not go with-oute my leve.' Than tolde Grisandolus how he dide laugh
be-fore the abbey and in the chapell, for the squyer that hadde smyten
his maister, and the dyuerse wordes that he hadde spoken, whan he
asked where-fore he dide laugh, and he seide that neuer wolde he
nought sey till he com be-fore yow, and now is he here, and therfore
aske hym why he hath so often laughed by the wey, and than the
Emperour hym asked, and he seide he sholde it knowe all in tyme, but
sendeth first for all youre barouns and than shall I tell yow that and
other thinges, with that entred the Emperour in to his chamber and
the sauage man and his prive counseile, and ther thei rested and dis-
ported, and spake of many thinges, and on the morowe the Emperour
sente to seche his barouns hem that he supposed sonest to fynde, and
than thei come a-noon bothe oon and other from alle partyes.

On the fourthe day after the sauage man was comen, where that the
lordes were assembled in the maister paleise, and the Emperour [brought

in] this sauage man and made hym to sitte down by hym, and whan the barouns hadde I-nough hym be-holden thei asked why he hadde for hem sente, and he tolde hem for a vision that hym be-fill in his slepynge, 'ffor I will that it be expowned be-fore yow,' and thei seide that the significacion wolde thei gladly heren. Than the Emperour comaunded this man to telle the cause why that he was sought, and ansuerde and seide that he wolde nothinge telle till that the Emperesse and hir xij maydones were comen, and she com a-noon with gladde semblaunce as she that yaf no force of nothinge that myght be-falle, whan the Emperesse and hir xij maydones were come a-monge the barouns, the lordes roos a-gein hir and dide hir reuerence, and as soone as the sauage man hir saugh comynge he turned his heed in trauerse an be-gan to laughe in scorne, and whan he hadde a-while laughed he loked on the Emperour stadfastly, and than on Grisandolus, and than on the Emperesse, and than on hir xij Maydenys that weren with hir, and than he turned toward the barouns, and he be-gan to laughe right lowde as it were in dispite, whan the Emperour saugh hym so laughe he preied hym to telle that he hadde in couenaunt, and whi that he lough now and other tymes, with that he stode vp and seide to the Emperour so lowde that all myght it heren. 'Sir, yef ye me graunte as trewe Emperour be-fore youre barouns that ben here that I shall not be the werse ne no harme to me therfore shall come, and that ye will yeve me leve as soone as I haue yow certefied of youre a-vision I shall telle yow the trew significacion,' and the Emperour hym ansuerde and graunted that noon harme ne annoye to hym sholde be don, ne that he sholde come hym no magre to telle hym that he was so desirouse for to heren, and that he sholde haue leve to go whan hym liste. 'But I praye the telle me myn a-vision in audience of alle my barouns what it was, and than shall I the better be-leve the significacion whan thow haste me tolde, of that I neuer spake to no creature,' and he ansuerde as for that sholde hym not greve, and ther-fore wolde he not lette and than he be-gan the a-vision.

'Sir,' seide the sauage man to the Emperour, 'it fill on a nyght that ye lay by youre wif that is here, and whan ye were a-slepe ye thought ye saugh be-fore yow a sowe that was feire and smothe, and the heer that she hadde on her bakke was so longe that it trailed to grounde more than a fadome, and on hir heed she hadde a cercle of goolde bright shynynge, and yow semed that ye hadde norisshed that sowe in youre house, but ye cowde it not verily knowe, and ther-with yow semed that ye hadde hir othir tymes sein, and whan ye hadde longe thought on this thinge ye saugh come out of youre chamber xij lyonsewes full feire and smothe; and thei com by the halle thourgh the courte to the sowe and lay by hir oon after a-nother, and whan thei hadde do that thei wolde thei wente a-gein in to youre chamber; than com ye to your

barouns and hem asked what sholde be do with this sowe, that he saugh
thus demened, and the barouns and alle the people seide she was
nothinge trewe, and thei Iuged to be brent, bothe the sowe and the
xij lyonsewes, and than was the fier made redy grete and merveillouse
in this courte, and ther-ynne was the sowe brente and the xij lyonsewes.
Now haue ye herde youre sweuene[18] in the same forme as ye it saugh
in your slepinge, and yef ye se that I haue eny thinge mys-taken, sey
it be-fore your barouns.' And the Emperour seide he hadde of nothinge
failed.

'Sir Emperour,' seide the barouns, 'seth that he hath seide what was
youre a-vision, hit is to be-leve the significacion yef he will it telle, and
it is a thinge that wolde gladly heren.' 'Certes,' seide the man, 'I shall
it declare to yow so openly that ye may it se, and knowe a-pertly[19] that
I yow shall sey. The grete sowe that he saugh signifieth my lady the
Emperess, youre wif, that is ther; and the longe heer that she hadde
on hir bakke betokeneth the longe robes that she is ynne I-clothed;
and the sercle that ye saugh on her heed shynynge be-tokeneth the
crowne of goolde that ye made her with to be crowned; and yef it be
youre plesier I will no more sey at this tyme.' 'Certes,' seide the
Emperour, 'yow be-hoveth to sey all as it is yef ye will be quyte of youre
promyse.' 'Certes,' seide man, 'than I shall telle yow. Tho xij lyonsewes
that he saugh come oute of a chamber, betokeneth the xij maydenes
that be ther with the Emperess; and knowe it for very trouthe that thei
be no wymen for it be men, and there-fore make hem be dispoiled,
and shull se the trouthe; and as ofte as ye go oute of the town she maketh
hem serue in hir chamber and in hir bedde. Now haue ye herde youre
a-vision and the significacion, and ye may se and knowe yef that I haue
seide to yow the soth.'

Whan the Emperour vunderstode th vntrouthe that his wife hadde don,
he was so a-baisshed that he spake no worde a longe while; and than
he spake and seide that that wolde he soone knowe, and than he cleped
Grisandolus, and seide, 'Dispoile mo tho dameseles, for I will that alle
the barouns that be here-ynne knowe the trouthe'; and a-noon Grisandolus and other lept forth and dispoiled hem be-fore the Emperour
and his barouns, and fonde hem formed alle as other men weren; and
than the Emperour was so wroth that he wiste not what to do. Than
he made his oth that a-noon ther sholde be do Iustice soche as was
right to be a-warded; and the barouns Iuged seth she hadde don hir
lorde soch vntrouthe that she sholde be brente and the harlottes hanged,
and some seide that thei sholde be flayn all quyk;[20] but in the ende
thei acorded that thei sholde be brente in a fier, and a-noon as the
Emperour herde the Iugement of the barouns, he comaunded to make
the fier in the place, and a-noon it was don, and thei were bounde hande

and foot, and made hem to be caste in to the brynynge fier, and in short tyme thei were all brent, ffor the fier was grete and huge. Thus toke Emperour vengaunce of his wif, and grete was the renomede that peple of hym spake whan it was knowen.

When the Emperesse was brente, and thei that she hadde made hir maydenes, the barouns returned a-gein to the Emperour, and seide oon to a-nother that the sauage man was right wise and avisee, ffor yet shall he sey some other thinges wher-of shall come some grete merveile vs, and to all the worlde; and the Emperour hym-self seide that he hadde seide his a-vision as it was in trouthe. Thus wiste the Emperour the lyvinge of his wif, and than the Emperour hym called, and asked yef he wolde sey eny more, and he seide, 'Ye yef he asked hym whereof.' 'I wolde wite,' quod he, 'wherefore thow didist laughe whan thow were in the f[o]reste, and loked on Grisandolus, and also whan thow were ledde be-fore an abbey, and in the chapell whan the squyer smote his lorde, and why thow seidest tho wordes to my stiwarde whan he asked why thow loughe, and after telle me what be-tokeneth the laughter here-ynne whan thow saugh the Emperesse come.'

'Sir,' seide the sauage man, 'I shall telle yow I-nowgh. I do yow to wite that the firste laughter that I made was for that a woman hadde me taken by her engyn',[21] that no man cowde not do; and wite ye well that Grisandolus is the beste maiden and the trewest with-ynne youre reame, and therefore was it that I lough; and the laughter that I made be-fore the abbey, was for ther is vnder erthe be-fore the yate[22] the grettest tresour hidde that eny man knoweth, and therefore I lough for that it was vnder feet of hem that a-boode after the almesse, ffor more richesse is in that tresour than alle the monkes beth worth, and all the abbey, and all that ther-to be-longeth, and the pore peple that ther-on stoden cowde it not take; and Avenable youre stywarde, that Grisan-dolus doth her clepen, saugh that I lowgh and asked me wherefore, and the couerte wordes that I to hir spake was for that she was chaunged in to the fourme of man, and hadde take a-nothir habite than hir owne; and alle the wordes that I spake thei ben trewe, ffor by woman is many a man disceyved, and therefore I cleped hir disceyaunt for by women ben many townes sonken and brent, and many a riche londe wasted and exiled, and moche people slayn; but I sey it not for noon euell that is in hir, and thow thy-self maist well perceyve that be women be many worthi men shamed and wratthed that longe haue loued to-geder, yef it were not for debate of women; but now rech the not for thy wif, that thou haste distroied, ffor she hath it well deserued, and haue there-fore no mystrust to other, for as longe as the worlde endureth it doth but apeire, and all that cometh to hem be the grete synne of luxure that in hem is closeth; ffor woman is of that nature, and of that disire, that whan she hath the moste worthi man of the worlde to hir lorde,

she weneth she haue the werse, and wite ye fro whens this cometh of
the grete fragelite that is in hem; and the foule corage and the foule
thought that thei haue where thei may beste hir volunte acomplish;
but therefore be not wroth, for ther ben in the worlde that ben full
trewe, and yef[23] thow haue be desceyved of thyn, yet shall thow haue
soche oon that is wthy to be Emperesse, and to resceyve that high dig-
nite, and yef thow wilt it be-leve thow shalt wynne ther-on more than
thowe shalt lese.

'But the prophesie seith that the grete dragon shall come fro Rome
that wolde distroie the reame of the grete Breteyne and put it in his
subieccion; and the fierce lyon crowned maugre[24] the diffence of the
turtill that the dragon hath norisshed vndir his wynges, and as soone
as the grete dragon shall meve to go the grete Breteigne, the lyon
crowned shall come hym a-geins, and shull fight so to-geder, that a
fierce bore that is prowde, whiche the lyon shall bringe with hym smyte
so the dragon with oon of his hornes that he shall falle down deed,
and thereby shall be delyuered the grete lyon. But I will not telle the
significacion of these wordes, for I owe it nought to do, but all this shall
falle in thy tyme, and therfore be well ware of euell counseile, for grete
part longeth to the.

'The tother laughter that I made in the chapell was not for the buffetes
that the squyer yaf his lorde, but for the be-tokenynges that ther-ynne
ben. In the same place ther the squyer stode was entred, and yet ther
is vndir his feet a merveillouse tresour. The firste buffet that the squyer
yaf his lorde signifieth that for avoure the wo[r]lde becometh so prowde,
that he douteth nother god ne his soule, no more than the squyer douted
to smyte his maister, but the riche wolde oppresse the pore vnder theire
feet; and that make these vntrewe riche peple whan enythinge cometh
to hem be myschaunce thei swere and stare and sey maugre haue god
for his yeftes,[25] and wite ye what maketh this nothinge but pride of
richesse. The seconde buffet be-tokeneth the riche vserer[26] that deli-
teth in his richesse and goth s[c]ornynge his pore nyghebours that be
nedy whan thei come to hym ought for to borough, and the vserer so
leneth hem litill and litill that at laste thei moste selle theire heritage
to hym that so longe hath it coveyted. The thridde buffet signifieth these
false pletours, men of lawe, that sellen and a-peire theire neyghbours
be-hinde here bakke for couetise and envye of that thei se hem thrive,
and for thei be not in her daungier, ffor whan these laweers sen that
her neighbours don hem not grete reverence and servise, thei thenken
and a-spien how thei may hem a-noyen in eny wise, and to make hem
lese that thei haue, and therfore men seyn an olde sawe, who hath a
goode neighbour hath goode morowe. Now haue ye herde the sig-
nificaciouns why the buffetes were yoven, but the squyer delited
nothinge ther-ynne whan that he smote his maister, but he wiste not
fro whens this corage to hym com. But god that is almyghty wolde haue

it to be shewed in exsample that men sholde not be prowde for worldly
richesse, for to the couetouse theire richesse doth hem but harme that
slepen in auerice, and for-yete god and don the werkes of the deuell,
that ledeth hem to euerlastinge deth, and all is for the grete delite that
thei haue in richesse.

'But now shall I telle yow whi I lough to day whan I saugh the
Emperesse comynge and hir lechours, I do yow to wite that it was but
for dispite, ffor I saugh that she was youre wif, and hadde oon of the
worthiest men of the worlde that eny man knoweth of youre yowthe,
and she hadde take these xij harlottes and wende euer for to haue ledde
this foly all hir lif; and ther-fore hadde I grete dispite for the love of
yow and of youre doughter, ffor she is youre doughter with-oute doubte,
and draweth litill after hir moder. Now haue ye herde alle the laugh-
tres and wherefore thei were, and therfore may I go yef it be youre
plesier.' 'Now a-bide a little,' seide the Emperour, 'and telle vs the
trouthe of Grisandolus, and also we shull sende to digge after the tresour
for I will wite yef it be trewe.' and he ther-to dide assent; than the
Emperour comaunded that Grisandolus were sought, and so she was
founden oon of the feirest maydenes that neded to enquere in eny londe,
and whan the Emperour knewe that Grisandolus, his stiwarde, that
longe hadde hym serued was a woman, he blissed hym for the wonder
that he ther-of hadde.

Than he asked the sauage man counseile what he sholde do of that
he hadde promysed to yeve his doughter, and half his reame, ffor loth
he was to falsen his promyse of couenaunt. 'I shall telle yow,' quod the
man, 'what he shull do yef ye will do my counseile, and wite it well,
it is the beste that eny man can yeven.' 'Sey on, than,' seide Emperour,
'ffor what counseile that thow yevest I shall it well be-leve, for I haue
founde thy seyinge trewe.' Than seide the sauage man, 'Ye shall take
Avenable to be yowre wif, and wite ye whos doughter she is. She is
doughter to the Duke Matan that the Duke Frolle hath disherited and
driven oute of his londe for enveye with grete wronge, and he and his
wife be fledde, and his sone, that is a feire yonge squyer, in to Province
in to a riche town that is called Monpellier; and sende to seche hem
and yelde hem her heritage that thei haue loste with wronge, and make
the mariage of youre doughter and Auenables brother that is so feire,
and ye may her no better be setten.' And whan the Barouns vndirstode
that the sauage man seide, thei spoke moche a-monge hem, and seiden
in the ende that the Emperour myght do no better after theire advis;
and than the Emperour asked his name, and what he was, and the hert
that so pertly spake vnto hym, and than seide he, 'Sir, of that enquere
no more, ffor it is a thinge the more ye desire to knowe the lesse ye
shall witen.'

'Ffor sothe,' seide the Emperour, 'now suppose I well what it may
be, but shull ye telle us eny more.' 'Ye,' quod he, 'I tolde yow right now

of the lyon crowned and of the lyon volage, [27] but now shall I telle yow
in other manere, for that ye shull be better remembred whan tyme
cometh. Emperour of Rome,' quod he, 'this is trewe prophesie that the
grete boor of Rome that is signified by the grete dragon, shall go a-
gein the lyon, crowned of the bloy[28] Breteyne a-gein the counseile of
the turtell that hath an heed of golde and longe hath ben his love. But
the boor shall be so full of pride that he will nothir be-leve, but shall
go with so grete pride with all his generacion in to the parties of Gaule
to fight with the crowned lyon that shall come a-geins hym with alle
his beestes. Ther shall be grete slaughter of beestes on both sides. Than
shall oon of the fawnes of the lyon crowned sle the grete boor, and
ther-fore I praye the yef thow wilt ought do for me er I departe that
thow do nothinge a-gein the volunte of thy wif, after that day that thow
haste her wedded, and wite well yef thow do thus thow shalt haue pro-
fite, and now I take my leve for here haue I no more to do.'

And the Emperour be-taught hym to god seth it myght no better be,
and ther-with he wente on his wey, and whan he com to the halle dore
he wrote letteres on the lyntell of the dore in grewe that seide, 'Be it
knowe to alle tho that these letteres reden, that the sauage man that
spake to the Emperour and expounded his dreme, hit was Merlin of
Northumberlande, and the hert brancus with xv braunches that spake
to hym in his halle at mete a-monge alle his knyghtes, and was chaced
thourgh the Citee of Rome, that spake to Auenable in the foreste whan
he tolde hir how she sholde fynde the man sauage; and lete the
Emperour well wite that Merlin is maister counseller to kynge Arthur
of the grete Breteyne.' And than he departed and spake no mo wordes.
Whan this sauage man was departed from the Emperour, he sente in
to Province to seche the fader and the moder of Auenable and Patrik
hir brother, in the town of Monpellier, whider as thei were fledde; and
a-noon thei com gladde and ioyfull of the auenture that god hadde
hem sente, and whan thei were comen thei hadde grete ioye of theire
doughter that thei wende neuer to haue seyn. Than thei a-bide with
the Emperour longe tyme, and the Emperour restored hem to here
herytage that Frolle hadde hem be-rafte. But as ffrolle myght he it a-
gein seide, ffor he was of grete power, and so endured the werre longe
tyme.

But in the ende the Emperour made the pees, and than he maried
his doughter to Patrik, and hym-self toke Auenable to his wif, and grete
was the ioye and the feeste that the Barouns maden, for moche was
she be-loved bothe of riche and pore, and as the Emperour was in ioye
and deduyt[29] of his newe spouse, ther com a massage to hym oute of
Greece for a discorde that was be-twene the barouns of Greese and
the Emperour Adrian, that sholde hem Iustise, ffor the Emperour Adrian
myght vn-ethe ride for febilnesse of age, and whan the messagers hadde
spoke to the Emperour and don all that he sholde, he toke his leve to

go, and as he caste vp his yie vpon the halle dore and saugh the lettres
that Merlin hadde writen in griewe, and a-noon he redde hem lightly,
and than he gan to laughe right harde, and shewed hem to the
Emperour, and seide, 'Sir, is this trewe that these lettres seyn.' 'What
sey thei,' quod the Emperour, 'wote ye neuer.' Quod the messager, 'Thei
seyn that he that tolde yow the vntrouthe of youre wif, and yoe dreme
expowned, and spake to yow in gise of an herte, that it was Merlin of
Northumbirlande, the maister counseller of kynge Arthur of Breteyne,
by whos counseile ye haue spoused youre wif Auenable.' And whan
the Emperour vndirstode these wordes he merveiled sore; and than
be-fill a grete merveile, wherof alle that were ther-ynne hadde wonder,
and the Emperour hym-self; ffor as soone as the Emperour herde what
the lettres mente, a-noon the lettres vanyssed so sodeynly that no man
wiste how, and ther-of hadde their grete wonder, and moche it was
spoken of thourgh the contrey. But now cesseth the tale of the Emperour
of Rome that a-bode in his paleise gladde and myry with his wif Auenable, and ledde goode lif longe tyme, for bothe were thei yong epeople,
ffor the Emperour was but xxvij yere of age at that hour, and his wife
was xxij, and yef thei ledde myri lif, yet Patrik and Foldate, the doughter of the Emperour, lyved in more delite.

1 *xij* = 12.
2 *Serue* = serve.
3 *CC* = 200.
4 *Bourdinge* = jesting.
5 *Lyonsewes* = lioncels (little lions—heraldic term).
6 *Iuged* = judged.
7 *Brente* = burnt.
8 *viij* = 13.
9 *Auenable* = avenable.
10 *Cleped* = named.
11 *Pilche* = vest-like tunic.
12 *Lowgh* = laugh.
13 *Yaf* = gave.
14 *Be leyser* = at leisure.
15 *Guerdon* = reward.
16 *Brocheland* = Broceliande Forest (in Brittany).
17 *Hir* = her.
18 *Sweuene* = dream.
19 *A-pertly* = frankly.
20 *Flayn all quyk* = flayed alive.
21 *Engyn* = cunning.
22 *Yate* = gate.
23 *Yef* = if.
24 *Maugre* = despite.
25 *Yeftes* = gifts.
26 *Vserer* = usurer.
27 *Volage* = wanton.

[28] *Bloy* = great.
[29] *Deduyt* = pleasure.

Chapter 3.

Merlin

by Walter Stein

Walter Johannes Stein (1891-1957) is one of the most fascinating exponents of the Matter of Britain ever to set pen to paper. His theories concerning the history of the Grail, set forth in *Weltgeschichte in Lichte des Heiligen Gral* (World History in the Light of the Holy Grail) have found support among several more recent writers, though Stein is generally not acknowledged. Unfortunately there is still no English language version of this seminal book, which sets out to discover parallels between actual historical personages in 8th century Europe and the heroes of the German Grail cycle represented by the Parzival of Wolfram von Eschenbach.[1]

Unfortunately for Stein his ideas caught the attention of someone whose interest in the Grail was also great, though for very different reasons—Adolf Hitler. Stein was forced to flee from Germany with the rise of the Nazis to power, subsequently settling in England and continuing his researches whilst teaching at various Evening Institutes and Rudolf Steiner schools throughout Britain.

During World War II he became an occasional adviser to Winston Churchill on the Astrological and Occult orders patronized by the Nazis. Stein's pupils have described him as a powerful and commanding speaker, whose knowledge of everything from Mathematics, Physics and Medicine, to History, Art and Economics, was truly encyclopedic.

From 1935 Stein edited a far-sighted journal, *The Present Age*, and it is from the pages of this that the following article, which bears all the hallmarks of Stein's imaginative and mystical approach, is taken.

❦

Legend relates that Merlin had the gift of knowing everything that was going on in the world at any given moment. His consciousness and perception were all-embracing; all that was happening at any present moment, no matter where in the world it might be, was accessible to him.

The legend goes on to tell that this consciousness was later on transmuted and that Merlin was thereafter able to embrace the future rather than the present. Indeed, there are many prophecies attributed to him.

There can be no doubt that Merlin was a seer, to whose vision the spiritual beings of Nature were perceptible. In woods and caves he would encounter the Nature-spirits. In the Bay of Tintagel to this day we are shown 'Merlin's cave'. Out of the trees, too, spiritual beings came to meet him and he was able to converse with them. They took the form

of nymphs and he united with them in love. For modern consciousness such things are difficult to understand; yet they were a reality for
that other kind of consciousness which existed in all parts of the world
in ancient times, and to the dreamlike impressions of which we must
ascribe the origins of all Mythology. It was due really to a mutual
penetration of the dreaming and waking life. What a man saw as a tree
by day appeared to him in dreams by night as a spiritual being. The
more active forces of Nature appeared in the figure of a masculine and
the more passive forces in the figure of a feminine being.

Trees have indeed a dual nature. Out of the Cosmos, out of the
Universe beyond the Earth they are formed—endowed with characteristic form after their kind. Take an apple-tree for example. Not only the
fruits, the apples, but the leaves, too, are round, and the tree as a whole
has the same rounded form. The identical principle of form works
throughout the tree and appears again in every detail. A pear-tree has
more longish leaves and fruit, and the entire form of the tree is like
the pear itself once more.

Such is the formative principle in trees. But there is also another force
at work there. Unlike the plastic forces which give the tree its form,
this other force comes not from the surrounding Universe, but from
within the Earth. It opens out and ramifies as it goes upwards. To begin
with it shoots upward in the trunk, then it divides and divides again
in branch and twig. This second force is more musical than plastic.
Indeed, for spiritual hearing the basic note or 'tonic' resounds in the
main trunk, the 'second' in the first main branches, the 'third' in the
next stage of ramification, and so on, and we shall find that most trees
come to an end of the branching process in the 'fifth'.

In the human being, too, these twofold forces are at work. The plastic forces, coming from the Universe outside the Earth, form and mould
our head and nervous system. The brain, above all, is a most perfect
work of plastic modelling. In the skeleton on the other hand, in the
repetition, sequence, and enhancement of the several bones, the more
musical forces are at work. Where the two polar forces—plastic and
musical—encounter one another, rhythm arises in the human being.
This finds expression in the repeated vertebrae and ribs. We see
the same rhythm in the plant, in the sequence of the nodes along the
stem.

Now the primeval clairvoyant consciousness saw on the one hand
the physical appearance of the tree, while on the other hand with dream-
like imagination it apprehended the dynamic working of these inner
forces, which was so like the play of the same forces in the human being
that the seer of old time, in his dreaming consciousness, actually perceived a human figure that emerged out of the tree and came to meet
him. And so it was in Merlin's case; nay, more, we are given to understand that his experiences of this kind were so real and so intense as

to make possible for him a personal relationship of love to such a being or spirit of a tree. Such experiences would lead to the development of an ever widening cosmic consciousness, to which the secrets of Nature would be unfolded.

Not only Merlin but a great number of spiritual seekers of olden time experienced the world of Nature in this way. Beings spoke to them— Beings were revealed to them out of the Stars, the Planets, and the elements of Earth. Indeed, this kind of consciousness was the prevalent one through many thousands of years. But in the course of time human consciousness underwent definite changes, which it is most important for us to observe and study. In Merlin's time the Nature-beings spoke to Man out of the woods and forests, out of the world of plants, and from the waves of the sea, surging and beating into the caverns of a rocky cliff. In still more ancient times it was the Heavens themselves, the world of the fixed Stars, which spoke to man. Orpheus brought forth Eurydice from the nether world, from which man had to take his leave when he turned his soul's attention to the Heavens, to the Stars. The Orphic songs, preserved, for example, by Appollonius of Rhodes, are a description of geological events, which in their turn were a terrestrial echo of the changing constellations, the varying positions of the axis of the Earth in its relation to the fixed Stars.

Stage by stage, the Universe was bereft of living soul. The first to fade away were the great pictures of the Heavens and of the constellations, which at long last became dead symbols—'signs of the zodiac' as we now know them. But in intermediate period the planetary Gods still spoke to man, until they too at length grew dumb, one after another. The realm of Chronos or *Saturn* fell away when Zeus or *Jupiter* began his reign. Thereafter came the epoch of *Mars* or of the Titans. Comparative study of all religions will prove that the dream-picture-world of mankind drew nearer and nearer to the Earth, while stage by stage the farther reaches of the Cosmos faded away—their Word reduced to silence.

It was as though the Gods descended to the Earth to unite with men. And at the last, the Logos Himself became flesh. The cosmic distances were now unpeopled of the Gods, and the time when John the Baptist had to prophesy: 'Change the way of your thinking, for the distant realms of the Heavens have now come near at hand.'

At the time of Merlin an important transition was just taking place. During the period immediately before him, the gods and demi-gods, whom the human being met in his dreams by night and in his daydreams, too, had still been revealing themselves in the phenomena of air and water. The adventures of the Knights of King Arthur have to do with this stage in the evolution of human consciousness. The

Figure 2: 'The Gifting of Excalibur by the Lady of the Lake to Arthur'
by A.G. Walker.

nineteenth century artist, Böcklin, reproduces very truly in his paintings the mood and feeling of this epoch.

Then came the time of Christianity. Long, long ago Persephone, the power of clairvoyance, had disappeared in the dark realm of Pluto. Isis, the human soul, wandered a widow through the world, filled with longing for the realm of Light and Imagination—for Osiris, her husband. The time had come when this universal realm of Light and spiritual Imagination was dismembered into so many isolated symbols. Sadness and grief spread out among the seekers of the Spirit. The fair world of their dreams receded ever more, and the plain, matter-of-fact everyday world alone remained. This was the time when the Round Table of King Arthur gradually became a place of loneliness. When the Knights, for lack of spiritual experiences, had nothing more to relate, they stayed away.

The point of time was not always the same in different lands. The peoples, it is true, all of them, passed through the different phases of consciousness, but they did not all do so at the same time. Yet for every nation, sooner or later, the moment came for which the word of Christ was spoken: 'Blessed are now no longer they who behold, blessed are they who believe.'

In Christianity itself, the historical event of Palestine and the tradition which took its start from thence replaced the ancient spiritual visions. Christian tradition tells of the Crucified One, no bone of whom was to be broken. The Prophets had foretold this, for it answered to a piece of ancient knowledge out of the Mysteries. The meaning of it is that in Christ the Spirit penetrated even to the skeleton, to the most mineral-like, most death-like substance in the human body. Indeed, it was only thus that the Spirit overcame Death. Thereafter the power of the visionary Light rayed forth renewed, out of the very symbol of Death—out of dead mineral substance.

The blood of Christ must be sought for in the crystal cup. Thus did the Knights of King Arthur seek. They took their departure from the Round Table and set out on their quest of the Holy Grail. The word 'Grail' is derived from the Latin word *gradalis*, signifying a gradual or step-by-step descent. The Grail in pre-Christian time had been a vessel the interior of which was graduated in a threefold form. Dedicated to the God[2] Ceridwen, it had contained the mysterious 'red substance' of Alchemy—that which became in Christian times the sacred Blood of Christ. It was the substance which induced the power of clairvoyant vision, which at one time had still borne witness to the realm of the fixed Stars, which at a later stage spoke only of the Planetary Spheres, and in the latest pre-Christian times became restricted to the kingdom of the Elements.

Clairvoyant vision was henceforth to be enclosed in the cup of crystal, that is to say the very substance of the Earth. This was the point in evolution when Christ celebrated the first Holy Mass, in the institution of the Last Supper as described in the Gospels. He took the Heavenly bread of Imagination which had once upon a time rayed forth from the entire Cosmos, and, as Osiris of old had been broken into many fragments, so now He broke the bread and distributed it among the twelve disciples. The 'white substance' of Alchemy, erstwhile the silvery power of the Moon, which leads us out into the world of dreams, was now transformed into the sacred Host. And in place of the 'red substance' of Alchemy Christ distributed the wine. Wine is, in fact, the substance which brings about in man the eventual extinction of clairvoyance. This was the darkest moment in the world's evolution. The ancient world of Mythologies was blotted out; the new world of Light, or of the Gnosis in which the Risen Christ should shine forth, had not yet dawned—for the Resurrection was not yet accomplished. Judas had received the Sacrament. The Lord had steeped the bread in the wine and had given it to him. Judas went forth; it was night. He took the wages of betrayal, for he knew not that the absolute darkness would only last for three-and-a-half days, from Holy Thursday until Easter Sunday.

Christ died and was laid in a rocky tomb, and Joseph of Arimathea gathered up His blood in the crystal cup. Ancient clairvoyance and inspiration were extinguished. The Spirit penetrated through and through the skeleton. The world lay dumb and blind, bereft of vision. The Sun was darkened and the Earth trembled. The power of the Light, the power of spiritual vision, penetrated into the very depths of the mineral kingdom.

This moment had been forseen in the great Mystery Schools of antiquity. They knew that Dionysos would be seized by the Titans and dismembered in the realm of the elements. They knew too that Persephone would be robbed by Pluto and would dwell in Pluto's kingdom under the tree of dreams, in whose interweaving branches the dream-pictures weave to and fro. They knew, too, that in Pluto's kingdom the cup would be offered to her with the potion in whose surface nothing else could be reflected than her own human countenance.

This I- or Ego-point of human evolution, the point where man utterly loses the Divine world and is alone with himself, had been foreseen in the mysteries of Iacchos. It was this moment which Christ Himself experienced in the Garden of Gethsemane on the Mount of Olives. In a little chapel somewhere in Hungary this scene is remarkably portrayed. Christ prays in Gethsemane to the Father from whom he receives the cup. On the one side we see the disciples sleep; mankind is asleep during the greatest event of all history. On the other side we see the Angels turning their faces away. They, too, do not understand what is going on; they cannot comprehend how an immortal God should undergo death. Then Christ in utter loneliness takes the crystal cup. The

eternal *I Am* of man is here revealed at the historic moment of decision.

English mythology has experienced this event of human evolution
in the Merlin legend. Merlin was the seer whose power of vision had
at one time embraced the Universe. But the visionary power had receded
and nothing more was left—only the Nymph of the tree with whom
he was to unite in love. She would grant him her love only on condition that he communicated to her all his secrets. He told her all he knew,
but still she was unsatisfied. She would fain know how she might hold
him prisoner for ever. This secret, too, he had to tell her. It was Merlin's destiny, in fact, to experience as his own personal fate the historic
destiny of the power of clairvoyance in mankind. And so it came about
that the Nymph imprisoned him in the rock, calling as she did so upon
the nine spheres, the nine Hierarchies, through whose circle the Spirit
had descended.

Here Gawain found him, by whom the narrative is told. Such is the
secret of Merlin: he was the one who experienced the tragic destiny
of the Spirit in mankind as his own personal fate. Yet by this very fact
he was elected to become the teacher and guardian of Arthur.

Merlin knew what was going on at any present moment, no matter
where upon earth the event was taking place. Through the Arthurian
tradition this form of knowing was bequeathed to British history. But
the legend with good reason goes on to tell that in the later course of
evolution Merlin learned to transform his universal present consciousness into a consciousness of the future. Through the consciousness of
things present man attains to Nature, whose works and beings he thus
learns to love and to revere. He learns to master the forces of the Nature-
beings, so much so that he grows able to elaborate the whole mineral
kingdom, to work it through and through. Yet strong as are the spiritual
forces which he applies in so doing, he cannot free himself in this kind
of work from being prisoner of matter. His love for the Nature-being
holds him spell-bound and imprisoned in the world of matter. But there
is also a second 'Nature'—a Nature not yet there in present time,
but which Man himself can bring to birth as he goes on towards the
future.

This 'second Nature' is the social world. Original Nature was created
and enspirited by the Divine powers. This second world is being created
by Man, in whom the Divine-spiritual world, having once become flesh
in man, comes more and more to realization and to creative activity.
Stage by stage in the long course of evolution, the old world of Nature—
Nature from out of which we are born—lost its Divine essence. The
Divine withdrew from the great Cosmos, that it might live on in the
free and autonomous responsibility of Man. When the Divine takes

leave of Nature, Nature takes on a character which is indeed still worthy of man's love and reverence, but which will none the less take
prisoner the human Ego. Moreover, man can only free himself from
this imprisonment by social deeds which have their origin in the
individual I, in the true human Ego.

In the creative development of social structure by mankind, a second
Nature is, indeed, being brought to birth within the Universe. It is as
yet only in process of becoming. And in this new world which is aris-
ing towards the future, Merlin, too, must find salvation. The moment
when the Round Table of King Arthur became a place of loneliness and
when the Knights set out upon the quest of the Grail, is the point in
evolution whereat man learns courageously and willingly to lose the
old clairvoyance which was Nature-given but therefore also Nature-
bound. Man enters bravely upon the intermediate period of quest and
search within the world of the physical senses, whereafter he is destined to give birth again to a new clairvoyance. This new clairvoyance,
unlike the old, does not unveil the secrets of Nature in cosmic Imagi-
nations, but in prophetic pictures no less significant foresees the evolution of the social life. The true quest of the Grail begins only at the
point where Merlin dies. It is the quest of the Spirit in the crystal cup
of matter; it is the seeking of that social love whose coming cannot
merely be awaited but will be brought forth by our creative action. This
newly awakened love is not the love of antiquity—the love of Nature
and of the Nature-spirits—it is the love within the human kingdom,
linking man with man, nay, more, linking whole groups of human beings
one with another. Through this alone shall we find the returning way
from matter to the Stars.

The ancient Norse Mythology beheld this path of evolution. It saw
the human God hang crucified for nine days long on the cosmic ash-
tree, whose ninefold branches are indeed the nine spheres of the
Cosmos, and it gives the three its true name: 'Iggdrasyl'—Ego-bearer.
Humanity is crucified upon the tree that bears the Ego, and indeed,
only by this means attains the turning-point of individualization. But
at this turning-point the ancient Gods of Nature die. It is the Twilight
of the Gods. One God alone outlives the world-wide downfall, namely
the God who Himself took human form. By the power of the Divine-
spiritual Word, which in Hum underwent humanity, evolution will be
guided back to its Divine origin, albeit this time in full consciousness
and Egohood.

Merlin experienced this passage of the Divine through matter. And
as the legend does not tell us of his eventual release from the spell of
matter, we are thus left to feel the more deeply that at this point something is still left unfulfilled—something for us to do.

¹ Trans. A. T. Hatto, Penguin Books, 1981.
² This must be a slip of the pen. Stein was far too knowledgeable to mistake the Celtic Goddess for a god. (Ed.)

Chapter 4.

The Early Days of Arthur

by Geoffrey of Monmouth

Geoffrey of Monmouth's *Historia Regum Britanniæ* (c.1136) is the earliest surviving text which deals not only with the historical or pseudo-historical figure of Arthur, but also with the mythical dimension which becomes such an essential part of the stories thereafter. Geoffrey's Arthur is a military genius, a strong and forthright king, and above all a typically mediaeval man—despite the fact that Geoffrey tells us he is writing a 'history' of the Britons which he found in an ancient book. Of this book we now have no knowledge, and it is generally supposed never to have existed, but to have been a spurious source of the kind often adopted by mediaeval writers to give their word an added quality of veracity.

However, it must be said that the *Historia* contains so much of an ancient and traditional nature, that Geoffrey was almost certainly drawing upon much earlier, possibly aural, sources for his work. In particular the sections dealing with the life and prophecies of Merlin, have about them an air of authenticity which, as Bob Stewart has shown in his two books on Merlin,[1] cause us to think of Geoffrey in a very different way—as a poet and an embellisher of history rather than as a forger as was hitherto the case.

The sections quoted here relate to the early days of Arthur's reign and show him extending his sway over much of Europe and Scandinavia. The strength of Geoffrey's narrative, so ably captured the early translation of J. W. Giles, holds true for the whole of the text, which contains many fascinating stories of ancient British Kings. Of particular interest is the description of Arthur's coronation, which not only shows the way the story was already tending towards the spectacle of the later romances, but also contains a very revealing list of names. This catalogue, which I have dealt with more fully elsewhere,[2] shows clearly that Geoffrey had access to ancient documents relating to the earliest heroes of Britain. The fantastic chronicle of Arthurian conquest, which as the translator notes is so unlikely that it is a matter for some wonder that anyone ever took it seriously, also indicates, at a deeper level, the breadth of Arthur's hold over the imagination of that particular time.

I. *Arthur succeeds Uther in the kingdom of Britain, and besieges Colgrin.*

Uther Pendragon being dead, the nobility from several provinces assembled together at Silchester, and proposed to Dubricius, archibishop of Legions, that he should consecrate Arthur, Uther's son, to be their king. For they were now in great straits, because, upon hearing of the king's death, the Saxons had invited over their countrymen from Germany, and, under the command of Colgrin, were attempting to exterminate the whole British race. They had also entirely subdued all that part of the island which extends from the Humber to the sea of Caithness. Dubricius, therefore, grieving for the calamities of his country, in conjunction with the other bishops, set the crown upon Arthur's head. Arthur was then fifteen years old, but a youth of such unparalleled courage and generosity, joined with that sweetness of temper and innate goodness, as gained him universal love. When his coronation was over, he, according to usual custom, showed his bounty and munificence to the people. And such a number of soldiers flocked to him upon it, that his treasury was not able to answer that vast expense. But such a spirit of generosity, joined with valour, can never long want means to support itself. Arthur, therefore, the better to keep up his munificence, resolved to make use of his courage, and to fall upon the Saxons, that he might enrich his followers with their wealth. To this he was also moved by the justice of the cause, since the entire monarchy of Britain belonged to him by hereditary right. Hereupon assembling the youth under his command, he marched to York, of which, when Colgrin had intelligence, he met him with a very great army, composed of Saxons, Scots, and Picts, by the river Duglas; where a battle happened, with the loss of the greater part of both armies. Notwithstanding, the victory fell to Arthur, who pursued Colgrin to York, and there besieged him. Baldulph, upon the news of his brother's flight, went towards the siege with a body of six thousand men, to his relief; for at the time of the battle he was upon the sea-coast, waiting the arrival of duke Cheldric with succours from Germany. And being now no more than ten miles distant from the city, his purpose was to make a speedy march in the night-time, and fall upon the enemy by way of surprise. But Arthur, having intelligence of his design, sent a detachment of six hundred horse, and three thousand foot, under the command of Cador, duke of Cornwall, to meet him the same night. Cador, therefore, falling into the same road along which the enemy was passing, made a sudden assault upon them, and entirely defeated the Saxons, and put them to flight. Baldulph was excessively grieved at this disappointment in the relief which he intended for his brother, and began to think of some other stratagem to gain access to him; in which if he could but succeed, he thought they might concert measures together for their safety. And since he had no other way for it, he shaved his head and beard, and put on the habit of a jester with a harp, and in this disguise walked up and down in the camp, playing upon his instrument as if he had been a harper. He thus passed unsuspected, and by a little and little went up to the walls of the city, where he was at last discovered by the besieged, who thereupon drew him up with cords, and conducted him to his brother. At this unexpected, though much desired meeting,

they spent some time in joyfully embracing each other, and then began
to consider various stratagems for their delivery. At last, just as they
were considering their case desperate, the ambassadors returned from
Germany, and brought with them to Albania a fleet of six hundred sail,
laden with brave soldiers, under the command of Cheldric. Upon this
news, Arthur was dissuaded by his council from continuing the siege
any longer, for fear of hazarding a battle with so powerful and numerous an army.

II. *Hoel sends fifteen thousand men to Arthur's assistance.*

Arthur complied with their advice, and made his retreat to London,
where he called an assembly of all the clergy and nobility of the kingdom, to ask their advice, what course to take against the formidable
power of the pagans. After some deliberation, it was agreed that ambassadors should be despatched into Armorica, to king Hoel, to represent
to him the calamitous state of Britain. Hoel was the son of Arthur's
sister by Dubricius, king of the Armorican Britons; so that, upon advice
of the disturbances his uncle was threatened with, he ordered his fleet
to be got ready, and, having assembled fifteen thousand men, he arrived
with the first fair wind at Hamo's Port,[3] and was received with all
suitable honour by Arthur, and most affectionately embraced by him.

III. *Arthur makes the Saxons his tributaries.*

After a few days they went to relieve the city Kaerliudcoit, that was
besieged by the pagans; which being situated upon a mountain, between
two rivers in the province of Lindisia, is called by another name Lin-
docolinum.[4] As soon as they arrived there with all their forces, they
fought with the Saxons, and made a grievous slaughter of them, to the
number of six thousand; part of whom were drowned in the rivers,
part fell by the hands of the Britons. The rest in a great consternation
quitted the siege and fled, but were closely pursued by Arthur, till they
came to the wood of Celidon, where they endeavoured to form themselves into a body again, and make a stand. And here they again joined
battle with the Britons, and made a brave defence, whilst the trees that
were in the place secured them against the enemies' arrows. Arthur,
seeing this, commanded the trees that were in that part of the wood
to be cut down, and the trunks to be placed quite round them, so as
to hinder their getting out; resolving to keep them pent up here till
he could reduce them by famine. He then commanded his troops to
besiege the wood, and continued three days in that place. The Saxons,
having now no provisions to sustain them, and being just ready to starve
with hunger, begged for leave to go out; in consideration whereof they
offered to leave all their gold and silver behind them, and return back

to Germany with nothing but their empty ships. They promised also that they would pay him tribute from Germany, and leave hostages with him. Arthur, after consultation about it, granted their petition; allowing them only leave to depart, and retaining all their treasures, as also hostages for payment of the tribute. But as they were under sail on their return home, they repented of their bargain, and tacked about again towards Britain, and went on shore at Totness. No sooner were they landed, than they made an utter devastation of the country as far as the Severn sea, and put all the peasants to the sword. From thence they pursued their furious march to the town of Bath, and laid siege to it. When the king had intelligence of it, he was beyond measure sur-prised at their proceedings, and immediately gave orders for the execution of the hostages. And desisting from an attempt which he had entered upon to reduce the Scots and Picts, he marched with the utmost expedition to raise the siege; but laboured under very great difficulties, because he had left his nephew Hoel sick at Alclud. At length, having entered the province of Somerset, and beheld how the siege was carried on, he addressed himself to his followers in these words: 'Since these impious and detestable Saxons have disdained to keep faith with me, I, to keep faith with God, will endeavour to revenge the blood of my countrymen this day upon them. To arms, soldiers, to arms, and courageously fall upon the perfidious wretches, over whom we shall, with Christ assisting us, undoubtedly obtain the victory.'

IV. *Dubricius's speech against the treacherous Saxons. Arthur with his own hand kills four hundred and seventy Saxons in one battle. Colgrin and Baldulph are killed in the same.*

When he had done speaking, St Dubricius, archbishop of Legions, going to the top of a hill, cried out with a loud voice, 'You that have the honour to profess the Christian faith, keep fixed in your minds the love which you owe to your country and fellow subjects, whose sufferings by the treachery of pagans will be an everlasting reproach to you, if you do not courageously defend them. It is your country which you fight for, and for which you should, when required, voluntarily suffer death; for that itself is victory and the cure of the soul. For he that shall die for his brethren, offers himself a living sacrifice to God, and has Christ for his example, who condescended to lay down his life for his brethren. If therefore any of you shall be killed in this war, that death itself, which is suffered in so glorious a cause, shall be to him for penance and absolution of all his sins.' At these words, all of them, encouraged with the benediction of the holy prelate, instantly armed themselves, and prepared to obey his orders. Also Arthur himself, having put on a coat of mail suitable to the grandeur of so powerful a king, placed a golden helmet upon his head, on which was engraven the figure of a dragon;

and on his shoulders his shield called Pridwen; upon which the picture of the blessed Mary, mother of God, was painted, in order to put him frequently in mind of her. Then girding on his Caliburn, which was an excellent sword made in the isle of Avallon, he graced his right hand with his lance, named Ron, which was hard, broad, and fit for slaughter. After this, having placed his men in order, he boldly attacked the Saxons, who were drawn out in the shape of a wedge, as their manner was. And they, notwithstanding that the Britons fought with great eagerness, made a noble defence all that day; but at length, towards sunsetting, climbed up the next mountain, which served them for a camp: for they desired no larger extent of ground, since they confided very much in their numbers. The next morning Arthur, with his army, went up the mountain, but lost many of his men in the ascent, by the advantage which the Saxons had in their station on the top, from whence they could pour down upon him with much greater speed, than he was able to advance against them. Notwithstanding, after a very hard struggle, the Britons gained the summit of the hill, and quickly came to a close engagement with the enemy, who again gave them a warm reception, and made a vigorous defence. In this manner was a great part of that day also spent; whereupon Arthur, provoked to see the little advantage he had yet gained, and that victory still continued in suspense, drew out his Caliburn, and, calling upon the name of the blessed Virgin, rushed forward with great fury into the thickest of the enemy's ranks; of whom (such was the merit of his prayers) not one escaped alive that felt the fury of his sword; neither did he give over the fury of his assault until he had, with his Caliburn alone, killed four hundred and seventy men. The Britons, seeing this, followed their leader in great multitudes, and made slaughter on all sides; to that Colgrin, and Baldulph his brother, and many thousands more, fell before them. But Cheldric, in this imminent danger of his men, betook himself to flight.

V. *The Saxons, after their leader Cheldric was killed, are all compelled by Cador to surrender.*

The victory being thus gained, the king commanded Cador, duke of Cornwall, to pursue them, while he himself should hasten his march into Albania; from whence he had advice that the Scots and Picts were besieging Alclud, in which, as we said before, Hoel lay sick. Therefore he hastened to his assistance, for fear he might fall into the hands of the barbarians. In the meantime the duke of Cornwall, who had the command of ten thousand men, would not as yet pursue the Saxons in their flight, but speedily made himself master of their ships, to hinder their getting on board, and manned them with his best soldiers, who were to beat back the pagans in case they should flee thither: after this he hastily pursued the enemy, according to Arthur's command, and allowed no quarter to those he could overtake. So that they whose behaviour before was so cruel and insolent, now with timorous hearts fled for shelter, sometimes to the coverts of the woods, sometimes to mountains and caves, to prolong a wretched life. At last, when none of these places could afford them a safe retreat, they entered the Isle of Thanet with their broken forces; but neither did they there get free from the duke of Cornwall's pursuit, for he still continued slaughtering them, and gave them no respite till he had killed Cheldric, and taken hostages for the surrender of the rest.

VI. *Arthur grants a pardon to the Scots and Picts, besieged at the Lake Lumond.*

Having therefore settled peace here, he directed his march to Alclud, which Arthur had relieved from the oppression of barbarians, and from thence conducted his army to Mureif, where the Scots and Picts were besieged; after three several battles with the king and his nephew, they had fled as far as this province, and entering upon the lake Lumond, sought for refuge in the islands that are upon it. This lake contains sixty islands, and receives sixty rivers into it, which empty themselves into the sea by no more than one mouth. There is also an equal number of rocks in these islands, as also of eagles' nests in those rocks, which flocked together there every year, and, by the loud and general noise which they now made, foreboded some remarkable event that should happen to the kingdom. To these islands, therefore, had the enemy fled, thinking the lake would serve them instead of a fortification; but it proved of little advantage to them. For Arthur, having got together a fleet, sailed round the rivers, and besieged the enemy fifteen days together, by which they were so straitened with hunger, that they died by thousands. While he was harassing them in this manner Guillamurius, king of Ireland, came up in a fleet with a very great army of barbarians, in order to relieve the besieged. This obliged Arthur to rise the siege, and turn his arms against the Irish, whom he slew without mercy, and compelled the rest to return back to thheir country. After this victory, he proceeded in his first attempt, which was to extirpate the whole race of the Scots and Picts, and treated them with an unparalleled severity. And as he allowed quarter to none, the bishops of that miserable country, with all the inferior clergy, met together, and bearing the reliques of the saints and other consecrated things of the church before them, barefooted, came to implore the king's mercy for their people. As soon as they were admitted into his presence, they fell down upon their knees, and humbly besought him to have pity on their distressed country, since the sufferings which he had already made it undergo, were sufficient; nor was there any necessity to cut off the small

remainder to a man; and that he would allow them the enjoyment of
a small part of the country, since they were willing to bear the yoke
which he should impose upon them. The king was moved at the manner of their delivering this petition, and could not forbear expressing
his clemency to them with tears; and at the request of those holy men,
granted them pardon.

VII. *Arthur relates the wonderful nature of some ponds.*

This affair being concluded, Hoel had the curiosity to view the situation of the lake, and wondered to find the number of the rivers, islands,
rocks, and eagles' nests, so exactly correspond: and while he was reflect-
ing upon it as something that appeared miraculous, Arthur came to
him, and told him of another pond in the same province, which was
yet more wonderful. For not far from thence was one whose length
and breadth were each twenty feet, and depth five feet. But whether
its square figure was natural or artificial, the wonder of it was, there
were four different sorts of fishes in the four several corners of it, none
of which were ever found in any other part of the pond but their own.
He told him likewise of another pond in Wales, near the Severn, called
by the country people Linligwan, into which when the sea flows, it
receives it in the manner of a gulf, but so as to swallow up the
tide, and never be filled, or have its banks covered by it. But at the
ebbing of the sea, it throws out the waters which it had swallowed,
as high as a mountain, and at last dashes and covers the banks with
them. In the meantime, if all the people of that country should stand
near with their faces towards it, and happened to have their clothes
sprinkled with the dashing of the waves, they would hardly, if at all,
escape being swallowed up by the pond. But with their backs towards
it, they need not fear being dashed, though they stood upon the very
banks.

VIII. *Arthur restores York to its ancient beauty, especially as to its churches.*

The king, after his general pardon granted to the Scots, went to York
to celebrate the feast of Christ's nativity, which was now at hand. On
entering the city, he beheld with grief the desolation of the churches;
for upon the expulsion of the holy Archbishop Sanxo, and of all the
clergy there, the temples which were half burned down, had no longer
divine service performed in them: so much had the impious rage of
the pagans prevailed. After this, in an assembly of the clergy and people, he appointed Pyramus his chaplain metropolitan of that see. The
churches that lay level with the ground, he rebuilt, and (which was
their chief ornament) saw them filled with assemblies of devout per-

sons of both sexes. Also the nobility that were driven out by the disturbances of the Saxons, he restored to their country.

IX. *Arthur honours Augusel with the sceptre of the Scots; Urian with
that of Mureif; and Lot with the consulship of Londonesia.*

There were there three brothers of royal blood, viz. Lot, Urian, and
Augusel, who, before the Saxons had prevailed, held the government
of those parts. Being willing therefore to bestow on these, as he did
on others, the rights of their ancestors, he restored to Augusel the
sovereignty over the Scots; his brother Urian he honoured with the
sceptre of Mureif; and Lot, who in time of Aurelius Ambrosius had
married his sister, by whom he had two sons, Walgan and Modred,
he re-established in the consulship of Londonesia, and the other
provinces belonging to him. At length, when the whole country was
reduced by him to its ancient state, he took to wife Guanhumara,
descended from a noble family of Romans, who was educated under
duke Cador, and in beauty surpassed all the women of the island.

X. *Arthur adds to his government Ireland, Iceland, Gothland, and the
Orkneys.*

The next summer he fitted out a fleet, and made an expedition into
Ireland, which he was desirous to reduce. Upon landing there, he was
met by king Guillamurius before mentioned, with a vast number of
men, who came with a design to fight him; but at the very beginning
of the battle, those naked and unarmed people were miserably routed,
and fled to such places as lay open to them for shelter. Guillamurius
also in a short time was taken prisoner, and forced to submit; as were
also all the other princes of the country after the king's example, being
under great consternation at what had happened. After an entire conquest of Ireland, he made a voyage with his fleet to Iceland, which he
also subdued. And now a rumour spreading over the rest of the islands,
that no country was able to withstand him, Doldavius, king of Gothland, and Gunfasius, king of the Orkneys, came voluntarily, and made
their submission, on a promise of paying tribute. Then, as soon as winter
was over, he returned back to Britain, where having established the
kingdom, he resided in it for twelve years together in peace.

XI. *Arthur subdues Norway, Dacis, Aquitaine, and Gaul.*

After this, having invited over to him all persons whatsoever that were
famous for valour in foreign nations, he began to augment the number of his domestics, and introduced such politeness into his court,

as people of the remotest countries thought worthy of their imitation.
So that there was not a nobleman who thought himself of any consideration, unless his clothes and arms were made in the same fashion
as those of Arthur's knights. At length the fame of his munificence and
valour spreading over the whole world, he became a terror to the kings
of other countries, who grievously feared the loss of their dominions,
if he should make any attempt upon them. Being much perplexed with
these anxious cares, they repaired their cities and towers, and built towns
in convenient places, the better to fortify themselves against any enter-
prise of Arthur, when occasion should require. Arthur, being informed
of what they were doing, was delighted to find how much they stood
in awe of him, and formed a design for the conquest of all Europe.
Then having prepared his fleet, he first attempted Norway, that he might
procure the crown of it for Lot, his sister's husband. This Lot was the
nephew of Sichelin, king of the Norwegians, who being then dead, had
appointed him his successor in the kingdom. But the Norwegians, dis-
daining to receive him, had advanced one Riculf to the sovereignty,
and having fortified their cities, thought they were able to oppose
Arthur. Walgan, the son of Lot, was then a youth twelve years old, and
was recommended by his uncle to the service of pope Supplicius, from
whom he received arms. But to return to the history: as soon as Arthur
arrived on the coast of Norway, king Riculf, attended with the whole
power of that kingdom, met him, and gave him battle, in which, after
a great loss of blood on both sides, the Britons at length had the advantage, and making a vigorous charge, killed Riculf and many others with
him. Having thus defeated them, they set the cities on fire, dispersed
the country people, and pursued the victory till they had reduced all
Norway, as also Dacia, under the dominion of Arthur. After the conquest of these countries, and establishment of Lot upon the throne of
Norway, Arthur made a voyage to Gaul, and dividing his army into
several bodies, began to lay waste that country on all sides. The province
of Gaul was then committed to Flollo, a Roman tribune, who held the
government of it under the emperor Leo. Upon intelligence of Arthur's
coming, he raised all the forces that were under his command, and
made war against him, but without success. For Arthur was attended
with the youth of all the islands that he had subdued; for which reason he was reported to have such an army as was though invincible.
And even the greater part of the Gallic army, encouraged by his bounty,
came over to his service. Therefore Flollo, seeing the disadvantages he
lay under, left his camp, and fled with a small number to Paris. There
having recruited his army, he fortified the city, and resolved to stand
another engagement with Arthur. But while he was thinking of strength-
ening himself with auxiliary forces in the neighbouring countries, Arthur
came upon him unawares, and besieged him in the city. When a month
had passed, Flollo, with grief observing his people perish with hunger

sent a message to Arthur, that they two alone should decide the conquest for the kingdom in a duel: for being a person of great stature,
boldness and courage, he gave this challenge in confidence of success.
Arthur was extremely pleased at Flollo's proposal, and sent him word
back again, that he would give him the meeting which he desired. A
treaty, therefore, being on both sides agreed to, they met together in
the island without the city, where the people waited to see the event.
They were both gracefully armed, and mounted on admirably swift
horses; and it was hard to tell which gave greater hopes of victory. When
they had presented themselves against each other with their lances aloft,
they put spurs to their horses, and began a fierce encounter. But Arthur,
who handled his lance more warily, struck it into the upper part of
Flollo's breast, and avoiding his enemy's weapon, laid him prostrate
upon the ground, and was just going to despatch him with his drawn
sword, when Flollo, starting up on a sudden, met him with his lance
couched, wherewith he mortally stabbed the breast of Arthur's horse,
and caused both him and his rider to fall. The Britons, when they saw
their king lying on the ground, fearing he was killed, could hardly be
restrained from breach of covenant, and falling with one consent upon
the Gauls. But just as they were upon rushing into the lists, Arthur
hastily got up, and guarding himself with his shield, advanced with
speed against Flollo. And now they renewed the assault with great rage,
eagerly bent upon one another's destruction. At length Flollo, watching his advantage, gave Arthur a blow upon the forehead, which might
have proved mortal, had he not blunted the edge of his weapon against
the helmet. When Arthur saw his coat of mail and shield red with blood,
he was inflamed with still greater rage, and lifting up his Caliburn with
his utmost strength struck it through the helmet into Flollo's head, and
made a terrible gash. With this wound Flollo fell down, tearing the
ground with his spurs, and expired. As soon as this news was spread
through the army, the citizens ran together, and opening the gates, sur-
rendered the city to Arthur. After the victory, he divided his army into
two parts; one of which he committed to the conduct of Hoel, whom
he ordered to march against Guitard, commander of the Pictavians;
while he with the other part should endeavour to reduce the other
provinces. Hoel upon this entered Aquitaine, possessed himself of the
cities of that country, and after distressing Guitard in several battles,
forced him to surrender. He also destroyed Gascony with fire and sword,
and subdued the princes of it. At the end of nine years, in which time
all the parts of Gaul were entirely reduced, Arthur returned back to
Paris, where he kept his court, and calling an assembly of the clergy
and people, established peace and the just administration of the laws
in that kingdom. Then he bestowed Neustria, now called Normandy,
upon Bedver, his butler; the province of Andegavia upon Caius, his
sewer; and several other provinces upon his great men that attended

him. Thus having settled the peace of the cities and countries there, he returned back in the beginning of spring to Britain.*

> XII. *Arthur summons a great many kings, princes, archbishops, etc. to a solemn assembly at the City of Legions.*

Upon the approach of the feast of Pentecost, Arthur, the better to demonstrate his joy after such triumphant success, and for the more solemn observation of that festival, and reconciling the minds of the princes that were now subject to him, resolved, during that season, to hold a magnificent court, to place the crown upon his head, and to invite all the kings and dukes under his subjection, to the solemnity. And when he had communicated his design to his familiar friends, he pitched upon the City of Legions as a proper place for his purpose. For besides its great wealth above the other cities, its situation, which was in Glamorganshire upon the river Uske, near the Severn sea, was most pleasant, and fit for so great a solemnity. For on one side it was washed by that noble river, so that the kings and princes from the countries beyond the seas might have the convenience of sailing up to it. On the other side, the beauty of the meadows and groves, and magnificence of the royal palaces with lofty gilded roofs that adorned it, made it even rival the grandeur of Rome. It was also famous for two churches; whereof one was built in honour of the martyr Julius, and adorned with a choir of virgins, who had devoted themselves wholly to the service of God; but the other, which was founded in memory of St Aaron, his companion, and maintained a convent of canons, was the third metropolitan church of Britain. Besides, there was a college of two hundred philosophers, who, being learned in astronomy and the other arts, were diligent in observing the courses of the stars, and gave Arthur true predictions of the events that would happen at that time. In this place, therefore, which afforded such delights, were preparations made for the ensuing festival. Ambassadors were then sent into several kingdoms, to invite to court the princes, both of Gaul and all the adjacent islands. Accordingly there came Augusel, king of Albania, now Scotland; Urian, king of Mureif; Cadwallo Lewirh, king of the Venedotians, now called the North Wales men; Sater, king of the Demetians, or South Wales men; Cador, king of Cornwall; also the archbishops of the three metropolitan sees, London, York, and Dubricius of the City of Legions. This prelate, who was primate of Britain, and legate of the apostolical see, was so eminent for his piety, that he could

*It is wonderful that the contents of this book should ever have passed for authentic history; our ancestors of the eleventh, twelfth, and thirteenth centuries must have been singularly ignorant of every thing concerning the latter ages of the Roman empire, and the formation of the modern kingdoms of France and Germany, etc., if they could believe that king Arthur ever held his court in Paris.

cure any sick person by his prayers. There came also the consuls of the principal cities, viz. Morvid, consul of Gloucester; Mauron, of Worcester; Anaraut, of Salisbury; Arthgal, of Carguiet or Warguit; Jugein, of Legecester; Cursalen, of Kaicester; Kinmare, duke of Dorobernia; Galluc, of Salisbury; Urgennius, of Bath; Jonathal, of Dorchester; Boso, of Ridoc, that is, Oxford. Besides the consuls, came the following worthies of no less dignity: Danaut, Map Papo; Cheneus, Map Coil; Peredur, Mab Eridur; Guiful, Map Nogoit; Regin, Map Claut; Eddelein, Map cledauc; Kincar, Mab Bagan; Kimmare; Gorboroniam, Map Goit; Clofaut, Rupmaneton; Kimbelim, Map Trunat; Cathleus, Map Catel; Kinlich, Map Neton; and many others too tedious to enumerate. From the adjacent islands came Guillamurius, king of Ireland; Malvasius, king of Iceland; Doldavius, king of Gothland; Gunfasius, king of the Orkneys; Lot, king of Norway; Aschillius, king of the Dacians. From the parts beyond the seas, came Holdin, king of Ruteni; Leodegarius, consul of Bolonia; Bedver, the butler, duke of Normandy; Borellus, of Cenomania; Caius, the sewer, duke of Andegavia; Guitard, of Pictavia; also the twelve peers of Gaul, whom Guerinus Carnotensis brought along with him: Hoel, duke of the Armorican Britons, and his nobility, who came with such a train of mules, horses, and rich furniture, as it is difficult to describe. Besides these, there remained no prince of any consideration on this side of Spain, who came not upon this invitation. And no wonder, when Arthur's munificence, which was celebrated over the whole world, made him beloved by all people.

XIII. *A description of the royal pomp at the coronation of Arthur.*

When all were assembled together in the city, upon the day of the solemnity, the archbishops were conducted to the palace, in order to place the crown upon the king's head. Therefore Dubricius, inasmuch as the court was kept in his diocese, made himself ready to celebrate the office, and undertook the ordering of whatever related to it. As soon as the king was invested with his royal habiliments, he was conducted in great pomp to the metropolitan church, supported on each side by two archbishops, and having four kings, viz. of Albania, Cornwall, Demetia, and Venedotia, whose right it was, bearing four golden swords before him. He was also attended with a concert of all sorts of music, which made most excellent harmony. On another part was the queen, dressed out in her richest ornaments, conducted by the archbishops and bishops to the Temple of Virgins; the four queens also of the kings last mentioned, bearing before her four white doves according to ancient custom; and after her there followed a retinue of women, making all imaginable demonstrations of joy. When the whole procession was ended, so transporting was the harmony of the musical instruments and voices, whereof there was a vast variety in both churches, that the

knights who attended were in doubt which to prefer, and therefore
crowded from the one to the other by turns, and were far from being
tired with the solemnity, though the whole day had been spent in it.
At last, when divine service was over at both churches, the king and
queen put off their crowns, and putting on their lighter ornaments,
went to the banquet; he to one palace with the men, and she to another
with the women. For the Britons still observed the ancient custom of
Troy, by which the men and women used to celebrate their festivals
apart. When they had all taken their seats according to precedence,
Caius the server, in rich robes of ermine, with a thousand young noble-
men, all in like manner clothed with ermine, served up the dishes. From
another part, Bedver the butler was followed with the same number
of attendants, in various habits, who waited with all kinds of cups and
drinking vessels. In the queen's palace were innumerable waiters,
dressed with variety of ornaments, all performing their respective offices;
which if I should describe particularly, I should draw out the history
to a tedious length. For at that time Britain had arrived at such a pitch
of grandeur, that in abundance of riches, luxury of ornaments, and
politeness of inhabitants, it far surpassed all other kingdoms. The
knights in it that were famous for feats of chivalry, wore their clothes
and arms all of the same colour and fashion: and the women also no
less celebrated for their wit, wore all the same kind of apparel; and
esteemed none worthy of their love, but such as had given a proof of
their valour in three several battles. Thus was the valour of the men
an encouragement for the women's chastity, and the love of the woman
a spur to the soldier's bravery.

XIV. *After a variety of sports at the coronation, Arthur amply rewards
his servants.*

As soon as the banquets were over, they went into the fields without
the city, to divert themselves with various sports. The military men composed a kind of diversion in imitation of a fight on horseback; and the
ladies, placed on the top of the walls as spectators, in a sportive manner darted their amorous glances at the courtiers, the more to encourage
them. Others spent the remainder of the day in other diversions, such
as shooting with bows and arrows, tossing the pike, casting of heavy
stones and rocks, playing at dice and the like, and all these inoffen-
sively and without quarrelling. Whoever gained the victory in any of
these sports, was rewarded with a rich prize by Arthur. In this manner
were the first three days spent; and on the fourth, all who, upon account
of their titles, bore any kind of office at this solemnity, were called
together to receive honours and preferments in reward of their services,
and to fill up the vacancies in the governments of cities and castles,
archbishoprics, bishoprics, abbeys, and other posts of honour.

[1] *The Mystic Life of Merlin*, Arkana, 1987, and *The Prophetic Vision of Merlin*, Arkana, 1986.
[2] *Warriors of Arthur* by John Matthews & Bob Stewart, Blandford Press, 1987.
[3] Southampton.
[4] Lincoln.

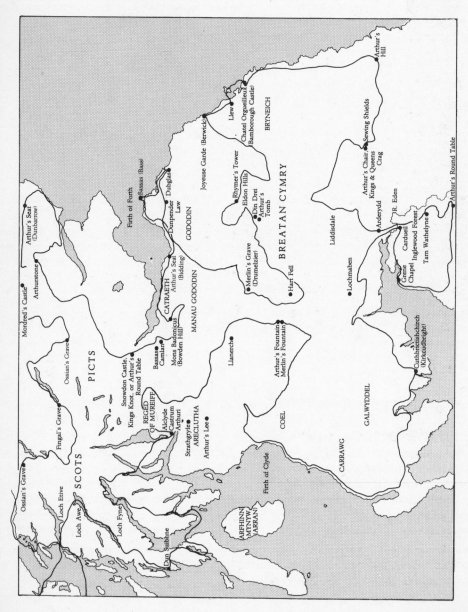

'THE NORTH'
in the Sixth
Century

OR

ARTHURIAN
SCOTLAND
to illustrate
MR STUART
GLENNIE'S
Journeyings

Scale of English Miles

5 0 5 10 15 20

Mr Glennie's route
indicated by
bold line

Ossian's Grave

Loch Etive

Fingal's Grave

Loch Awe

Loch Fyne

SCOTS

PICTS

Mordred's Castle

Arthurstone

Arthur's Seat
(Dunbarrow)

Ossian's Grave

Snowdon Castle.
Kings Knot, or Arthur's
Round Table

REGED
OF MUREIFF

Dun Suibhne

Alclyde
Castrum
Arthuri

Strathgyte

ARECLUTHA

Arthur's Lee

Firth of Clyde

ARFHINN
MYNYW
(ARRAN)

CARRAWG

COEL

GALWYDDEL

Bassas
Camlan

Mons Badonicus
(Bowden Hill)

CATRAETH

Arthur's Seat
(Bidding)

MANAU GODODIN

Llanerch

Firth of Forth

Bassas (Bassi)

Dubglas

Dunpender
Law

GODODIN

Arthur's Fountain
Merlin's Fountain

Merlin's Grave
(Drumelzier)

Hart Fell

Lochmaben

Joyeuse Garde (Berwick)

Llew

Chatel Orgueilleux
(Bamborough Castle)

Rhymer's Tower

Eldon Hills

Din Drei
Arthur's
Tomb

BREATAN CYMRY

BRYNEICH

Arthur's Hill

Arthur's Chair
Kings & Queens
Crag

Sewing Shields

Liddisdale

Arderydd

R. Eden

Carduell

Grene
Chapel

Inglewood Forest

Tarn Wathelyne

Arthur's Round Table

Cuthbrictiscurch
(Kirkcudbright)

Chapter 5.
Arthurian Localities
by J. S. Stuart Glennie

Ever since the beginning of modern Arthurian Scholarship in the 19th century, debate has raged over the position of the sites associated with the great stories. Where was Camelot, which was the site of the Round Table? Was Arthur a Cornishman, or did he hail from Somerset, Wales or even further North? While no conclusive evidence one way or the other has yet been produced, there has been a persistent argument for placing Arthur in Scotland.

Recently, Norma Lorre Goodrich, in her curious book King Arthur (Franklin Watts, 1967) has re-opened this old theory; but one of the first attempts to investigate the idea was the respected antiquarian J. S. Glennie from whose pioneering *Arthurian Localities*, originally published in 1869, the following extracts are taken.

Much of Glennie's scholarly apparatus is now defunct, having been superceded by more up-to-date archaeological evidence. But much remains unchallenged, and contains some fascinating speculations about the sites of Arthur's famous 12 battles against the Saxons, his court of Camelot, his deeds and the deeds of his champions. Above all, Glennie walked the land himself, covering some 12,000 miles, mostly on foot, and visiting every known site that his extensive reading and research could discover. Many of these sites are now lost, ploughed under or built over in the succeeding years. But for all those concerned with the living history of the land, the magical *temenoi* where the figures of Arthur and his men live on in the realms of imagination and magic, here is a quarry that bears a rich lode.

INTRODUCTION—THE OLD ARTHUR-LAND.

One of the many indications of that synthetic, and reconstructive, rather than analytic, and destructive, tendency which marks this second half of the nineteenth century is the fact that historical scholars are beginning to look on popular legends and romances, not certainly with the uncritical credulity of the days before Niebuhr, but with the belief of finding in them such records of historical events as will well repay the trouble of investigating them. It seems desirable, therefore, in this introductory chapter, in order at once to indicate the point of view of this Essay, to set-forth, in the first place, the general relation which it seeks to establish between Mediaeval Romance and Pre-mediaeval

History. I shall, then, in the second section, bring before the reader
the chief traditional Arthurian Localities of Southern Scotland, Western
England, and North-Western France. After such a survey of the Old
Arthur-land, I shall, in the third section, state the question which I
propose in this Essay more particularly to consider, point-out its interest,
and explain the method by which I hope to attain a definitive answer.
And, in conclusion, I shall state the general subjects of the succeeding
chapters.

THE RELATION OF MEDIAEVAL ROMANCE TO PRE-MEDIAEVAL HISTORY

The age of the Arthurian, and other great Cycles of Romance, is that
which, in the opinion of both the great thinkers who have chiefly
influenced the intellectual development of Modern Europe—in the opinion both of Hegel and of Comte—began in the eleventh, and culmi-
nated in the thirteenth century. For, about that century, it is—as has
been conclusively shown by the researches of later scholars verifying
and confirming philosophical speculation—that the distinctively Christian, or Catholico-Feudal organization of society attains its highest perfection; that the Crusades afford their brightest examples of heroism,
and chivalric magnanimity; that Art achieves its most original, most
variedly beautiful, and majestic triumphs; and that Literature presents,
in the Romances, at once the highest, and most popular Ideals of the
Age. And thus culminating in the thirteenth century, the Mediaeval
Age may, as a great historic period, be defined as the five centuries
from the eleventh to the fifteenth inclusive. With the sixteenth century begins our present Modern or Transition Age; a period marked,
not as was the Mediaeval Age, by the general acceptance of an established system of thought, and of government; but a period distinguished
by the manifestly progressing destruction of all the political forms, and
intellectual foundations of the social system of the Age preceding it,
and a no less certain, though perhaps less manifest preparation of a
new and higher system of social organization.

But for a thousand years before the opening of the Mediaeval Age,
Christianity had been working in the European world, completing the
destruction of the antique system of thought and of society, and laying the foundations of a new world-system. The first half of this
millennium I would distinguish as the Imperial Age. For it is the age
of the Roman Empire of the East and West. It is the age also of the
Apostles, the Fathers, and the Martyrs of Christianity. And the latter
five hundred years of this first millennium of the Christian era I would
distinguish as the Barbarian, or Pre-mediaeval Age. The Roman Empire
no longer extends its sway over Northern and Western Europe; and
the various tribes of barbarians—Celtic and Teutonic—are engaged in

perpetual conflicts—miserable and disheartening when looked at in their details, but, regarded as a whole, found to be in their great issues conflicts that laid the foundations of the nationalities of a New Europe.[1] For, by the end of this age, there has been constituted in France the first of the Romanic or Neo-Latin nationalities; in England, a preponderatingly Teutonic; and, in Scotland, a predominantly Celtic nationality. And as this Pre-mediaeval Age was occupied by the elemental wars of the tribes ultimately consolidated in these three national unities; so, the Mediaeval Age was filled with the contests of these nations with each other, and with the rising nationalities around them. But, on taking a wide view of European history, we shall see these Mediaeval wars preparing, as all conflict does, in fact, prepare, a higher unity. And, as the name of Scotland is first heard towards the close of the Pre-mediaeval wars of the tribes of North Britain; so, the idea of Europe emerges from the Mediaeval conflict of the races of this Asiatic promontory.

Now that which, I trust, will be found the most clearly established, as it is the most general view in this Essay maintained, is that in the Romances of the Mediaeval Age, and more particularly in those of the Arthurian Cycle, there is not only a mythological element, as I hope in another Essay fully to show; but that there is a very important historical element; a record, legendary indeed, and hardly to be deciphered for its extraordinary flourishes, but still a record of certain real, and not purely fictitious characters, incidents, and conflicts of the Premediaeval Age. And if this should be established, we shall certainly have a result which will reward the labour of this investigation of Arthurian localities; a result not only for the general Mediaeval history of European literature; but for the Pre-mediaeval history of that particular region in which our researches may localize the events from which the historic element of the Arthurian Romances is derived. Of no slight historic interest can it be to show that Arthur and Merlin are neither purely mythic personages, nor mere poetic creations; but that the legends and traditions that the Mediaeval trouveres and troubadours wrought-out into their magnificent romances, were records of actual Pre-mediaeval personages, whose characters and histories had forcibly impressed the popular imagination; and that the country where the heroic Arthur fought, and the forests where the wild Merlin wandered, can be now, on no doubtful evidence, pointed-out. The one, no doubt, was but a leader of barbarians, and the other but a barbarian compound of madman and poet, of prophet and bard. But it is these very circumstances that give their characters an historic interest in relation to their Mediaeval idealisation.

And not only shall we thus see the Mediaeval connected with the Pre-mediaeval Age in the relation between the Romantic Ideals of the one, and the Traditional Heroes of the other; but, in showing that the

Mediaeval Romances had an historic element, and that the age and country of those characters who lived-again in the Romantic Ideals, can be now assigned; we shall connect also with that Pre-mediaeval, our present Modern Age. For there are many indications, not only in the needs of the time, and in the characteristic advantages of the Arthurian Mythology; but in the actual fact of the use already made of it by so many modern poets;[2] that the Mediaeval Romances of King Arthur will be the chief formal material of the New Poesy. To show, therefore, that these Mediaeval Romances had in them a definite historical element, is to give that New Poesy also an historic basis; to discover for its characters and incidents 'a iocal habitation'; and to connect by a new bond the Present, not only with the Mediaeval, but with the Pre-mediaeval Age.

Another, a still higher, a moral interest this investigation seems also to me to have; and I trust that, before entering upon it, I may be pardoned for alluding for a moment to these higher, these moral aspects of our subject. Let me but desire my readers to reflect how the establishment of such a relation, as will here occupy us, between Mediaeval Romance and Pre-mediaeval history, brings home the great idea of the continuity of human development; how it shows the traditions of the barbarian conflicts of one age taken up by the next, and used as the formal material of the creations of a magnificient poesy; how it shows the rude lives of an earlier period living again in the ideal heroes of succeeding ages; how it shows that, though the tribes of whom these traditions are the historic memorials, were conquered, absorbed and extinguished as separate political organizations, yet they died not; how it shows that, in the succession of Humanital, as in the sequence of Natural phenomena, there is, in fact, no such thing as Death; that there is but Decease only, and Transformation. And thus it is but a great historic truth mythically expressed, that legend of Merlin's prophecies from his Tomb. 'Lady,' replied Merlin, 'the flesh upon me will be rotten before a month shall have past; but my spirit will not be wanting to all those who shall come here.'[3]

> 'Vive la voce; e come chiara emerga,
> Udir potrai da la marmorea tomba;
> Che le passate e le future cose,
> A chi gli domandó sempre rispose.'[4]

THE ARTHURIAN LOCALITIES OF SOUTHERN SCOTLAND, WESTERN ENGLAND, AND NORTH-WESTERN FRANCE

Let us now proceed to our preliminary survey of the traditional Arthurland. Localities with Arthurian names, or Arthurian traditions attached to them, are to be found, in greater or less abundance, in Scotland, in Wales, Somersetshire, and Cornwall, and in Brittany. In Scotland, there is still pointed out in the churchyard of Meigle, on the borders of Perthshire and Forfarshire, an ancient sculptured stone said to mark 'Ganore's Grave', or the tomb of Guenivere. Arthur's Seat still connects Edinburgh with the mythic hero's fame. And at Drummelziar on the Tweed is still to be seen the perennial thorn that has not yet ceased, in an offshoot at least, to bloom over the grave of Merlin. How many more Arthurian localities are to be found in Scotland will, in the third chapter of this essay, be shown in detail. Postponing, then, any further notice of the Arthurian localities of Southern Scotland, I shall at once proceed to those of Western England.

In North Wales, between Mold and Ruthin, near Colomendy Lodge, in Flintshire, is Maen Arthur, a stone which, in popular fancy, bears and impression of the hoof of the hero's steed. Between Mold and Denbigh is Moel Arthur, an ancient British fort, defended by two ditches of great depth. Near Denbigh, 'there is, in the Paroch of *Llansannan* in the Side of a Stony Hille, a Place wher there be 24 Holes or Places in a Roundel for Men to sitte in, but sum lesse, and some bigger, cutte oute of the mayne Rok by Mannes Hand; and there Children and Young Men cumming to seke their Catelle use to sitte & play. Sum caulle it *the Rounde Table.* Kiddes use ther communely to play & skip from Sete to Sete.'[5] The remains of what would appear to have been a Roman Camp overlooking Redwharf Bay, or Traeth Coch, in Anglesea, is locally called Burdd Arthur, or Arthur's Round Table. Also in Anglesey, in the grounds of Llwydiarth, a seat of the Lloyd family, is a famous Maen Chwf, or rocking stone, called Arthur's Quoit. In Caernarvonshire, to the south of Snowdon, 'overlooking the lower end of Llyn y Ddinas, is Dinas Emrys, a singular isolated rock, clothed on all sides with wood, containing on the summit some faint remains of a building defended by ramparts,' with which a legend of Merlin and Vortigern is connected:

> 'And from the top of Brith, so high and wondrous steep,
> Where Dinas Emris stood, shewed where the serpents fought,
> The White that tore the Red; from whence the prophet wrought
> The Briton's sad decay then shortly to ensue.'[6]

In this same county at Llyn Geirionydd, as also at Aberystwith, and other localities on the Cardiganshire coast, Taliessin, another of the four great bards of the sixth century, is said to have been found on the shore, like Moses in the bulrushes, by Gwyddno Garanhir. And, on the south of Caernarvon Bay, is Nant Gwrtheyrn, the Hollow of Vortigern, a precipitous ravine by the sea, said to have been the last resting place of the usurper—so, at least, he is represented in the *Romance of Merlin*[7]—when he fled to escape the rage of his subjects on finding themselves betrayed to the Saxons. In Merionethshire, there is a river with the Arthurian name of Camlan flowing into the Eden. And the Church of Llanover, near the Bala Lake in this county, is said

to have been the burial place of one of the four most famous bards
of the Arthurian Age, Llywarch Hen, or Llywarch, the Aged. To the
address of this bard to his Crutch Mr Arnold refers in illustration of
'the Titanism of the Celt, his passionate, turbulent, indomitable reac-
tion against the despotism of fact.'[8]

> 'O my Crutch! is it not the first day of May? The furrows, are they not
> shining? The young corn, is it not springing? Ah! the sight of thy handle
> makes me wroth.'

In South Wales, near the turnpike road from Reynoldstone to Swan-
sea, on the north slope of Cefn Bryn, there is the famous cromlech
called Arthur's Stone. About five miles to the south of Brecon on the
Usk, rise the twin peaks of the Beacons called Arthur's Chair. On an
eminence adjoining the park of Mocras Court, in Brecknockshire, is
a large and peculiar kind of British cromlech, called Arthur's Table.
And at the once famous city, now the decayed village, of Caerleon upon
Usk—the *Isca Silurum* of Antoninus, where the second Augustan Legion
was, during a long period, in garrison—are the remains of a Roman
Amphitheatre, in a bank of earth heaped up in an oval form sixteen
feet high, and now also called Arthur's Round Table. Some four miles
from Caermarthen, itself said to be derived, but quite erroneously, from
Caer Merddin, the city of Merlin, is Merlin's Grove, and Hill. And on
the bank of the Towy, within the domain of Dynevor Park, Spenser has
placed the cave of Merlin:

> 'There the wise Merlin, whilom wont, they sey,
> To make his wonne low underneath the ground,
> In a deep delve far from the view of day,
> That of no living wight he might be found,
> When so he counselled with his sprights around.
>
> It is a hideous, hollow, cave-like bay,
> Under a rock that has a little space
> From the swift Tyvi, tumbling down apace
> Amongst the woody hills of Dynevowr.'[9]

In Somersetshire, may first be mentioned Bath, the *Aquae Solis* or *Sulis*
of the Romans. But the reasons against here localizing the Arthurian
Battle of Badon Hill mentioned by Nennius are well stated by Mr Guest,
though, as will be seen hereafter, I cannot agree with his suggestion,
'Why may not the Mons Badonicus be the Badbury of Dorsetshire?'
Between Castle Cary and Yeovil, on the escarpment of the oolite, abut-
ting on the plain which extends to Ilchester, is Cadbury, 'a hill of a
mile compass at the top, four trenches encircling it, and twixt every
of them an earthen wall; the content of it, within about twenty acres
full of ruins and reliques of old buildings. . . ''Dii boni (saith Leland)
quot hîc profundissimarum fossarum? quot hîc egestae terrae valla? quae
demum praecipita? atque ut paucis finiam, videtur mihi quidem esse

et Artis at Naturae miraculum.'' Antique report makes this one of
Arthur's places of his Round Table.' Cadbury is mentioned in old records
under the name of Camelot, a name still perpetuated in the adjoining
villages of Queen's Camel and West Camel. In the fourth ditch is a spring
called King Arthur's Well. And the relics found in the fortress prove
it to have been occupied by the Romans, though, as we have seen, tradition assigns its origin to King Arthur, who, in the opinion of Camden, probably fought a battle with the Saxons in this neighbourhood.
The other famous Arthurian locality of Somersetshire is Glastonbury,
which, once encircled by the arms of the Brue, or Brent, formed the
Roman Insula Avalonia, or Isle of Avalon.

> 'O three times famous Isle, where is that place that might
> Be with thyself compared for glory and delight,
> Whilst Glastenbury stood? exalted to that pride,
> Whose monastery seemed all other to deride.
>
> To whom didst thou commit that monument to keep
> When not great Arthur's tomb, nor holy Joseph's grave,
> From sacrilege had power their holy bones to save?'[10]

Selden's annotation on this passage seems worth giving, at least in part.
'Henry the Second in his expedition towards Ireland entertained by
the way in Wales with bardish songs, wherein he heard it affirmed that
in Glastenbury (made almost an isle by the river's embracements)
Arthur was buried betwixt two pillars, gave commandment to Henry
of Blois, then abbot, to make search for the corps, which was found
in a wooden coffin (Girald saith oaken, Leland thinks alder), some sixteen foot deep; but after they had digged nine foot, they found a stone
on whose lower side was fixt a leaden cross (crosses fixt upon the tombs
of old Christians were in all places ordinary) with his name inscribed,
and the letter side of it turned to the stone. He was then honoured
with a sumptuous monument, and afterwards the sculls of him and
his wife Guinever were taken out (to remain as separate relics and spec-
tacles) by Edward Longshanks and Eleanor... Worthily famous was
the Abbey also from Joseph of Arimathea (that Εὐσχήμων βουλητής, as
S. Mark calls him) here buried, etc.'[11] But, notwithstanding the
inscription on the leaden cross, 'Hic jacet sepultus inclytus rex Arthurus in insula Avalonia'; or as it is otherwise more epigrammatically given,
'Hic jacet Arthurus, Rex quondam, Rexque futurus'—

> 'His Epitaph recordeth so certaine
> Here lieth K. Arthur that shall raigne againe—'

it is hardly necessary to add that there is almost every reason to believe
that this extraordinary 'find' could have been nothing but a pious fraud,
in majorem monasterii gloriam.

In Cornwall (Cornus Galliae), Camelford and Tintagel have a pre-
eminence in Arthurian tradition similar to that maintained by Cad-

bury and Glastonbury in Somersetshire. Not far from Camelford is a
little entrenchment, known as Arthur's Hall. On the Camel or Alan
(*Crum hayle,* crooked river) the final battle is said to have been fought
between Arthur and his rebellious nephew, or rather, bastard son,
Mordred.

> 'Let Camel of her course & curious windings boast,
>
> . . .her proper course that loosly doth neglect,
> As frantic, ever since her British Arthur's blood,
> By Mordred's murtherous hand was mingled with her flood.'[13]

Between Camelford and Launceston, on Wilsey Downs, is Warbelow
Barrow, an ancient fortification of considerable size, in the centre of
which is a large mound, popularly called King Arthur's Grave. At
Slaughter Bridge, between Camelford and Tintagel, on the Bristol Channel, a stone, with the hero's name on it, is pointed out. Tintagel, though
in the romances of Sir Tristrem it is made the Castle of King Mark,
is the reputed birthplace and residence of Arthur. Some of the rock
basins in the slate of the promontory are fantastically called King
Arthur's Cups and Saucers; and south of Tintagel, near St Colomb,
is the eminence of Castle an Dinas, or the earth-fort, crowned with
an elliptical doubly entrenched camp of six acres, which tradition affirms
to have been the hunting-seat of King Arthur, who, according to the
legends, chased the wild deer on the Tregon Moors. Some miles north
of Liskeard are several rocky tors, one group of which is called King
Arthur's Bed (*Beth, i.e* Grave?). Lyonnesse, the possession of Sir Tristrem, is said to have been that submerged tract of slate by which the
Scilly Isles, the outlying members of that series of granitic highlands
which extends through Cornwall to Dartmoor, were traditionally united
to the mainland; and two of the most eastern isles of this little
archipelago are distinguished by the names of Great, and Little Arthur.

Crossing the Channel, we find in Little Britain, or Brittany, another
district boasting itself to be the cradle of romance. In the Cornuailles
and Leonais, two of its ancient divisions, we have another Cornwall
and Lyonnesse. In the latter, is situated Kerduel, where Arthur is said
to have held his Court. A short distance off the coast is the island of
Aiguilon or Avalon, where, as in the Insula Avalonia of Glastonbury,
he is said to have been buried. And near this also is Mount St Michael,
with its legend of the hero's rescue of the fair Helena, the niece of Hoel,
from the hateful embraces of the giant.

> ' . . . great Rython's self he slew in his repair
> Who ravish'd Howell's niece, young Hellena the fair;
> And for a trophy brought the giant's coat away,
> Made of the beards of kings.'[14]

'On the banks of the Elorn are still pointed out the sites of the castles

and forts of Launcelot du Lac, and of La Blonde Yseult. In the Morbi-
han, the next Celtic division to that of Cornuailles is shown the Forest
of Broceliande, where Merlin ''drees his weird''; and there also is the
consecrated fountain of Baranton, which is still believed to possess
miraculous properties. There also may be found Caradoc and Madoc,
and other names peculiar to the ancient legends of British History.'[15]

Figure 3: 'Sir Percival vanquishes the Knights of the Evil custom in the
Enchanted Forest' by Christian Loring.

THE QUESTION PROPOSED, ITS INTEREST, AND THE METHOD OF ITS SOLUTION

Thus we find Arthurian localities in all the five districts, in modern
times known as Southern Scotland, Wales, Somersetshire, Cornwall,
and Brittany. And hence the first result of a general inquiry into Arthurian topography is the outlining of a continuous region from the Grampians, in Scotland, to the Loire, in France, distinguished by localities
with Arthurian names, or Arthurian traditions attached to them. This
region may be briefly described as including what is now the south
of Scotland, the west of England, and the northwest of France.[16] And

the question which I propose in this Essay mainly to consider, and, if possible, definitively to answer, is:- Which of these three divisions of the old Arthur-land, that of Scotland, of England, or of France, was the original birth-land of Arthurian tradition?

To show the importance of this question, and to excite an interest in its solution, I trust that the following brief remarks will be sufficient. In the first place, then, it opens up to the philosophic historian the general question of the origin of traditional topographies; a question which has not only not been, as yet, so far as I am aware, treated scientifically, except with respect to some of the Syrian localities of Christian tradition; but which is connected in its general bearings with all those other questions of origin which so directly affect the validity of popular religious beliefs. But, farther, it is an inquiry, the result of which will be to draw back the veil from ancient centuries of the history of mankind, and to connect, with still existing monuments, long past events of that struggle for existence, which, of all others, must chiefly interest us of the human race.

But, besides these general results, the inquiry on which we would now enter, ought, at length, to present us with the local historical basis of that vast cycle of Romance the large place of which in the history of European literature, and the great influence of which on the development of modern civilization, is now more or less fully acknowledged. Yet, further, if I am right in the conclusion that the two chief elements determining the form of the Mediaeval Arthurian Romances are to be found in historical events of the Premediaeval Age, and in Celtic myths, which may be traced back to the earliest forms of speech distinctive of the Indo-European Races, this inquiry will appear as the necessary preliminary to the investigation of the Arthurian branch of a mythology which is second in interest only to that which has gathered round the historical facts of Christian tradition. And yet, further, if, as seems probable, not only from their special characteristics, but from the use increasingly made of them, the Arthurian Romances are destined to become the chief formal material of European poesy; such an inquiry as the following should, in determining the original locality of Arthurian tradition, fix also the site of a new classic land, in which, as of old, in Greece, the creations of poesy in all its different forms, may have a common 'local habitation', and gain all the advantages, thus only given, of vivid realization in the popular fancy.

For those to whom the force of these considerations in illustration of the importance of the question above proposed, and the interest of its solution, may not be at once apparent, let me add, what may to some antiquarians be the most stimulating circumstances of all, the facts, simply, that this question has been eagerly discussed; that the answer here given, though it has been suggested, cannot be held to have been hitherto proved; and that the method of proof which has

been followed is new, inasmuch as it is in adaptation of physical methods
in antiquarian researches.

That method has consisted, first, in examining the results of the
modern scientific criticism of Celtic history, political, and literary, in
as far as these results more particularly bear on the definite localiza-
tion of events which may have been the origin of those traditions which,
in our investigation of Arthurian topography, we have found to be so
widely diffused. Our deduction from these critical results has been that
it was in Southern Scotland, and neither in Western England, nor in
North-western France that the Arthurian traditions, still attached to
so much of the topography of all these districts, originated. This deduction, however, standing alone, could hardly in any case, and especially
considering the scantiness of the materials on which it is founded,
be received as satisfactory scientific proof of the historical origin of
Arthurian localities. And hence the necessity of an inductive verification of our deductive theory. How was such a verification to be
gained?

By the second step of the method which has guided these researches.
This was founded on the postulatte, or assumption, that, except special reasons could be shown to the contrary, that district in which the
Arthurian traditions had their local historical origin would be found
to be the chief country of Arthurian localities. I therefore noted, in the
course of a great many perambulations of the region thus critically indicated, all the localities there to be found with Arthurian names, or
Arthurian traditions attached to them. The general result of these journeys was a determination of that district of Southern Scotland and the
English Border, in which the Arthurian traditions had, according to
our critical theory, had their local origin, as, to this day, the chief country
of Arthurian localities. This, on the principle above stated, I seemed
justified in regarding as the required inductive verification. And thus
it is in the fact of the accordance of the deduction from the results of
literary and historical criticism with the induction from the results of
topographical investigation, that the main proof of the thesis in this
essay maintained, namely, that Scotland is the original seat of Arthurian tradition, consists.

But our conclusions both as to the historical origin and the chief country of the Arthurian localities, having been found to be thus accordant
and mutually confirmatory in their indication of Southern Scotland,
it did not appear that our investigation would be scientifically complete without an examination of the relations of the Scottish Arthurian topography to that Fingalian topography which has been long
known to be possessed by Scotland, as well as Ireland. Nor will, I trust,
this third step in our investigation of Arthurian localities be thought
other than a necesary part of our discussion of Arthurian localities,
if, instructed by the results of that most powerful of modern scientific

instruments, the Comparative Method, one has been led to see how necessary is the study of the Fingalian Myths in the scientific investigation of the Arthurian Romances; if one considers the importance of the fact that the local relations, discovered in Scotland, of Arthurian to Fingalian tradition, are nowhere else to be found; and if, especially, I am successful in showing in these unique relations a confirmation of the theory here maintained as to the original birthland of the traditions of King Arthur.

Having thus set-forth the general relation which I seek to establish between Mediaeval Romance and Pre-mediaeval History; having briefly noted the chief traditional localities of the Old Arthur-land, considered as a continuous European region; and having stated the method by which I propose to determine the special district in which Arthurian traditions originated, the subjects of the succeeding chapters will be as follows. A summary account will be given of the very numerous perambulations of the Arthurian district of Scotland, from the result of which arises the verificative induction as to the chief country of Arthurian localities.

Let me now, then, endeavour to show that that part of those far Islands of the West where terminated, until their new exodus in the present age and where were reunited, at length, the two great northern and southern streams of Celtic migration from the Asian birthland of the Aryan tribes—that part of the Old Arthur-land in which the Premediaeval events which are the chief historical bases of the Arthurian Romances of the Mediaeval trouveres and troubadours actually occurred, and where the tradition of these events has to this day the most numerous topographical monuments—is that district of the largest of the British Isles which, bounded on the north by the chain of the Grampians, and on the south by the Tyne and the Derwent, was formerly known as *Y Gogledd*, or 'the North', and which I would distinguish as Arthurian Scotland.[18]

THE CHIEF COUNTRY OF ARTHURIAN LOCALITIES, AS GENERALIZED FROM AN EXPLORATION OF SOUTHERN SCOTLAND AND THE ENGLISH BORDER

Let me now proceed to give the generalized result of my exploration of the existing Arthurian Topography of the region indicated by the criticism of Cymric history as the birthland of Arthurian tradition, in a narrative of a single hypothetical journey in which a very great number of actual journeys through particular districts are connected, as in the route on the accompanying map. Let us suppose ourselves, then, to start from the Braes of Mar, at the foot of Ben-Muich-Dhui, the central dome of that mountain range of the Grampians, which, as we shall find in the next chapter, separates Arthurian, from Fingalian Scotland. For journeying, and it must be on foot, up Glen Cluny, and Glen Callater—ascending the wild, and solitary heights at the head of Loch Callater to the plateau of the Kinlochan Forest—passing along the eastern edge of the deep glen which runs up through this plateau, with hawks and eagles over head, and great herds of red deer in the woody pastures of the glen below—and travelling through Upper and Lower Glen Isla; we shall, in a single day's journey—but of some thirty or forty miles—pass through scenery which will remain in our recollection as a grand background to that of Arthurian Scotland; and, coming down on the most north-eastern group of Arthurian localities, our route will be southwards, through the eastern part of the Arthurian region, and then up again, northwards, on its western side.

We shall thus explore successively three great divisions of Arthurian localities—an Eastern, a Southern, or Border, and a Western Division; and the very numerous localities of each of these divisions we shall find to lie in three naturally distinguished districts, giving us, thus, in 'the North', no less than nine distinct Districts of Arthurian Localities. And, further, we shall find these localities to be of three different classes, which may be distinguished as Traditional, Historical, and Poetical; the first, being localities which, in their names and the still living traditions attached to them, are Arthurian; the second, being identifications of places connected with the Arthurian story as it is found in the earliest historical sources; and the third, being identifications of places mentioned in those Four Ancient Books of Cymric Poetry which we have found to belong, in their subject-matter, to the Arthurian Age, meaning by that term, not merely the generation of Arthur, but the century which opens with his exploits. That, side by side with these identifications of historical and poetical sites, we should find a very great number of traditional localities, is evidently, in itself, and apart from other considerations, no slight proof of the correctness of these identifications.

THE EASTERN DIVISION OF ARTHURIAN SCOTLAND

Lower Glen Isla lies between the main line of the Grampians and the lower range of hills, through the eastern end of which the road passes. Here we find ourselves with a wooded hill on the right, and, on the left, a steep, furze-covered hill, the last of the range in this direction, and with the remains of what has apparently been a formidable stronghold on its summit. It is Barry-hill (*Barra*, fortified hill), and the first Arthurian locality of what I would distinguished as **District I— Strathmore.** I ascend its grassy sides, crossed by many a sheep-track, and am sorry its rabbit-inhabitants disturb themselves so much to get out of my way. Seated on the higher of the two lines of entrenchment,

and looking down on the great valley of Strathmore, stretching across
to the seaward range of the Sidlaw Hills, and with the Isla winding
through it, past the 'bonnie house o' Airlie', I recall its Arthurian traditions. For innumerable legends agree in representing it as the Castle
to which the Pictish king Mordred, having defeated King Arthur in a
great battle, carried off as a prisoner his queen Quenivere, or, as she
is locally named, Ganora, Vanora, or Wander.[19] This, however, it
seems, she found by no means so unpleasant as she ought to have done.
For 'Vanora', says tradition, 'held an unlawful intercourse with Mordred;
and Arthur, when he received her again,' did not act with the mag-
nanimty of Mr Tennyson's *flos regum*, but, 'enraged at her infidelity,
caused her to be torn to pieces by wild horses.'[20] As an old fellow,
however, with whom I got into talk on the road near this, and who
told me a legend I had not previously heard of the four places in this
neighbourhood where the parts of Queen Vanora's dismembered body
were buried, sagely remarked: 'Thae auld histories are maistly lees, I'm
thinkin'.'

Her tomb (or principal tomb), 'Ganore's Grave', lies but a few miles
off. For 'she was buried at Meigle, and a monument erected to per-
petuate her infamy'. Gray, who visited the place from Glammis Castle,
notes: 'Passed through Meigill, where is the tomb of Queen Wander,
that was riven to death by stoned horses for nae gude that she did. . .
so the woman here told me, I assure you.'[21] And on examining the
curious sculptured stones in Meigle churchyard, said to be the remains
of this monument, we do actually find 'two representations of wild
beasts tearing a human body. . . and one where the body seems tied,
or close to chariot wheels. . . which may relate to Vanora, or may have
given rise to the tradition'. This is otherwise described by Archdeadon
Sinclair, of Glasgow, in a MS of the year 1560, as, 'Ane goddess in ane
caert and twa hors drawand her.'[22] But the scene of her last resting
place, when I visited it, seemed suggestive of some less rude, some
nobler version of her story. It was the close of autumn. Along the broad
valley of Strathmore, ending northwards in the Howe of the Mearns,
and sheltered from the sea by the Sidlaw Hills, with their many legends
of Duncan, Macbeth, and Banquo, the farm-yards were closely stacked
with the ingathered corn; the leaves, whirled by gentle breezes, were
falling through the sunny air; and beneath the lofty range of the snow-
capped Grampians, lay the dying year in the beauty of an ineffable
repose.

Mordred thus appears, in Scottish tradition, as both the political *hostis*,
or foe, and the domestic *inimicus*, or unfriend, of Arthur; but in Mediaeval Romance he commonly occupies the former position only, while
his traditional part, as the lover of Guenivere, is taken by Lancelot.
The question then arises, can Lancelot, as well as Mordred, be local-
ized in Scotland? Now M. de la Villemarqué very ingeniously identi-

fies Lancelot, or L'Ancelot, with the Cymric chieftain Mael: 'Les plus anciens manuscrits... portent souvent Ancelot... *Ancel,* en langue romane, signifie *servant,* et Ancelot est son diminutif... Si, par hasard, Ancelot était la traduction du nom d'un personnage gallois, dont l'histoire s'accorderait en tout point avec le roman? Eh bien, c'est ce que je crois avoir découvert. On trouve, en effet dans les traditions cel-tiques, un chef dont le nom *Mael (serviteur)* répond exactement à celui *d'Ancelot,* et à qui les anciens bardes, les triades, les chroniques, les legends, et toutes les autorités armoricanies, galloises on étrangeres prê-tent les mêmes traits, le même caractère, les mêmes moeurs, les mêmes aventures qu'au héros du roman français.' And, if we accept this iden-tification, then Lancelot, as well as Mordred, belongs to Scotland. For 'le chef Mael, selon les bardes gallois, avait dans l'Ecosse des domaines où il la mena'. But we may far more directly identify the country of Lancelot with a Scottish district, for he is uniformly spoken of in the Romances as the son of 'le roy Ban de Benoic'; and in the Scottish *Lancelot* of 1478, this 'Benoic' is at once identified for us in the lines

> 'a knycht clepit Lancelot of ye Laik,
> That sone of Bane was king of Albanak'

Albanak, or Alban, being the well-known name applied to Scotland beyond the Firths of Forth and Clyde. And that it was in the eastern part of that region that the kingdom of Lancelot's father was situated, we may presume from the fact of its having been 'le roy Claudas de la terre d'Escosse' (the western kingdem of the Scots of Dalriada?) who 'mena guerre contre le roy Ban de Benoic et le roy Boort de Ganues (or Gannes) tant quil les desherita de leurs terres'.[25] Thus, the Mael of tradition, and the Lancelot of romance, and the Mordred both of tradition and romance, are as closely connected in the scenes, as in the stories of their lives.

In very remarkable proximity to the Castle of Mordred, and the Grave of Guenivere, we find near Meigle, and in the parish of Cupar Angus, a standing stone called the Stone of Arthur; near it, again, a gentle-man's seat, called Arthur's Stone; and not far from it a farm called Arthur's Fold. And 'a rock on the north side of the hill of Dunbar-row, in Dunnichen parish (in the adjoining county of Forfar), has long borne, in the tradition of the country, the distinguished name of Arthur's Seat'.[26] This parish, it may be noted, is further remarkable as the scene of that great defeat of the Saxon Ecfrid, in 680, which per-manently secured the country between the Tay and the Forth from the influences that would have made it part of England.

And the Tay—of which the old name was Tava, from the Gaelic *Tamh,* smooth, of which *Taw* is the Cymric equivalent—is more than once men-tioned in the *Four Ancient Books,* as, for instance, in the *Black Book of Caermarthen:*

'It is not the nearest Tawy I speek to thee,
But the furthest Tawy.'[27]

And the Scottish Tay, and not the river of that name in South Wales,
seems to be also alluded to in the Dialogue between Merlin and his
sister Ganieda in the *Red Book of Hergest:*

'Rydderch Hael, the feller of the foe,
Dealt his stabs among them,
On the day of bliss at the ford of Tawy.'[28]

Between Perth on the Tay, and Stirling on the Forth, we find no Arthurian localities. But at the latter river, we enter on **District II—Firth
of Forth**. The banks of the Forth should seem to have been the scene
of a dispute as to who should lead in crossing the river, of which a curious legend is preserved in the Venedotian code of the *Old Welsh Laws*
(p. 50). And on the Links of Forth, Mr Skene would find the site of
Arthur's tenth battle, 'in litore fluminis quod vocatur Treuruit'. 'There
is much variety in the readings of this name, other MSS reading it "Trath
truiroit"; but the original Cymric form is given us in two of the poems
in the *Black Book;* it is in one *Trywruid,* and in the other *Tratheu
Trywruid.* There is no known river bearing a name approaching to this.
Tratheu, or shores, implies a sea-shore or sandy beach, and can only
be applicable to a river having an estuary. An old description of Scotland, written in 1165 by one familiar with Welsh names, says that the
river which divides the "regna Anglorum et Scottorum et currit juxta
oppidum de Strivelin" was "Scottice vocata *Froch,* Britannice *Werid*".
This Welsh name for the Forth at Stirling has disappeared, but it closely
resembles the last part of Nennius' name, and the difference between
wruid, the last part of Nennius' name Try-wruid, and Werid is trifling.
The original form must have been Gwruid or Gwerid, the G disappear-
ing in combination.'[30] So far Mr Skene. And it must be, at least,
remarked that not only has no more probable site been found for this
tenth battle, but that we have a strong confirmation of the above argument in favour of the Links of Forth, in the fact of Stirling being undoubtedly a traditional Arthurian locality.

For William of Worcester tells us that 'Rex Arturus custodiebat le
round table in Castro de Styrlyng, aliter Snowden West Castell'.[31] And
Snowdon, which is also the official title of one of the Scotish heralds,
has no connection with the Welsh mountain of that name, but is simply the descriptive name of Stirling—Snua-dun, the fort, or fortified
hill, on the river.

'Stirling's tower
Of yore the name of Snowdoun claims,'

says Sir Walter Scott,[32] and, in a note, quotes Sir David Lindsay:

'Adew, fair Snawdoun, with thy towris hie,
Thy Chapell-royall, park, and *Tabyll Round:*
May, June, and July would I dwell in thee,
Were I a man, to hear the birdis sound,
Whilk doth agane thy royal rock rebound.'[33]

The Table Rounde here mentioned, and which I found to be now more generally known as the King's Knot, is a singular flat-surfaced mound within a series of enclosing embankments, which would appear to be of very great antiquity; and where, 'in a sport called "Knights of the Round Table", the Institutions of King Arthur were commemorated',[34] at least, to the close of the Mediaeval Age. How current, in Scotland, where Arthurian tales in the fourteenth and fifteenth centuries is witnessed-to by the poet I have just quoted, who, in his *Dreme*, speaks of having diverted James V. when young, ' with antique storeis, and deidis martiall',

'Of Hector, *Arthur*, and gentile Julius,
Of Alexander, and worthy Pompeius.'

But, indeed, such evidence is unnecessary, considering that we still possess Scottish Arthurian Romances of that period.

Near Larbert, and not far from where are now the Carron Ironworks, is, or rather was—for it was destroyed many years ago by its barbarian proprietor—what would appear to have been a Roman structure, but which, since the thirteenth century, at least, had been known as Arthur's O'on (Oven). For in 1293, in the reign of Alexander III, William Gourley granted to the monks of Newbotle 'firmationem unius stagni ad opus molendini sui del Stanhus quod juxta *Furnum Arthuri*, infra Baronium de Dunypas est'.[35]

Proceeding up the Carron, which even Mr Pearson identifies with the Carun Fluvius of Nennius, we are struck with the appearance of two very singular conical hills, or mounds, in the park of Dunipace House. These Mr Skene would make the site of Arthur's sixth battle 'super flumen quod vocatur Bassas'.[36] There is now no river of this name in Scotland; but, as Mr Skene remarks, 'the name Bass is also applied to a peculiar mound having the appearance of being artificial, which is formed near a river, though really formed by natural causes. There is one on the Ury river in Aberdeenshire, termed the Bass of Inverury, and there are two on the bank of the Carron, now called Dunipace, erroneously supposed to be formed from the Gaelic and Latin words *Duni pacis*, or hills of peace, but the old form of which was *Dunipais*, the latter syllable being no doubt the same word Bass. Directly opposite, the river Bonny flows into the Carron, and on this river I am disposed to place the sixth battle'.[37]

But I venture to think that a personal inspection of the ground would not only have convinced Mr Skene that the Park of Dunipace was a very unlikely place for a great battle, but have shown him, on the opposite side of the Carron, almost directly opposite these mounds, and in the angle formed by the junction of the Bonny with the Carron, another, and vastly larger Bass; a moraine (?) with three of its sides (those towards the Bonny and Carron) as steep and sharply defined at the edges as walls, and forming a natural stronghold, the broad flat summit of which, waving—when I scaled it from the river side—in acres of clover, would scarce need defence except in the rear, where it slopes gradually to the south. This natural fortress must certainly have been the scene of many a conflict between Cymry, Picts and Saxons in the Arthurian Age; and all Mr Skene's arguments would, as it appears to me, apply with ten-fold more force to this Bass than to those he has fixed on, as the site of the sixth battle of the Arthur of Nennius. From an old man, with whom I had some talk on the Bridge of Carron, I found that, in spates, the river not unfrequently overflowed to the very base of this hill, and that it, and the farm to which it belongs, is called Roughmute. And many a rough moot, or council, has no doubt been held there.

After the old man left me, I suddenly remembered, as I looked over the bridge, and up the river, that the Carron was one of Ossian's favourite streams.

> 'I behold not the form of my son at Carun; nor the figure of Oscar in Crona.
> The rustling winds have carried him far away, and the heart of his father
> is sad.'[38]

And so, instead of proceeding on my way, I wandered up its southern banks for a mile or two, coming down to the bridge again on the other side. Moraines, or whatever else they may be geologically, there is, on this southern bank, such a number of 'Basses'—of beautiful knolls, with woody dells, and shadowy braes—such Fairy Highlands, as I do not remember to have elsewhere seen. Well might the Doric Muse have been here inspired with these fine pastoral lines:

> 'O bonnie are the greensward howes,
> Whar through the birks the burnie rowes,
> An' the bee bums, an' the ox lowes,
>   An' saft winds rustle,
> An' shepherd lads, on sunny knowes,
>   Blaw the blithe whistle.'

Then, on again towards the scene of the final battle between Arthur and Mordred; having some talk on the way with a bridge-keeper whom I found beguiling the time with Brougham's 'Discourse on the Study of Science'. 'However ignorant we may be,' he modestly remarked, 'we may benefit a little.' Now, where is the site of the 'Gweith Camlan in qua Arthur et Medraut coruere', to be more probably found than at the little town of Camelon where we now are? 'It is surprising,' says

Mr Skene, 'that historians should have endeavoured to place this battle in the south, as the same traditions, which encircle it with so many fables, indicate very clearly who his antagonists were. Medraut or Mordred was the son of that Llew to whom Arthur is said to have given Lothian, and who, as Lothus, king of the Picts, is invariably connected with this part of Scotland. His forces were Saxons, Picts, and Scots, the very races Arthur is said to have conquered in his Scottish campaigns. If it is to be viewed as a real battle at all, it assumes the appearance of an insurrection of the conquered districts, under Medraut, the son of that Llew to whom one of them was given.'[39] Remark, further, not only that the site bears still the very same name as the battle; but that it is, as we have already in part seen, in the centre of a group of Arthurian localities; and further that, as history has shown it is well fitted to be a great battle-field. For, in later historical times, two great battles have been fought at, or near Camelon; that of Falkirk, but a mile distant, in 1298, between the Scots and the English; and that of Falkirk-muir, in 1746, between the Hanoverian forces, under General Hawley, and the Highlanders, commanded by Prince Charles Stuart.

But 21 years before this final Arthurian battle of the year 537, namely, in 516, was fought that twelfth battle 'in Monte Badonis', of Nennius, the 'obsessio Montis Badonici', of Gildas, the site of which has given rise to so much discussion. 'It has been supposed to have been near Bath, but the resemblance of names seems alone to have led to this tradition. Tradition equally points to the northern Saxons as the opponents, and in Ossa Cylellaur,[40] who is always named as Arthur's antagonist, there is no doubt that a leader of Octa and Ebissa's Saxons is intended; while at this date no conflict between the Britons and the West Saxons could have taken place so far west as Bath. The scene of the battle near Bath was said to be on the Avon, which Layamon[41] mentions as flowing past Badon Hill. But on the Avon, not far from Linlithgow, is a very remarkable hill, of considerable size, the top of which is strongly fortified with double ramparts, and past which the Avon flows. This hill is called Bouden Hill. Sibbald says, in his *Account of Linlithgowshire*, in 1710, "On the Buden Hill are to be seen the vestiges of an outer and inner camp. There is a great cairn of stones upon Lochcote Hills, over against Buden, and in the adjacent ground there have been found chests of stones, with bones in them, but it is uncertain when or with whom the fight was." As this battle was the last of twelve which seem to have formed one series of campaigns, I venture,' says Mr Skene, 'to identify Bouden Hill with the Mons Badonicus.'[42]

After enjoying the beautiful view from the top, with the Little Bouden and Cockleroy Hills on my right, as I looked north over the undulating country about Linlithgow, with its ancient royal palace on the lake, across to the fine estuary of the Forth, the shores of Fife and Clackmannan, and the Ochil Hills (Sliabnochel, or Ocelli Montes); I found, in talk with an old man of upwards of fourscore ('81 on the 21st of last July'), who was breaking stones on the roadside, what appeared to me an interesting confirmation of Mr Skene's hypothesis, in a tradition of Arthur's presence here, at least, if not also, of an Arthurian siege of Bouden Hill. After pointing out to me the 'Fechtin' Fuird,' about three-quarters of a mile below Bouden Hill, 'from which they say that the Romans lifted their camp to gang to besiege Jerooslem';[43] and telling me that on Cockleroy there was 'a bit hollow on the tap, whaur twa or three men micht lie, ca'd the Bed o' Wallace'; I asked him how the hill got so curious a name? 'Ou,' said he, chuckling, and taking a pinch from his snuff-mull, 'They say it was because the king was cockled (cuckolded) there.' 'What king?' said I, 'any of the Stuarts?' 'Na, I never heard it was ony o' the Stuarts at the pailace doon by; but it's mentioned in history[44] that King Arthur's wife was na' faithfu', an maybe it was her that was ouer cosh (too intimate) wi' anither man on the tap there.'

Then, on to Linlithgow, which appears in Mr Pearson's *Index* as the Llechlleuteu of Aneurin, and thence down, some three miles, to the shore of the Firth and Caredin.

'Let the Caer of Eiddyn deplore
The dread and illustrious men clothed in splendid blue.'[46]

For this, as it would appear, was the site of the conflict which is the subject of the first part of that great poem of the 'Gododin' which 'has attracted so much attention, from its striking character, its apparent historic value, and the general impression that, of all the poems, it has the greatest claims to be considered the genuine work of the (Arthurian) bard (Aneurin) in whose name it appears.[47] After criticizing the various theories, as to the site of this conflict, which have been put forward by Mr Williams, M. de la Villemarqué, Mr Stephens, Mr Nash, and Mr Vere Irving, Mr Skene thus proceeds:

'It is plain from the poem that two districts, called respectively Gododin and Catraeth, met at or near a great rampart; that both were washed by the sea; and that in connection with the latter was a fort called "Eyddin"... The name of Eyddin takes us at once to Lothian, where we have Dunedin or Edinburgh, and Caredin on the shore, called by Gildas "antiquissima civitas Britonum". That the Edin in (the former of?) these two names is the Eyddin of the poem is clear from a poem in the *Black Book of Caermarthen*, where Edinburgh is called Mynyd Eiddin'; and in a poem in the *Book of Taliessin* there is the expresion 'Rhuing Dineiddyn ac Dineiddwg', where Dineiddyn can hardly be anything but Dunedin. At Caredin the Roman wall terminated... And Caredin is not far from the river Avon, and parallel to it flows the river Carron, the two rivers enclosing a district at the west end of which is a great moor still called Slamannan; in old Gaelic 'Sliabh Manand', the moor or plain of Manand. This is the 'Campus Manand' of Tighernac, and the Avon and Carron are meant by the Haefe and Caere of the *Saxon Chronicle*, and the Heue and Cere of *Henry of Huntingdon*. Now Gododin contained this district. For the *Guotodin* of the 'Manau Guotodin', mentioned by Nennius as 'regio in sinistrali parte insulae' (an expression equivalent in Welsh to 'y gogledd', or the North), is plainly the same as the Gododin of Aneurin; and the Cymric *Manau* of Gododin is, in its Gaelic form, *Manand*. Gododin was, therefore, equivalent to the north part of Lothian, and was washed by the Firth of Forth.[48] So much for the identification of Eyddin and Gododin. Now as to Catraeth. 'The *Irish Annals* frequently mention a district called *Calathros*; as in Tighernac... in 736, "Bellum Cnuice Cairpre i Calathros uc etar linn du", which latter place can be identified as Carriber on the Avon, near Linlithgow. Calathros, therefore, adjoined this district. Its Latin form was Calatria... Now, in the address of Walter L'Espec at the battle of the Standard in 1130, as reported by Ailred... Calatria is placed between Lothian and Scotland proper, north of the Firths. And Calatria is surely the Cymric Galtraeth,[49] which we know was the same place as Catraeth.[50]All the requirements of the site seem, therefore, satisfied in that part of Scotland where Lothian meets Stirlingshire, in the two districts of Gododin and Catraeth, both washed by the sea of the Firth of Forth; and where the great Roman Wall terminates at Caredin, or the fort of Eidin.'[51]

'As to the date of the battle we are not without indications... The combatants were, on the one side, the Britons and the Scots under Aidan; the enemy or "Barbari" were the Pagan Saxons and half-Pagan Picts of Manau Guotodin, called in the poem the "bedin" or host of Gododin. And the identity of the battle of Catraeth with the "bellum Miathorum" of Adomnan enables us to fix its date... at 596. But the first part alone of the poem of the Gododin relates to this battle; the second part, or continuation, contains in it an allusion to the death of Dyfynwal Vrych, or Domnal Breck, which the bard (*not* Aneurin) saw from the heights of Adoyn. The date of this event is known to be in 542. The site is not difficult to fix. *Tighernac* calls it Strathcauin; the *Annals of Ulster*, Strathcairinn. The upper part of the vale of the Carron, through which the river, after rising in the Fintry Hills, flows, is called Strathcarron; but it also bore the name of Strathcawin... And in the Statistical Account of the parish of Fintry there is the following notice: "At the foot of the rock which encircles the western brow of the Fintry Hills there is a considerable extent of table-land, and on the descent below this starts out a knoll, *commonly known by the name of the Dun or Down*, of a singular appearance. Its front is a perpendicular rock, fifty feet high. The western extremity of this rock is one solid mass." This is surely the height of Adoyn.'[52] And having here, at Caredin, viewed the site of the battle which is the subject of that first part of the Gododin, composed by Aneurin, we shall, in exploring the

Lennox on our returning northern route, have an opportunity of visiting the scene of the battle celebrated by the later bard, who was the
author of the second part of the poem.

I found that there had been recently discovered, near Caredin, a stone
with an inscription in admirable preservation, of the Second Augustan
Legion, on completing a certain distance of the wall under Antoninus
Pius. And near this, at the eastern end of the wall, was that linguisti-
cally famous town 'qui sermone Pictorum Peanfahel, lingua autem
Anglorum Peneltun appellatur', as Bede writes;[53] and as Nennius
names it,[54] 'Penguaul, quae villa Scottice Cenail... dicitur.' Passing
through the dismally dirty town of Burrowstowness, I turned up towards
Linlithgow again. While enjoying, towards the top of the steep ascent,
the splendour of the sunset over the river, and estuary of the Forth,
the Frenessicum, or Frisicum Mare, (Frisian Sea) of Nennius; the Frisian shore, where stood in the Arthurian Age that monastery of Cul-
ross in which the young Kentigern was placed under the discipline of
St Servanus; the sands on which, in a later age, Sir Patrick Spens was
walking when he received the king's (Alexander III) 'braid letter',

> 'To Noroway, to Noroway,
> To Noroway o'er the faem,
> The king's daughter to Noroway,
> It's thou maun tak her hame;'

the royal Dunfermline in the Abbey of which, the chief Burial-place
of the kings of Scotland, is the tomb of Robert the Bruce; and Loch
Leven, with its romantic memories of Mary Queen of Scots, a fine-
looking fellow, but of unmistakably English aspect, came-up, with whom
our common admiration of the glorious scene drew me into conversa-
tion. Walking on with him, he invited me into his house to have a cup
of tea; and I found that he and his wife, a fair and hearty girl with a
charming Northumbrian *burr,* one 'darrlin' in her arms, and another
at her feet, as she bustled about, were one of many English families
of the artisan class, now invited into, and peacefully settled in this district, where their ancestors had had to maintain themselves by such
hard fighting. Their happy looking home, kindness, and hospitality,
could not but bring into vivid contrast in my mind the present times,
and those we may hope they are preparing, with those of that Premediaeval Arthurian age of which I had been thinking, and which had been
so truly described by my last road-side acquaintaince, the old stone-
breaker of Bouden Hill, when he said, 'I'm thinkin' that in thae days—
aye, it'll be mair nor a thoosan years ago—there were hereawa jist vawri-
ous wild tribes a' fechtin thro' ither.'

Irongath Hill on the east side of the river Avon near Linlithgow appears
to be the Agathes of the *Book of Taliessin.*[55] For the Avon is, in the
Gododin, called the Aeron, and probably appears in the first part of

the name 'Iron'. Sir R. Sibbald in his *History of Linlithgowshire* says 'The tradition is current that there was a fight between the Romans and the natives under Argadus in this hill, and that it had its name from Argad'; which was the name of a son of Llywarch Hen.[56] Journeying to Edinburgh, we pass Dalmeny, which appears to be identifiable with the Caer Govannon of the Red Book of Hergest.[57] For in an old list of the churches of Linlithgow, printed by Reiner, appears 'Vicaria de Qumanyn'; and Dalmeny was formerly called Dumanyn.[58] Abercorn on the Firth, where was anciently a famous monastery, is the Abercurnig of Gildas. Cramond or Caer Amond, which may be identified with Caer Vandwy.[59]

> 'Before Caer Vandwy a host I saw
> Shields were shattered and ribs broken.[60]
> ...And when we went with Arthur of anxious memory
> Except seven, none returned from Caer Vandwy.'[61]

Caer Sidi of the *Book of Taliessin*[62] would appear to have been upon an island, and is, according to Mr Skene, probably the Urbs Judeu of Nennius,[63] and Bede's island city of Giudi, which we may with great probability place on Inchkeith, in the Firth of Forth.[64] And between six or seven miles from Edinburgh we find the famous Catstane, the inscription on which Sir James Simpson reads as recording the grave of Vecta, the grandfather of Hengist and Horsa.[65]

At Edinburgh we find the site of Arthur's eleventh battle, which was fought 'in monte qui dicitur Agned'—that is, Mynyd Agned, the Painted Mount, which seems to be clearly identified with Edinburgh, the southern stronghold of the Picts;[66] against whom, under the name of *Cathbregion*, 'contra illos que nos Cathbregyon appellamus', and not against the Saxons, this eleventh battle would appear to have been fought. And it may be noted that the words which form the root of the epithets Cath Bregion and Brithwryr, are, '*Brith*, forming in the feminine *Braith*, Diversicolor, Maculosus, and *Brych*—the equivalent in Cymric of the Gaelic *Breac*—Macula. Both refer to the same Picti, or painted: and Agned probably comes from an obsolete word, *agneaw*, to paint, *agneaid*, painted'.[67] In a poem referring to Arthur the Guledig, in the *Black Book of Caermarthen*, we read, for example:

> 'In Mynyd Eiddin
> He contended with Cynvyn
> By the hundred there they fell,
> There they fell by the hundred,
> Before the accomplished Bedwyr.
> On the strands of Trywruid.'[68]

Edinburgh, or rather its Castle, appears also under the name of Castrum Puellarum, in the Charters, and of the Castle of Maidens, and Dolorous Valley in the Romances. 'Arthur's Seat,' says Chalmers—in a note to which he had been incited by the remark of 'a late inquirer', who had said that it was 'a name of yesterday'—'had that distinguished name before the publication of Camden's *Britannia* in 1585, as we may see in p. 478; and before the publication of Major in 1521, as appears in fol. 28; and even before the end of the 15th century, as Kennedy, in his flyting with Dunbar, mentions *Arthur Sate* or ony Hicher Hill.'[69]

Proceeding from Edinburgh towards Haddington, we may make an excursion to Trapender, formerly Dunpender, and more anciently Dunpeledur Law. Here is said to have been buried that Llew, or Lothus, in whose establishment by Arthur, as a (tributary?) king of Lothian, the battle of Mynyd Agned seems to have resulted. On Dunpeledur also, as likewise on the three fortified rocks of Edinburgh, Stirling, and Dumbarton, at Dundonald, in Ayrshire, and Chilnacase, in Galloway, S. Monenna or Darerca of Kilslleibeculean, in Ulster, founded a church, and nunnery.[70] These foundations appear to synchronise with the re-establishment of the Christian Church in these districts by Arthur, who was pre-eminently a Christian hero fighting against pagan Saxons and apostate Picts. And it seems not improbable that Thenew, the daughter of King Lothus, was one of the virgins in the church in Dunpeledur. About the time of S. Monenna's death, however, in the year 518, this royal virgin had the misfortune to give birth to a fine boy, who afterwards became the apostolic missionary Kentigern, now more commonly remembered as S. Mungo. And as her story of an immaculate conception did not meet with due credence among the barbarians; after an attempt to put her to death, in one legend on Dunpeledur (or Dunpender), in another on Kepduff, now Kilduff, she was cast adrift in a boat from Aberlady Bay.[71] And this romantic incident, putting us in mind of the similar story of Custaunce being sent adrift by the constable of Alla, King of Northumberland

> 'But in the same schip as he hire found,
> Hire and hire yonge sone, and all hire gere,
> He shulde put, and croude here fro the londe,
> And charge hire, that sche never eft come there.
> Hir litel child lay wepyng in hire arm,
> And in hire arme sche lulleth it ful faste.
> And unto heven hire eyghen up sche caste'[72]

may be an inducement to visit the scene of it.

In this district also, we must at least notice, if we do not think it worth while to visit, the sites which that writer in the *Gentleman's Magazine* of 1842, before mentioned,[73] fixed on as the probable scenes of Arthur's four battles on the Dubglas, or Duglas, and is sixth battle on the Bassas. The former battle he places on 'the little river Dunglas, which has formed through successive ages the southern boundary of Lothian'; and, he continues, 'When the Saxons were driven from their entrenchments on the Dunglas, their flight was directed' northwards; and, 'forced again to face their foes beside the channel which separates the mainland from the remarkable isolated rock in the Firth of Forth, near the town of North Berwick, called the Bass, and which, by a trivial error, the historian designates ''the river Bassas'', the Saxons sustained a sixth defeat.'[74] The battles on the Du(b)glas 'in regione *Linnuis*' we shall, however, before the end of our journey, find, I think, to have been more probably situated on the Douglas in the *Lennox*, than here on the Dunglas in *Lothian*. And a more probable site of the battle on the Bassas we have, I venture to think, already found on the Bonny, at Dunipais (or Dunipaice). Finally, on our way into the next Arthurian district we shall pass on the borders of the counties of Edinburgh and Peebles, the Moss of Maw mentioned in the *Book of Taliessin* as the Bush of Maw.[75]

We enter now on the exploration of **District III—Tweeddale**. At Peebles on the Tweed, or Tywi of the *Four Ancient Books*, we find one of the many wells, or fountains, dedicated to S. Mungo, the legend of whose birth we have just noticed. And we are here in the heart of the Nemus Caledonis whither Merlin is said, in the Latin *Vita Merlini*, to have fled after the battle of Arderyth, and where, according to the tradition reported by Fordun, he met Kentigern, and afterwards was slain by the shepherds of Meldredus, a regulus of the country on the banks of the Tweed, 'prope oppidum Dunmeller'. So, from the Broughton station I set out on foot for Merlin's Grave at Drummelzier, in which the name of Meldredus is preserved, according to Mr Skene,[77] and that of Merlin according to M. de la Villemarqué.[78]

'Questa è l'antiqua e memorabil grotta,
Ch'edificò Merlino, il savio Mago
Che forse ricordare odi tal' otta, ·
Dove ingannollo la Donna del Lago.'[79]

Crossing to the south bank of the Tweed, and reaching the ancient parish church and kirkton, or hamlet, by the Pausayl (i.e. Willow) Burn, I was fortunate in making the acquaintance of the intelligent shoemaker of the place. From his account there seemed to be some doubt as to which of two localities here had the best traditional right to be called the Grave of Merlin. That now certainly the most picturesque, and maintained by the late Dr Somerville, the minister of the parish, to be the true site of the tomb, is by an ancient thorn-tree, of which there is now a younger thriving offshoot (fair augury of a renewal of Merlin's fame), by the burnside, a little above its junction with the Tweed, and at the foot of the moraine, on which stands the kirk and manse. But it seems that, at the corner of what is now a corn-field, there used to be a cairn, called Merlin's Grave; and though the Pausayl does not at present meet the Tweed at this spot, yet it did so for a time, in consequence of a great spate or overflow of the river, when the Scottish James VI became the king of England, and so the prophecy was fulfilled that:

'When Tweed and Paysayl meet at Merlin's grave,
Scotland and England one king shall have.'[80]

For me, not only the weight of authority, but the perennial thorn-tree
decides the matter. For this is always introduced in the romantic fic-
tions that represent his ladye-love, Viviana,[81] as imprisoning Merlin,
not, in the earlier romances, at least, that she might basely triumph
over him, but that he might be with her for evermore. And though,
in its present disafforested state, the scenery of the here narrow valley
of the Tweed, and its enclosing hills is somewhat disappointing; it cannot
be looked on with indifference by any one who knows how a 'plus
ancienne tradition romanesque a fait agir Merlin, comment elle a per-
sonnifié et idéalisé en lui le dévouement passionné à tout ce que la
grande epoque chevaleresque jugeait digne de son respect; je veux dire
la religion, la patrie, la royauté, l'amour, l'amour pur, discret, délicat,
la solitude à deux éternellement enchantée'.[82] And well may the
French *savant* in his history of the bard, his works, and influence, refuse
to follow him—

> 'a travers les fantaisies des continuateurs et des imitateurs de son noble
> panégyriste, Robert de Borron. L'esprit grivois et goguenard y remplace
> progressivement l'esprit moral et grave passé de la tradition bretonne dans
> l'oeuvre française primitive. Le sentiment est chassé trop souvent par le
> rire; ce qui est élevé par ce qui est plat; le sérieux par l'amusant. A la
> fin, Merlin sera plus on moins moulé sur le type scolastique et vulgaire
> du savant devenu fou d'orgueil, du sage Salomon que séduisent les femmes
> étrangères, du poëte Lucrèce que la perfide Lucile empoisonne, du vieil-
> lard de la comédie, victime de sa sotte passion. Et la verve de Rabelais,
> pas plus que l'art de Tennyson, ne parviendront complétement à vaincre
> la pitié qu'inspirera cette figure tombante.'[83]

In the legends and romances of Merlin mention is ever made of a fountain, by which he used to meet his lady fair, and around which, as is
the wont of love, he caused to spring up an enchanted Garden of Joy.
Of no well, or fountain, however, could I hear either with the name,
or a tradition, of Merlin attached to it. The sources, or wells of Tweed,
though at an elevation of 1500 feet, lie in a hollow of the mountains,
and, therefore, do not, as I should have liked to find, correspond with
the description of the Fountain of the Caledonian Merlin, given in the
Vita Merlini, of the 12th century, ascribed to Geoffrey of Monmouth.
But in crossing the mountains here, that central mountain-district of
the east of Scotland, which separates Tweeddale from Annan-dale and
Moffat-dale, and where, at no great distance apart, are to be found the
sources of the eastward-flowing Tweed, the westward-running Clyde,
and the southward-falling Annan, I found many other fountains to
which Geoffrey's (?) lines would apply:

> 'Fons erat in summo cujusdam vertice montis,
> Undique praecinctus corulis, densisque frutectis,

Illic Merlinus consederat; inde per omnes
Spectabat silvas, cursusque, jocosque ferarum.'[84]

After journeying past deep ravines, and shadowy mountain nooks; through dales, over the steep green sides of which swept the swift shadows of the clouds, and fell, in silver torrents, many a waterfall; through a country, in which the long presence of a large Saxon element in its population was witnessed-to by the vulgarity of the names—Devil's Beef-tub, Grey Mare's Tail, etc.—by which so many of its finest scenes were profaned;[85] I passed a night at the famous cottage of Tibbie Shiels, where I was sorry to find the old housekeeper of the Ettrick Shepherd on her death-bed; and so, the next day, on, through Ettrick Forest. Somewhere in this district must have been fought Arthur's seventh battle 'in silva Caledonis id est cat Coit Celeddon'—that is, the battle was so called, for *Cat* means 'battle', and *Coed Celyddon,* ''the wood of Celyddon'',... of which the forests of Selkirk and Ettrick formed a part;'[86] and which is mentioned along with the Teifi or Teviot in a poem relating to the battle of Arderydd in the *Black Book of Caermarthen.*

'Seven score generous ones have gone to the shades;
In the wood of Celyddon they came to their end.'[87]

On the Teviot, also, Mr Pearson[88] places the Din Guortigern, mentioned by Nennius.

Coming to Melrose by Abbotsford we pass through the Rhymer's Glen and by the Huntly Burn:

'True Thomas lay on Huntlie bank;
A ferlie he spied wi' his ee;
And there he saw a ladye bright,
Come riding down by the Eildon Tree.'[89]

Immediately to the south of Melrose, the Melros of Nennius, rise those three summits of the Eildons, the *Tremontium* of the Romans, which Mr Nash identifies with the Din Drei of Aneurin, and near which he places the site of the battle celebrated in the *Gododin.*[90] These three summits also with their various weirdly appurtenants—the Windmill of Kippielaw, the Lucken Hare, and the Eildon Tree—mark the domes of those vast subterranean Halls, in which all the Arthurian Chivalry await, in an enchanted sleep, the bugle-blast of the Adventurer who will call them at length to a new life. And it is to be noted also that there are on the Eildons the remains of a fortified camp, and at their foot a Bowden Burn and Bowden Moor, at the further end of which is another hill with the remains of fortifications. There is not, however, an Avon here to enable us to oppose this site to that which Mr Skene has identified as the *Mons Badonis* of Arthur's twelfth battle.

Crossing the winding Tweed, we find 'six miles to the west of that

heretofore noble and eminent monastery of Meilros', Gwaedol, or
'Wedale, in English Wodale, in Latin Vallis Doloris'. Here, at Stowe, was
the church of Saint Mary, where were once 'preserved, in great veneration, the fragments of that image of the Holy Virgin, Mother of God',
which Arthur, on his return from Jerusalem,[91] 'bore upon his shoulders, and through the power of our Lord Jesus Christ, and the Holy
Mary, put the Saxons to flight, and pursued them the whole day with
great slaughter'.[92] Not far from this church at Stowe, dedicated to S.
Mary, General Roy places a Roman fort; and thus the site of Arthur's
eighth battle 'in Castello Guinnion' is very plainly indicated.[93] This
Guinnion also appears in the Garanwynyon mentioned in the poem
in the *Book of Taliessin* on the battle of Gwenystrad or the White Strath,
thus also identified with the valley of the Gala Water.

> 'In defending Gwenystrad was seen
> A mound and slanting ground obstructing. . .
> Hand on the cross they wail on the gravel bank of Garanwynyon.'

And the White Stone of Galystem (in which the name Gala seems contained), referred to in the succeeding lines,

> 'I saw a brow covered with rage on Urien,
> When he furiously attacked his foes at the White Stone
> Of Galystem,'[94]

is probably the stone mentioned in the *Statistical Account:* 'A little above
it (S. Mary's Church of Stow) is a very fine perennial spring, known
by the name of the Lady's Well, and a huge stone, recently removed
in forming the new road, but now broken to pieces, used to be pointed
out as impressed with the print of the Virgin Mary's foot.' In the Verses
of the Graves also this valley seems to be alluded to.[95]

Crossing from Stowe to Lauder, and journeying down the Leader Water
we come to the Rhymer's Tower, on a beautiful haugh or meadow by
the waterside. Here in his Castle of Ercildoune, of which these are the
ruins, lived Thomas the Rhymer, whom so many traditions connect
with Arthurian Romance, in representing him as the unwilling, and
too quickly vanishing guide of those adventurous spirits who have
entered the mysterious Halls beneath the Eildons, and attempted to
achieve the re-awakening of Arthur and his knights, but only to be cast
forth, amid the thunders of the fateful words:

> 'Woe to the Coward that ever he was born,
> Who did not draw the Sword, before he blew the Horn.'[96]

And hence it is to 'True Thomas', still 'doomed to revisit Eildon's fated
Tree', that Leyden appeals to

> 'Say who is he with summons long and high,
> Shall bid the charméd sleep of Ages fly;
> Roll the long sound through Eildon's caverns vast,

> While each dark warrior kindles at the blast;
> The Horn, the Falchion grasp with mighty hand,
> And peal proud Arthur's march from Fairyland.'[97]

From Ercildoune, or Earlston, we journey to Kelso, which is mentioned in the *Book of Taliessin* as Calchvynyd.[98] This literally means 'Chalk mountain', and Chalmers says, 'It seems to have derived its ancient name of Calchow from a calcareous eminence which appears conspicuous in the middle of the town, and which is still called the Chalk Heugh.'[99] At no great distance to the south of Kelso is Jedburgh, identified by Mr Pearson with the Judeu and Atbret Judeu of Nennius,[100] and Mr Nash and the Ven. Archdeacon Jones, placing Manau Guotodin further south than Mr Skene would do, extend it beyond Jedburgh, and so as to include Northumberland.[101]

Though properly, perhaps, belonging to the next district, we shall find it more convenient to include in our exploration of *Tweeddale* that river Glen, one of the indirect tributaries of the Tweed, which the above-quoted writer in the *Gentleman's Magazine* identifies with the Glein or Gleni, at the mouth of which took place the first battle in which Arthur was engaged. 'Near the junction of the Glen with the Till rises a lofty hill, called from its shape "Weavering Bell", on the summit of which are to be seen to this day the remains of a rude fortress of immense strength, and nearly inaccessible position. The hill rises abruptly to the height of upwards of 2000 feet, the summit being attained by a winding path on its south-east side, and presenting a level plain of about 12 acres... In the midst is an elevated citadel... That this was at a later period a royal fortress of the Saxons we know on the authority of Bede... And that Weavering was a fortress of the Britons, before it fell into the hands of the Saxons... is supported by the tradition of ages... On the invasion of their country by a superior force, the Ottodeni naturally sought refuge in this fortress... In their behalf, Arthur first drew his sword upon the Saxons... Its position near the capital of Bernicia, and its celebrity from the ministration of Paulinus and the narrative of Bede, account for this river being mentioned without any allusion (as in the case of the Duglas) to the region in which it flowed.'[102]

Along the Border-country we note an almost endless number of places, famous in story, among which we must, at least, name Carham as the scene of the battle which finally added the Saxon Lothians to the Celtic kingdom of Malcolm II in 1018.[103] And so, on to Berwick, formerly Aberwick. And, though now fallen into comparative decay and insignificance—crowning, as it does, the northern heights at the mouth of the Tweed, looking eastward on the sea, that dashes up to high caverned cliffs, and commanding westward the vale of the beautiful river, here flowing between steep braes, shadowy with trees, or bright with corn and pasture—Berwick, but for the dullness within its walls,

seems still almost as worthy of being called Joyeuse Garde as, both from
its real and romance history of siege, conquest, and reconquest, it is
of being remembered as Dolorous Garde.[104]

THE SOUTHERN DIVISION OF ARTHURIAN SCOTLAND

From the still preserved ramparts of Berwick I observed, away to the
south, a great pyramid-like mass by the sea; and, on asking what this
was, I was told it was Bamborough Castle. 'Ah,' said I to myself, 'the
Chatel Orgueilleux of Romance[105] and the Dinguaroy and Bebban-
burgh of Nennius.' So, entering on the exploration of **District IV—
Northumberland**, I went by train to the Belford station, whence it
is some five miles to the little model village under the Castle-rock. And
whatever may on other grounds be said of the expenditure of the funds
vested for certain charitable purposes in the Trustees to whom this
ancient Castle, with its valuable estates, now belongs, an Arthurian anti-
quary can hardly but be grateful to them for enabling him to enter,
what might easily be imagined one of the very castles of which he has
been reading. Occupying the whole extent of a solitary eminence, it
stands among sandy downs, close by the sea, and overlooking a wide
plain at the foot of the Cheviots. Nearly opposite the Castle are the
Faroe Islands. And journeying five or six miles over the sands when
the tide is out, and a mile by boat, one reaches Lindisfarne, the Medg-
aud of Nennius, opposite which, on the mainland, is the Lleu. Having
visited the Abbey of the Holy Island of St Cuthbert—like Iona, whence
the saintly Aidan came here as a missionary, a primitive seat of
Christianity—and where, as I thought, there ought to have been a tradition of its having been the retreat of Sir Lancelot after the discovery
of his treason, and his final separation from the Queen; I regained the
mainland, and Beal station, in a slow, jolting cart, chased by the too
swiftly incoming tide, but amusing myself thinking of the still worse
jolting Sir Lancelot underwent, and the ludicrous disgrace brought upon
him by his accepting the offer of the dwarf to guide him to the captive
Guenivere, would the knight but leave his disabled horse, and get into
'la charette', the filthy cart of the dwarf.

The references to Northumberland in the Romances are very frequent.
It was in the forest of Northumberland that dwelt the Hermit Blaise
to whom Merlin is represented as so often repairing, in order that being
'a nobill clerk and subtle', he might put in writing all the wonderful
things that befell in those days. And one chapter, for instance, of the
French Romance of Lancelot is headed, 'Comment la Dame de Noe-
hault envoya deuers le Roy Artus, luy supplier quil luy envoya secours
contre le Roy de Norhombellande qui luy menoit guerre'. Northumberland also formed part of the Berneich of Nennius, the Tir Brenech
of Llywarch Hen, and the Brenneich of Aneurin, the Anglic kingdom

of Bernicia. And in the suburbs of its chief town, Newcastle, we find Arthur's Hill.

We are now on the Tyne, the south-eastern boundary of Arthurian Scotland. But, before turning westward, we must note that, but a little way over the frontier is York, Eboracum, with which the name of the father of Perceval, that famous knight of the Quest of the Holy Grail is connected. For he is always mentioned as Ebrauk or Evrok of the North.[106] But, under his earlier Cymric name of Peredur, Perceval is brought into more direct connection with Arthurian Scotland in his relations with Merlin in the Caledonian Forest

'Venerat ad bellum Merlinus cum Pereduro. . .
Solatur Peredurus eum,'[107]

and as one of the chiefs mentioned by Aneurin in the *Gododin* as having fallen at the battle of Cattraeth:

'Peredur with steel arms, Gwawrddur, and Aeddan,
A defence were they in the tumult, though with shattered shields.'[108]

Turning now westward, and passing through the picturesquely-situated old town of Hexham, with its Moot Hall and Abbey Church, on a wooded ridge over-hanging the Tyne, we stop either at the Haydon Bridge, or the Bardon Mill station of the Carlisle and Newcastle Railway. For six or eight miles to the north of these stations, and in the neighbourhood of Housesteads, the most complete of the stations on the Roman Wall, are the principal Arthurian Localities of this Northumbrian District. The scenery here is very remarkable. The green, but unwooded grazing hills—wide and wild-looking from their want of enclosures, and the infrequency of farm-houses—seen like the vast billows of a north-sweeping tide. Along one of these wave-lines runs the Roman Wall, with the stations of its garrison. In the trough, as it were, of this mighty sea, and to the north of the Wall, were, till a few years ago removed and ploughed over, the ruins of the ancient castle of Sewing Shields, referred to by Sir Walter Scott as the Castle of the Seven Shields,[109] and by Camden as Seavenshale.[110] Beneath it, as under the Eildons, Arthur and all his court are said to lie in an enchanted sleep. And here also tradition avers that the passage to these Subterranean Halls, having once on a time, been found, but the wrong choice having been made in the attempt to achieve the adventure, and call the Chivalry of the Table Rounde to life again, the unfortunate adventurer was cast forth with these ominous words ringing in his ears:

'O woe betide that evil day
On which this witless wight was born,
Who drew the Sword, the Garter cut,
But never blew the Bugle-horn'[111]

the very opposite mistake, it will be observed, to that of which the equally luckless Eildon adventurer was guilty.

The northern faces of three successive billows here, if I may so call them, present fine precipitous crags—whinstone and sandstone strata cropping out. These are called respectively Sewing Shields Crags, the King's, and the Queen's Crags. Along the crest of the first of these the Roman Wall is carried. The others take their name from having been the scene of a little domestic quarrel, or tiff, between King Arthur and Queen Quenivere. To settle the matter, the king sitting on a rock called Arthur's Chair, threw at the queen an immense boulder which, falling somewhat short of its aim, is still to be seen on this side of the Queen's Crags. And on the horizon of the immense sheep farm of Sewing Shields, and beyond an outlying shepherd's hut, very appropriately named Cold-knuckles, is a great stone called Cumming's Cross, to which there is attached another rude Arthurian tradition. For here, they say, that King Arthur's sons attacked and murdered a northern chieftain who had been visiting their father at Sewing Shields Castle, and who was going home with too substantial proofs, as they thought, of the king's generosity.

Thence, over a most bracingly wild, wide-horizoned, and open Border-country to Liddesdale.[112] At the head of this famous dale we find Dawston, which may be reckoned among localities of the Arthurian Age, as the scene of that great battle of Dagsestan of 603, in which Aidan, who seems to have been, like Arthur some sixty years before, performing the functions of *Guledig* or 'Dux Bellorum' in the North, led a combined force of Scots and Britons against the Angles of Bernicia, under Ethelfrid; only, however, to meet with a crushing defeat.[113]

But our next and more strictly Arthurian locality, a hill, on the eastern side of the valley, called Arthur's Seat—the third locality of that name we have found in the course of our journey—we must place in **District V—Cumberland**. The chief object, however, of our exploration of Liddesdale, is the locality of the great battle of Arderydd, so often mentioned in the *Four Ancient Books*, in the *Triads*, and in the *Vita Merlini*. 'Concealed under these extravagant fables, we can see,' says Mr Skene, 'the outlines of one of those great historical struggles which alter the fate of a country. . . It was, in short, a great struggle between the supporters of the advancing Christianity and the departing Paganism, in which the former were victorious. That it was an historical event, and that this was its character, appears from this, that it occurs in the *Annales Cambriae*, as a real event about the year 573; "Bellum Armterid inter filios Elifer et Gwendoleu filium Keidau in quo bello Gwendoleu cecidit. Merlinus insanus effectus est"; and that 573 is the first year of the reign of Rhydderch over Strathclyde, and of Aidan, over Dalriada,'[114]—these being the leaders of the Christian party.

Where, then, was this battle fought? It was a passage in the *Vita S. Kentigerni*, quoted by M. de la Villemarqué,[115] that induced me to look in Liddesdale for its site. Shortly before, however, the same passage had been similarly suggestive to Mr Skene; though his *Notice of the Site of the Battle of Arderyth* was not published till after the identification which was the result of my visit to the place. This passage is as follows. One day that the saint was praying in a wild solitude of the Caledonian Forest, there sprang across his path 'quidam demens, nudus et hir sutus, ab omni solatio mundiali destitutus, quasi quoddam torvum furiale'. The saint asked this strange being who, or what he was, and received for answer, 'Olim Quortigerni vates, Merlinus vocitatus, in hac solitudine dura patiens. . . Eram enim caedis omnium causa interemptorum qui interfecti sunt in bello, cunctis in hac patria constitutis satis noto, quod erat *in campo inter Lidel et Carvanolow situato*.'[116]

Carwhinelow is a burn, on which there is a village of the same name, and which flows from Nicholl Forest into the Esk. And some little way above the junction of the Esk, with the Liddel is what is called in the *Statistical Account*, the Moat of Liddel, though known in the country only as the Roman Camp. It is situated on the top of a high bank overhanging the river, to which, on the north side, the rock goes sheer down; while on the other side it is defended by prodigious earthen ramparts which rise from the field to a height of nearly thirty feet. There is a well in the enclosure, and on the west side a second great rampart. 'It is obviously,' says Mr Skene, 'a native strength.' On its east side the ground slopes down till it comes to the level of the river at a place called Ridding, not quite half a mile off. Between the fort and the village of Carwhinelow is a field extending to the ridge along the stream of that name. This, then, is certainly the 'campus inter Lidel et Carwanolow situato'. The name of Erydon which Merlin gives to the battle probably remains in Ridding at the foot of the fort. 'And I have no doubt,' says Mr Skene, 'that the name Carwhinelow is a corruption of Caerwenddolew, the Caer or city of Gwenddolew,'[117] who, as we have seen, was the leader of the Pagan party, and slain in the battle.

Looking westward from the fort, the eye rests on the gleaming Solway, and southwards, on the knolls of Arthuret, beyond which the Cumberland hills bound the horizon. To Arthuret, then, let us next proceed. For double *d* in Welsh being equivalent to *th*, we can hardly now refuse to recognise in it the name of Arderydd[118] by which the battle is commonly mentioned. Should any doubt remain, it will be dispelled by a visit to the place, which is but some two miles from Longtown. Standing there, on the knolls by Arthuret Church and looking west, with Liddel and Carvanolow behind, a grander battle-plain could hardly be imagined, could the enemy be manoeuvred to attack one in a position of which that eminence should be the centre. In the distance behind

and around, low hills, except where they rise to a greater height on
the Scottish border; in front, the Esk, flowing across the plain, to fall
into the Solway Firth, after having been joined by the Line; and bound-
ing the plain, the sea, into which, should the enemy have been unsuc-
cessful in their attack, the victors, fording the river, might drive them
in irreparable rout.

At Camelon on the Firth of Forth, we found the site of the battle
that closed the career of the historical Arthur in 537. But it was on
this scene of the great battle of Arderydd in 573, that it seemed to me,
standing on the knolls of Arthuret, that the final Arthurian battle of
the Romances might best be imagined to have been fought—the enemy,
driven down from the Moat of Liddel, we have just visited, here making a last stand. For it is Merlin who is the romantic character, *par excellence* of the Romances; and it seemed fitter to make the scene of the
last great battle of the Romance Arthur the same as that in which Merlin, who is in the Romances so intimately connected with Arthur, historically 'bore the golden torques', than to make the scene of that battle
which, in its event, was the departing out of this world of all the Arthurian chivalry, the same as that in which the historical Arthur fell, but
at which Merlin was not present. And, besides, here we have a great
Western Lake, which suits that primitive mythological element which
can, I think, be shown cropping-out with singular frequency in the
Arthurian Romance-cycle.

With such thoughts, then, I wandered over the old battle plain, past
great farms, or rather agricultural manufactories, with their steam-
engines and chimney-stalks, down to and by a primitive wooden bridge
mounted on stilts, across the Line. Then, getting on the turnpike-road
to Glasgow, I crossed the Esk by an iron bridge, and, a mile or so on
the south side of the border, I turned down towards the sea, but some
five minutes distant now. The scene I beheld as I went down to the
tide, 'washing among the reeds', struck me as of a weird and magical
beauty. Behind, in the middle of the great plain, was still clearly visible the mound of Arthuret; before me, in the far distance to the right,
was the Scottish Criffel, and, to the left, the English Skiddaw; between
these, in the sheen of the setting sun, and stretching away amid points
of land to the west, so that, whether it was land-locked as a lake, or
boundless as a sea, one could not tell, was the Solway. 'Here,' I thought
'well may one feign that here, even at such a sunset hour as this, after
the last fatal battle on the plain above, Excaliber was thrown into the
sea; that here it was caught by the fairy hand, and borne aloft, symbol
of the hope, and ultimate triumph of the genius of the Celtic race; and
there, in the infinite Beyond, is Avalon.'

Coming up to Gretna Green from the Solway, we proceed to Carlisle,
which would appear to be the Caer Lliwelydd of the *Book of Taliessin*,[119] and the Cardueil of Romance, even still more famous than the

hardly yet identified Camelot, as the favourite residence of King Arthur. And with reason. For beautifully does the Castle- and Cathedral-crowned eminence, swept round by the Eden, the Peteril, and the Caldew, rise from the wide plain that stretches from the Border Hills down to, and along the Solway Firth. Of the Eden there is a tradition that King Arthur's father tried to turn it out of its course:

> 'Let Uther-pendragon do what he can,
> Eden shall run where Eden ran.'[120]

But a visit to the populous modern manufacturing quarter, in the evening, when the hands are loose, (how meaningful is the phrase!) may profitably disturb antiquarian memories, and romantic associations.

From Carlisle, near which would appear to have been the Guasmoric of Nennius,[121] our Arthurian pilgrimage takes us southward again through the Inglewood Forest of Romance. From the Southwaite station, we have a walk of something more than two miles, through a beautifully-wooded lane, its waysides luxuriant with wild flowers, to the village of Upper Hesket. At the 'White Ox' I had the good fortune to encounter an intelligent old man, who, taking me to the back of the farmyard, pointed out, down in the hollow, what I was in search of, the famous Tarn Wahethelyne of Ballad and Romance. But Tarn Wadling, as it has been called in later times, has been for the last ten years a wide meadow, grazed by hundreds of sheep. Of the draining of it the old man, the innkeeper as it turned out, who had come from Yorkshire, but had been here for the last fifty years, had a great deal to say. Among the rest, what fun it was to see the swine that belonged to a cottager at the far end of the tarn, get tired of the dead carp, that were cast on the land, and wade in to fish for the 'quick uns'. But of the story of the Grim Baron whom King Arthur chanced to meet here, whose

> 'Strokes were nothing sweet'[122]

and who refused all other ransom than that the King should, within a year and a day, bring him word 'what thing it is that women most desire'; and of the Foul Ladye, who, at length, gave, for the courteous Sir Gawayne's sake, the true answer, and who, on her marriage, was so transformed that

> 'The Queen sayd, and her ladyes alle,
> She is the fayrest nowe in this halle;'

of how

> 'This ferly byfelle fulle sothely to fayne
> In Iggillwode Foreste at the Tarn-wathelayne;'[122]

of all this, neither my old friend nor his dame had ever heard, till, sitting by their kitchen fire to dry my clothes, wet with a heavy shower,

I told them the tale. And all he knew about King Arthur was that

'When as King Arthur ruled this land,
He ruled it like a swine;
He bought three pecks of barleymeal
To make a pudding fine.

'His pudding it was nodden well,
And stuffed right full of plums;
And lumps of suet he put in
As big as my two thumbs;'

a tradition of the 'Flos Regum', hitherto, I believe, unnoticed.

Crossing the south end of the Tarn, or rather meadow, and passing through a fir wood, I ascended Blaze Fell, and, from the quarry on its summit, had a fine view over the undulating, mountain bounded, and still finely wooded ancient forest of Inglewood. Below me was the Tarn; to the west of it, the ridge of Upper Hesket; to the east, an eminence with the site, though no more than the ruins, of the Castle Hewin of Romance, the stronghold of the Grim Baron. And behind this eminence the Eden flows past still another locality that recalls his fame, and, with it, the legend of the Marriage of Sir Gawayne—Baron-wood. This legend belongs, as I think, to the class of Sun-myths; and it may be instructive to compare with it that of the Laidley Worm of Spindleston Heugh, near Bamborough Castle, celebrated in the ballad of 1270 by Duncan Frazier the Bard of Cheviot. As the Foul Lady is transformed into 'the fairest in hall,' so also is the Laidley Worm, or Loathsome Dragon. For her brother, coming over the Eastern Sea, in a ship with Rowantree masts,

'...sheathed his sword, and bent his bow,
And gave her kisses three;
She crept into a hole a Worm,
And stepped out a Ladye.'[123]

Returning to the Southwaite Station, we proceed next to Penrith, passing on our way the Plumpton Park and Hatton Hall which Sir Frederic Madden identifies with places of similar names in the Romances of Sir Gawayne.[124] Thence, crossing the narrow but picturesque old bridge of the Eamont, which, flowing from Ulleswater, here separates the counties of Westmoreland and Cumberland, we find, closely adjoining the fine Celtic monument of Mayborough, another such set of circular embankments round a flat-surfaced central mound as we have found, but on a larger scale, under the battlements of Stirling Castle. But what is there now called the King's Knot, is here named Arthur's Round Table. And, connected with a cave in the demesne of Brougham Castle in this neighbourhood, we still find a tradition of a giant killed by the most famous knight of the Table Rounde, Sir Lancelot du Lac. Continuing our journey, we come on the Winster, which is another stream separating the counties of Cumberland and Westmoreland, and would appear to be the Gwensteri of the *Book of Taliessin*;[125] as the Derwent should seem to be the Derwennydd of the *Gododin Poems*.[126]

Here we have come to the south-western limit of what I venture to designate Arthurian Scotland. And now, turning northwards, again, I determined, if possible, to verify Sir F. Madden's conjecture that the Grene Chapel spoken of in the Scottish Romance of *Syr Gawayne and the Grene Knight* (by 'Huchowne of the Awle Ryale'[127]?) is the same with the 'Chapel of the Grene', which, in the older maps of Cumberland, is marked as existing on the point of land on the western coast, running into the estuary of the Wampool, not far from Skinburness. So from Silloth, which seems to be getting a favourite sea-bathing and health-recruiting place, I wandered up the Solway beach to the extreme point of Skinburness. And this much, at least, by way of verification of Sir F. Madden's conjecture, I may say, that there is near this a beautifully embayed shore, covered with the brightest green down to the very water's edge, from which, if, indeed, the site of the Chapel of the Grene, it might well have taken its name; and, further, that Volsty or Vulstey Castle, so long associated with the necromantic fame of the wizard Michael Scott, and which once stood in the fair wide plain which rises gradually to the foot of Skiddaw, might, from its site with reference to this bright green shore, the seaward border of the plain, well be that in which Sir Gawayne took up his abode, and which is stated to have been but two miles distant from the Grene Chapel, the object of his quest.

Away, from here, over the sea, is the Castle of the King of Man—

'He lett him see a castle faire,
Such a one he neuer saw yare,
Noe where in noe country.
The Turke said to Sir Gawaine,
"Yonder dwells the King of Man,
A heathen soldan is hee." '[128]

And the Isle of Man, is the Mynaw of Taliessin;[129]the Manau and Eubonia of Nennius.[130] May it possibly be also the Ermonie of the *Romance of Sir Tristem?* Merlin, at any rate, is traditionally connected with the Isle of Man, as well as Gawayne. For, by Merlin the giants, who had overpowered the primitive population of Fairies, are in their turn said to have been overpowered, and spell-bound in subterranean chambers.[131]

A shower falling with the turn of the tide, I took shelter in a little cottage, where I found a pretty young woman with her firstborn in her arms. Crowing, instead of crying, at sight of the stranger, I remarked what a fine big boy he was; and his proud mother, turning her face modestly a little away, replied: 'And yet they say that foresons are ordinarily sma'.' Looking from the cottage door, she pointed out to me where, on the opposite shore of the gleaming water, Annan might just be distinguished, and where, up the estuary of the Nith, lay Dumfries. And I was delighted with the beautiful lake-like Firth; the charm of which, I imagined must be mainly owing to the variety of its coast-outlines, and the undefined, mysterious recesses of its bays and estuaries; though there were also, indeed, the fine distant forms of the Scottish and English mountains, and the lights and shades of a bright, though beclouded summer's day.

Returning to Carlisle, thence crossing the Border, and turning along the northern shore of the Solway, the Galwudiae Mare of Gildas,[132] we enter **District VI—Galloway**; including under that name the western part of Dumfriesshire, Kircudbrightshire, and Wigtonshire. This district is mentioned in the poems of the Arthurian age as *Gallwyddel*, of which *Galgaidel* is the Gaelic, and *Galweithia* the Latin form, or equivalent;[133] and it may be described as lying between the Nith and Loch Ryan.[134] In the Mediaeval romances, it is referred to as the patrimony of Sir Gawayne,[135] son of Loth, or Lothus, King of Lothian. And thus Galloway may be viewed also as the birthland of the many other knights of whom the only description is but such as this: 'al they were of Scotland, outher of Syr Gawaynes' kynne, outher well-willers to his brethren'.[136]

The localities, however, which we have to note in this, as also in the next district, belong rather to the Arthurian age than to King Arthur. But the first two I have to mention may be considered as exceptions to this rule, as they refer to S. Kentigern, whom so many traditions connect with Merlin. At Hoddam or Hodelem on the Annan, it is stated by Joceline[137] that this saint, on this recall from Wales, after the great Christian victory of Arderydd, placed, for a time, his episcopal seat. And some way higher up on the opposite side of the river is a chuch dedicated to him as S. Mungo. The whole of Nithsdale, and the country about Lochmaben appears in the *Book of Taliessin*, under the name of Mabon;[138] and Lochar Moss (near which we may visit the famous Caer-laverock Castle, where Murdoch, second Duke of Albany, was for a time a prisoner in 1425), should seem to be the Man-Llachar of these poems.[139] Near Dumfries, with its tragical memories of the later years, and premature death, of Burns, we find on the north bank of the Cluden—the Cludvein or Cledyfein of the poems—where it falls into the Nith, the scene of the battle also commemorated in the *Book of Taliessin*, where

> 'lay the Peithwyr prostrate
> At the end of the wood of Celyddon.'[140]

For the author of the *Statistical Account* says, 'The lower part of this parish was unquestionably at an early period a *quercetum*, or oak-forest, extending most probably to Snaid, a distance of eight miles.' It was

termed the Holywood, and a monastery was afterwards founded here
called 'Abbatia Sacri Nemoris'. Not more than a quarter of a mile south-
west of the church eleven large stones are placed in an oval form. They
are situated near the lower end of the Sacred Grove; and should seem
to be a record of this battle of Pencoed. The Peithwyr were no doubt
the Picts of Galloway.[141] The Carron which flows into the Nith, in the
upper part of its course, is probably the stream mentioned in the same
Ancient Book as the 'boundary of Garant'.[142] And the Caer Rywe,
mentioned in another of these poems, 'probably refers to Sanquhar
or Senchaer, the old city which is on the Crawick, a name formed from
Caer Rawick as Cramond is from Caer Amond.[143]

Journeying westward past the mediaeval ruins of Sweetheart Abbey,
of romantic fame, and Kirkcudbright, with its pre-mediaeval memories
of S. Cuthbert, we come to Wigton; and near this we find what would
appear to be the tomb of that Gwallawg ap Lleenawg, relating to whom
there is a whole class of poems in the *Four Ancient Books*.[144] For 'in
the highway between Wigton and Portpatrick about three miles westward of Wigton is a plaine called the Moor of the Standing Stones of
Torhouse, in which there is a monument of three large whinstones, called
King Galdus's Tomb, surrounded, at about twelve feet distance, with
nineteen considerable great stones, but none of them so great as the
three just mentioned, erected in a circumference.'[145] And of Galdus,
or Gallawg, Boece says 'Elatum est corpus... in vicino campi ut vivens
mandaverat, est conditum ubi ornatissimum ei monumentum patrio
more, immensis ex lapidibus est erectum';[146] and he identifies him
with Galgacus who fought against Agricola.[147] Leaving Whitehorn, or
Candida Casa, with its memories of the apostolic S. Ninian, to the
south, we journey on, passing Kirkcowan, with the query whether there
is here to be found a topographical record of Gawayne, and come at
length to the neighbourhood of Loch Ryan. Here there seems to be
a record of the

'Battle in the Marsh of Terra, at the dawn,'[148]

in 'four large unpolished stones placed erect and forming a circle. At
a distance of some yards stands a single stone. They are called by the
country people the "Standing Stones of Glenterra".' Near this, 'about
three feet deep in a peat moss, there is a regular pile of stepping-stones,
extending about a quarter of a mile. These must have been placed in
this position to form a passage through a swamp previous to the growth
of the peat moss.'[149] It remains but to add that Caer Rheon, now
Cairnryan, Llwch Rheon, now Loch Ryan, and Rhyd Rheon, or Ford
of Ryan, are all mentioned in these poems of the Arthurian Age;[150]
and that the Mull of Galloway is the Novant of Aneurin.[151]

THE WESTERN DIVISION OF ARTHURIAN SCOTLAND

We now enter on **District VII—Ayr**. And here we have first to note that
the three immemorial divisions of this country—Carrick, Kyle, and Cunningham, all appear in the poems of the Arthurian Age under the more
primitive Cymric forms of Carrawg, Coel, and Canowan. In the *Book
of Taliessin*, [152] we find

> 'Of the many-citied Cymri, Carawg,
> The father of Caradawg.'

This Caradawg is obviously the Caractacus of Boece, who appears to
have used local traditions whenever he could find them, and who says
that in Carrick 'erat civitas tum maxima a qua Caractani regio videtur
nomen sortita. In ea Caractacus natus, nutritusm educatus,'[153] And a
similar monument to that we have found in Galloway to the memory
of Galdus, is described in a MS quoted by Dr Jamieson, in his edition
of Bellenden's *Boece* as existing in Carrick. 'There is 3 werey grate
heapes of stonnes, callit wulgarley the Kernes of Blackinney, being the
name of the village and ground. At the suthirmost of thir 3 cairnes
are ther 13 great tall stonnes, standing upright in a perfyte circkle, about
some 3 elle ane distaunt from ane other, with a gret heighe stonne in
the midle, which is werily esteemed to be the most learned inhabitants
to be the buriall place of King Caractacus.'[154] In reference to this division of Ayr I have only to add that the Gafran of the poems would appear
to be Girvan,[155] Caer Caradawg the Caractonium of Boece,[156] and
Dunduff the Dindywydd of Aneurin.[157]

In the same poem, and a few lines after those last quoted, we find

> 'Who will pay the precious reward?
> ...Or Coel, or Canowan?'[158]

Carrick, Kyle, and Cunningham thus mentioned together. And in those
Verses of the Graves in the *Black Book of Caermarthen*, from which
Mr Arnold takes one of his illustrations of what he calls the *Pindarism*
of the Celtic, as contrasted with the *Gemeinheit* of the Teutonic
style,[159] we read

> 'Whose is the Grave on the slope of the hill?
> Many who know it do not ask;
> The Grave of Coel, the son of Cynvelyn.'[160]

Boece tells us 'Kyl dein proxima est vel Coil potius nominata, a Coilo
Britannorum rege ibi in pugna caeso';[161] and a circular mound at
Coilsfield, in the parish of Tarbolton, on the highest point of which
are two large stones, and in which sepulchral remains have been found,
is pointed out by local tradition as his tomb.[162] The name of 'Auld
King Coil' is also perpetuated in the Crags of Kyle, the burn of Coyl,
and the parish of Coylton.

Coilsfield has fresher, and more romantic memories as the residence, in the humble capacity of a dairy-maid, of Burns' 'Highland Mary'. For Kyle is the Land of Burns;[163] as Carrick, we have just left, was the patrimony of Bruce, through the marriage of his father Robert Bruce, son of the Lord of Annandale, with the widowed Countess of Carrick.[164] And local traditions of both the national heroes—Wallace as well as Bruce having been natives of this south-west part of Scotland—may not a little have deepened the enthusiastic patriotism of the national poet. But we must proceed with our exploration of that Arthurian stratum of Romance which far underlies all those of mediaeval and modern times.

The next locality we have to note is the promontory of Troon, which would appear[165] to be the site of the

'battle in the region of Bretrwyn,'

mentioned in the *Book of Taliessin*.[166] On Dundonald, 'in cacumine montis qui appellatur Dundevenel', S. Monenna founded one of her churches after Arthur's victories over the pagan oppressors of his country. And Mr Skene places his first battle 'in ostium fluminis quod vocatur Glein', at the mouth of the river Glen, which rises in the mountains that separate Ayrshire from Lanarkshire, and falls into the Irvine in the parish of Loudon. And it appears to Mr Skene more probable that 'Arthur advanced into Scotland on the West', just as in after days, Bruce, 'through the friendly country peopled by the Cymry, than through Bernicia', where, as we have seen,[167] there is another river of this name, but 'which was already occupied by large bodies of Angles'.[168]

In Cunningham, the third division of Ayr, and which we have already noted as mentioned in the poems under the name of Canowan, was the

'battle in the wood of Beit at the close of the day,'

referred to by Taliessin.[169] And the place meant would appar to be the Moor of Beith in this district, where there was formerly a wood.[170] There should seem, however, to be no other locality of the Arthurian Age now discoverable here; so we may turn southwards again, and cross the mountains to the upper waters of the Clyde.

We now enter **District VIII—Strathclyde**, 'the region of the Clyd' of the *Red Book of Hergest*.[171] Upper Strathclyde would appear to be the Arfynydd of the Poems.[172] And here we may first note that, though, as we found, the Wells of the Tweed would not, the Sources of the Clyde, on the western slope of the same mountain-range would, very well accord with the twelfth century description of the Fountain of the Caledonian Merlin.[173] But if Merlin's Fountain is not clearly identifiable, we find, in the parish of Crawford, a well called Arthur's Fountain. That this name is of very ancient date we have evidence in a grant of 'David de Lindesay, in 1339, to the monks of Newbotle of the lands of Brotheralwyn in that district which were bounded on the west part, "a Fonte Arthuri usque ad summitate montis"'.[174] And other memories of Merlin are here recalled, for proceeding down the Clyde, we are in the ancient territory of his friend Rydderch Hael. For it is with this king of Strathclyde, not with Arthur, the Guledig, that the historical Merlin is associated. And in one of Merlin's poems relating to the Battle of Arderydd, preserved in the *Black Book of Caermarthen*, he seems to refer to Lanark, in its Cymric form *Llanerch*, a glade,[175] where in one of the apostrophes with which the stanzas of the poem commence, he exclaims—

> 'Sweet apple tree that grows in Lanark!
> ...Sweet apple tree that grows by the river side!'[176]

Overhanging the brawling Avon, and on the skirt of the noble chase which, with its wild cattle and ancient oaks, is all that now remains of that Caledonian Forest, once haunted by Merlin, and which stretched from sea to sea, stands Cadzow Castle. It preserves the name of that district of Godeu, or 'regina de Caidzow', as it is called in the life of S. Kentigern, which corresponded with what is now the middle ward of Lanarkshire,[177] and which is so often mentioned in the poems, and particularly in that called the Battle of Godeu:

> 'Minstrels were singing,
> Warrior bands were wondering,
> At the exaltation of the Brython,
> That Gwydyon effected.'[178]

'This,' says Mr Skene, 'was the alliance between the Brython, represented by Lleu (or Lothus) and the Gwyddel by Gwydyon which resulted in the insurrection of Medraut (or Mordred), son of Llew against Arthur, with his combined army of Picts, Britons, and Saxons, and which arose from a section of the Britons in the North being drawn over to apostasy by the pagan Saxons and semi-pagan Picts.'[179]

Calderwood would appear to be the Calaterium Nemus of Geoffrey.[180] Cambuslang is the 'regio Lintheamus', or Linthcamus, where S. Cadoc, to whom the parish is dedicated, built a monastery. And the adjoining parish of Carmunnock, formerly Carmannock, preserves the name of the mountain Bannawc—B, in combination, passing into M in Welsh—mentioned in the life of S. Cadoc, and now called the Cathkin Hills. 'Between Strathclyde and Ayrshire lay the district of Strathgryfe, now the county of Renfrew, and this part of Cumbria seems to have been the seat of the family of Caw, commonly called Caw Cawlwydd, or Caw Prydyn, one of whose sons was Gildas.[181] For in one of the lives of Gildas he is said to be the son of Caunus who reigned in Arecluta... And this name signifies a district lying along the Clyde'[182] as Strathgryfe or Renfrewshire does.[183] But in Neilston parish, in this county, we find more directly Arthurian localities in the places called Arthur Lee, Low Arthur Lee, and West Arthur Lee.

We conclude our exploration of Strathclyde with Glasgow. It appears in the *Book of Taliessin* as Caer Clud, the City on the Clyde.

'...they shall pledge the rich plains
From Caer Clud to Caer Caradawg,
The support of the land of Penprys and Gwallawg,
The king of the kings of tranquil aspect.'[184]

And in a poem in the same Book, connected by its title with the legends of the sons of Llyr, the Lear of Shakspeare, and finely beginning with

'I will adore the love-diffusing Lord of every kindred,
The sovereign of hosts manifestly round the Universe,'

Glasgow appears under the name of Penryn Wleth:

'From Penryn Wleth to Loch Reon
The Cymry are of one mind, bold heros.'[185]

For 'Joceline describes Kentigern as proceeding from the Clyde, and sitting "super lapidem in supercilio montis vocabulo Gwleth" (c. xiv.) *Gwleth*, forming in combination *Wleth*, signifies dew, and this hill was afterwards known as the Dew of Dowhill in Glasgow.'[186] But a better known memorial of the Arthurian founder of the city, three of whose miracles are commemorated on its arms,[187] in S. Mungo's Well, in the crypt of the Cathedral.

We leave Glasgow for the exploration of **District IX—Lennox**. That part of it to the east of Loch Lomond is identified by Mr Skene with Murief or Reged. The district intended by this name appears from a passage in the *Bruts*, where Arthur is said to have driven the Picts from Alcylde into Mureif, a country which is otherwise termed Reged, and that they took refuge there in Loch Lomond. Loch Lomond was, therefore, in it, and it must have been the district on the North side of the Roman Wall or *Mur*, from which it was called *Mureif*.[188] It is frequently mentioned in the poems; in one, for instance, in the *Book of Taliessin*, beginning

'Extol the career of the kings of Reged.'[189]

And among special localities in or adjoining this district may be mentioned Mugdock, in Strathblane, which would appear to be the place meant by the latter of the two names in the line

'Between Dineiddyn and Dineiddwg,'[190]

the former being clearly Edinburgh. It was certainly the scene of the great battle of 750 between the Britons of Strathclyde and the Picts at a place called by the Welsh chronicles Magedauc or Maesedauc.[191] And near this is Ardinny, the scene of the 'battle of Ardunnion',[192] referred to by Taliessin.

On the western brow of the Fintry Hills, we find that 'Dun or Down
of singular appearances—its point a perpendicular rock fifty feet high',
identified, as above,[193] with the 'Height of Adoyn, from which the
Bard of the second part of the *Gododin* saw the battle which he
describes. And the Hills of Kilsyth, of which the old form was Kilvesyth,
seem to be referred to in the 52nd stanza of the poem—

> 'Gododin, in respect of thee will I demand
> The dales beyond the ridges of *Drum Essyd.*'[194]

Beyond this, along the north-eastern shores of Loch Lomond, Mr Skene
places Argoed Llwyfain.[195] Here Urien and Owen his son are
described in a poem in the *Book of Taliessin* as fighting against Flamdd-
wyn, or the Flamebearer—

> 'And because of the affair of Argoed Llwyfain,
> There was many a corpse.
> The ravens were red from the warring of men,
> And the common people hurried with the tidings.'[196]

Dumbarton appears to be mentioned under the name of Nemhhur,
or Nevtur, in a dialogue between Merlin and Taliessin in the *Black Book
of Caermarthen.*[197] For this name occurs in the *Life of S. Patrick* by
Fiech, written in the eight century, after which it is unknown, and is
identified by his scholiast with Dumbarton.[198] And Arthur's ninth battle, 'in urbe Leogis qui Britannice Kairlium dicitur', is, by Mr Skene,
added to the innumerable conflicts which have been witnessed by this
magnificent fortified rock, where the sword of Wallce is now preserved.
For, as he says, 'it seems unlikely that a battle could have been fought
at this time with the Saxons at either Caerleon on the Esk, or Caerlon
on the Dee, which is Chester; and these towns Nennius terms, in his
list, not Kaerlium or Kaerlion, but Kaer Legion. It is more probably
some town in the north, and the *Memorabilia* of Nennius will afford
some indication of the town intended. The first of his *Memorabilia* is
"Stagnum Lumonoy", or Loch Lomond; and he adds: "non vadit ex
eo ad mare nisi unum flumen quod vocatur *Leum*"—that is, the Leven.
The Irish Nennius gives the name correctly, *Leamhuin*, and the Balli-
mote text gives the name of the town, *Cathraig in Leomhan* (for *Leamhan*), the town on the Leven. This was Dumbarton, and the
identification is confirmed by the *Bruts,* which place one of Arthur's
battles at Alclyd; while his name has been preserved in a parliamen-
tary record of David II in 1367, which denominates Dumbarton "Castrum Arthuri".[199] And it may be added that, according to tradition,
it was the birthplace of Mordred, Arthur's nephew or bastard son.[200]
Under the name of Alclyde, the city on the Clyde—a name as applicable to it as Kaer Leum, or Cathraig in Leomhan, for it is at the junction of the Leven with the Clyde—Dumbarton is frequently mentioned
in the *Four Ancient Books:*

'A battle in the ford of Alclud, a battle at the Inver.'[201]
'A battle in the ford of Alclud, a battle in the Gwen.'[202]
'There will come from Alclud, men, bold, faithful,
To drive from Prydein bright armies.'[203]

And on the Rock of Clyde, Petra Cloithe, another appropriate name for Dumbarton, 'rex Rodarcus filius Totail regnavit', when, as recorded by Adomnan,[204] he sent a message to S. Columba, to ask him, as supposed to possess prophetic power, whether he should be slain by his enemies.

Lennox, Leven, and Lomond are all one word; and district, river, and lake are all mentioned in the poems and old historical sources. The original word is, in its Cymric form, *Llwyfain*; in its Gaelic form, *Leamhain*, an elm-tree. From the latter comes *Leamhanach*, corrupted into Levenachs or Lennox, of which the Cymric equivalent is *Llwyfenydd*. But the old form of *Leamhan* of which Leven is a corruption, was *Leoman*, with the *m* not as yet aspirated; and from this comes Lomond. Thus we have the old form adhering to the loch and the mountain, while the river adopts the more modern.[205] In one of the poems in the *Four Ancient Books* the Lennox is mentioned as having been given to Taliessin in reward for his songs:

'And a fair homestead,
And beautiful clothing,
To me has been extended,
The lofty Llwyvenydd,
And requests open.'[206]

Sailing up the Lago Maggiore of Scotland there comes, like a dark shadow, across our delight in the loveliness of its fairy islands, the memory of the tragic story connected with the ruins on the largest of them. For here it was that Isabel, Duchess of Albany lived after the death on the scaffold of her father, her husband, and her two sons,[207] in 1424. Yet most singular it is, that it is in her, and her husband's descendants, that is the representation of what is now the eldest legitimate male line of the Royal House of Stuart.[208] But proceeding on our voyage, and landing on the western shore of the Lake, about half way up, we find ourselves in Glen Douglas. Here Mr Skene places Arthur's second third, fourth, and fifth battles 'super aliud flumen quod dicitur Dubglas et est in regione Linnuis'. 'Here,' says he, 'Arthur must have penetrated the ''regiones juxta murum'', occupied by the Saxons. Dubglas is the name now called Douglas. There are many rivers and rivulets of this name in Scotland; but none could be said to be ''in regione Linnuis,'' except two rivers—the Upper and Lower Douglas which fall into Loch Lomond, the one through Glen Douglas, the other at Inveruglas, and which are both in the district of the Lennox, the Linnuis of Nennius. Here, no doubt, the great struggle took place; and the hill called Ben Arthur at the head of Loch Long, which towers over this district between the two rivers, perpetuates the name of Arthur in connection with it.'[209]

Here, on Ben Arthur, our Arthurian wanderings terminate; and here we may fitly review in their connection the localities we have identified as the sites of Arthur's great battles. For, thus viewed, the probable correctness of each identification will, I think, become more apparent. 'According to the view I have taken,' says Mr Skene, 'Arthur's course was first to advance through the Cymric country, on the west, till he came to the Glen, where he encountered his opponents. He then invades the regions about the Wall, occupied by the Saxons in the Lennox, where he defeats them in four battles. He advances along the strath of the Carron as far as Dunipace, where, on the Bonny, his fifth battle is fought; and from thence marches south through Tweeddale, or the Wood of Celyddon, fighting a battle by the way, till he comes to the valley of the Gala, or Wedale, where he defeats the Saxons of the east coast. He then proceeds to take four great fortresses: first, *Kaerlium* or Dumbarton; next, Stirling, by defeating the enemy in the *tratheu Tryweryd,* or Carse of Stirling; then *Mynyd Agned,* or Edinburgh, the great stronghold of the Picts, here called *Cathbregion;* and, lastly, Bouden Hill, in the centre of the country between these strongholds. Twenty-one years after, is fought at Camelon the battle of Camlan, in which both Arthur and Medrant perished.' Mr Skene concludes with the judicious remark, that 'in thus endeavouring to identify the localities of those events connected with the names of Cunedda and of Arthur, I do not mean to say that it is all to be accepted as literal history, but as a legendary account of events which had assumed that shape as early as the seventh century, when the text of the *Historia Britonum* was first put together, and which are commemorated in local tradition'.[210]

Such, then, is the verification of the theory, deduced from the criticism of Cymric history, which is afforded by an exploration of the topography of Southern Scotland and the English Border. In the first place, we find in the Lennox, on the Firth of Forth, and in Tweeddale, sites for all the great battles of the Arthur of History, highly probable, to say the least, both considered separately, and in their sequence. This only I would remark on Mr Skene's theory as just stated, that, as it seems to me improbable that Arthur had Saxon foes so far west as the Lennox, I would, on this ground, be inclined to prefer the sites given by the writer in the *Gentleman's Magazine,* as those of his first, and next four battles. But whether we accept Mr Skene's theory in its entirety, or thus modified, the fact remains that very probable sites may be found for all Arthur's battles, not only in Arthurian Scotland, but just in those districts of it which we know to have formed a debatable-land between Cymry, Saxons, and Picts during the Arthurian Age. And further, it is to be remarked that at, or in the near neighbourhood of every one of these battlesites thus identified, we find existing, from the time of our oldest charters, and other documents, to this day, places with Arthur's name, or traditions of Arthur's history. Not far from the Glen, we have Arthur's Lee, etc.; towering over the battle-fields on the Douglas, Ben Arthur; near the battlefield of Dunnipais (Bassas), as also near that of the final battle of Camlan, Arthur's O'on; near the fields of battle of the Wood of Celyddon, and of Wedale, the Eildon Hills with their traditions of the departing out of this world of all the Arthurian Chivalry, and of the coming again of King Arthur; Dumbarton, where, as above, his ninth battle was fought, bears his name as Arthur's Castle; near the scene, according to Mr Skene, of his tenth battle, we find Arthur's Round Table; near that of his eleventh battle, Arthur's Seat; and near his twelfth battle-field, the tradition I have above given of Cockleroy Hill. And not only are these battle-sites in the neighbour-hood of traditional localities, but what is, perhaps, an equally im portant confirmation of the correctness of these identifications, they are in the neighbourhood of the great Roman roads.[211] We find also, from the foregoing exploration, that the Arthurian Traditions of the various districts, in which so many historical and poetical sites of the Arthurian Age have been identified, are not only distinctively differ-ent in each district, but that, in such difference, these traditions are in singular accordance with historical facts. In Strathmore, we have the tradition of Guenivere carried off by the Pictish Mordred; and the fact of the country beyond the Forth having been in the possession of the Picts. Lothian and Galloway we find connected by traditions of Lothus and his son Gawayne; and we know as a fact that, though separated by a wide extent of Cymric territory, these two districts were inhabited by the same Pictish race. Cumberland is distinguished by traditions of the Court of King Arthur, of which Gawayne, who is particularly mentioned as 'of Scotland', 'de l'Escosse', in the French Romances, is the principal hero; and Cumberland marched with his patrimony of Galloway. The Isle of Man is spoken of as inhabited by a foreign and hostile race; and it was in fact inhabited, not as the mainland by Cymry, but by Irish Scots. And so on. I do not, indeed, know of any tradition of Arthurian Scotland which, in its general features at least, is not in accordance with the results of our later historical researches.

I trust that the chief country of these localities will appear, without question, to be 'the North'; and that, in this general fact, and those to which I have, in the fore-going remarks, more particularly called atten-tion, there will be admitted to be an important inductive verification of our deductive theory that the birthland of the Traditions of King Arthur was Arthurian Scotland.

[1] As a writer of such authority as Mommsen has said 'Solche Eigenschaften guter Soldaten und schlechter Bürger erklären die geschichtliche Tatsache, dass die *Kelten alle Staaten erschüttert und keine gegründet haben,*' (*Romische Geschichte* B. II., K. IV., b. I., s. 329, *English Translation,* v. I., p. 359), one would not be justified in thus speaking of the consolidation of the tribes of North Britain into a predominantly Celtic nationality without, at least, briefly referring to one's proofs. These are to be found in the unquestionable facts, firstly, that, both in number, and in extent of territory occupied, Celts—Cymry, Picts and Scots, or Gael—were the chief basis of the Scotish nationality; secondly, that it was by one of the Celtic tribes, the Scots, namely, or Gael, that, not only all the other Celtic elements of the population, but the Saxon element also, was, towards the end of the Pre-mediaeval age, united under one monarch, whose dynasty, or the heirs of whose dynasty, lost their sovereignty only with the fall of the Stuarts, and the substitution of the present German Family; and, thirdly, that, in the opinion of the most competent authorities, not only were the tribes of North Britain thus united into the Scotish nationality by a Celtic race; not only, that is, have we here, at least, an exception to what Mommsen declares thus absolutely to be an historical fact, 'that the Celts have shaken all states and have founded none,' but the language of Scotland, both in the Highlands and Lowlands, except a narrow strip of sea-coast, was, at least till the reign of Malcolm Caenmore (1058-1093), and the opening of the Mediaeval Age, Gaelic. See Innes, *Sketches of Early Scottish History,* pp. 85-6; compare also Robertson, *Scotland under Her Early Kings,* vol. I., pp. 125, et seq. and v. II., pp. 142-3, and p. 374; and Tytler, *History of Scotland,* v. II., p. 188, et seq. That, during the Mediaeval Age, a Teutonic dialect, allied to the English, took the place of Norman-French, and of Gaelic, at the Court, and further extended itself in the Lowlands, was due to many causes. Among these, may, for instance, be named, the marriage of Malcolm Caenmore with the sister of Edgar Atheling, and the encouragement thence given to the settlement in Scotland of Saxon refugees from the Norman conquest; the policy of the Scotish monarchs generally in encouraging the settlement both of Saxons and Normans, as allies against their own turbulent subjects; and the naturally preponderating influence of the inhabitants of sea-coasts. See note 16 *infra* p. xliii*. And yet to this hour one may, in a day's journey from such a vast centre of an English-speaking population as Glasgow, find the simplest English question answered with 'No English!' Celts *have,* therefore, once, at least, succeeded in *founding,* though not in long maintaining, a state with a purely Celtic organization and language. But have Saxons founded or long maintained a State with a purely Teutonic organization? These current generalizations about the Celts will seldom bear being strictly examined. See Robertson, as above, *Appendix B. The Celt and the Teuton,* v. II. p. 197 et seq.

[2] I need here only recall Mr Tennyson's *Idylls of the King,* Mr Arnold's *Tristram and Iseult,* Mr Morris's *Defence of Guenivere,* Edgar Quinet's epic *Merlin,* and Richard Wagner's 'Poèms d'Opera', *Lohengrin,* and *Tristan et Iseult.*

[3] *Prophecies de Merlin,* F. 76.

[4] Ariosto, *Orlando Furioso,* c. III. s. 11.

[5] Leland, *Itinerary,* v. V. pp. 62, 63.

[6] Drayton, *Poly-Olbion, Song the Tenth. Works,* v. III. p. 843.

[7] Chapters II. and III. (Early English Text Society).

[8] *On the Study of Celtic Literature,* p 155. See also *Four Ancient Books,* v. I. p. 326.

[9] '*Faerie Queene,*' iii. 3.

[10] Drayton, *Poly-Olbion, Song the Third, Works,* v. II. p. 712.

[11] Ibid. v. II. p. 722.

[12] Lidgate, *Boccace Lib.* VIII. *Cap.* 24.

[13] Drayton, *Poly-Olbion, Song the First, Works,* v. II. p. 660.

[14] Drayton, *Poly-Olbion, Song the Fourth, Works,* v. II. p. 735.

[15] Forbes-Leslie, *The Early Races of Scotland and their Monuments,* v. I. p. 12.

[16] Arthurian traditions, it must, however, be noted, attach also to some places beyond the limits of the region thus described, and rather in the south, than the west of England. For instance,

> 'And for great Arthur's seat, her Winchester perfers,
> Whose old Round Table yet she vaunteth to be hers;'

sings Drayton in the Second Song of the *Poly-Olbion*, so often above quoted (*Works*, v. II. p. 691).

[17] Chalmers remarks that 'the valourous Arthur of History and the redoubtable Arthur of Romance has supplied the topography of North Britain with such significant names, as seem to imply, either that the influence of the real Arthur was felt, or the remembrance of the fictitious Arthur was preserved, for many ages after the Pendragon had fallen by the insidious stroke of treachery from the kindred hand of Mordred.' *Caledonia*, v. I. p. 244. Sir Walter Scott, in a note on his *Vision of Don Roderick, Introduction*, s. iv., observes that 'much of the ancient poetry preserved in Wales refers less to the history of the Principality to which that name is now limited, than to events which happened in the north-west of England, and south-west of Scotland, where the Britons for a long time made a stand against the Saxons'. And he further refers to the connection of Aneurin, Llywarch Hen, and Merlin with Scotland rather than with Wales. Compare also his introduction to *Sir Tristrem*, pp. xxxiv-viii.; and to *Thomas the Rhymer*, Part II. in *Minstrelsy of the Scottish Border*. A writer in the *Gentleman's Magazine* of 1842 was, however, the first, I believe, distinctly to maintain that 'the seat of Arthur's power was. . . adjacent to the Saxon settlement of Lothian';' and that 'in connection with that settlement his victories are recorded by Nennius'. And he adds that the mistake of assigning to Arthur a kingdom in the south-western extremity of the island 'was possibly confirmed by the casual similarity of name between Arthur's real subjects in the north, and those assumed for him in the Cornish promontory, the former bearing the designation of Damnii, the latter of Dumnonii' v. XVII. p. 486. But the incompleteness of the evidence advanced in support of this conclusion was probably the reason of its attracting but little attention. Mr Nash also asserts, but does not even attempt to prove a theory similar to that in this essay maintained. 'The original locality,' he says, 'of the traditions which have furnished the groundwork of these world-renowned romances (of King Arthur) is probably the Cumbrian region taken in its widest extent from the Firths of Forth and Clyde southward and westward along the borders of the Northumbrian kingdom, in which the famous exploits of the British Cymric struggle with the Northumbrian Angles became the theme of a native minstrelsy, transplated into Brittany by the refugees from the Saxon conquest, and moulded into the romances with which we have been made acquainted by the Norman trouveres.' *Merlin the Enchanter and Merlin the Bard*, p. iv. And Mr Burton at least admits that, 'if any reality could be extracted from the Arthurian histories, Scotland would have its full share, since much of the narrative comes northward of the present border'. *History of Scotland*, v. I. pp. 174-7. On the other hand, however, Dr Guest identifies Arthur with Owen Finddu, the son of Aurelius Ambrosius, and places him in the south-west of England; remarking that his being called the son of Uter arose from Geoffrey of Monmouth's having mistaken the meaning of the term applied to him by Nennius, *map uter*, 'the terrible boy, because he was cruel from his childhood'. *Welsh and English Rule in Somersetshire after the Capture of Bath*, AD 577. *Archaeological Journal*, 1859, p. 123 et seq. And Mr Pearson also makes Arthur sovereign of a territory in the south-west of England of which Camelot, or Cadbury, in Somersetshire, was the capital. *Early and Middle Ages of England*, v. I. p. 56-8. See also *Bishop Percy's Manuscript*, v. I. pp. 401-4. And Col. Forbes-Leslie, without appearing to have a suspicion that Scotland may be the true birthland of Arthurian tradition, says: 'I do not presume to give an opinion on the rival claims of Wales, Corn-

wall, and Armorica, to the domicile of King Arthur and his Paladins, and Merlin with his magical powers'. *Early Races of Scotland and their Monuments*, v. I. p. 167 (1866).

[18] This term is thus used to include part of what is now England. But, I think, justifiably: not only because it is a more convenient, though, perhaps, less excact term than 'Southern Scotland and the English Border'; but because the dominion of the early Scottish kings extended, though precariously, beyond the present border; and because Cumberland and Northumberland were not finally annexed to the Crown of England till the third of Henry II. See Hinde, *On the Early History of Cumberland*, in *The Archaeological Journal*, 1859, p. 217 et seq.

[19] Called Wanore and Vanore in the Scottish Romance of *Lancelot of the Laik* of 1478 or 1490. See pp. 230 and 575. Edit. E.E.T. Soc.

[20] *New Statistical Account of Scotland*, v. X. 118.

[21] *Works* (1825) v. II. p. 274.

[22] Quoted by Chalmers (of Auldbar) *Sculptured Stones of Angus and Mearns*.

[23] *Les Romans de la Table Ronde*, pp. 58-9.

[24] Ibid. p. 64, citing *The Myryrian Archaeology*, v. I. p. 175.

[25] *Lancelot du Lac*, f. 1.

[26] *New Stat. Ac.*, v. I. p. 419

[27] *Four Ancient Books*, v. I. p. 294.

[28] Ibid. p. 463.

[29] *Chronicle of the Picts and Scots*, p. 136. 'It may seem strange,' says Mr Skene,'that I should assert that Gwryd and Forth are the same word. Bu *Gwr* in Welsh is represented by *Fear* in Irish, the old form of which was *For*, and final *d* in Welsh is in Irish *ch*, in Pictish *th*. The river which falls into the Dee, near Bala, in North Wales, is called Try-weryn, a very similar combination.'

[30] *Four Ancient Books*, v. II. pp. 56-7.

[31] *Itinerary*, p. 311.

[32] *Lady of the Lake*, Canto VI. S. xxviii.

[33] *Complaynt of the Papingo*.

[34] *New Stat. Ac.*, v. VIII. p. 407, citing William of Worcester, Barbour, Gough's, Camden's *Britannica*, and Chalmers, Caledonia, v. I. p. 244-5.

[35] *Charta Newbotle*, No. 239, cited by Chalmers, *Caledonia*, v. I. p. 245.

[36] 'The printed text of the Vatican MS of Nennius has *Lussas*, but this is a mistake, the original MS reads Bassas.'—Skene's note.

[37] *Four Ancient Books*, v. I. pp. 53-4.

[38] Macpherson, *The Poems of Ossian. The War of Caros*.

[39] *Four Ancient Books*, v. I., pp. 59-60.

[40] May there not be a reminiscence of this name in the Gallehault of the French, and the Galyot of the Scotish, Romance of *Lancelot?*

[41] 'There sank to the bottom five and twenty hundred, so that all Avon's stream was bridged with steel.'—*Brut*. Edit. Madden, v. II. p. 469.

[42] *Four Ancient Books*, v. I. pp. 57-8.

[43] Would it be too much to consider this legend of a camp under Bouden as a memory of the Arthurian Obsessio Montis Badonici which had got attributed to the Romans; and this particularly, as there are many legends of Arthur's having gone to Jerusalem; as there is no considerable historical improbability in his actually having done so; and as, if he made an Eastern pilgrimage, it would probably have been after this twelfth victory, which gave the kingdom peace till the fatal battle of Camlan, in which Arther fell, twenty-one years later. Very probably, had I asked the old man whether he did not mean that it was Arthur, and not the Romans, who 'lifted' the camp, he would have assented. But one cannot get truth if one does not guard against the temptation to put such leading questions in support of one's theories.

[44] I found that such phrases as 'auld histories', and 'mentioned in history', did not

mean, with these old men, written, but traditional history.

[45] *Historical Maps—Britannica Cumbria.*

[46] *Four Ancient Books,* v. I. p. 413 and v. II. p. 394. See also v. I. p. 378 and v. II. p. 374.

[47] *Four Ancient Books,* v. II. p. 359.

[48] This is also the opinion of Mr Beale Poste; but Mr Nash and Archdeacon Jones place Munau Guotodin in the district about Jedbugh, and extend it into Northumberland.

[49] For a further account of Calatria see *Chronicles of the Picts and Scots. Introduction,* p. lxxx.

[50] Catraeth is placed by Mr Pearson 'about Galashiels, or near Kelso, and not far from the Kale'. *Historical Maps—Britannica Cambrica.* Compare also Madden, *Layamon's Brut.* v. III. p. 324.

[51] *Four Ancient Books,* v. II. . 366-8.

[52] *Four Ancient Books,* v. II. pp. 369-70. Compare also v. I. pp. 177-8.

[53] *Historica Ecclesiae,* 1. c.

[54] *Historia Britonum,* 23.

[55] *Four Ancient Books,* v. I. p. 337.

[56] Ibid. v. II. p. 401.

[57] Ibid. v. I. p. 287.

[58] Ibid. v. II. p. 452.

[59] Ibid. v. Ii. p. 411 and 352.

[60] Ibid. v. I. p. 294.

[61] Ibid. v. I. p. 265

[62] Ibid. v. I. p. 276.

[63] The Judeu, however, of Nennius, Mr Pearson places in the Jedburgh district.

[64] *Four Ancient Books,* v. II. p. 408.

[65] *On the Catstane, Kirkliston,* etc., in *Proceedings of the Society of Antiquaries of Scotland,* v. IV. p. 119 *et seq.*

[66] Madden, *Layamon's Brut,* v. III. pp. 315-6.

[67] *Four Ancient Books,* v. I., p. 84.

[68] Ibid. v. I. p. 263; cf. also p. 276.

[69] *Caledonia,* v. I., p. 245; and Ramsay's *Evergreen,* v. II., p. 65.

[70] Hence, perhaps, the name of *Castle of Maidens* applied to Edinburgh?

[71] Compare *Four Ancient Books,* v. I. pp. 85-6, and the *Vita S. Kentigerni,* by Jocelyn in Pinkerton's *Vitae Antiquissimorum Sanctorum.*

[72] Chaucer, *The Man of Lawe's Tale.*

[73] See note 17, p. 113.

[74] *Gentleman's Magazine,* v. XVII., N. S., 1842, p. 598.

[75] *Four Ancient Books,* v. I. p. 337, and v. II. p. 401.

[76] *Scotichronicon,* B. III. C. xxvi.

[77] *Four Ancient Books,* v. I. p. 54.

[78] *Myrdhin, ou L'Enchanteur Merlin,* p. 3.

[79] Ariosto, *Orlando Furioso,* C. III. S. 10.

[80] See Chambers, *History of Peebleshire,* and Pennycuick, *History of Tweeddale,* p. 26.

[81] 'It also seems evident,' says the Revd T. Price, 'that it is to the Hwimleian, or Chwifleian of Merlinus Silvestris,' the historical Merlin of Scotland, 'that we are to attribute the origin of the Viviane of the romances of Chivalry, and who acts so conspicuous a part in those compositions, although it is true there is not much resemblance betwixt the two names. But if we look into the poems of Merlin Sylvestris, we shall find that the female personage of this name, which by the French romances might easily be modified into Viviane, is repeatedly referred to by the bard in his vaticina-

tions. It also seems probable, as Chwifleian signifies a female who appears and disappears, and also as the word bears some resemblance in sound to Sybilla, that the bard, by a confusion of terms and ideas, not uncommon in early writers, coined this name as an appellation for some imaginary character, and thus furnished the original of Viviane'. (*Literary Remains*, v. I. p. 144). This Merlin also had a twin-sister Gwendydd or Ganieda, who supplied her brother with food in his solitary wanderings in the Caledonian Forest. In a poem in the *Red Book of Hergest* (*Four Ancient Books*, v. I. p. 462) she addresses him as *Llallogan* or twin-brother. 'And this,' says Mr Price, 'will explain a passage in the life of S. Kentigern, in which it is said that there was at the court of Rydderch Hael, a certain idiot named *Laloicen*, who uttered predictions: "In curia ejus quidam homo fatuus vocabulo Laloicen"; and in the *Scotichronicon* it is stated that this Laloicen was *Myrddin Wyllt*. By connecting these several particulars we find an air of truth cast over the history of this bard, as regards the principal incident of his life, and there can be no reason to doubt that some of the poetry attributed to him was actually his composition' (*Literary Remains*, v. I. p. 143; cited *Four Ancient Books*, v. II. pp. 353 and 424).

[82] Villemarqué, *Merlin*, p. 234.

[83] Ibid.

[84] *Vita Merlini*, ll. 138-141 in San-Marte (Schultz) *Die Sagen von Merlin*, p. 277.

[85] 'As the Saxon names of places, with the pleasant wholesome smack of the soil in them—Weathersfield, Thaxted, Shalford—are to the Celtic names of places, with their penetrating lofty beauty—Velindra, Tyntagel, Caernarvon—so is the homely realism of German and Norse nature to the fairy-like loveliness of Celtic nature' (Arnold, *Study of Celtic Literature*, p. 159). Sir Walter Scott certainly makes the best of the *Grey Mare's Tail* when he says of this cataract of 200 feet that it,

'White as the *snowy charger's tail*,
Drives down the pass of Moffatdale.'

(Marmion, Introd. to Canto 2).

[86] *Four Ancient Books*, v. I. p. 54.

[87] Ibid. v. I. p. 370; v. II. pp. 18 and 337.

[88] *Historical Maps—Britannia Cambrica*.

[89] Scott, *Minstrelsy of the Scotish Border*, Thomas the Rhymer, Part 1.

[90] On the History of the Battle of Cattraeth and the Gododin of Aneurin, in The Cambrian Journal, 1861.

[91] Pilgrims from Britain are mentioned by S. Jerome. There is, therefore, no historical improbability in the legends of Arthur's pilgrimage to the Holy Sepulchre.

[92] *Harleian MS* of the *Historia Britonum*. Henry of Huntingdon, who likewise gives this account, says the image was upon his shield; and, as in Welsh, *ysgwyd* is a shoulder, and *ysgwydd*, a shield, a Welsh original must have been differently translated by the two authors.

[93] *Four Ancient Books*, v. I. p. 55.

[94] Ibid. v. I. pp. 343-4.

[95] Ibid. v. II. p. 412.

[96] See *Appendix to General Preface to Waverley*.

[97] *Scenes of Infancy*, Part II.

[98] *Four Ancient Books*, v. I. p. 363, and v. II. p. 162.

[99] *Caledonia*, v. II. p. 146.

[100] *Historical Maps—Britannica Cambrica*.

[101] On the History of the Battle of Cattraeth, etc., in The Cambrian Journal, 1861.

[102] *Gentleman's Magazine*, v. XVII. (1842), p. 59.

[103] See Robertson, *Scotland under Her Early Kings*, v. I. p. 96, n.

[104] See Scott, *Romance of Sir Tristrem, Introduction,* p. xxxvii. See also Burton, *History of Scotland,* v. I. p. 177.
[105] Scott, *Romance of Sir Tristrem, Introduction, p. xxxvii.*
[106] Villemarqué, *Romans de la Table Ronde,* pp. 321 and 395.
[107] *Vita Merlini,* l. 31 and l. 68. San Marte (Schultz), *Die Sagen von Merlin,* pp. 274-5.
[108] *Four Ancient Books,* v. I. p. 386. Compare also Guest (Lady Charlotte) *Mabinogion, Notes to Peredur the Son of Evrawc,* v. I. p. 371.
[109] *Harold the Dauntless,* s. VI.
[110] Bruce, *The Roman Wall,* p. 175.
[111] Hodgson, *History of Northumberland,* Part II. v. III. p. 287.
[112] Liddesdale is, of course, known to be within the political frontier of Scotland, though its Arthurian localities are here treated of partly as belonging to the district of Northumberland, and partly to that of Cumberland.
[113] *Four Ancient Books,* v. I. pp. 177-8; also v. II. p. 365, where it is said that Mr Stephens now considers this battle to have been that celebrated in the poems of the Gododin. Donald Brec, who was defeated in the battle of Strathcawin—the subject according to Mr Skene, of the second part of these poems—was the son of this Aidan.
[114] *Notice of the Site of the Battle of Arderyth—Proceedings of the Society of Antiquaries of Scotland,* v. VI. P. I. p. 95 (published in 1867, my visit being in 1866).
[115] *Myrdhin, ou L'Enchanteur Merlin,* p. 72.
[116] *Vita S. Kentigerni,* MSS. Mus. Britann. Cf. Fordun *Scotichronicon,* lib. III. cxxxi. p. 135, ed. Edinb. 1769. See also Scott, Introduction to *Thomas the Rhymer,* Part II., in *Minstrelsy of the Scottish Border.*
[117] *Notice of the Site,* etc., above quoted, p. 98.
[118] Arthuret, as a name, therefore, has nothing whatever to do with Arthur, as Hutchinson supposes (*History of Cumberland,* v. II. p. 545), making it a corruption of Arthur's head; and is mentioned among these Arthurian localities, not because of its connection with Arthur, but with the Arthurian Merlin.
[119] *Four Ancient Books,* v. I. p. 257, and v. II. pp. 200 and 419.
[120] As an illustration of the unlikely places in which one may find the objects of one's search, I may note that I found this tradition mentioned in Mr Mortimer Collins' novel, *Who is the Heir?* v. I. p. 253.
[121] Pearson, *Historical Maps—Britannia Cambrica.*
[122] Madden, *Romances of Sir Gawayne* (Bannatyne Club).
[123] See White, *Northumberland and the Border,* p. 249 et seq. Compare also Fergusson, *Tree and Serpent Worship,* p. 32, n.
[124] Madden, *Romances of Syr Gawayne,* p. 309.
[125] *Four Ancient Books,* v. I. p. 338, and v. II. p. 402.
[126] Ibid. v. I. p. 406, v. II. p. 449.
[127] Madden, *Romances of Syr Gawayne.*
[128] Madden, *Romances of Syr Gawayne.* See also *Bishop Percy's Folio MS.,* v.I. p. 95.
[129] Pearson, *Historical Maps—Britannica Cambrica.*
[130] 'Tres magnas insulas habet, quarum una vergit contra Armoricas, et vocatur Inisgueith; secunda sita est in umbilico maris inter Hiberniam et Britanniam et vocatur nomen ejus Eubonia, id est Manau.' This name was also, as we have above seen, applied to a district in North Britain; 'regio qui vocatur Manua Guotodin'. It should seem that 'the island was associated with the name of the Scots, and the region with that of the Picts'. *Four Ancient Books,* v. I. p. 83.
[131] See Waldron, *History and Description of the Isle of Man.*
[132] *De Excid Brit.* c. xi.
[133] *Four Ancient Books,* v. II. p. 452, etc.
[134] Ibid. p. 401.
[135] Madden, *Romances of Syr Gawayne.*

136 Malory, *The Byrth, Lyf, and Actes of Kyng Arthur*.
137 *Vita S. Kentigerni* in Pankerton's *Vitae Antiquissimorum Sanctorum*.
138 *Four Ancient Books*, v. I. pp. 363, 562 and v. II. pp. 420-6.
139 *Four Ancient Books*.
140 Ibid. v. I. p. 338.
141 Ibid. v. II. p. 402.
142 Ibid. v. I. p. 429, and v. II. p. 407.
143 Ibid. v. II. p. 401.
144 Ibid. v. I. p. 336 *et seq*.
145 Symson, *Description of Galloway* (1684).
146 Quoted in *Four Ancient Books*, v. I. p. 171.
147 The antiquarian controversy about the Mons Grampius, and the site of the battle between Galgacus and Agricola is well known. See Burton, *History of Scotland*, v. I. p. 12 et seq. But, if I am not deceived by the partiality of a grandson, a very probable case seems to be made out for that site on the Grampians in the neighbourhood of Stonehaven in Kincardineshire, where we find, on the plain, within a mile of the sea, a Roman Camp, and directly opposite, on the face of the hills, at the distance of not more than two miles, a native, or Caledonian entrenchment (Re-dykes). Stuart (of Inchbreck), *Essays on Scottish Antiquities*, pp. 79-80 *et seq*. See also Roy, *Military Antiquities, Introduction*, p. iv.
148 *Four Ancient Books*, v. I. p. 338.
149 *Statistical Account of Insch*, in the county of Wigton, quoted in *Four Ancient Books*, v. II. p. 402.
150 Ibid. v. I. pp. 241, 276, v. II. pp. 337, 401.
151 Pearson, *Historical Maps—Britannia Cambrica*.
152 *Four Ancient Books*, v. I. p. 429.
153 Quote, Ibid. v. I. p. 171.
154 Quoted in *Four Ancient Books*, v. I. p. 172.
155 Ibid. v. II. p. 403.
156 Ibid. v. II. 415.
157 Pearson, *Historical Maps—Britannia Cambrica*.
158 *Four Ancient Books*, v. I. p. 430.
159 Ibid. v. I. p. 316, Cynvelyn would become Cymbeline in English.
160 Ibid. v. I. p. 170.
161 *Study of Celtic Literature*, p. 145. The verse he quotes is as follows:

> 'The Grave of March is this, and this the Grave of Gwythyr;
> Here is the grave of Gwgawn Gleddyvrud;
> But unknown is the Grave of Arthur.'

Compare Skene, *Four Ancient Books*, v. I. p. 315.
162 Whatever truth there may be in Mr Fergusson's theory that the so-called Druidical Circles of Britain had nothing whatever to do with the Druids, but are sepulchral monuments of the Arthurian Age; it seems worth noting that in these Tombs of Gwallawg (Galdus) of Caradawg (Caractacus) and of Coel, we have monuments similar to those elsewhere called Druidical circles, but with traditions attached to them which seem to give support to such a theory as Mr Fergusson's.
163 It must, however, be noted that it was only the father of Burns who migrated to Ayrshire. His ancestors are traceable for three centuries as tenants of farms on the estate of Inchbreck, on the southern slope of the Grampians in Kincardineshire, a property that still belongs to the representative of the Stuarts of Castleton, etc., a branch of the family of the Earl of Castle-Stuart. See *infra*, note 208. p. cv.
164 Bruce was thus 'the representative of a Gaelic line of princes which had ruled over Galloway from time immemorial; whilst his paternal grandfather's mother, through

whom he inherited his claim on the throne, was a daughter of the (Gaelic) royal house of Atholl'. (Robertson, *Scotland under Her Early Kings*, v. II., p. 142 n). The representation of the family of the Bruce passed into that of the Stuarts (*Infra*, p. cv. n. 208); the Bruces, Earls of Elgin, being descended but from a knight of whom all that is known is that he was a contemporary of the heroic king.

[165] *Four Ancient Books*, v. II. p. 402.

[166] Ibid. v. I. p. 337.

[167] *Supra*, p. lxxviii.

[168] *Four Ancient Books*, v. I. p. 52. But see *infra*, p. cxxv.

[169] Ibid. v. I. p. 337.

[170] Ibid. v. II. p. 402.

[171] Ibid. v. I. p. 463. See also p. 431, and v. II. p. 399.

[172] Ibid v. II. p. 413.

[173] *Supra*, p. lxxiv.

[174] *Chart. Newbotle*, N. 148, quoted by Chalmers, *Caledonia*, v. I. p. 245. See also Irving and Murray, *Upper Ward of Lanarkshire*.

[175] *Four Ancient Books*, v. II. p. 336.

[176] Ibid. v. I. p. 371-2.

[177] Ibid. II. p. 414.

[178] Ibid. v. I. p. 278.

[179] *Four Ancient Books*, v. I. p. 204.

[180] Pearson, *Historical Maps—Britannia Cambrica*.

[181] Another, the Cueil, or Hueil, king of Scotland, 'quem occidit rex Arthurus?'

[182] *Four Ancient Books*, v. I. p. 173.

[183] It was in this county that the Normanno-Celtic family of the FitzAlans, who, from their hereditary office, took the name of Stewart, had their first grants of lands in Scotland. See Skene, *History of the Highlanders*, v. II. p. 308 et seq.; and Stuart (Hon. and Rev. Godfrey), *Genealogical and Historical Sketch of the Stuarts of the House of Castle-Stuart*. Paisley, the chief town of the county, was founded by Walter Stuart in 1160; and in its Abbey is the tomb of Marjory, daughter of Robert the Bruce, and mother of Robert the Second, the first of the Stuart dynasty.

[184] *Four Ancient Books*, p. 340.

[185] *Four Ancient Books*, v. I. p. 276.

[186] Ibid. v. II. p. 404.

[187] Burton, *History of Scotland*, v. I. p. 249.

[188] *Four Ancient Books*, v. I. p. 59.

[189] Ibid. p. 350.

[190] Ibid. p. 270.

[191] *Four Ancient Books*, p. 404.

[192] Ibid. p. 337.

[193] *Supra*, p. lxvi.

[194] *Four Ancient Books*, v. I. p. 893.

[195] Ibid. v. II. p. 413.

[195] Ibid. v. I. p. 366.

[197] Ibid. v. I. p. 368.

[198] Ibid. II. 321.

[199] *Four Ancient Books*, v. I. pp. 55-6.

[200] Campbell, *West Highland Tales*.

[201] *Four Ancient Books* I. 350.

[202] Ibid. I. 363.

[203] Ibid. I. 441.

[204] *Life of S. Columba*.

[205] Compare *Four Ancient Books*, v. I. p. 159, and v. II. p. 413.

[206] Ibid. v. I. 347.

[207] To Walter, the younger of the two, the beautiful and pathetic ballad of 'Young Waters' is believed, on good ground, to refer.

[208] On the death of Prince Charles Edward without legitimate issue, the eldest son of Robert II (James I) was left without descendants in the male line. The representation, therefore, of the Royal Family of Stuart, as also of that of Bruce, fell to the Earl of Castle-Stuart, the representative in direct male descent of the Duke of Albany, the second son of Robert II, the first of the Dynasty. See Stuart, (Hon. and Rev. Godfrey), *Genealogical and Historical Sketch of the Stuarts of the House of Castle-Stuart*. The connection of our present German sovereign with the ancient line of native English and Scottish kings is of a most remote, and collateral description. On personal conduct, and popular affection, not on 'right divine', is the throne now fortunately established.

[209] *Four Ancient Books*, v. I. p. 53.

[210] *Four Ancient Books*, v. I. pp. 58 and 60.

[211] Compare Roy, *Military Antiquities*. One is the more struck on observing this as Mr Skene's identifications seem to have been made without any reference to these roads.

Chapter 6.
Arthur and Accolon
by Sir Thomas Malory

No selection of Arthurian material would be complete without something from the *Le Morte D'Arthur* of Sir Thomas Malory. Written in 1485 and published by William Caxton on one of the first printing presses in this country in 1485, its incomparable prose style and richness of story, still constitutes the finest single attempt to tell the whole story of Arthur and his knights. It was based upon a massive 13th Century French prose compilation known as the *Vulgate Cycle*, but it is much more than a slavish translation. Everywhere Malory shapes and changes his material, adding to and omitting so much that his book is clearly an independent work of art and the work of a single mind.

We know virtually nothing about the owner of that mind, though several contenders for the title have been put forward in recent years. Sir Thomas Malory of Newbold Revel in Warwickshire is the senior by a number of years,[1] and has given rise to a mythology of his own. For this Malory was far from the paragon of Chivalry one might expect, but a thief and rapist who spent much of his life in prison. Malory's own repeated requests in the glosses of his book to 'Pray for him' who was a 'knight prisoner', have led credence to this.

More recently William Matthews[2] has put forward another contender, Sir Thomas Mallory of Hutton Conyers in Yorkshire, who spent much of his life as a prisoner-of-war in France, where he would certainly have had access to the works he used for his own account of Arthur.

Whichever portrait one chooses—each has its own validity—it is the text itself which finally draws one back. Countless numbers of people know it from the sometimes bowdlerized versions prepared for children; its true riches await those who are led to explore further.

The episode included, which comes from one of the earliest critical editions, that of Thomas Wright, printed in 1858, concerns the early days of Arthur's reign, when he was still active among his knights. Here, too, is an explanation of sorts for the enmity which existed hereafter between Arthur and his sister Morgan le Fay. It is a curious episode altogether, and contains many clues to the inner history of the legend, which have been dealt with more fully elsewhere.[3]

<hr />

Then it befell that king Arthur and many of his knights rode on hunting into a great forrest, and it happened king Arthur, king Urience, and Sir Accolon of Gaule followed a great hart, for they three were well horsed, and they chased so fast that within a while they three were ten mile from their fellowship, and at the last they chaced so sore that they slew their horses under them. The wer they al three on foot, and ever they saw the hart afore them passing weary and embushed.

'What will we doe?' said king Arthur, 'we are hard bested.'

'Let us goe on foote,' said king Urience, 'till we may meete with some lodging.'

Then were they ware of the hart that lay on a great water-banck, and a brachet biting upon his throate, and many other hounds came after. Then king Arthur blew the price[4] and dight the hart there. Then king Arthur looked about him, and saw afore him in a great water a little ship al apparelled with silke downe to the water, and the ship came straight unto them, and landed[5] on the sands. Then king Arthur went to the bank and looked in, and saw none earthly creature therein.

'Sirs', said the king, 'come thence and let us see what is in this ship.' So they went in all three, and found it richly behanged with cloath of silk, and by that time it was darke night; there suddainly were about them an hundred torches set on all the sides of the shippe bords and gave a great light. And therewith came out twelve faire damosels, and saluted king Arthur on their knees, and called him by his name, and said he was welcome, and such cheere as they had he should have of the best. And the king thanked them faire. Therewith they led the king and his two fellowes into a faire chamber, and there was a cloth laid richly beseene of all that belonged to a table, and there they were served of all wines and meates that they could thinke of, that the king had great marvaile, for he fared never better in his life for one supper.

And so when they had supped at their leisure, king Arthur was led into a chamber, a richer beseene chamber saw he never none, and so was king Urience served, and led into another chamber, and sir Accolon was led into the third chamber, passing rich and well beseene. And so were they laid in their beds right easily, and anon they fell on sleepe, and slept mervailously sore[6] all that night. And on the morrow king Urience was in Camelot abed in his wives armes, Morgan le Fay. And when he awok he had great mervaile how he came there, for on the even afore hee was about a two dayes journey from Camelot. And also when king Arthur awoke, he found himselfe in a darke prison, hearing about him many complaints of wofull knights.

Then said king Arthur, 'What are ye that so complaine?'

'We are here twentie good knights prisoners,' said they, 'and some of us have lien here seaven yeere, and some more and som lesse.'

'For what cause?' said king Arthur.

'We shall tell you,' said the knights. 'The lord of this castle is named sir Damas, and he is the falsest knight that liveth, and full of treason, and a very coward as any liveth, and hee hath a yonger brother, a good knight of prowesse, his name is sir Ontzlake, and this traitor Damas, the elder brother, wil give him no part of his livelihood but that sir Ontzlake keepeth through his prowesse, and so he keepeth from him

a full faire mannor and a rich, and therin sir Ontzlake dwelleth worshipfully, and is well beloved of the people and commonalty. And this
sir Damas our master is as evil beloved, for he is without mercy and
he is a very coward, and great war hath bene between them both, but
sir Ontzlake hath ever the better, and ever he proffereth sir Damas to
fight for the livelihood,[7] body for body, but he will doe nothing; or
else to find a knight to fight for him. Unto that sir Damas hath granted
to find a knight, but he is so evill and hated that there is no knight
that wil fight for him. And when sir Damas saw this, that there was
no knight that would fight for him, he hath dayly layen in a waite with
many knights with him to take all the knights in this countrey to see
and espie their adventures; he hath taken them by force and brought
them into his prison, and so hee tooke us severally as wee rode on our
adventures, and many good knights have died in this prison for hunger, to the number of eighteene knights, and if any of us al that is here
or hath beene would have foughten with his brother Ontzlake, he would
have delivered us; but because this sir Damas is so false and so full
of treason, we would never fight for him to die for it. And we be so
leane for hunger, that unnethes we may stand on our feete.'

'God deliver you for His mercy!' said king Arthur.

Anon therewith came a damosell unto king Arthur, and asked him,
'What cheere?'

'I can not tel,' said he.

'Sir,' quoth she, 'and ye will fight for my lord, ye shall be delivered
out of prison, or else ye shall never escape with your life.'

'Now,' said king Arthur, 'that is hard; yet had I rather to fight with
a knight then to die in prison, if I may be delivered with this and all
these prisoners,' said king Arthur, 'I will doe the battaile.'

'Yes,' said the damosell.

'I am ready,' said king Arthur, 'if I had a horse and armor.'

'Yee shal lacke none,' said the damosell.

'Me seemeth, damosell, I should have seene you in the court of king
Arthur.'

'Nay,' said the damosell, 'I came never there, I am the lord's daughter of this castle.' Yet was shee false, for she was one of the damosels
of Morgan le Fay. Anon shee went unto sir Damas, and told him how
hee would doe battaile for him. And so he sent for king Arthur, and
when hee came hee was well coloured and well made of his limbes,
and that all the knights that saw him said it were pittie that such a
knight should die in prison. So sir Damas and he were agreed that he
should fight for him upon this covenant, that al the other knights should
be delivered, and unto that was sir Damas sworne unto king Arthur,
and also to doe this battaile to the uttermost. And with that all the
twentie knights were brought out of the darke prison into the hall and
delivered. And so they all abode to see the battaile.

Turne we unto sir Accolon of Gaule, that when he awoke he found
himselfe by a deepe wel side within halfe a foote in great perill of death,
and there came out of that fountaine a pipe of silver, and out of that
pipe ranne water all on high in stone of marble. And when sir Accolon
saw this, hee blessed him and said, 'Jesus, save my lord king Arthur
and king Urience! for these damosells in this ship have betraied us,
they were divels and no women, and if I may escape this misadventure
I shall destroy all where I may find these false damosels that use inchant-
ments'. And with that there came a dwarfe with a great mouth and
flat nose, and saluted sir Accolon, and said how he came from queen
Morgan le Fay, 'and she greeteth you well, and biddeth you to bee strong
of hart, for yee shall fight to morrow with a knight at the houre of prime,
and therefore she hath sent you here Excalibur, king Arthurs sword,
and the scabbard, and she desireth you, as you love her, that ye doe
the battail to the uttermost without any mercy, like as ye have promised
her when ye spake together in private; and what damosell that bringeth her the knights head that ye shall fight withall, shee wil make her
a rich queene for ever.'

'Now I understand you well,' said sir Accolon, 'I shall hold that I
have promised her, now I have the sword. When saw yee my lady queene
Morgan?'

'Right late,' said the dwarfe. Then sir Accolon tooke him in his armes,
and said, 'Recommend me unto my lady queen Morgan, and tell her
that all shall be done as I have promised her, or else I will die for it.
Now, I suppose,' said sir Accolon, 'she hath made all these crafts and
enchantments for this battel.'

'Yee may wel beleeve it,' said the dwarfe.

Right so came a knight and a lady with sixe squires, and saluted sir
Accolon, and praied him to arise and come and rest him at his manor.
And so sir Accolon mounted upon a voide horse, and went with the
knight unto a faire manor by a priorie, and there he had passing good
cheere. Then sir Damas sent unto his brother sir Ontzlake, and bad
him make him ready by to-morrow at the houre of prime and to be
in the field to fight with a good knight, for he had found a good knight
that was ready to doo battaile at al points. When this word came unto
sir Ontzlake, he was passing heavie, for he was wounded a little tofore through both his thighes with a speare, and made great mone;
but for all hee was wounded he would have taken the battell in hand.

So it happened at that time by the meanes of Morgan le Fay, sir Accolon was lodged with sir Ontzlake, and when he heard of that battaile,
and how sir Ontzlake was wounded, he said he would fight for him;
because Morgan le Fay had sent him Excalibur and the scabbard for
to fight with the knight on the morrow, this was the cause sir Accolon
tooke the battaile in hand. Then sir Ontzlake was passing glad, and
thanked sir Accolon hartily, that he would doe so much for him. And

therewith sir Ontzlake sent word to his brother sir Damas, that he had a knight that for him should be ready in the field by the houre of prime.

So on the morrow king Arthur was armed and well horsed, and asked sir Damas 'When shall we goe to the field?'

'Sir,' said sir Damas, 'ye shal heare masse.'

And when masse was doone, there came a squire on a great horse and asked sir Damas, if his knight were ready; 'for our knight is ready in the field'. Then king Arthur mounted on horsebacke, and there were al the knights and commons of the countrey, and so by al advises there were chosen twelve goodmen[8] of the countrey for to waite upon the two knights. And as king Arthur was upon horsebacke, there came a damosell from Morgan le Fay, and brought unto king Arthur a sword like unto Excalibur and the scabbard, and said unto king Arthur, 'Morgan le Fay sendeth you here your sword for great love'. And he thanked her, and wend it had beene so; but she was false, for the sword and the scabbard was counterfeit, brittle, and false.

And then they dressed them on both parties of the field, and let their horses run so fast, that either smote other in the middest of their shields with their speares, that both horses and men went to the ground; and then they started up both and drew out their swords. And in the meane while that they were thus fighting came the damosel of the lake into the field, that had put Merlin under the stone, and she came thither for the love of king Arthur, for she knew how Morgan le Fay had so ordained that king Arthur should have beene slaine that day, and therefore she came to save his life. And so they went egerly to doe their battaile, and gave manie great strokes. But alway king Arthurs sword was not like sir Accolons sword, so that for the most part every strooke that sir Accolon gave wounded king Arthur sore, that it was marvaile that he stood, and alway his blood fell fast from him. When king Arthur beheld the ground so sore beblooded,[9] hee was dismaied, and then he deemed treason that his sword was changed, for his sword was not still[10] as it was wont to doe; therefore was he sore adread to be dead, for ever him seemed that the sword in sir Accolons hand was Excalibur, for at every strooke that sir Accolon strooke, he drew blood on king Arthur.

'Now knight,' said sir Accolon to king Arthur, 'keepe thee well from me.' But king Arthur answered not againe, and gave him such a buffet on the helme that he made him to stoope, nigh falling to the ground. Then sir Accolon withdrew him a little, and came on with Excalibur on high, and smote king Arthur such a buffet that he fell nigh to the earth. Then were they both wroth, and gave each other many sore strookes, but always king Arthur lost so much blood thas it was marvaile that he stood on his feete, but he was so full of knighthood that knightly he endured the paine. And sir Accolon lost not a drop of blood, therefore he waxed passing light; and king Arthur was passing feeble,

Figure 4: 'Arthur and Annolure the Sorceress' by Dora Curtis.

and thought verily to have died. But for all that he made countenance
as though he might endure, and held sir Accolon as short as he might,
but sir Accolon was so bold because of Excalibur, that he waxed passing hardy. But al men that beheld them said they saw never knight fight
so well as did king Arthur, considering the blood that he bled, and
all the people were sory for him, but the two brethren would not accord.
Then alway they fought together as fierce knights, and king Arthur withdrew him a little for to rest him, and sir Accolon called him to battaile,
and said, 'It is no time for me to suffer thee to rest'. And therewith
he came fiersly upon king Arthur, and king Arthur was wroth for the
blood that he had lost, and smote sir Accolon upon the helme so mightily that hee made him nigh fall to the earth, and therewith king Arthurs
sword brak at the crosse[11] and fel in the grasse among the blood, and
the pomell and the handle he held in his hand. When king Arthur saw
that, he was greatly afeard to die, but alwayes he held up his shield
and lost no ground, no bated noe cheere.

Then sir Accolon began to say thus with words of treason: 'Knight,
thou art overcome and maist no longer endure, and also thou art
weaponlesse, and thou hast lost much of thy blood, and I am full loth
to sley thee, therefore yeeld thee to mee as recreaunt.'

'Nay,' said king Arthur, 'I may not so, for I have promised to doe
the battaile to the uttermost by the faith of my body while my life lasteth,
and therefore I had rather to die with honour then to live with shame,
and if it were possible for me to die an hundred times, I had rather
so often die then to yeeld me to thee; for though I lacke weapon and
am weaponlesse, yet shall I lacke no worship, and if thou sley me
weaponlesse it shall be to thy shame.'

'Well,' said sir Accolon, 'as for the shame I wil not spare. Now keepe
them from me,' said sir Accolon, 'for thou art but a dead man.' And
therewith sir Accolon gave him such a strooke, that he fel nigh to the
earth, and would have king Arthur to crie him mercy. But king Arthur
pressed unto sir Accolon with his shield, and gave him with the pomell
in his hand such a buffet that he went three strides back. When the
damosell of the lake beheld king Arthur, how full of prowesse and wor-
thinesse his body was, and the false treason that was wrought for him
to have slaine him, she had great pittie that so good a knight and so
noble a man of worship should be destroyed. And at the next strooke
sir Accolon strooke him such a stroke, that by the damosel's enchaunt-
ment the sword Excalibur fell out of sir Accolon's hand to the earth.
And therewith king Arthur lightly leapt to it, and quickly gate it in
his hand, and forthwith he perceived clearly that it was his good sword
Excalibur, and said, 'Thou hast beene from me al too long, and much
domoge hast thou done to me.' And therewith he espied the scabbard
hanging by sir Accolon's side, and suddenly hee leapt to him, and pulled
the scabbard from him, and anon threw it from his as farre as he might

throw it. 'O, knight,' said king Arthur, 'this day thou hast don me great domage with this sword. Now are ye come to your death, for I shall not warrant you but that he shall be as well rewarded with this sword or we depart asunder as thou hast rewarded me, for much paine have yee made me to endure, and have lost much blood.' And therewith king Arthur rushed upon him with all his might, and pulled him to the earth, and then rushed off his helme, and gave him such a buffet on the head that the blood came out of his eares, nose, and mouth. 'Now will I sley thee,' said king Arthur.

'Sley me yee may,' said sir Accolon, 'and it please you, for ye are the best knight that ever I found, and I see well that God is with you; but for I promised to doe this battaile,' said sir Accolon, 'to the uttermost, and never to be recreaunt while I lived, therefore shall I never yeeld me with my mouth, but God doe with my body what he wil.' And then king Arthur remembred him, and thought he should have seene this knight.

'Now tel me,' said king Arthur, 'or I will sley thee, of what countrey art thou? and of what court?'

'Sir knight,' quoth sir Accolon, 'I am of the court of king Arthur, and my name is sir Accolon of Gaule.' Then was king Arthur more dismaied then he was before, for then he remembered him of his sister Morgan le Fay, and of the enchantment of the ship.

'O, sir knight,' said he, 'I pray thee tell me who gave thee this sword and by whom had ye it?'

Then sir Accolon bethought him, and said: 'Woe worth this sword, for by it have I gotten my death.'

'It may wel be,' said king Arthur.

'Now sir,' said sir Accolon, 'I wil tel you. This sword hath beene in my keeping the most of these twelve monethes, and queene Morgan le Fay, king Urience wife, sent it me yesterday by a dwarfe to this intent, that I should sley king Arthur her brother, for ye shall understand that king Arthur is the man which shee most hateth in this world, because that he is the most of worship and of prowesse of any of her blood. Also she loveth me out of measure as her paramoure, and I her againe. And if she might bring about for to sley king Arthur with her crafts, she would sley her husband king Urience lightly, and then had she me devised to be king in this land, and so for to raigne, and she to be my queene; but that is now done,' said sir Accolon, 'for I am sure of my death.'

'Well,' said king Arthur, 'I feele by you ye would have beene king in this land; it had beene great domage for me to have destroyed your lord,' said king Arthur.

'It is truth,' said sir Accolon, 'but now have I told you the truth, wherefore I pray you that ye will tell me of whence ye are, and of what court?'

'Oh, sir Accolon,' said king Arthur, 'now I let thee to wit that I am king Arthur, to whom thou hast done great domage.'

When sir Accolon heard that, he cried out aloud: 'Oh, my gracious lord, have mercy on me, for I knew you not!'

'Oh, sir Accolon,' said king Arthur, 'mercy shalt thou have, because I feele by thy words at this time thou knewest not my person. But I understand well by thy words that thou hast agreed to the death of my person, and therfore thou art a traitor. But I blame thee the lesse, for my sister Morgan le Fay, by her false crafts, made thee to agree and consent to her false lusts; but I shall so be avenged upon her and I live, that all Christendome shall speake of it. God knoweth, I have honoured her and worshiped her more then any of my kin, and more have I trusted her then mine owne wife and all my kin after.'

Then king Arthur called the keepers of the field, and said, 'Sirs, come hither, for here we be two knights that have fought unto a great domage to us both, and like each one of us to have slaine other, if it had happened so; and had any of us knowen other, here had beene no battaile nor stroke stricken.'

Then aloud cried sir Accolon unto all the knights and men that there wer gathered together, and said to them in this manner wise: 'Oh, my lords, this noble knight that I have fought withall, which me full sore repenteth, is the most man of prowesse, of manhood, and of worship that in all the world liveth, for it is himselfe king Arthur, our most soveraigne liege lord and king, and with great mishap and great misadventure have I done this battaile against my king and lord, that I am holden withall.'

Then all the people fell downe on their knees, and cried king Arthur mercie. 'Mercie shall ye have,' said king Arthur; 'here may ye see what adventures befalleth oftentimes to erraunt knights; how I have fought with one of mine owne knights to my great domage and his hurt. But, sirs, because I am sore hurt and he both, and have great neede of a little rest, ye shall understand my opinion betweene you two brethren. As to thee, sir Damas, for whom I have beene champion and won the field of this knight, yet will I judge because ye, sir Damas, are called a very proud knight and full of vilany, and nothing worth of prowesse of your deedes, therefore I will that ye give unto your brother all the whole manor with the appurtenance under this maner of forme, that sir Ontzlake hold the manor of you, and yearely to give you a palfrey to ride upon, for that will become you better to ride on then on a courser. Also, I charge thee, sir Damas, upon paine of death, that thou never distresse none erraunt knights that ride on their adventures. Also, that thou restore these twentie knights which thou hast long kept in prison of all their harneis, and that you content them, and if any of them come to my court and complaine of thee, by my head thou shalt die therefore. Also, sir Ontzlake, as to you, because ye are named a good knight and ful of prowesse, and true and gentle in your deedes,

this shal be your charge. I will that in all goodly hast ye come to me
and to my court, and ye shal be a knight of mine, and if your deedes
be therafter, I shall so advance you by the grace of God that ye shall
in short time be in case for to live as worshipfully as doth your brother
sir Damas.

'God thanke you of your largesse and of your great goodnesse,' said
sir Ontzlake, 'and I promise you that from henceforth I shall be at all
times at your commandement. For sir,' said sir Ontzlake, 'as God would
I was hurt but late with an adventurous knight through both my thighes
which grieved me sore, and else had I done this battaile with you.'

'Would to God,' said king Arthur, 'it had been so, for then had not
I beene hurt as I am, I shall tell you the cause why; for I had not beene
hurt as I am had not it beene mine owne sword that was stolen from
me by treason, and this battaile was ordeined aforehand for to have
slaine me, and so it was brought to the purpose by false engine,[12] and
treason, and false enchantment.'

'Alas!' said sir Ontzlake, 'that is great pittie that so noble a man as
you are of your deedes and prowesse, that any man or woman might
find in their hearts to work any treason against your person.'

'I shal reward them,' said king Arthur, 'in short space by the grace
of God. Now tel me,' said king Arthur, 'how far am I from Camelot?'

'Sir, ye are two daies journey therfro.'

'I would fain be at some place of worship,' said king Arthur, 'that
I might rest my selfe.'

'Sir,' said sir Ontzlake, 'heereby is a rich abbey of nuns of our elders
foundation, but three miles hence.'

So then the king tooke his leave of all the people, and mounted on
horseback, and sir Accolon with him. And when they were come to
the abbey, he let fetch surgions and leeches for to search his wounds,
and sir Accolon's both; but sir Accolon died within foure days afer,
for he had bled so much blood that hee might not live, but King Arthur
was well recovered. And when sir Accolon was dead, he let send him
on horsbacke with six knights to Camelot, and said, 'Beare him to
my sister Morgan le Fay, and say that I send him hir for a present, and
tel her that I have my sword Excalibur and the scabbard.' So they
departed with the body.

---

[1] Proposed in Sir John Rhys' Introduction to *Le Morte D'Arthur*, Dent, 1906.
[2] *The Ill-Framed Knight* by William Matthews, University of California Press, 1966.
[3] *Arthur & the Sovereignty of Britain* by Caitlín Matthews, Arkana, 1989.
[4] *Blew the price*—The *prise* was the note blown on the death of the deer.
[5] *Landed*—i.e. came to land.
[6] *Sore*—Hard; soundly.
[7] *For the livelihood*—i.e. for the property which sir Damas withheld from him.
[8] *Goodmen*—The term *good-men (boni homines)* was equivalent with freemen.

[9] *Beblooded*—Covered with blood. The use of the prefix *be* in an intensive or distributive sense is very common in this book, and it will be hardly necessary to point it out except in particular instances where the passage requires explanation.

[10] *Was not still*—An error of the printer of the edition of 1634. Caxton has, *boote not styl*, i.e. did not bite or cut into the steel as it used to do.

[11] *Crosse*—The piece of metal which crossed the sword above the handle, to guard the hand.

[12] *Engine*—Ingenuity; contrivance.

PART TWO: THE QUEST FOR THE GRAIL

Chapter 7.
Mystic Gleams from the Holy Grail
by Francis Rolt-Wheeler

The Grail is at the heart of the Matter of Britain and has led many people to go in search of it since the mediaeval writers first described the great Quest. Its origins are too complex to go into here and are more fully dealt with elsewhere.[1] But part of its importance lies in the fact that it spans both Christian and pagan world-views and draws all kinds of seekers from every walk of life to go in search of it.

Still one of the best of the many books written from a magical and mystical point of view is *Mystic Gleams from the Holy Grail* by Francis Rolt-Wheeler, which begins this section devoted to the subject of the Grail. Wheeler founded at least one Grail-orientated group, *Les Amis de Montségur*, and edited the occult journal *L'Astrosophie*, as well as writing numerous books on esoteric subjects. He moved in the same circles as the redoubtable Colonel Seymour, then a foremost member of the Society of the Inner Light.

His book gives a deeply magic over-view of the Grail cycle, with many insights for those in search of a solution to its mysteries. He also speaks, as might be expected from someone who lived much of his life in France, of the Cathar and Templar connection with the Grail—a fascinating and much discussed topic which has still to be satisfactorily dealt with. His approach is radically different from that of Hannah Closs, whose essay will found in Chapter 9.

Much of what Rolt-Wheeler writes is speculative and intuitive—but such an approach is a wise one when dealing with the Grail, and those who are true seekers will find much in his works to guide him further on the path.

⌥✦⌥

THE HOLY GRAIL, THE NATURE OF ITS DIVINE MYSTERY AND ITS INITIATORY POWER

The soul of man, inheritor and guardian of a Divine Spark wherein dwells an ever-shining and vital mirroring of the Divine Soul, possesses thereby an inherent receptivity to the Good. This faculty enables him to distinguish between that which is spiritually true and that which is false. Too often this inner receptivity, source of our Moral Consciousness, is neglected or obstructed by other organs of reception, or resonators, attuned either to lesser emotions or to material vibrations.

None the less, this 'sensitive ear of the soul' is never completely dulled. It acts upon the egregore of a people or an era. This it is which gives 'The Judgement of the Centuries', that decision which consigns a commercial Carthage to the limbo of forgetfulness, and which enshrines Athens in imperishable beauty.

The Judgement of the Centuries rules impartially and its decrees have no appeal. Among the thousand myths and legends, which have cradled Humanity since the beginnings of Thought, rare indeed are those which have acquired immortality. They bear within themselves that Mystery which is known as 'Initiation'. As examples of these immortal myths may be named: Adam and Eve in the Earthly Paradise and The Quest of the Holy Grail.

We are yet far from a full understanding of the cosmogony, the anthropogony, and the spiritual significance of the Garden of Eden. Much remains to be deciphered (or revealed) of Adam-Kadmon as a Vesture of God; of the descent of Adam-Macroprosopus and Adam-Microprosopus; of the Fall of Adam and of the Mystery of Redemption—all concealed in the ancient traditions of the Earthly Paradise. Esoteric students know well that it is one of the most profound teachings in initiatory literature.

The Legend of the Holy Grail glows likewise with an inner light of esoterism. Few, indeed, be those who have sought to follow the silver thread of Spiritual Initiation in this strange and mysterious cycle of miracle, of faërie, of chivalry, and of a super-sacrament. Constantly, in this mystical legend, there is a glimpse of the unknown; the reader may lose his way in a thicket of visions. The texts themselves are so overburdened that any effort to set them in order produces an overlaid recital, full of sensational but secondary incidents, obscuring the higher aim.

It is customary to say that this Legend is known to everybody; it would be more just to say that it is unknown, to save to the very few. Philology may guide us through a labyrinth of texts, history may show a psychological stratification, exegesis may give us a dozen possible interpretations, and the mystics—who see further and higher—may illumine the Way, showing it as thorny, or as blossoming, according to their particular enlightenment. But of 'The Legend of the Holy Grail', taken as a whole, no interpreter has yet come to explain fitly.

Far be it from us to attempt the impossible! A restatement would lead nowhere. Great scholars have laboured, and great works bear witness to their labours. Yet the Legend of the Holy Grail is so rich in mystery, so revealing in vision, so subtle in its high teaching, so prophetic in its initiation that it is possible to put before the reader certain esoteric meanings he may have overlooked. It may be permitted to mirror forth some gleams of a Mystic Light too dazzling unless viewed with reflected vision.

It is therefore our intention to limit our research to such parties of the vast Legend as may permit some mystical or spiritual meaning. The incidents will not be drawn from any single text.

Little will be said of the prowess of knights in combat or in tourney; nor shall stress be laid—save insofar as may serve an allegorical purpose—on romantic or passionate attachments to the maidens of Faërie and of Chivalry. True it is that there is rhythm and beauty in the love-singing of trouvère and troubadour, but such is not our theme.

The Legend of the Holy Grail, in its origin and in its development, is essentially Christian. Yet we shall miss the spiritual uplift in the story if we fail to realize that the rites and sacraments of which it tells are no celebrated on the earthly plane, but rather in 'a temple not made with hands'. The 'Lost Word' may not be known on this Earth, but it resounds eternally where the Celestial Hierarchies abide.

This Way will also lead us into the astral world and into the kingdoms of Faërie, where Merlin, the Enchanter, serves as a guide. Those who know how to read in the Book of Nature will find the link of Celtic Initiation in these sagas, and may even hear the tread of 'The Lordly Ones'.

The deeds and adventures of the Knights of the Round Table form but a thin disguise for the setting forth of a Spiritual Chivalry, such as may war with the Powers of Darkness in that conflict of the soul that leads to the Holy Grail. The Grail itself is that Cup of Immortality which contains—in addition to the Precious Blood—that draught of Living Water whose source is the fourfold river that flows from the Throne of God.

Above all, this high romance is of the Supreme Quest. It is the search for God in the soul, for spiritual contact, for the ecstatic communion received in the Sanctuary of the Grail. Even if the Holy Grail itself be hidden from description, the Luminous Chalice, symbol of its glory, is not withdrawn from our spiritual vision. The accolade of knightliness awaits him who is worthy of the Quest.

Sublime, indeed, is the Reality of the Ideal to one who has entered into this Mystery. A Joy of Possession is his, and in the mystical words of the ancient authors: 'he is nourished of the Grail'. It is thus that we seem to see the high esoteric meaning and the sacred inspiration of that marvellous vision of spiritual chivalry: 'The Legend of the Holy Grail'.

THE MYSTICAL NATURE OF THE HOLY GRAIL, AS IT APPEARS ON THE SEVERAL PLANES

The Mystery of the Holy Grail is of so interior a nature, so apart from any concrete organisation, that it may be well to show forth the inner meaning of the Legend before giving a brief summary of the story to those who may have forgotten it. Only thus can we understand its extraordinary shining athwart the ages.

Truly it may be said that the Holy Grail is the Cup of the Last Supper; it is also the Heavenly Vessel borne by an angel to the Divine Sufferer in the Garden of Gethsemane; and it is the Mystic Chalice wherein Joseph of Arimathea received the drops of the Precious Blood at the Descent from the Cross. But these three Cups are not one and the same, save in a spiritual understanding.

Likewise, the Castle of the Grail may be found at Corbenic, at Montsalvatch, at Montségur and at other places. But, like the Golden Stair of Celtic Legend, it can be found only by him who is worthy. It awaits the coming of the elect, for the Castle of the Grail. like to the Grail itself, is real but as a mystical reality.

To seek a tangible vessel as the Holy Grail, whether of gold, of silver or of emerald, is but simple-wittedness. It reveals the seeker to be a sordid materialist, to whom the higher understanding is closed. More than a dozen false 'Grails' exist. One may mention those at Bruges, at Mantua, at Weingarten, at Fécamp, not to speak of the famous 'Sacro Catino' of Genoa—supposed to have been made from a single emerald, which is but common glass. In reducing the Cup of the Holy Grail to the level of cunning handiwork, vulgar incomprehension can no further go.

The mystical interpretation abides. The Holy Grail is definitely the supreme symbol of the Immanent Presence of Christ on Earth, inspiration of a sublime faith, enshrining a sacramental mystery whose communion is of the soul.

The Holy Grail is not only a mystical symbol; it is the Mystic Life. In reverent hesitation, yet with undoubted sincerity, the trouvères and the poets sought to set forth this high truth. The time for its understanding was not yet come. It is for us—to whom a key may be given—to evoke from this ancient Legend its imperishable beauty, and to invoke its indwelling power.

Let us try, briefly, to set forth the main lines of the central plot which is common to these several cycles, for the texts contain more than 800,000 lines, and the incidents are complex, confused and bewildering.

Tradition tells of the events of the night of the Last Supper, of the Blessing of the Cup, of the Agony at Gethsemane, of the condemnation of Jesus by Caiaphas, Herod and Pilate, and of the Crucifixion.

When Pilate accorded to Joseph of Arimathea the privilege of the sepulture of Christ, he gave him, also, the precious Cup. During the Descent from the Cross, some drops or clots of blood were caught by Joseph in this Chalice. Thus the 'sang real' became the 'sang Graal,' or 'San Graal'. (There are other derivations for this term.)

Hate-filled, the Jews threw Joseph into a windowless tower, wherein he dwelt for forty years, visited only by the Risen Christ and nourished only by the Holy Grail. Vespasian, son of the Roman emperor Titus, having been healed from leprosy by the Veil of St Veronica, liberated Joseph of Arimathea.

During his incarceration Joseph had learned much from the Risen Saviour, and had been ordered to travel to the West. Traces of his voyagings may be found in Sicily, at Marseilles, on both sides of the Pyrenees, in the Landes, in Brittany, and finally in Great Britain and Wales.

'The Times Adventurous', a period of bewitchment in the Kingdom of Logres (an esoteric term), which is said to have lasted for centuries, caused the Holy Grail to remain in hiddenness.

At this point, the Christian Legend encountered the ancient initiatory Celtic myths and hero-cycles of Ireland, of Wales and of Cornwall. After centuries of literary contact, a certain fusion occurred. Thus Merlin, the bard, becomes enchanter and initiator. The Legends of the Round Table (a grouping of the hero-cycles of Arthur, of Lancelot, of Merlin, of Percival, of Galahad, etc.) came to include the Legend of the Holy Grail, which, in time, served to inspire the whole. This fusion gives an atmosphere of faërie and chivalry to a legend purely Christian in its origin and symbolism.

During the Great Awakening of the twelfth century, era of the Sacramental Controversy (settled in 1214), the trouvères chanted to the barons, knights and ladies in feudal castles these legends and their lays. There was no standard text; each minstrel sang after the joy of his heart. Some had a vision of higher things. The Holy Grail became a sacrament, even a super-sacrament of an extra-terrestrial consecration, whereof the partakers were a Spiritual Chivalry.

It is told how the Holy Grail, veiled, passed on a shaft of light about the Great Hall of the Round Table, at Camelot, and how every knight present vowed to follow the Quest for a year and a day, that he might more clearly see the Holy Grail and understand its mystery.

Wondrous were the adventures that befell the knights-errant on the Quest, and many other hero-cycles were grafted on the Legend. In this present short study, the deeds of only four of the knights of the Quest will be followed: Gawain, who found disgrace therein; Lancelot, who, by reason of his love for Guinevere, received but a partial vision; Percival, to whom the vision of the Graal was given, but not an understanding of its mystery; and Galahad, the High Prince, glory of knighthood and hero of the Quest.

It is Galahad, the Pure and Perfect Knight, who apears in a Messianic light in several of the versions, who frees the Kingdom of Logres from its sorcery-held bondage, who heals the Maimed King and participates in the Apostolic Rite of the Holy Grail. At the last, guarding the Holy Grail and the Lance of Longinus—together with other Hallows—Galahad sets forth on the Mystical Ship of Solomon, set afloat two thousand years before, for the last voyage to the Initiate City of Sarras, of whose whereabouts no man knoweth.

After the death of Percival and Galahad, the Grail was 'withdrawn' from this Earth and from terrestrial vision, nor dare any man say that he has seen it since, earthly-wise. But the high Mystery of the Holy Grail calls ever to the elect and to those who have within them the will to tread this High Way of Initiation.

MONTSEGUR, BROCELIANDE AND GLASTONBURY; THE MANY VOYAGES OF THE GUARDIANS OF THE GRAIL

Not of this Earth, truly, are the Wood of Ambush, the Field of the Second Table and the City of Sarras; each is a stage on a mystic journey, unreal and yet real. From its beginning, the Way of the Holy Grail westward is of a spiritual content. Whether, indeed, the Holy Grail symbolize the Presence of God in the soul, or the continuing regeneration of the soul by the Holy Spirit, shall discover itself as the Quest goes on. It may be remembered that when, at the Second Table, Joseph invoked the Holy Spirit by means of the Grail, it was the figure of Jesus which appeared.

The voyagings of the Grail are on many planes, of which the material plane is the least important. Truth in history and truth in allegory form a harmonious whole, though this may call for inner understanding.

It is undoubted that the origin of the Legend of the Holy Grail is in Palestine. It is no less evident that the cult of the Grail and the Quest of the Grail belong in the Celtic countries of the West. The miraculous incidents that accompany the travels of the Guardians of the Grail do in no sense alter the historical fact that the Legend was developed and made real in a Celtic atmosphere and not otherwise.

If the versions of the Legend differ greatly in their details, it is because the trouvères, of another race and of another era, did but lightly grasp the spiritual power of their theme. Yet each sought, after his manner, to seize the undiscernible, to poetize an unworldly beauty or to ennoble an abstract ideal, heeding little of historical accuracy or biographical succession.

Even as concerning the voyage of Joseph of Arimathea the versions disagree. We prefer to follow the earliest record, as it appears in the writings of Nennius and William of Malmesbury, rather than the later trouvères, Chrétien de Troyes, Robert de Borron and their successors. It is not impossible that, during the centuries, there were two recensions of the ancient tradition, one in favour of St David, the apostle of Wales, the other to uphold the claims of the Abbey of Glastonbury. The earlier verison will suffice.

Joseph of Arimathea, according to this tradition, was no stranger to the coasts of Britain. As a youth, he had accompanied his uncle, a wealthy merchant who traded with the Phoenicians, on a voyage to the Scilly Isles for tin, and to the Mendip Hills, in Somersetshire, for lead. The Phoenicians had maintained trading posts there for centuries.

In sailing up the Bristol Channel, the early navigators (who had no compass) took as a landmark a conical hill, rising out of the marshes south of the Mendips. Many years later, when in the tower, Jesus told Joseph that he should voyage to the utter West and settle near a peak resembling Mount Hor in the Syrian Desert, the memory of this little Somersetshire hill came back to him.

While Josephe II, now Pontiff and Guardian of the Grail, together with Brons, Alain, and the greater number of the pilgrims, left Sarras to continue their westward journey, Joseph of Arimathea remained. It was for him to follow when Josephe II had partly evangelized the unknown country and prepared a place of refuge for his father, nearly a hundred years old.

Soon after their departure, Joseph of Arimathea disappeared from Sarras. A legend tells how a skiff, having neither sails or oars, slitting the water like an arrow, carried him to 'the mountains which have their feet in two seas', most notably the Pyrenees. He may have disembarked at the Roman port of Elna (now sanded up). His trace is lost in the Pyrenees, but missionaries who penetrated that region in the second century learned that 'there were Christians in the mountains'.

It is of all things tempting to link this tradition to the Cathare-revered mountain of Montségur. Such a link might help to explain the many references to the cult of the Grail in the Pyrenean region, so far from 'la Bloie Bretagne'. It is not permissible to call Montségur 'The Castle of the Grail', for the Ark with the Grail therein had already gone before in the charge of Josephe II; moreover, feudal watch-towers (such as Montségur) were not built until a much later date. Yet it is nowise forbidden to hold Montségur as a Castle Spiritual of the Grail, for a Divine Presence knows neither time nor place, and its Essence may ensoul many sacred sites. To this, the writer bears personal witness.

It is likely that Joseph took ship at Bordeaux (Tyrus was dead, but the fame of Jesus remained) and set sail for Britain and the Mendip Range. At sight of the conical hill (now called Glastonbury Tor), Joseph diembarked with two companions. (These must have been Celt-Iberians, for he started alone from Sarras.)

There, on an islet of firm ground amid the marshes, he built a little church of wattle-and-clay, the first Christian fane in England. Years later, Josephe II came to visit his father, bearing with him the Holy Grail. Joseph of Arimathea died at Glastonbury and was buried before the altar of this humble sanctuary.

The voyages and adventures of Josephe II make a confused story. It is told how, at his arrival on the shores of the English Channel, he and the bearers of the Ark walked on the water, as did the Christ. Josephe II laid his mantle on the waters; it spread even as a vast carpet and the elect crossed the unruffled water on this raft, following the steps of those who bore the Holy Grail. The unworthy were left behind on the shore.

Josephe II, with the Ark of the Holy Grail, wandered over Wales, Northumbria and Scotland, and may even have visited Ireland. Thence he came to Somerset to see his father, and afterwards returned to Wales, where he was taken and made captive. Freed by Evalach, he returned at long last to the bedside of his rescuer (become 'the Maimed King') and died there, having consecrated Alain, the eldest son of Brons, his successor as the Guardian of the Grail.

The work of Brons, brother-in-law of Joseph of Arimathea, is on a higher plane than that of Josephe II. 'The Fisher King' was an Initiate of the Grail, but not its Guardian. He came to Britain with Alain, in the company of Josephe II, but did not follow the Grail in its missionary journeyings. His place of retreat became a holy site where, from time to time, appeared the Vision of the Grail. According to Robert de Borron (but not to Chrétien de Troyes), the Castle of the Fisher King is the Castle of the Grail. It is not to be confounded with Corbenic.

Brons and Alain lived on for centuries ere their task was done. After the birth of Percival, Alain 'passed into the Eternal Peace', but Brons lingered dolorously until the moment when he could transmit to Percival the 'Mysterious Words' received from Joseph of Arimathea. His lips had just pronounced them when his soul slipped its earthly shell and was received by angels. Percival, in ecstasy, beheld the splendour of their wings above the death-bed of this most aged of the Initiates of the Grail.

THE CASTLES OF THE GRAIL, REAL AND UNREAL, AND THE TIMES ADVENTUROUS

A mystery of silence broods over the intervening centuries. There is a halt in the sequence between the first period, when the Holy Grail was a tangible relic of incomparable saintliness, and the second period in the time of King Arthur, when the Grail had become the intangible goal of an ideal Quest.

Little less obscure is the succession of the Guardians of the Grail, through these centuries, for the Initiates are sometimes of the hiddenness, and sometimes beings of symbol.

As for the Castle or Sanctuary of the Grail, here it has no abiding term, for the Divine Presence cannot be bound to form or place. To treat the Castle of the Grail as history, or to give it permanent of site is to misinterpret its reality. Spiritual experiences are measured by states of soul, not by leagues of space, nor yet by years and hours measured upon the dial.

Revelations and indications—some real and some less real—may be found. They are to serve as a thread of light linking the happenings of these half-known times. It may be possible to find a beginning with

Alain, consecrated Guardian of the Grail by Josephe II, the day before his death.

The legend tells how, shortly after his consecration, Alain, led a hundred of his followers, with the Holy Grail, to the 'terre Forayne' ('Lystenoys', Lyonesse') in South Wales, to the kingdom of Calafas, a monarch of renown, but paynim and a leper. The king received the pilgrims honourably, and, on learning that they had come from Jerusalem, asked if his malady were incurable. Alain promised a cure if the king would abandon the 'evil custom' (heathendom) and embrace the 'good custom' (Christendom).

After his baptism, under the name of Alphasan, the king received permission to behold the Grail. He was forthwith cured, and in gratitude he offered to build a castle for the Grail and proposed that his daughter should marry Joshua, brother of Alain. The Guardian agreed, convinced that thus the Grail would be in surety. The very day that the construction of the castle was finished there appeared on the door in scarlet letters these words: 'Corbenic, the Sanctuary of the Holy Grail.' Joshua married the princess and was crowned as heir-apparent of the 'Terre Forayne'.

The night following, King Alphasan declared his intention of sleeping in the new Keep. He was awakened a few minutes after midnight, and was witness of a Mass of the Grail. This suggests that Corbenic was 'keep' or 'sanctuary' rather than castle, and that the king was sleeping in the holy place. At the close of the ceremony a fiery seraph appeared, and, with a lance, mortally wounded the king for his impious intrusion. Alphasan died ten days later, since which time the Sanctuary of Corbenic was known as 'The Castle Adventurous'.

The name 'Corbenic' (cor-arbenig'—the Sovereign Chair) recurs many times in these writings of chivalry, but never twice in the same way, nor yet of the same place. Chrétien de Troyes situated the Castle of the Grail in a smiling valley; in the Queste of Walter Map, it is on a rockbound coast. Wauchier de Denain describes a colossal and much-peopled castle; the Didot Percival speaks of the retired dwelling of the Fisher King. In the Perlesvaus, the castle is protected by three moats and three bridges of the purest faërie; the Parzival makes of it a feudal fortress.

All agree that he who is worthy shall find it, 'whether he wend to East or West'; this is to say whether he lift his soul to God or open his soul that God may enter in. He who is wholly unworthy will never find; the Quest is not for him.

The Castle of the Grail is also called 'The Castle of Souls', which term gives no meditation. It behoves to remember that the Quest is of the soul, and spiritual. The Castle of the Grail, even as 'The Temple of the Holy Ghost', of which the Christ speaks, is subjective and objective, within and without, immanent and transcendent.

The succession of the Guardians of the Grail is vaguely historical, but poignantly initiatory. The order gives: Joseph of Arimathea, Josephe II, Alain, Eminadab (son of Joshua and nephew of Alain), four kings of the Terre Forayne closing with King Pelles and his brother, Pellahan. A more spiritual line, which is rather that of the Initiates of the Grail, lists only Joseph of Arimathea, Brons and Percival, keeper of 'the High Word'.

Stranger still is the teaching hidden in the sufferings of the Guardians of the Grail. In vicarious expiation, their sufferings bring about the 'Times Adventurous', those sorcery-bound centuries which darkened the Realm of Logres. Brons and Evalach, even Pellahan—wounded by the Lance of Longinus at a moment of the Quest—set forth this mingling of spiritual honour and earthly suffering.

Here, again, comes a Gleam from the Holy Grail to lighten a Mystery of the Inner Man. That soul which is become conscious of the Divine Presence, realizing its own imperfections, is inevitably pierced by the Lance of Self-Reproach; without grace, this is a mortal wound. The Legend of the Holy Grail shows at every turn how the visible interpenetrates the invisible, and the invisible the visible.

Although the enchantments, the magic and the phantasmagoria of the Times Adventurous are on another plane than the miraculous events accompanying the Holy Grail in its voyagings, there is no lack of continuity in the theme. The astral illusions and the deeds of chivalry in the World of Faërie and of Knight Errantry are strictly true in their own domain. Who shall be so blind to wonder as to assail them in the rigour of material fact?

Athwart these untoward adventures, told in all sincerity, there pierces a higher truth. Historic verity obtains in the descriptions of the rude and warring centuries, in the clash of monk with initiate, of priest with pagan, of devotee with druid. In the forests, on wild wastes, by hills and vales for ever unexplored, this subtle conflict raged unceasingly.

It is not otherwise in the Quest of the Holy Grail whose battleground is our own soul, that 'Realm of Logres' whose frontiers no man can define. Blessed indeed is he who has seen the Grail, or felt the Divine Presence in outer vision or inner consciousness; his feet are already on the Way. The Times Adventurous await him.

A thousand obstacles intervene to halt us on the Way or to lead us into by-paths, often to blind us to the seeing of the Castle of the Grail before our eyes. We are ourselves enchanted, lost in the thicket of our own bewilderments.

But the Grail is ever there!

Brons, burdened with the weight of centuries, waits but to give us the Mysterious Words. If we be stricken like to the Maimed King, Galahad will come with healing, that Galahad who is born in us, and we in him.

In our personal worth, in the intensity of our ardour, lies our admission to Spiritual Chivalry. Merlin, Arthur, Lancelot, Percival and Galahad offer us their help, their trials, their very lives, to guide us on the Way—that Way of Christic Initiation which is known as 'The Quest of the Holy Grail'.

THE WORLD OF FAERIE AND OF GRAMARYE; THE ASTRAL PLANE AND CELTIC INITIATION

Older and deeper-rooted, reaching to the nature-sources of Being, the traditions and initiatory strivings of the Celtic Race strike athwart the Christian content in the Legends of the Holy Grail. They do neither change nor colour it, but Initiates of 'The Green Ray' will recognize a focused simultaneity on two planes, very different from the fenced thoroughfare of Mosaic monotheism. No Celtic tradition will give us a Garden of Eden with pot-herbs and fruit-trees cunningly planted; nor will God appear as an exclusive tribal possession or a totem in border war.

Such is not the Celtic Way. The Celtic peoples, so richly blessed in poesy and mystic fervour, have also their holy legends, their secret lore and their hidden initiations. High Gods are theirs. They have a story of Creation, and who shall take upon him to judge the inner truth of Cosmogony!

He knows not the Holy Grail to whom the fairy portals have not been opened. As A.E. points out, 'Poesy must always be more than it can be.' It is not enough to hold the Cup; one must be free of the Fountain. Seen on the two planes, the Holy Grail becomes something quite other than a holy relic, however sacrosanct. The Celtic harp vibrates to a Cosmic touch; Merlin is as vital to the Great Epic of Saintly Chivalry as is Joseph of Arimathea.

Be it remembered historically that when the trouvères wrote and sang, England had been robbed of her birthright. The Celt had been driven to fastnesses and wild places by Dane, Angle and Saxon. If the Normans were less barbaric, their Latin admixture made them even less able to see 'the world of Faërie'. To this day—save in Brittany, which is Celt—the Latin peoples are alien to the Land of Gramarye.

This abyss of misunderstanding was one of the chief causes of 'The Times Adventurous'. To a monk of the Roman rite, Aengus of Eternal Youth was but a pagan deity; in no wise could Tir-na-n 'Og be made to fit into an earthly Paradise of Semitic source. There is no need that this misunderstanding should continue. It may then be permitted to lift a corner of the veil and glimpse the beauty and the heart-stir of the fairy spell in Celtic lore.

The Initiation bestowed by the gods and demi-gods of Nature was once widely spread. Unknowingly, it is so still. The Greeks held Dionysian and Orphic rites on wooded mountain and vine-clad slope; at Eleusis, Demeter was goddess of meadow and planted field. In the ruder zone of the oak forest, where Druids counselled and bards sang, the gods of the woodland gave the word of Acceptance to Aspirant and Neophyte.

Is the enchantment past and all forgotten? Not so. Let those answer who feel the Divine Presence more readily in a shadowed glade than in a parish church, and who prefer the hymning of the wood-thrust to that of the urchin chorister. Are there not still Neophytes of hill and dale? How many more souls would respond, if they did but hear!

The Holy Grail of blessed Palestine, a hallow of high sanctity, given to Joseph of Arimathea and his successors, is a symbol whereby we may pierce to the Divine Transcendence. The Holy Grail of the Celtic peoples is Nature itself, the Cup in which all Life is consecrated. The 'sang real' of the Celt is God Immanent, not Transcendent; it is the Absolute in Manifestation, not in Withdrawal.

The pilgrims of the Grail who followed Joseph of Arimathea beheld before them, as a Pillar of Fire, the Mystery of the Redemption. The pilgrims and children of the Dagda Môr feel, deeply and convincingly, the Divine Presence in every leaf of tree and hear the Message in every note of a bird's song. Not all men can translate that message.

The early Christians, as yet unloosed from Hebraic bondage, saw, in the Celestial Hierarchies, nought but the messengers of Jehovah; the Celts knew well their 'Lordly Ones', personifications of Great Forces in perpetual activity but real and vital to be seen of those who have the Seeing. 'The Lords of the Flame' and 'the Lords of Form' of another cosmogony have their parallels in the Celtic theogony. God, watching over all his worlds, 'slumbers not, nor sleeps'; to the Celt, the gods were never far away.

From the fairy of the field-flower to the mighty elementals who upheave mountain ranges, from the sylph to the moulder of worlds, every Nature-Being vibrates with the Divine Immanence. Divinity homes in a tuft of moss or a cedar of Lebanon, in a drop of dew or the whirling of a hurricane. The Initiate of Nature, even as the mystic, establishes the Unitive Life with God. These be the higher regions of the World of Faërie.

The Astral or Sublunary World—to use the ancient name—is a borderland, twilight-lit, the ante-chamber of the Beyond, a land of traverse wherein no one should too long time dwell. Its frontiers run with the World of Faërie; sometimes it is hard to tell where one begins and the other ends.

It is the dwelling-place of the Great Elementals, and on a very different plane, of the Welcomers, who come to meet the newly dead. Ethereal guides await the hardy adventurer and there are always deeds of rescue awaiting him to do. There is a knight-errantry of the Astral also. But it is also the abode of lying spirits, of the tormented earthbound, of enmagicked soul-shells, of larvae and lemures. A region terribly vast, terribly real, largely uncharted, wherein sorcerers may ply their noxious trade. Yet not one of all these hosts of evil and half-evil can touch the innocent and the unknowing. This shows out clearly, where the Legends of the Round Table touch the Astral World.

Not only does the Holy Grail operate differently on all these planes, it is different in itself. In the earlier centuries of Christianity, the Grail was a material relic of precious metal, chased with gems; something that might be held and lifted with the hands. It needed a Tabernacle for its hiding-place and was often accompanied with emblems which spoke of physical suffering: such Hallows as the Lance, the Nails, the Sword, the Scourge and the Crown of Thorns. It served as a chalice at Mass. It was a Cup of Miraculous Healing for Evalach, Pellahan and other sufferers of mystical wounds, the restoration being by Faith, as in the miracles of Jesus Christ.

In the days of Chivalry, when the Legend rings the note of the Quest of the Holy Grail, all this is changed. That which was sacred becomes magical. The presence of the Grail suffices to heap up dishes of food and to fill the beakers of drink, without distinction of number. This like to the Bowl of Plenitude of Celtic origin. The Cauldron of Dagda or Awen, the Caire of Alba and many other vessels of pre-Christian legend have the same character.

It is almost impossible not to bracket together the Four Talismans of the Tuatha na Danaan and the Four Hallows of the Holy Grail. Who were the Tuatha na Danaan? Heroes all, kin to the demi-gods of Homer, kin also to the dwellers of the Lands beneath the Moon, living an enchanted life in dignity and peace. Their Talismans were (1) the Cup or Cauldron of Dagda, giving food and drink in plenty to all who came to the feast; (2) the Magic Lance or Javelin, known as the Lance of Redemption; (3) the Invincible Sword of Lugh of the Long Hand; and (4) the Lia Fail or the Stone of Destiny. In the Hallows of the Grail we find the Cup, the Lance of Longinus, the Sword of David and, in *Parzival,* the Grail itself is the Stone of Destiny.

The last phase of the Legend of the Holy Grail, which transmutes the Grail to a spiritual plane, touches sublimity. It finds the Voice of Chivalry in the Great Hall at Camelot, when the Knights of the Round Table took the vow to follow the Quest for a year and a day, that they might see it clearly and understand its mystery.

Here is no Bowl of Plenitude, nor Stone of Destiny. All material significance disappears. The Grail becomes the abiding-place of the Divine Presence. The Castle of the Grail is the Temple of the Holy Spirit. And, in the Higher Mass of the Holy Grail, the Celebrant is the Christ Himself, 'a priest for ever after the Order of Melchizedek'.

THE ESOTERIC RELATIONSHIP BETWEEN THE
TEMPLARS AND THE QUEST OF THE HOLY GRAIL

The cycle of Galahad, at its best in *La Queste del Saint Graal* attributed to Walter Map, moves on a different plane from that of Percival and the *Perlesvaus*. The atmosphere changes. It is not Symbolism, but Sanctification. It presents the Quest otherwise, while adding its luminous quote to the Mystic Rays from the Holy Grail.

It would not be right to ignore nor to deny that this latest of all the texts presents many critical problems and establishes some remarkable analogies. Among these will be found the parallelisms in the esoterism of the Militant Orders of Chivalry. This is especially so in the case of the Knights Templar, or, to give them their own title: 'The Poor Knights of Christ and of the Temple of Solomon'.

It may be well to affirm—and with emphasis—that the innocence and probity of the Knights Templar, as concerned the charges brought against them, is definitely and finally established in history. In every case, in England (Oxford), in Castile (Salamanca), in Arragon (Tarragona), in Portugal (Lisbon) and in Germany (Mainz) all the high lay tribunals acquitted the Order. Ecclesiastical councils at Trèves, at Messina, at Bologna, in Cyprus, etc., held the charges against the Templars to be unfounded and formally upheld the Order. France, alone, could find tribunals that could be bought or menaced to give any ruling that might please authority.

The torture and savage criminal procedure in France (the disgrace of Europe in those times—and later) was put in force against the Templars. The Order was rich, a most heinous crime in the eyes of the French State. A vain and treacherous king (Philippe IV, *le Bel*) and a sly intriguer of a pope (Clement V, born in France, crowned in Lyons, who moved the papacy to Avignon) combined to condemn the Order, to torture the knights, to assassinate the Master, to cram full their own pockets and to vilify the reputation of the Knights Templar to hide their own villainy. Foul politics and sordid venality never went further than in these irregular trials in France.

All the great historians of modern times: Dollinger, Wendt, Gmelin, Lea and Finke, for example, are of one voice in declaring that the few confessions wrung from individual Templars under torture, in France, do not offset the universal witness of Europe to the well-doing and organized charity of the Knights Templar in their 9,000 'manors' established in Europe, Africa and Asia Minor.

To prove the rightly-used power of the Knights Templar does not necessarily relate them to the Knights of the Quest. Such a direct comparison is unjustified in fact. It is inadmissible to follow the immoderate and unhistorical German cycles of the Grail, all of them as destitute of spirituality as they are replete with materialism and magic. He rides a false road who would link the Arthurian Chivalry of the Quest with the 'Tempeleisen' of Wolfram von Eschenbach (*Parzival*), the 'Knights of the Grail' of Heinrich (*Diu Crône*), or of Albrecht (*Titural*). Still less can be accepted the low vulgarity of the Minnesingers with their 'lais' of the 'Venusberg'. Such is but profanation.

Of a variety, the Order of Knights Templar, beside its military ardour, monastic charcter, religious chivalry, initiatory devotion, administrative authority and financial power, was definitely antagonistic to a corrupt and static orthodoxy and did defy emperors, kings and popes. It had an aim, an ideal, a faith and a vision of the Divine Beauty and Light which rendered it suspect to all ecclesiastics enslaved in the Scholastic doctrines.

Beauty and Light were the two things most openly and violently hated by the Church of the Middle Ages. The Church taught ugliness and darkness, mortification and fasting, self-flagellation and weeping, hairshirts and austerity, hate and heresy-hunting under the threat of a dire Purgatory or a worse Hell. The Religion of Rancour took satisfaction in excommunication and interdict, and the Inquisition was its favourite child.

Its thunders of anathema were at their most violent when directed against the 'Religions of Light': the Albigenses, the Cathares, the Bogomils, the Poor Men of Lyons, the 'Faithful to Love', the Children of the Resurrection and the Knights Templar. Their thrice-damned sin— in the eyes of the Church—was that they told of Heaven rather than Hell, they adored the Risen Christ and not the Crucified Christ, they held to holiness of life even among the clergy, they asserted that Pardon and Grace came from God and were not marketable commodities in the monopoly of the Church, and held the Symbol of the Radiant Light a truer symbol of Christ than the Crucifix. For such, according to Pope Clement V, 'burning at the stake was far too good'.

Many passages in the Legends of the Round Table show a parallelism with the Knights Templar, even as the *Divine Comedy* of Dante is mainly an esoteric study of the Religions of the Light. Witnesses (under torture) declared that the Templars spat on the wood of the Crucifix (not on the figure) on Good Friday and decorated the Crucifix with flowers at Easter. (The Rose + Cross links back to the Religions of the Light). In the *Perlesvaus* it is told how, one Good Friday, Percival saw a priest whipping the Crucifix, and was told that the Mystery was one that could not be explained to a non-Initiate.

The symbol of Light was an accepted proof of heresy. It was also an accepted symbol of opposition to the Roman Church. Roger Bacon was imprisoned by the Church for having a medallion of the Sun in his possession. Spiritual Alchemy was under a ban because of 'the Rising Sun'. The 'Radiant Sun' of initiatory fraternity was a hidden and secret sign. No Cabbalist dared speak, save to brother-Cabbalists, of the 'glory of

Shekinah' or 'the Divine Beauty of Tiphereth'. The luminous Chalice of the Grail was suspect. How much more the 'perpetual Light' of the Templars and of the Rose + Cross!

If the *Perlesvaus* gave some parallelisms with the Templar symbolism, even more striking are those in *La Queste del Saint Graal*. Walter Mapp's authorship is doubtful, but, had his hand been therein, this archdeacon of Oxford and chaplain to King Henry II, of Angevin stock, certainly would be hostile to the papacy and friendly to the Templars.

The text is more likely to be from the pen of a Cistercian monk, and this Order had Templar chaplains. St. Bernard, founder of the Cistercians, was practically the founder of the Knights Templar as well; he wrote their Rule and obtained authorization for the Order from the Pope. The Rule provided that Templars should be received in Cistercian Abbeys as brothers. There were Templars residing in the Abbey of Citeaux when *La Queste del Saint Graal* was being written.

In the year 1208, just before the period of the text in question, a Cistercian monk, Martin de Pairis, brought from Constantinople two relics of untold sanctity. These were: some drops of the Blood of Jesus of Nazareth ('the Grail') and a piece of the True Cross. In the records of Citeaux it is told that 'angels served at the Mass of the Grail', and exactly these words are used in *La Queste*, apropos of a Mass of the Grail in which Galahad, Percival, and Bohors were the participants.

Pauphilet, the great authority on this text, says: 'It is not possible to find a tale more preciously close to the *Queste* than that of Walter de Birbach, as told by the Cistercian, César de Heisterbach. Truly a singular figure is this knight, so worldly and yet so religious. All his Adventure takes place on the very borders of Citeaux, at the frontiers of the chivalric and monastic worlds.

'Once, for example,' says Pauphilet, 'Walter de Birbach was prevented from attending a tournament, having to say an Office for the Virgin. An angel in full armour with his blazon took his place, and won all the prizes in the tournament. In Walter de Birbach,' concludes Pauphilet, 'we have a perfect Cisterican prefigurement of the Knights of the Grail.'[1]

Many of these correspondences and these parallelisms turn on a Celestial Paradise, a New Jerusalem, a Spiritual Chivalry and an Innermost Sanctuary of Sanctuaries. These are of the esoterism of the Holy Grail, and also of the Knights Templar, who claimed their right to continue as a Spiritual Chivalry in Heaven, and who had a Mass of their own in an Inner Sanctuary.

A further link is found in the comparison of the Holy Grail to the Spiritual or Interior Church, of which the External Church was a veil. With the Religions of the Light, the Knights Templar sought to raise Christianity from the mire in which it wallowed during the Middle Ages, when, for example (as Council decrees show), priests paid monthly for prostitutes whom the bishops had on hire. Such a desire for epuration of course was heresy. But was it not better so? Is not the upspringing of the soul more dear in the eyes of God than a clinging to a turgid doctrine?

Again, the Liturgy in *La Queste del Saint Graal* is not Latin. It is Oriental, and hence at this period, in heated opposition to Rome. Phrases are taken from the Gospel of St. John—a Gospel hated of the Church—and it was a formal accusation of heresy in the trials of the Knights Templar that they used this Gospel. The 'Apostolic Communion' wherein there are twelve participants at High Mass is Oriental, and also Templar; it is described in detail at the Mass of the Grail in the *Queste*.

Here, then, is neither identity nor succession between the Quest of the Holy Grail and the Knights Templar, but the spiritual content is the same. The spirit of the Quest is found in the works of the Knights Templar; the faith and ardour of the Templar is found in the Quest of the Holy Grail.

THE SUBLIME MYSTERY OF THE HOLY GRAIL; THE SPIRITUAL PLANE OF THE QUEST

Sursum corda! Two noble texts in the cycles of the Round Table serve to lead us to planes of high spiritual beauty. These are far other than the plane of Faërie where Merlin is guide, or the plane of Chivalry, wherein moves Lancelot, the Best Knight in the World. The world of Faërie opens its gates and those of the astral world to those who are akin; earthly knighthood appears in its due place as a preparation for the Fellowship of Celestial Knighthood. On the spiritual plane, there are moments when Percival will speak to the soul, and Galahad shall be the Pillar of Light, to lead.

The *Perlesvaus* or *The Longer Prose Percival* is a very special text. It has been translated into English with exquisite care and artistry of style by Dr Sebastian Evans, and is known as *The High History of the Holy Grail*. It tells specially of the adventures of Percival (and Gawain), but begins only in the middle of their career. This is not the lay of a trouvère, but an esoteric rendering of a part of the Legend, revealing initiatory factors held as a Mystery.

As Waite has pointed out, in the whole field of Christian literature there is not one text that speaks so richly of a Mysterious Faith, of an Esoteric School and of a Secret Church, as does the *Perlesvaus*.[2] If its tales of wonder be always crowned with a morning Mass, be sure that the Chapel is of a surpassing fairness, and the Mass is not according to the Ordinary. Every Sanctuary seems to be the ante-chamber to some higher Sanctuary, the sacrament is a super-sacrament, the order of priesthood is of celestial ordination. It is written within and without, and for those who can receive it, there is the Bread of Heaven and the Wine of the Spirit.

There are mystic emanations from the Holy Grail on many planes. There is a Mysticism that may be called 'Divine' and its protagonist is Joseph of Arimathea. There is a Mysticism of Faërie and of the Celtic Initiation and the wand of Merlin ponts to the Lordly Ones. There is a mysticism of Chivalry on Earth which prefigures a Celestial Fellowship. So, also, earthly symbols have spiritual values, and ecclesiastical rites foreshadow heavenly mysteries.

Whoso has read deeply into mystical literature and especially into the mysticism of Symbolism will not have failed to note its specific desire to be in contact with a plane that is both immanent and transcendental in its simultaneity. Though difficult to express, Jakob Boehme has made a fusion of the in-going and the out-going will. The matter is far more difficult if it is to be expressed in rite and symbol; it is an inner problem in the Quest of the Holy Grail.

In all the Legends of the Round Table may be seen this recognition of an Outer or exoteric sense of Right and of an Inner or esoteric sense. The Knight Errant was missionary as well as judge. The Holy Grail, veiled in symbol (the External Church), is not enough, its meaning and mystery (the Inner Church) must be known. 'The Word that was with God', in Manifestation, is also 'the Word that was God', in non-manifestation. This is a deep force in mystical Christian feeling. It has been overlaid by a material interpretation, as in St Augustine, where

Figure 5: 'They took their vessel and came into this land' by Ann Alexander.

Rome is the be-all and end-all of everything, but the Celtic note—so strong in the legends—is always ready to go deeper.

In the Middle Ages, The Brethren of an Interior Life, precursors of a liberal yet esoteric tradition, worked on this basis. Its most definite expressions are in *The Cloud Upon the Sanctuary* by Eckartshausen, and *The Character of the Interior Church* by Loupuhin. These two didactic works evoke a definite memory of the *Perlesvaus*.

Without overstretching the point, it may be said that a number of the specific conditions set down by Eckartshausen are foreshadowed in the Legends of the Round Table, and more especially that part of those Legends which has to do with the Holy Grail. Nine such may be mentioned:

1. That there exists an Interior Church, founded by Christ between his Resurrection and Ascension, the teaching of which was confined to a few depositaries, among them Joseph of Arimathea and St John.
2. That the External Church reflects these teachings, more or less justly, according as the mystical and initiatory contacts are kept or lost.
3. That there is a spiritual Temple, invisible to those who cannot read the soul, but where the elect may gather, and to which, after death, they will be formally admitted. (Spiritual Chivalry is of the same line of thought).
4. That the Inmost Sanctuary is Christ and is Eternal, knowing no change, being both pre-Incarnation and post-Incarnation.
5. That the three stages of Regeneration are ecclesiastic, interior, and spiritual; they are not secret, but shown forth in the words of Christ.
6. That the Two Paths are Wisdom and Love, the mind and the heart, and that these were combined in Jesus.
7. That the Incarnation is a continuing process in the soul of Man.
8. That all Mysteries which may be accomplished on Earth are inadequate of themselves and do not give salvation.
9. That the Eucharist on Earth is a pre-figurement, and the priesthood a forth-shadowing; their offices are not valid unless consummated in Heaven (this is definitely the setting-forth of Galahad.)

If, to the line of Mysticism already mentioned, be added the Mystery of the Interior Church, many problems in the Legends become clear. It is thus shown why Joseph of Arimathea avoided Jerusalem and Rome; why the Holy Grail was brought to the countries of the Celtic Church; why there are Mysterious Words of Consecration that must be handed on orally; why the Question of the Grail requires that he who asks it shall be conscious of its inner meaning; why the Earthly Chivalry is but a prefigurement of the Spiritual Chivalry; and why the Mass of the Grail has Christ Himself as celebrant, or, at least, one of the translated saints, made a priest after the Order of Melchizedek. The esoteric teaching of the *Perlesvaus* opens great spiritual horizons.

The second text to which reference has been made, while not more spiritual, is more devotional. It is churchly, even churchy. It suggests Rule rather than ecstasy, conformity rather than the liberty of the soul, ecclesiasticism rather than individualism, the liturgy rather than the Mystery. On its finer lines it reveals unsuspected heights and sublimates doctrine. This is *La Queste del Saint Graal*. The text is attributed to Walter Map or to a Cistercian monk. Its special character is so well analysed by Pauphilet that a few words of quotation may be permitted.

'It seems as though nearly all the apparitions of the Grail (in this text),' says Pauphilet, 'are of the nature of the immaterial. In a blaze of wonder it begets astonishment and enthusiasm in the half-worldly court of King Arthur; it passes before Lancelot in the heart of a forest; it accompanies the three elect (Percival, Bohors and Galahad) on the mystical Ship of Solomon; it shines in the heart of a prison. It is ubiquitous.

'Earthly hands to not touch it; angels may do so, martyrs descended from Paradise, or even the Divine Presences. The Grail is always veiled. A terrible punisment awaits those who would profane its mysteries. At its approach, life is halted, men are struck dumb, for the arrival of the Grail is a Judgement. Herein, then, the attributes of the Grail are those of God. Immaterial, omnipresent, encircled with celestial beings, it possesses Omnipotence and Miraculous Grace. The Grail is the love-bearing Manifestation of God.'

These conceptions are more spiritual than the cup as reliquary, as the Cosmic Cup of Nature, as the Bowl of Plenty or as the Chalice of the Mass. But even the *Perlesvaus* and *La Queste* do not reveal all the Mystery behind the age-old symbols. Its allegories are far other than the introspection of St John of the Cross or the pious Biblical simplicity of the *Pilgrim's Progress*.

Among its other Mysteries, the Quest of the Holy Grail thus appears as an illustrative initiatory rite for Adepts of some mystical Unitive Life, and its temple is 'not made with hands'. The 'Lost Words' are not lost to those to hear the Music of the Spheres, the Cosmic Mass knows no boundaries of church, place nor time; and the Spirit of the Grail reaches from the soul of Man to the Grace of God.

[1] Albert Panphilat 'Au Sujet du Graal', in *Romania 66* (1940), pp. 289-321, 481-504.
[2] See p. 203-219.

Chapter 8.
The High History of the Holy Grail

The mediaeval romance known as the *Perlesvaus*, or sometimes *The High History of the Holy Grail* was probably written at Glastonbury in the 13th century. It contains some of the most deeply mystical episodes of any of the Grail texts, and is justly famous for the insights it gives into the higher mysteries of the mysterious vessel.

Katherine Maltwood, who in the 1930s rediscovered what she believed to be the outlines of a vast terrestrial zodiac around Glastonbury, used the *Perlesvaus* as a map to the Arthurian cycle as a whole. Her theories have been much discussed and argued over since their publication in Glastonbury's Temple of the Stars in 1929, and various clues have come to light within the text from which the following excerpts are taken.

The part we have chosen to include here deals with the rare encounter between Arthur and the magical power of the Grail, and of the unique vision which arose from it. In particular the description of the Grail as having 'five mysterious shapes' is one of the key images within the whole cycle.

The present extracts come from the fine early translation by Sebastian Evans, published in 1898.

It was one Ascension Day that the King was at Cardoil. He was risen from meat and went through the hall from one end to the other, and looked and saw the Queen that was seated at a window. The King went to sit beside her, and looked at her in the face and saw that the tears were falling from her eyes.

'Lady,' saith the King, 'What aileth you, and wherefore do you weep?'

'Sir,' saith she, 'And I weep, good right have I; and you yourself have little right to make joy.'

'Certes, Lady, I do not.'

'Sir,' saith she, 'You are right. I have seen on this high day, or on other days that were not less high than this, when you have had such throng of knights at your court that right uneath might any number them. Now every day are so few therein that much shame have I thereof, nor no more do no adventures befall therein. Wherefore great fear have I lest God hath put you into forgetfulness.'

'Certes, Lady,' saith the King, 'No will have I to do largesse nor aught that turneth to honour. Rather is my desire changed into feebleness of heart. And by this know I well that I lose my knights and have the love of my friends.'

'Sir,' saith the Queen, 'And were you to go to the chapel of S. Augustine that is in the White Forest, that may not be found save by adventure only, methinketh that on your back-repair you would again have your desire of well-doing, for never yet did none discounselled ask counsel of God but he would give it for love of him so he asked it of a good heart.'

'Lady,' saith the King, 'And willingly will I go, forasmuch as that you say have I heard well witnessed in many places where I have been.'

'Sir,' saith she, 'The place is right perilous and the chapel right adventurous. But the most worshipful hermit that is in the Kingdom of Wales hath his dwelling beside the chapel, nor liveth he now any longer for nought save only the glory of God.'

'Lady,' saith the King, 'It will behove me go thither all armed and without knights.'

'Sir,' saith she, 'You may well take with you one knight and a squire.'

'Lady,' saith the King, 'That durst not I, for the place is perilous, and the more folk one should take thither, the fewer adventures there should he find.'

'Sir,' saith she, 'One squire shall you take by my good will, nor shall nought betide you thereof save good only, please God!'

'Lady,' saith the King, 'At your pleasure be it, but much dread I that nought shall come of it save evil only.' Thereupon the king riseth up from beside the Queen, and looketh before him and seeth a youth tall and strong and comely and young, that was hight Chaus, and he was the son of Ywain li Aoutres.

'Lady,' saith he to the Queen, 'This one will I take with me and you think well.'

'Sir,' saith she, 'It pleaseth me well, for I have heard much witness to his valour.'

The King calleth the squire, and he cometh and kneeleth down before him. The King maketh him rise and saith unto him, 'Chaus,' saith he, 'You shall lie within to-night, in this hall, and take heed that my horse be saddled at break of day and mine arms ready. For I would be moving at the time I tell you, and yourself with me without more company.'

'Sir,' saith the squire, 'At your pleasure.'

And the evening drew on, and the King and Queen go to bed. When they had eaten in hall, the knights went to their hostels. The squire remained in the hall, but he would not do off his clothes nor his shoon, for the night seemed him to be too short, and for that he would fain be ready in the morning at the King's commandment. The squire was lying down in such sort as I have told you, and in the first sleep that he slept, seemed him the King had gone without him. The squire was sore scared thereat, and came to his hackney and set the saddle and bridle upon him, and did on his spurs and girt on his sword, as it seemed him in his sleep, and issued forth of the castle a great pace after the

King. And when he had ridden a long space he entered into a great forest and looked in the way before him and saw the slot of the King's horse and followed the track a long space, until that he came to a launde of the forest whereat he thought that the King had alighted. The squire thought that the hoof-marks on the way had come to an end, and so thought that the King had alighted there or hard by there. He looketh to the right hand and seeth a chapel in the midst of the launde, and he seeth about it a great graveyard wherein were many coffins, as it seemed him. He thought in his heart that he would go towards the chapel, for he supposed that the King would have entered to pray there. He went thitherward and alighted. When the squire was alighted, he tied up his hackney and entered into the chapel. None did he see there in one part nor another, save a knight that lay dead in the midst of the chapel upon a bier, and he was covered of a rich cloth of silk and had around him waxen tapers burning that were fixed in four candlesticks of gold. This squire marvelled much how this body was left there so lonely, insomuch that none were about him save only the images, and yet more marvelled he of the King that he found him not, for he knew not in what part to seek him. He taketh out one of the tall tapers, and layeth hand on the golden candlestick, and setteth it betwixt his hose and his thigh and issueth forth of the chapel, and remounteth on his hackney and goeth way back and passeth beyond the grave-yard and issueth forth of the launde and entereth into the forest and thinketh that he will not cease until he hath found the King.

So, as he entereth into a grassy lane in the wood, he seeth come before him a man black and foul-favoured, and he was somewhat taller afoot than was himself a-horseback. And he held a great sharp knife in his hand with two edges as it seemed him. The squire cometh over against him a great pace and saith unto him, 'You, that come there, have you met King Arthur in this forest?'

'In no wise,' saith the messenger, 'But you have I met, whereof am I right glad at heart, for you have departed from the chapel as a thief and a traitor. For you are carrying off thence the candlestick of gold that was in honour of the knight that lieth in the chapel dead. Wherefore I will that you yield it up to me and so will I carry it back, otherwise, and you do not this, you do I defy!'

'By my faith,' saith the squire, 'Never will I yield it you! rather will I carry it off and make a present thereof to King Arthur.'

'By my faith,' saith the other, 'Right dearly shall you pay for it, and you yield it not up forthwith.'

Howbeit, the squire smiteth with his spurs and thinketh to pass him by, but the other hasteth him, and smiteth the squire in the left side with the knife and thrusteth it into his body up to the haft. The squire, that lay in the hall at Cardoil, and had dreamed this, awoke and cried in a loud voice: 'Holy Mary! The priest! Help! Help, for I am a dead man!' The King and the Queen heard the cry, and the chamberlain leapt up and said to the King: 'Sir, you may well be moving, for it is day!' The King made him be clad and shod. And the squire crieth with such strength as he hath: 'Fetch me the priest, for I die!' The King goeth thither as fast as he may, and the Queen and the chamberlain carry great torches and candles. The King asketh him what aileth him, and he telleth him all in such wise as he had dreamed it.

'Ha,' saith the King, 'Is it then a dream?'

'Yea, sir,' saith he, 'But a right foul dream it is for me, for right foully hath it come true!' He lift his left arm. 'Sir,' saith he, 'Look you there! Lo, here is the knife that was run into my side up to the haft!' After that, he setteth his hand to his hose where the candlestick was. He draweth it forth and showeth it to the King. 'Sir,' saith he, 'For this candlestick that I present to you, am I wounded to the death!'

The King taketh the candlestick and looketh thereat in wonderment for none so rich had he never been tofore. The King showeth it to the Queen.

'Sir,' saith the squire, 'Draw not forth the knife of my body until that I be shriven.'

The King sent for one of his own chaplains that made the squire confess and do his houselling right well. The King himself draweth forth the knife of the body, and the soul departed forthwith. The King made do his service right richly and his shrouding and burial. Ywain li Aoutres that was father to the squire was right sorrowful of the death of his son. King Arthur, with the good will of Ywain his father, gave the candlestick to S. Paul in London, for the church was newly founded, and the King wished that this marvellous adventure should everywhere be known, and that prayer should be made in the church for the soul of the squire that was slain on account of the candlestick.

King Arthur armed himself in the morning, as I told you and began to tell, to go to the chapel of S. Augustine. Said the Queen to him: 'Whom will you take with you?'

'Lady,' saith he, 'No company will I have thither, save God only, for well may you understand by this adventure that hath befallen, that God will not allow I should have none with me.'

'Sir,' saith she, 'God be guard of your body, and grant you return safely so as that you may have the will to do well, whereby shall your praise be lifted up that is now sore cast down.'

'Lady,' saith he, 'May God remember it.'

His destrier was brought to the mounting-stage, and the King mounted thereon all armed. Messire Ywain li Aoutres lent him his shield and spear. When the King had hung the shield at his neck and held the spear in his hand, sword-girt, on the tall destrier armed, well seemed

Figure 6: 'And there fell between them a fiery cloud, which burned up
both their shields' by H. J. Ford.

he in the make of his body and in his bearing to be a knight of great
pith and hardiment. He planteth himself so stiffly in the stirrups that
he maketh the saddlebows creak again and the destrier stagger under
him that was right stout and swift, and he smiteth him of his spurs,
and the horse maketh answer with a great leap. The Queen was at the
windows of the hall, and as many as five-and-twenty knights were all
come to the mounting-stage.

When the King departed, 'Lords,' saith the Queen, 'How seemeth
you of the King? Seemeth he not a goodly man?'

'Yea, certes, Lady, and sore loss is it to the world that he followeth
not out his good beginning, for no king nor price is known better learned
of all courtesy nor of all largesse than he, so he would do like as he
was wont.'

With that the knights hold their peace, and King Arthur goeth away
a great pace. And he entereth into a great forest adventurous, and rideth
the day long until he cometh about evensong into the thick of the forest.
And he espied a little house beside a little chapel, and it well seemed
him to be a hermitage. King Arthur rode thitherward and alighteth
before this little house, and entereth thereinto and draweth his horse
after him, that had much pains to enter in at the door, and laid his
spear down on the ground and leant his shield against the wall, and
hath ungirded his sword and unlaced his ventail. He looked before him
and saw barley and provender, and so led his horse thither and smote

off his bridle, and afterwards hath shut the door of the little house and locked it. And it seemed him that there was a strife in the chapel. The ones were weeping so tenderly and sweetly as it were angels, and the other spake so harshly as it were fiends. The King heard such voices in the chapel and marvelled much what it might be. He findeth a door in the little house that openeth on a little cloister whereby one goeth to the chapel. The King is gone thither and entereth into the little minster, and looketh everywhere but seeth nought there, save the images and the crucifixes. And he supposeth not that the strife of these voices cometh of them.

The voices ceased as soon as he was within. He marvelleth how it came that this house and hermitage were solitary, and what had become of the hermit that dwelt therein. He drew night the altar of the chapel and beheld in front thereof a coffin all discovered, and he saw the hermit lying therein all clad in his vestments, and seeth the long beard down to his girdle, and his hands crossed upon the breast. There was a cross above him, whereof the image came as far as his mouth, and he had life in him yet, but he was nigh his end, being at the point of death. The King was before the coffin a long space, and looked right fainly on the hermit, for well it seemed him that he had been of a good life. The night was fully come, but within was a brightness of light as if a score of candles were lighted. He had a mind to abide there until that the good man should have passed away. He would fain have sate him down before the coffin, when a voice warned him right horribly to begone thence, for that it was desired to make a judgement within there, that might not be made so long as he were there.

The King departed, that would willingly have reamined there, and so returned back into the little house, and sate him down on a seat whereon the hermit wont to sit. And he heareth the strife and the noise begin again within the chapel, and the ones he heareth speaking high and the others low, and he knoweth well by the voices, that the ones are angels and the others devils. And he heareth that the devils are distraining on the hermit's soul, and that judgement will presently be given in their favour, whereof make they great joy. King Arthur is grieved in his heart when he heareth that the angels' voice are stilled. The King is so heavy, that no desire hath he neither to eat nor to drink. and while he sitteth thus, stooping his head toward the ground, full of vexation and discontent, he heareth in the chapel the voice of a Lady that spake so sweet and clear, that no man in this earthly world, were his grief and heaviness never so sore, but and he had heard the sweet voice of her pleading would again have been in joy. She saith to the devils: 'Begone from hence, for no right have ye over the soul of this good man, whatsoever he may have done aforetime, for in my Son's service and mine own is he taken, and his penance hath he done in this hermitage of the sins that he hath done.'

'True, Lady,' says the devils, 'But longer had he served us than he hath served you and your Son. For forty years or more hath he been a murderer and robber in this forest, whereas in this hermitage but five years hath he been. And now you wish to thieve him from us.'

'I do not. No wish have I to take him from you by theft, for had he been taken in your service in suchwise as he hath been taken in mine, yours would he have been, all quit.' The devils go their way all discomfort and aggrieved; and the sweet Mother of our Lord God taketh the soul of the hermit, that was departed of his body, and so commendeth it to the angels and archangels that they make present thereof to Her dear Son in Paradise. And the angels take it and begin to sing for joy *Te Deum laudamus*, And the Holy Lady leadeth them and goeth her way along with them. Josephus maketh remembrance of this history and telleth us that this worthy man was named Calixtus.

King Arthur was in the little house beside the chapel, and had heard the voice of the sweet Mother of God and the angels. Great joy had he, and was right glad of the good man's soul that was borne thence into Paradise. The King had slept right little the night and was all armed. He saw the day break clear and fair, and goeth his way toward the chapel to cry God mercy, thinking to find the coffin discovered there were the hermit lay; but so did he not! Rather, was it covered of the richest tomb-stone that any might ever see, and had on the top a red cross, and seemed it that the chapel was all incensed.

When the King had made his orison therein, he cometh back again and setteth on his bridle and saddle and mounteth, and taketh his shield and spear and departeth from the little house and entereth into the forest and rideth a great pace, until he cometh at right hour of tierce to one of the fairest laundes that ever a man might see. And he seeth at the entrance a spear set bar-wise, and looketh to the right or ever he should enter therein, and seeth a damsel sitting under a great leafy tree, and she held the reins of her mule in her hand. The damsel was of great beauty and full seemly clad. The King turneth thitherward and so saluteth her and saith: 'Damsel,' saith he, 'God give you joy and good adventure.'

'Sir,' saith she, 'So may He do to you!'

'Damsel,' saith the King, 'Is there no hold in this launde?'

'Sir,' saith the damsel, 'No hold is there save a most holy chapel and a hermit that is beside S. Augustine's chapel.'

'Is this then S. Augustine's chapel?' saith the King.

'Yea, Sir, I tell it you for true, but the launde and the forest about is so perilous that no knight returneth thence but he be dead or wounded; but the place of the chapel is of so great worthiness that none goeth thither, be he never so discounselled, but he cometh back counselled, so he may thence return on live. And Lord God be guard of your body, for never yet saw I none aforetime that seemed more like to be good knight, and sore pity would it be and you were not, and never more shall I depart me hence and I shall have seen your end.'

'Damsel,' saith the King, 'Please God, you shall see me repair back thence.'

'Certes,' saith the damsel, 'Thereof should I be right fain, for then should I ask you tidings at leisure of him that I am seeking.'

The King goeth to the bar whereby one entereth into the launde, and looketh to the right into a combe of the forest and seeth the chapel of S. Augustine and the right fair hermitage. Thitherward goeth he and alighteth, and it seemeth him that the hermit is apparelled to sing the mass. He reineth up his horse to the bough of a tree by the side of the chapel and thinketh to enter hereinto, but, had it been to conquer all the kingdoms of the world, thereinto might he not enter, albeit there was none made him denial thereof, for the door was open and none saw he that might forbid him. Sore ashamed is the King thereof. Howbeit, he beholdeth an image of Our Lord that was there within and crieth Him of mercy right sweetly, and looketh toward the altar. And he looketh at the holy hermit that was robed to sing mass and said his *Confiteor*, he seeth at his right hand the fairest Child that ever he had seen, and He was clad in an alb and had a golden crown on his head loaded with precious stones that gave out a full great brightness of light. On the left hand side, was a Lady so fair that all the beauties of the world might not compare them with her beauty. When the holy hermit had said his *Confiteor* and went to the altar, the Lady also took her Son and went to sit on the right hand side towards the altar upon a right rich chair and set her Son upon her knees and began to kiss Him full sweetly and saith: 'Sir,' saith she, 'You are my Father and my Son and my Lord, and guardian of me and of all the world.'

King Arthur heareth the words and seeth the beauty of the Lady and of the Child, and marvelleth much of this that She should call Him her Father and her Son. He looketh at a window behind the altar and seeth a flame come through at the very instant that mass was begun, clearer than any ray of sun nor moon nor star, and evermore it threw forth a brightness of light such that and all the lights in the world had been together it would not have been the like. And it is come down upon the altar. King Arthur seeth it who marvelleth him much thereof. But sore it irketh him of this that he may not enter therewithin, and he heareth, there where the holy hermit was singing the mass, right fair responses, and they seem him to be the responses of angels. And when the Holy Gospel was read, King Arthur looked toward the altar and saw that the Lady took her Child and offered Him into the hands of the holy hermit, but of this King Arthur made much marvel, that the holy hermit washed not his hands when he had received the offering. Right sore did King Arthur marvel him thereof, but little right would he have had to marvel had he known the reason. And when the Child was offered him, he set Him upon the altar and thereafter began his sacrament. And King Arthur set him on his knees before the chapel and began to pray to God and to beat his breast. And he looked toward the altar after the preface, and it seemed him that the holy hermit held between his hands a man bleeding from His side and in His palms and in His feet, and crowned with thorns, and he seeth Him in His own figure. And when he had looked on Him so long and knoweth not what is become of Him, the King hath pity of Him in his heart of this that he had seen, and the tears of his heart come into his eyes. And he looketh toward the altar and thinketh to see the figure of the man, and seeth that it is changed into the shape of the Child that he had seen tofore.

When the mass was sung, the voice of a holy angel said *Ite, missa est.* The Son took the Mother by the hand, and they evanished forth of the chapel with the greatest company and the fairest that might ever be seen. The flame that was come down through the window went away with this company. When the hermit had done his service and was divested of the arms of God, he went to King Arthur that was still without the chapel.

'Sir,' saith he to the King, 'Now may you well enter herein and well might you have been joyous in your heart had you deserved so much as that you might have come in at the beginning of the mass.'

King Arthur entered into the chapel without any hindrance.

'Sir,' saith the hermit to the King, 'I know you well, as did I also King Uther Pendragon your father. On account of your sins and your deserts might you not enter here while mass was being sung. Nor will you to-morrow, save you shall first have made amends of that you have misdone towards God and towards the saint that is worshipped herewithin. For you are the richest King of the world and the most adventurous, wherefore ought all the world to take ensample of you in well-doing and in largesse and in honour; whereas you are now an ensample of evil-doing to all rich worshipful men that be now in the world. Wherefore shall right sore mishap betide you and you set not back your doing to the point whereat you began. For your court was the sovran of all courts and the most adventurous, whereas now is it least of worth. Well may he be sorry that goeth from honour to shame, but never may he have reproach that shall do him ill, that cometh from shame to honour, for the honour wherein he is found rescueth him to God, but blame may never rescue the man that hath renounced honour for shame, for the shame and wickedness wherein he is found declare him guilty.'

Chapter 9.

The Secret Heresy of the Middle Ages

by Hannah Closs

The connection between the mysterious group known as the Cathars or Albigensians and the Grail romances has already been mentioned in the writings of Francis Rolt-Wheeler (see Chapter 7) and has been much discussed elsewhere. There are those who believe (perhaps not without foundation) that the Cathars kept alive the secret inner tradition of the Grail and passed it on to the Templars and the troubadour poets who came after them. The Cathars themselves were virtually wiped out in a terrible crusade in the 13th century, but their memory has remained green in the hands of scholars and investigators like Hannah Closs, who have pursued their mystery through the ages. Certainly the ideas of Courtly love, which raised women to new heights as objects of passionate regard, the *agape* or holy love, are deeply embedded in both the histories of the Grail and the Cathars.

Hannah Closs (1905-1953) was a remarkable scholar and novelist of distinction whose understanding of the Cathars was unique. Her trilogy of novels, *High are the Mountains, Deep are the Valleys* and *The Silent Tarn* are still the best fictional treatment of the subject yet written—they await rediscovery and reprinting for a fresh audience.

The essay which follows first appeared in a collection published in 1937 and has not been reprinted since. It is the most conventionally scholarly of the works presented here and offers some challenging insights into a mystery which shook the mediaeval world to its foundations.

⸎

Courtly love—how remote sounds the phrase, what memories of lovesick knights and swooning troubadours it conjures up, what charming and absurd conceits! Visions of meadows and woodland, glades where rich repasts are spread in the shade of summer trees enwoven with the song of birds; where gallants clad in sumptuous velvets strike the lute and slender ladies trail their long kirtles over a carpet of flowers—the life depicted so often on mediaeval embroideries and tapestries or on the painted walls of turret-chamber and banquet hall. These manifold delights and graces of the *Vie seigneuriale* are reflected in the tapestries of the Cluny Museum at Paris. On the walls of the Palazzo del Concilio in Trient, in colours subtle and brilliant as those of a Persian miniature, knights and their ladies partake of delicious fare on a marble table set in a shady nook, or clad in long-sleeved scolloped robes amble beneath the trees, whilst a damsel crowns her lover's head with a wreath of flowers.

Or turn to those charming scenes in mediaeval manuscripts—two loves, hawk on wrist, dallying by the way, all forgetful, it seems, of the chase. So we see them in the Manesse Codex in Heidelberg— the *chef-d'oeuvre* of the German minnesong, the paintings dating from the 14th century, the poems from the 13th century and earlier.

In the same manuscript, too, we find depicted another side of courtly love—those wild escapades encountered to satisfy a lady's whim, and their frequently bitter reward; as here where Poro von Hamle, having been enticed to scale his lady's tower by means of a basket on a pulley, finds himself suspended halfway to suffer the mockery of the crown at break of dawn. So too, the minnesinger Ulrich von Lichtenstein, who rode from Venice to Vienna, clad as Dame Venus, was moved to prove his love by chopping off his little finger and sending it to the fickle lady of his heart. We are reminded of the Provençal poet, that poor fool Peire Vidal, of whom they tell that he ran mad for love of Loba (the she-wolf) of Penautier, and clad in the skin of a wolf, was chased by her hounds and torn, for which at least he received the guerdon of being nursed back to life and healed by her own hands!

Add to these fantasies the jousts and the tourneys, with their torrent of banners and pennons, of garlands and blood—and remoter yet, behind the impregnable battlements of time, that strange institution of female rights, the Courts of Love, where the cultured ladies of 12th and 13th-century France, holding discourse on the mysteries of Eros, rivalled the learned doctors themselves in hair-splitting arguments as to whether, for instance, since love in matrimony is quite impossible, one might not accept one's husband as lover after divorcing him first!

Scholarship has questioned whether such Courts of Love did in fact exist, but one thing is certain, that in the song of the troubadours and the cult of the *amour courtois*, woman is definitely allotted an extraordinarily high place—as an ideal. And however far the practices of mediaeval life may seem to gainsay such a status, does not poetic imagination often hold a deeper reality than actuality itself? We may discover under the troubadour's conventional and often seemingly artificial protestations of a consuming passion, a yearning far deeper and the search of a goal more absolute than the mere requiting of fleshly love.

COURTLY LOVE AND RELIGION

The origins of the *amour courtois* have given rise to continuous dispute amongst the learned, and we cannot enter upon all their arguments here. Some have regarded the cult of the Madonna as a formative influence in the development of the courtly ideal, some believe that the stimulus operated the other way round. But to prove at least how strong are the parallels, let us glance at a few representations of the Virgin in mediaeval cathedrals.

The grace, the subtlety that with the so-called early Gothic supersedes the Norman and Romanesque (that massive virile style so reminiscent of the heroic *chansons de geste*) betrays a growing susceptibility to the charms of the feminine—the feminine with all its subtleties and wiles so exquisitely expressed, for instance, in the face of the 13th-century statue of Eve at Bamberg Cathedral near Bayreuth in Germany.

This appreciation of feminine graces and charms is analogous to the growing adoration of the Virgin. For she too grows senuously beautiful, comporting herself with the fashionable elegance and mannerisms of a lady of the court. How remote is the *Vièrge dorée* of Amiens from the stark Madonnas of earlier centuries. So strong is this growing feeling for beauty, for life, that even the crown burgeons with leafy growth. Three angels hover about her head holding the aureole like some huge halo hat.

One can well believe that she interceded with God for the sins of her earthly vassals, even as the Mary in the *Last Judgement* at Bamberg intercedes for the young king whom an angel leads by the hand to the throne of Christ. How remote is the spirit of this *Last Judgement* from those that threatened a fearful damnation on the porches of the 12th-century churches. The damned indeed do not look so unhappy at all and one is tempted to agree with the hero of that charming French romance *Auscassin and Nicolette* that it must be far more fun to go to Hell, whither fare all men of worth, than to go to Heaven with such smug-faced creatures as we see here.

This Mary, then, interceding in heaven, what is she but the *grande dame* craving pardon for her lord, her husband, for some erring vassal, who is her faithful knight, her troubadour?

We find many analogies between worship of the Virgin and the *amour courtois*. It was a very earthly, courtly Mary surely who could step down from her stone pedestal in the chapel to fight in a tourney, taking the place of the young knight who had forgotten all about time whilst praying before her image; or another time put in the habit of the nun who eloped from her convent with a handsome noble—the story on which Reinhard bases his miracle play.

How very near she often seems to the ideal lady whom the troubadours worshipped with heart and soul and of whom they sang, as does the Provençal Bernard de Ventadorn in one of his songs, 'Good lady, nothing I crave but that you accept me as serviter, that I may serve you even as I do my lord.'

Yes, it may well be that the Church felt compelled to encourage the worship of the Virgin in order to guide so overwhelming a passion into safer channels.

Time precludes entering into the possible relationships between Church and pagan ritual—suggested for instance by the spring songs which form one of the starting points of the Provençal lyric. These feast days (*Dies Rosae*, etc.) are themselves a christianized survival of pagan customs and here one must call to mind those other classical influences, Ovid and Latin love-letters which may have played some part in the development of the Courtly Ideal.

But we find still more curious parallels between religious and courtly love—parallels that make the courtly representation of Paradise on the walls of the Campo Santo in Pisa less bewildering, for one is surely tempted to ask whether that group of elegant lords and dames with their lutes and dulcimers, their lap dogs and hawks are engaged in a *santa conversazione* or the delights of a Garden of Love.

We must not forget that many of the troubadours who may appear to us gay frivolous sort of fellows, were men of learning who often spent the winter months in the cloister before they set out in spring to wander from castle to castle singing their songs. There was, then, a certain direct relationship between the cleric and chivalric life. Song was the *gaya sienzia* which celebrated 'amors, joi e joven.'

And how did this gay science define love? In the songs of many a Provençal troubadour we find a reference to the three degrees of love.

Now it is an interesting fact that we find a remarkable parallel to this concept in the teaching of that saintly Cistercian Bernard de Clairvaux, whose very language seems sometimes to employ almost the conventional troubadour pathos—'O la grande et suave blessure d'amour', whilst he cries even more explicitly, 'In vain must he who cannot love, read or listen to a love-song, for a heart that remains cold can scarcely understand that language.' True love, love that consumes the heart and arouses the intelligence becomes the primary and indispensable condition for being admitted amongst the elite; in short, of becoming, in courtly jargon, a *fin cuer leal*. Of love, St Bernard says, there are three degrees: the first, sensual; the second, rational; the third, spiritual; a concept that leads us back to Duns Scotus Erigena, to St Denis the Areopagite and thence to Plato and the Neo-Platonists.

THE TENETS OF COURTLY LOVE: ITS EXPONENTS AND THEIR ENVIRONMENT

It is possible that behind the frivolties of the Courts of Love lurked memories half forgotten and misunderstood of that high intellectual Platonic ideal.

Let us turn for a moment to that strange book *De Amore libri tres* by Andreas Capellanus, chaplain of Marie de Champagne, that fascinating and enlightened lady who gathered around her some of the greatest

names of French 13th-century literature. In this book, Andreas seems
to be putting forth the ideas fashionable at her court. At first sight they
would seem almost a blasphemous parody of the spiritual ideal. According to André, Marie decrees that imagination alone constitutes love:
true love should endure without the presence of the beloved. There
is however no need at all for celibacy—marriage counts for nothing.
Love then, being incompatible with marriage, must be sought outside
it. How else can one become a *fin cuer leal?* Love must be an unreachable goal. Hence the knight must ever love a lady infinitely beyond him.
In courtly circles it followed of necessity that she must be a lady of
high estate, of far nobler blood than the knight or troubadour himself, in fact very often the wife of his liege-lord. Naturally he dare not
profess his love openly, he must nourish it in secret, only hoping to
draw attention to himself by noble deeds and song, rejoicing in veiled
terms at the slightest sign of recognition his worship may bring, and
lamenting, for the most part, his hapless lot—a state of affairs very
charmingly depicted on a little 13th-century casket from Bavaria, on
which some knight has had inscribed the story of his yearning, whilst
the dreamed-of fulfilment is suggested by the scenes and figures carved
on the sides.

   That a plethora of verse, product merely of an elegant vogue, should
result from such a state of affairs was as inevitable as the fashion for
sonnet writing amongst cultivated gentlemen of the Elizabethan age,
but here as there, amongst countless verses mediocre, formalistic, and
insincere, we find love poems unmatched in formal beauty and power
and even pscyhological insight, as for instance in that unforgettable
dawn-song of the 13th-century German minnesinger Heinrich von
Morungen, which seems almost modern in the depth and subtlety of
its emotion—one of the greatest love songs surely of all time:

O wè sol aber mir niemer mè	Alas, ne'er more shall glow For me,
geliuhten durh die naht	through darkest night,
Vil wîser als ein snê	Far whiter than the snow
îr lîp so wol geslaht...	Her shapely form's delight ...

with its refrain...

dô tagite ez	Then came the dawn

And speaking of the dawn song we may recall that lovely poem by an
anonymous 12th-century Provençal, translated so often into English,
amongst others by Swinburne, George Moore, and Ezra Pound:

   In orchard under the hawthorn tree...

with its re-iterate plaint:

   Ah God, ah God, that dawn should come so soon.

In what land did the dawn song, the *alba* and the idea of courtly love originate? One can still not be sure. Its earlier manifestations, however, certainly seem to point to the south of Europe, to Provence and its neighbouring lands, and it is perhaps significant that Marie of Champagne, who did so much to propagate the cult of courtly love, was the daughter of Alienor of Guyenne, queen of Henry II and mother of Richard Lionheart, herself grandmother of Guillem of Poitiers, one of the earliest known troubadours.

There were, I think, a number of reasons why the cult of the troubadour should have developed in the south of France. Incidentally, the term Provençal is here used to cover not only the Provence itself but the neighbouring lands—Languedoc, Aquitaine, the Pyrenees, etc.— a region once sown with the seeds not only of Latin but Hellenic culture through the Greek colonization of Marseilles. Side by side with the ruins of feudalism stand yet older remains—the aqueduct near Nimes, the triumphal arch and ancient Roman theatre at Orange which inspired Rainer Maria Rilke to a panegyric of the classic stage. The ghost of that past majesty haunts one everywhere in visiting these places, now reduced to the state of petty provincial towns and villages, retrieved from squalor by the sun of the south. The power of Rome still echoes in the stone galleries of the coliseum at Arles. At St Remy the triumphal arch has a lightness, a grace unconsciously inherited, may be, from a remoter Greek ancestry. Gazing on these ruins, one is overcome by elegiac melancholy at the thought of the rich civilization which blossomed here, not only in classic times, but again in the Middle Ages themselves—a phenomenal and in some ways almost modern civilization, that grew to such glory, only to be annihilated by the Albigensian wars. More of that anon.

Today the ruins of Les Baux, once an important town, now scarce differentiable from the rock from which it was hewn, might stand almost as a symbol of the wreck of a whole culture. In the 12th century, it flourished with all the refinements of aesthetic life. Here, it is said, were held some of those—perhaps legendary—Courts of Love. Here certainly the elite of southern France must often have foregathered—the greatest troubadours, Betran de Borne, Bernard de Ventadorn and Arnaut Daniel.

The long ridges of rock that rise from the plain in that district are actually those van Gogh so loved to paint during his sojourn at Arles; and yet as I stood here in 1938, it seemed to me that his distraught, torn brush stroke did not express the atmosphere of that land as fully as some of the verses of the mediaeval troubadours who leashed the vehemence of their passion to a close pattern of sound and word and rhyme, just as man had welded the walls and vaulted chambers of town and castle from the volcanic rock itself, had tamed the fecundity of the sun-drenched, umber soil to the patterned rows of the young vine stocks, the silvery grey of the olives above their writhing stems.

In this landscape, then, the form-wrought passion of troubadour verse, even the intricate virtuosity of the sestina, seems essentially at home. Master of the sestina was Arnaut Daniel, that incalculable, almost insolent figure amongst the troubadours of Provence who sang of himself:

> I am Arnatuz who binds the winds
> and chases the hare with the bull
> and swims against the current.

It was from him who loved to encase his vehement outbursts in the most intransigent form that Dante borrowed the form of the sestina, developing it to one of the most powerful and haunting poems of ideal love: 'Al poco giorno ed al gran cerchio d'ombra', transalted by Rossetti amongst his renderings of early Italian poets:

> To the dim light and the large circle of shade
> I have clomb, and to the whitening of the hills...

verses which with their reiteration of the word *stone* and the stark grandeur of their imagery appear as really inspired variations on the name of the lady Pietra, an example of the heights to which the virtuosity of the sestina can rise and the controlled passion of which it is capable.

Arnaut himself favoured a dark, obscure, and involved style, the *trobar clus* as it was called. But Provençal poets often adopt a gentler tone, as for instance, Bernard de Ventadorn in the tender love-plaint (possibly inspired by Alienor of Guyenne), in which he longs to be a swallow that he might follow his lady across the sea. 'Never,' he complains, 'was even Tristan tortured by such yearning for Iseult the fair.'

Or we may recall the gay spring-songs, in particular one by Raimbaud de Vaqueiras 'Kalenda maya...', in which the fourteen lines of each verse end always on the same sound; *aya* in the first verse, *ia* in the second, *uda* in the third, and so on.

One would like to hear this song sung to enjoy it to the full, and it is a great consolation, that unlike most of the melodies of the German *minnesänger*, many of the troubadours' tunes are preserved in MS.

In a certain 13th-century MS indeed we find imaginary portraits of the poets themselves: Bernard de Ventadorn, Jaufré Rudel dying in his lady's arms, Marcabru, one of the earliest troubadours of Provence, and many another. Nor must we forget to mention Bertran de Born, whom Dante met wandering through the gloom of the Inferno bearing his own head in his hand as a lantern and groaning, 'For that I sundered other men in life, so must I now myself walk sundered.' He refers evidently to the quarrels he was always instigating amongst his contemporaries and even his friends, for instance between Henry II of England and his two sons, Richard Lionheart and the other Henry.

Characteristic of Bertran's bellicose nature is a peculiarly gripping poem which swings over from praise of spring to a fierce eulogy of war, and which, though not absolutely identified as his own, is unmistakably born of his spirit. But the truculent Bertran was no mean lover as we see from that curiously artificial lyric of his in which he borrows the fair shape of Audiart, the hair of Anhes, throat and hands of the viscountess of Chalais, of Midons Aelis of Monfort her swift, free-running speech, together with sundry parts of one lady or another in order to create therefrom an 'ideal lady' who would recompense him for the heartlessness of Maent of Montignac. Possibly, as Ezra Pound suggests, Bertran's poems and adulation are a veil for political machinations. It is still more likely that a great deal of Provençal poetry contains a significance heterodox and even heretical. For though many of the troubadours may not consciously have infused a deeper meaning into their songs, they must have imbibed something of the spiritual atmosphere in which they moved and that was certainly pent with religious unrest and intellectual curiosity.

COURTLY LOVE AND MYSTIC IDEALISM

For one thing, knowledge of the great culture and discoveries of the Arabs must have filtered through from Spain, and with it very possibly, tenets of the Sufist doctrine and its mystic concepts. In this Eastern heresy, an ideal love on earth is a means of obtaining spiritual perfection—an idea which was particularly attractive to poets and painters, and resulted in a form of mystic eroticism that bears a striking analogy to troubadour concepts. For the Sufists, love is a way to Illumination, to Communion with the Absolute. Thus, after long trials, the initiate, reaching the far side of the Bridge of Sinvat is met by a lovely maiden who greets him with the words 'I am thyself.' One is frequently reminded of the unreachable lady, the soul's yearning of the troubadours, and of Dante's Beatrice. Indeed the pattern of the *Divina commedia* may owe some influence to the *Book of nocturnal wanderings* of the Arab mystic Ibu al Arabi.

A typical Sufi concept is that of the 'Garden of Love', which is reflected not only in love lyrics and romances but so frequently plays a part in the exquisite miniatures of the Persian MSS. Courtly lovers and musicians under flowering trees, trelissed gardens (an earthly paradise shut off from the hub-bub of existence), the cistern amongst the flowers—do not constitute the motifs of a concept only too familiar to European courtly love? And do they not point to relationships between East and West that were to be perpetuated, probably unconsciously, into far later times? We recall, for instance, the charming little painting in Frankfurt of the *Paradiesgärtlein* by a German artist of the 15th century—a garden of Paradise in which Mary sits reading under the

trees surrounded by her court of angels and saints, or rather, one would
say, damsels and gallants clad according to the latest fashion of the
time, whilst some make music and some converse and one maiden
fetches water from the well. How vividly it suggests the atmosphere
of *amour courtois*, and yet at the same time our imagination leaps forward to another age, to the paintings of Giorgione. For still, in his *Concert champêtre*, that atmosphere of idealism and dream shrouds the
perfected glory of the flesh, the glamour of rich-hued silk; and in the
noon-drowzed summer heat all breath has ceased, but for the music
of the pipe and strings, and the trickle of water where the girl dips her
crystal pitcher in the well. The trelissed palings, the battlemented walls,
have crumbled and vanished, and yet, wrapped in that magic hush,
this group of youths and women of the Veneta, earthly lovers though
they be, are withheld in a timeless world, inviolate, remote.

What secret, what initiation into hidden rites, apart from the magic
of his own personality, give Giorgione's paintings (we need but recall
his *Tempesta*) that quality of mystery? Many have speculated, none can
really tell.

What cult, what secrets may not underlie the formridden passion of
the troubadours?

COURTLY LOVE AND HERESY

Let us for a moment consider Provençal society of the 12th century.
To those accustomed to connect the Middle Ages with a hide-bound
and tyrannical feudalism, the liberties enjoyed by 12th-century Provence
and its neighbouring lands must seem truly remarkable. Women—at
any rate a good many of them—enjoyed a comparatively emancipated
state. They possessed full hereditary rights, and Ermengarde, countess
of Narbonne, stands out as a Provençal Portia with full powers of juris-
diction over her subjects.

The case of the towns and cities is equally significant. These nomi-
nally stood under the suzerainty of the counts of Toulouse, descendants
of the Visi-Goths and Celto-Iberian race. Their ancestors had played
a great part in the earlier crusades, founding the colony of Tripoli in
Syria, whilst their names are enwoven with the history of Saladin and
that lovely and mysterious Melissande whose dream-image inspired the
troubadour Jaufré Rudel to journey across the sea to this death—a story
retold in verse by Uhland and Heine.

Nevertheless, the cities of southern France, which enjoyed all the aesthetic virtues and vices of a metropolis, possessed liberties reminiscent
of the Roman Republic, electing their own council of *capitulari*, etc.
Rank and dignity were not the hereditary privilege of the feudal lords
and knightly feudal class alone, but were shared by poets and a highly
cultured bourgeoisie.

This enlightened outlook was extended also to religious questions. The Jews lived free from persecution, holding high positions as ministers of finance to the viscounts of Carcassone and Béziers. They possessed, moreover, their own world-famous academies. Heresy was tolerated far and wide. 'No one' cried one of the counts of Foix, 'shall dictate to me in what manner I worship or think of my God.' Yes, in the eyes of the Church, heresy was the canker gnawing at the heart of the South.

We have already touched on various influences, Christian, orthodox, pagan and oriental, which very probably played some part in saping the ideal of Courtly Love. It seems possible that a faith for which thousand were ready to lay down their lives in some way or other also tinged the aesthetic life of the time—a faith which ultimately caused both poor and rich alike to suffer massacres and persecutions that make the night of St Bartholomew and the persecution of the Huguenots pale before them. What is the Albigensian heresy which in the eyes of Rome raged like a pestilence through the land, bringing with it that fearful vengeance which in the space of a few decades wiped one of the freest civilizations from the earth, so that the troubadour Sicard de Marjevols, at sight of the ruin of the lands which once he had beheld in their full glory, burst forth in anguish:

Ai Tolosa e Provensa	Ah Toulouse and Provence,
E la terra d'Agenza	and the land of Agen,
Béziers e Carcassey	Béziers and Carcassonne.
Qui vos vi, qui vos voy.	What were you once,
	what are you now?

The Albigensian heresy embraces both the Waldensian and Cathar sects, themselves forms and branches of older heresies. Whilst the Waldensian appears as a type of Puritanical reform whose somewhat communistic tenets threatened the power and wealth of the Church, the Cathar faith appears to be veiled in a greater mystery. Based on dualistic Manichean beliefs and on the gospel of St John, the gospel of Love, it regards the world as the work of Lucifer. For the Cathars, hell existed on earth alone, a hell through which we must pass through countless reincarnations on earth and from star to star until our sins are retrieved by our own suffering, and purified, we merge in the Divine Essence, in God.

We are reminded perhaps of Indian concepts, and indeed Indian miniatures of ladies visiting a female hermit, though of a far later date, make the parallels more evident. For female Cathar hermits also frequented the mountains of the Pyrenees, whilst the pallor of the Indian's skin reminds one how during the Albigenisan persecution, a pale skin (considered a sure sign of fasting and vegetarianism) sufficed for man or woman to be suspected of heresy!

What is more, in considering the flesh as Satan's the Cathars were led to a scorn of all earthly ties, including that of marriage. Free or adulterous love, it was argued, is no more sinful than marriage, perhaps less so as it has fewer materialistic ends in view, and has not as its aim the propagation of the species—a sinful burden of the flesh.

It is clear that the Church must of necessity see in such teaching but anarchy—a complete disruption of Christian society. But can we not also see something else? These tenets seem to betray direct bearing on the cult of *Minne* and the *Amour Courtois*. It is not comprehensible that the Cathar chivalry of Montségur (a sort of Cathar Gralsburg or Mont Salvat of the Pyrenees) was able to find a happy analogy between the earthly religion of Love and the Cathar faith, the Church of Love— the more so as their church itself is founded on a feminine principle— a sort of paredia, the mother of Logos, the Mary of the pre-Christian theogonists?

In addition to which, take the parallels between the Cathar faith and Courtly Love—scorn of marriage, the pursuit of a love unreachable, ideal; above all a yearning for complete transcendance of the flesh. The symbolism itself, the one and only kiss which the worshipped lady bestowed on her troubadour, suggest an earthly analogy to the kiss of the *consolamentum*, the Cathar's one and only sacrament. The secrecy, the veiled language, the *trobar clus*, seem doubly significant as but a mask for a forbidden cult.

Courtly Love, then, may really, for some of its exponents, have had this heretical meaning, in all sincerity or just as the expression of a fashionable craze. For others it may have provided a vessel for the outpouring of a vaguer idealism. To others again, it may have meant no more than sensual desire. For in Courtly Love, the limits of spirit and flesh are as uncertain as in the love lyrics and romances of the East, with their inebriated sublimation of fleshly love, or in the exquisite miniatures of Sufist Persia, to which we have already referred, and those Indian MS paintings where Radha waits for her lover Krishna under the stars and the spectral trees, even as Iseult waited for Tristan.

We have spoken of spiritual parallels to orthodox ideas—St Bernard, etc.—of classic and oriental influences. But in the south, heresy, as represented by Catharism, was certainly a potent and irresisitble force, rousing a whole civilization to a spiritual intoxication which (though it ultimately brought so terrible a doom) first gave birth not only to a perfected art, but sublimated reality to the stature of myth. Even now the shepherds of the Pyrenees tell of Esclarmonde, who rescued the Cathar relics at the fall of Montségur, and then transformed into a dove, flew to the far mountains of Asia—an Esclarmonde into whose legendary person are fused the qualities of her three real namesakes: Esclarmonde of Foix, the Cathar priestess; Esclarmonde d'Alion, the passionate; and Esclarmonde de Perelha, who died for heresy at the stake. In this strange and lovely figure, we can find a perfect embodiment of troubadour idealism and romance.

Regarded in this light, as an expression of spiritual yearning, a dream of absolute transcendance, the strange cult of Courtly Love, the unfulfillable yearning of the troubadour gains a deeper and indeed far more lasting significance. And is it not feasible that it should have blossomed at first particularly in the south of France, the home of the Albigensian heresy, that transcendental cult? But further, it is also comprehensible that in ever-varying forms that yearning should persist in European literature even till modern times, bursting forth in its most violent and unbridled form in the *Tristan* of Wagner. 'Do I hear the Light?' Tristan's dying words express the ecstasy of absolute transcendence in the sense almost of St John of the Cross—a disembodiment, a disintegration of all finite form in Supernal Light—the light that has no likeness to that of the deluding day, at dawn of which Tristan, discovered at his secret tryst, so poignantly exclaims: 'The barren day— for the last time. . .' far echo of the *alba*, the dawn-song of the troubadours.

With Wagner, the mystic quality of passion, the root of Courtly Love is blatantly revealed. For most of us today (if we except the music) too much, far too much, is said.

In the *Tristan* of the mediaeval German poet Gottfried von Strassburg in which the courtly element is fused with Celtic motifs to a romance of perfect form, all is veiled, is secret. Superficially, Gottfried's tone is graceful, fluent, lucid, but somehow darkened like the wave by the underswell—reminding one almost of Mozart's music where frivolity seems ever to hover on the boundary of death. For beneath— what is it Gottfried is really telling his *edeliu herzen,* his rare hearts, his *fins cuers leals* but that only through yearning, through heart's distress can they reach the true world, the true life across whose threshold Tristan and Iseult are borne in the inebriation of the love-potion—a symbol as it were of their initiation into that secret realm in which alone we may apprehend its mystery? Henceforth, these two can only live consumed by *diu endelôse herzenôt*, an unquenchable yearning for the consummation of that mystery which through the power of passion they have apprehended—a yearning for complete transcendence.

How charmingly, though in a lighter, truly courtly way, that yearing is expressed by the fragile passion-attenuated figures in the illumination of a French MS of the 13th century (Fr. 2186). Here too we see the lovers as King Marc finds them, asleep in the forest, divided by Tristan's great sword. In the mediaeval poem, even this adventure seems to have a deeper significance, for according to the courtly ideal, only through repeated suffering and division, even self-inflicted parting, can the flame of love be kept burning till at last it has consumed away utterly the veil of the flesh.

Alas, Gottfried's poem lies unfinished, but we can be pretty sure that, unlike Wagner, he would have kept to the supremely tragic end, their divided death—drawing from it a deeper significance—that in the flesh there is no absolute union.

What is Gottfried von Strassburg really invoking in *Tristan* but a religion of Love—a secret mysticism—intimated only, and perfectly fused with the romance? What is the poem to us but a confession, at once angelic and diabolic, that mercilessly penetrates into each nerve and fibre, through every ravishment and anguish known to the heart of man, and yet again retreats unfathomable, inviolable, behind that exquisite and profoundly equivocal form?

How wonderfully Gottfried veils the secrets of the spirits in the exquisite frailties of the flesh. With what intuitive sense of form he makes word and sound themselves call forth a magic timelessness in the secret grotto of Love, where for one brief moment the lovers apprehend the consummation of their yearning.

Behind and before them, the wilderness, the precipices real and figurative of the apparent world. For this island of green meadows and flowers and streams, this earthly Paradise, is divided from the real world by a tract of wilderness and rock. It is *inclusus*, even as the Sufist garden of love or the garden of Mary's Paradise are fenced off from the world by a wall or by a hedge of blossoming thorns from the world of reality— rather say from the world of actuality, the world of transient appearances.

Often and in ever-varying shapes this Paradise, this mystic garden, appears in literature and art. Research into the subject will show that it may be traced far afield to Asia and relics of the ancient Mazdaian religion of Iran. The influence may often have been quite unconscious though we must not forget the part played by the Crusades and above all the Manichean and Cathar heresies as mediators between East and West. Here, I can only hope to point out possible paths of research and above all to suggest the deeper nature of an ideal that at first sight may seem incomprehensible and absurd. To many, the later and degenerate examples of the *Amour Courtois* (the *Roman de la Rose* and its derivatives) are far more familiar than the earlier stages of Courtly Love which we have been discussing here. Soon, all too soon, the secret house is violated, the mystery darkly imprisoned in the formal pattern of the *trobar clus*, is half revealed to the mundane light of day. No longer the monopoly of an initiated chivalry, the religion of love is secularized only to be tied by a new and more rigid constraint—the strait-jacket of allegory. The infinite bourn of yearning is plumbed and nicely regulated, guided into stony channels, clearly labelled with symbolic names, whilst the imagination, safely leashed, can exhaust itself trying to find the clue through a labyrinth of allegorical detail—a process not empty of delight when Chaucer leads us by the hand.

In countless late allegories of Love, the deeper sense is practically forgotten; often they appear as quasi-scientific treatises ornamented with every device of classic learning as in the quaint 15th-century French MS called *Love's Game of Chess*, where the walled garden now harbours classical goddesses, where Venus presides with her looking glass amongst the geometrical flowerbeds, and the chatelaine is Dame Nature. Or on another page, we meet Father Neptune with his bodyguard of trumpeting fishes; here again, three pig-tailed and decidedly flat-footed Graces foreshadow Botticelli, whilst Apollo appears on the scene in a fashionable mediaeval oufit, complete with scarlet cloak, troubadour harp and—white gloves! But the most intriguing of these late allegories is perhaps the *Cueur d'amour épris*, the work of that strange aesthete of a king, René of Anjou, whose knights rode into the lists clad as shepherds and bearing crooks instead of spears. It tells of the dream-like quest of the heart for the far island where lies imprisoned the lady of his desire, but its greatest attraction lies perhaps in the wonderful illuminations of the MS in Vienna, whose rich mysterious colouring and twilit scenes seem at once to symbolize a last flickering of the courtly ideal in mediaeval France, and to presage the surrealist dream of modern times.

To the well known persistence of the troubadour ideal in Italy in the *dolce stil nuovo* with Dante, Guido Cavalcanti and the early Italian poets I can but allude in passing; likewise to the far-spreading influence of Petrarca on the North and West. Only to one late and probably quite unconscious echo of that ideal would I refer in more detail here.

Amidst the voluptuous splendour of the Renaissance, amidst the masques and extravaganzas, the echoing fanfares of Medicean arrogance and pride, the dream of Courtly Love seems to flit like a ghost, made palpable for a brief moment in the fragile beauty of a girl—Simonetta Vespucci, Madonna or Venus. For seven years her being pervaded that court, indefinable yet inextinguishable; at twenty-three she was dead.

Already to the painter Piero de Cosimo, her fatality must have appeared so imminent that he could only match her profile against the changing clouds. Did he perhaps unconsciously steep himself in the intricate coils of the jewelled tresses and the allegory of the snake to divert from the unbearable clarity of her vision?

How many brought her homage—poets and painters and courtiers alike; foremost among them, Giuliano Medici, brother of the great Lorenzo himself—a homage so remote somehow from that inspired by the great heroines and courtesans of the age, Lucrezia Borgia, Diana Capelli, that the flaw in the apparently all-sufficing self-possession of the Renaissance seems suddenly revealed, and even the tournament

that Giuliana held in Simonetta's honour appears at root but a measure by which he sought to compensate his own torturing sense of inadequacy by heroics in the field of action, whilst the old unquenchable
yearning breaks like an old wound beneath the panoply of pagan and
humanistic conceit.

Even the verses of the pedantic Poliziano—the *Giostra* composed to
celebrate that very tournament, seem suddenly drenched in dew when
he describes how Giuliano, speeding far afield on the hunt, comes to
that sheltered grove where the Graces weave their white limbs in the
dance, and Flora scatters her blossoms over the sward. Where the years
have ceased their tireless course and Zephyrus blows in vain—revived
dream of a lost Paradise, that land of heart's desire transported now
to classic groves—Garden of Love where Simonetta reigns.

Did not Bottgicelli discover her there, he who had seen her always,
mirrored in the wistful eyes of his Virgins, the equivocal glance of Aphrodite herself—till now there was left of her mortality only Beauty's ghost
wrapped about in a crimson cloak whilst all her spirit had suffered trans-
mutation into the Spring?

So he painted her after her death—as Primavera—and unknowing
made visible for us, even today, that quality of eternal renewal her being
had possessed on earth for men. And here we have indeed still something of the yearning of the troubadours, of Courtly Love, the faith
that through the mystery of love we are purged, that in that death to
our former selves we are born anew.

In 1476, two years after Simonetta's death, on the very anniversary
of that day, 26 April, Giuliano was murdered by the Pazzi in the choir
of Santa Maria dei Fiori in Florence. Years later, Botticelli, penniless
and deserted, was laid to rest close beside Simonetta's grave.

There we must all but close our swift survey of Courtly Love. What
is so estranging to us in its mediaeval manifestations is perhaps its seemingly snobbish and artificial element—the adoration of the distant, the
high-born, unapproachable *dame*. But this seems really only a form
dictated by the age, a temporal mask for man's unabatable yearning
for the absolute. May it not be that reaching towards a goal which in
the body could have no fulfilment, he dreamed of outreaching all final-
ity, all earthly purpose, thus despite his abject avowals, unconsciously
reviving Plato's concept (recently given new life by Rainer Maria Rilke)—
that the lover excels the beloved?

Must such an ideal that harbours within it the danger of an almost
mystic sublimation of self lead to a deification of passion that threatens
Western Civilization with the doom predicted by Denis de Rougement
in his book *Passion and Society*? Are we already shaping a more con-
structive and objective concept of Love? We cannot enter on those speculations now, and in addition to the problems we have touched on here,
I would only recall the richness of that literature to which that Courtly

dream gave birth, in all its variety of form, from the lyrics of the troubadours and Gottfried's *Tristan*, to Shakespeare's *Romeo and Juliet*, from the *Vita Nuova* of Dante to the poetry of Hölderlin, Novalis and rilke. [cf. A. Closs, *The genius of the german lyric, an historical survey of its formal and metaphysical values*, London, 1938; *Hölderlin Gedichte*, London, 1942 and 1944; and *Tristan and Iseult*, Oxford, 1946.]

Lastly and on a lower plane too, one may argue: often enough the dream was violated: the high ideal lent itself all too easily to conventionalization, to travesty and vulgar suggestion. There are those who see in the *amour courtois* no more than a convenient excuse for adultery, and dispense with the troubadours as an immoral, dissolute lot of fellows. Certainly to some it will have meant no more than a frivolous adventure into the realms of Love. But who can say where begin and end the boundary of spirit and flesh?

In one and the same character even, desire will take on varied and conflicting shapes. The *Vita Nuova* of Dante led to his *Divina Commedia*. To how many the images of profane and heavenly Love became at last more than an allegory—along what labyrinthine paths that quest can lead one, through what thickets of mystic rose or rue; and once perhaps out of the densest shadow may gleam the whiteness of the unicorn; in the distance the horns, and the hounds baying in pursuit— that strange mysterious beast. See, he is ever at his lady's side, with the lion, in waiting where she stands or sits on her velvet island of grass, and all the animals enwoven in the meshes of the silk. And now her handmaiden has brought her casket of jewels. Which should she choose?

The pearls drop through her hand—day in, day out. When will he come? But the banners stand hoisted, the brocaded curtain of the tent is drawn apart, and on its azure ground the little flames quiver unquenched. 'A mon seul désir.'

What are they all about, these deep-rose tapestries of the Dame à Licorne in the Cluny museum in Paris that Rainer Maria Rilke loved? Each one of us perhaps must find it out for himself, and even Dante had to struggle through an earthly Purgatory before he won to the sight of his divine Beatrice;

Guardami ben,	Look at me well truly
ben son ben son Beatrice	truly I am Beatrice

So at least she greets him from the chariot of fire as though implying therewith a mocking rebuke for his long erring before Divine Grace can restore his failint heart. For is the *Visto Dei* really at last attainable to earthly eyes? In vision perhaps? But which of us can follow Dante on his spirit's flight? And in our own inadequacy we wish perhaps that in that far-off mystic realm upon the threshold of the Empyrean, his

Beatrice may still wear a shadow of her earthly frailty, and on her face through all that cold inviolable radiance, a flicker of the incalculable smile of Eve.

Chapter 10.

The Grail & the Rites of Adonis

by Jessie L. Weston

Jessie L. Weston was probably the most influential of the early 20th century scholars of the Arthurian legends. Her many books and papers pushed the frontiers of understanding and interest further than ever before, and caused people to look afresh at the magic country of mediaeval romance. Her best known book, *From Ritual to Romance*, influenced a whole generation of writers, including the poet T. S. Eliot, whose magnificent Grail poem *The Waste Land* made great use of Miss Weston's work.

She was the first to set forth the argument for an understanding of the Grail stories as ritually-based texts, and allowed herself to be indebted to such esoteric luminaries as A. E. Waite and G. R. S. Meade. In the postscript of *From Ritual to Romance* she proposed an analogy between the hallows of the Grail—spear, cup, sword and shield—and the suits of the Tarot—an idea which has been explored by almost every major esoteric writer on the subject ever since.[1]

The Grail & The Rites of Adonis is an early work, written during the foundation of Miss Weston's ideas. It draws inspiration from Classical myth and draws some exciting conclusions into the origins of the Grail cult, which, if allusions to Britain as an island once sacred to Apollo are to be believed, contains more than a grain of truth.

Much of J. L. Weston's writings remain out of print and hard to come by, but they are all worth searching out for the clarity of thought and openness to unusual influences which suggest so many new approaches to the study of the Grail.

⌘

In offering these remarks on the subject of the Grail origins, I should wish to be understood as seeking, rather than tendering, information. The result of my researches into the *Perceval* legend has been to cause me to form certain opinions as to the sources of the Grail story, which the exigencies of space, and the character of the *Studies* as a whole, prevented me from setting forth fully in the published volume. At the same time these conclusions bore so directly on folklore researches that I was strongly impressed with the desirability of bringing them to the attention of trained folklorists, that I might have the advantage of their criticism and judgement in finally formulating my theory. Not that I can claim to be the first to give expression to such views. Long since Simrock, in his translation of the *Parzival*, and Professor Martin, in his *Zur Gralsage Untersuchungen* (1880),[2] arrived at very similar conclusions, but at that time the critical material at their disposal was scanty. We lacked the illuminating labours of Mannhardt and his disciple, Dr J. G. Frazer. We had but one *Perceval* text, and that an extremely bad one, at our disposal, and in consequence the results obtained, though interesting and stimulating, were hardly convincing.

Hitherto, in criticizing the Grail legend, we have been under the grave disadvantage of uncertainty as to the relative position of the extant versions of the story; we were not sure which of the varying forms represented most faithfully the original *données* of the tale. It is obvious that this was a serious hindrance. You cannot safely theorize as to the original form of a story while you are still in doubt as to which of certain widely differing versions is the older. Inasmuch as, in point of MS date, the *Perceval* of Chrétien de Troyes is the oldest of our Grail romances, the tendency has been to regard the story as told by him as the most nearly approaching the original, and to argue from that; although the vague and unsatisfactory details there given left it open to conjecture whether the author were dealing with a tradition already formed, or with one in process of formation.

Now, owing to recent discoveries, the standpoint has been shifted back, and we know that the earliest attainable Grail story is that of which not Perceval but Gawain was the hero, and the authorship of which is ascribed not to Chrétien de Troyes, but to Bleheris the Welshman. The date at which Bleheris lived is uncertain, but his identity alike with the Bledhericus referred to by Giraldus Cambrensis, and the Bréri quoted as authority for the *Tristan* of Thomas, has been frankly accepted by the leading French and American scholars; so far the Germans have preserved silence on the subject.[3]

The passage in Giraldus is unfortunately very vague; he simply refers to Bledhericus as '*famosus ille fabulator*', and says he lived 'a little before our time', words which may mean anything. Giraldus may be using the editorial 'we', and may mean 'a little before my time', which, as he was writing in the latter half of the twelfth century, might imply that Bledhericus lived in the earlier half. But he may also have used the pronoun quite indefinitely; as M. Ferdinand Lot, with whom I discussed the question, remarked, 'it may mean anything from ten to a hundred years; we might say that Bonaparte lived "a little before our time"'. When we take into consideration the fact that only three direct references to Bleheris, or Blihis, as a source, have been preserved, while the name is more frequently found in the duplicated form of[4] Bleo-Bleheris, Blihos-Bliheris, or Bliobliheri, and generally attached to a knight of Arthur's court, it seems most probable that he lived at a period sufficiently remote to allow of the precise details concerning his life and work to become obscured, while the tradition of his close connection with Arthurian romance was retained. In any case this much is certain, and this is what principally concerns us, his version of the Grail

story is older than that of Chrétien, and we are justified in seeking for
indications of origin in the story as told by him rather than in the version of the younger poet.

This is the Bleheris Grail story, as given by Wauchier de Denain, in
his continuation of the *Perceval*.[5]

Arthur, at the conclusion of his successful expedition against Chastel
Orguellous, has given the queen *rendez-vous* at certain cross roads,
marked by four pine trees. Here the court awaits him. One evening
the queen is playing chess at the entrance of her pavilion when a stranger
knight rides past, and fails to offer any salutation. Indignant at the
apparent discourtesy, the queen sends Kay after him to command his
return. Kay, as is his wont, carries out his commission in so ungracious
and insulting a manner that he is overthrown for his pains, and returns
to court with an exaggerated account of the knight's bearing and language. Gawain is then dispatched on the same errand, and, overtak-
ing the stranger, courteously invites his return, but is told that he rides
on a quest that will brook no delay, and which none but he may achieve;
nevertheless, he thinks it possible that Gawain, whose identity he has
learned, might succeed. On his return he will gladly pay his respects
to the queen.

Gawain, however, by soft words, persuades him to return, pledging
his honour that he shall in wise suffer by the delay. They turn back,
but scarcely have they reached the tents when the knight, with a loud
cry, falls forward, wounded to death by a javelin cast by an unseen hand.
with his dying breath he bids Gawain don his armour, and mount his
steed, which shall carry him to the destined goal. Gawain, furious at
the slur cast on his honour by this breach of his safe-conduct, does
as requested, and, leaving the dead body to the care of the queen,
departs at once.

Through the night he rides, and all the next day, till he has passed
the borders of Arthur's land, and at nightfall, wearied out, he finds
himself in a waste land by the sea-shore. A causeway, bordered on either
side by trees, their roots in the water, runs out from the land, and at
the further end Gawain sees a light, as of a fire. The road is so dark,
and the night so stormy, he would fain delay till morning, but the steed,
taking the bit in its teeth, dashes down the pathway, and eventually
he reaches the entrance to a lighted hall. Here he is at first received
as one long-expected, but, having unhelmed, is seen to be a stranger,
and left alone. In the centre of the hall stands a bier, on which lies a
body, covered with a rich pall of crimson silk, a broken sword on the
breast, and four censers at the four corners of the bier. A procession
of clergy enters, headed by a silver cross, and followed by many folk.
Vespers for the dead are sung amid general lamentation, and Gawain
is again left alone. He now sees on the daïs a Lance, fixed in a silver
socket, from which a stream of blood flows continuously into a golden

cup, and thence, by a channel, is carried out of the hall. Servants prepare the tables for a meal, and the King of the castle, entering, greets
Gawain kindly, and seats him beside him on the daïs. The butlers pour
wine into the cups, and from a doorway there issues *the rich Grail,*
which serves them; otherwise there is *nor serjant nor seneschal,* and
Gawain marvels much at the service of the Grail, for now 'tis here, and
now there, and for fear and wonder he scarce dare eat. After supper
the King leads Gawain to the bier, and, handing him the broken sword,
bids him resolder it. This he fails to do, and the King, shaking his head,
tells him he may not accomplish the quest on which he has come;
nevertheless, he has shewn great valour in coming thither, and he may
ask what he will; he shall be answered. Gawain asks of the Lance: 'tis
the Lance of Longinus, with it the side of the Saviour was pierced, as
he hung on the Cross, and it shall remain where it now is, and bleed,
till the Day of Doom. The King will tell who it is who lies on the bier,
of the stroke by which he met his death, and the destruction brought
on the land thereby; but as he speaks, weeping the while, Gawain falls
asleep, and wakes to find himself upon the seashore, his steed fastened
to a rock beside him, and all trace of the castle vanished. Wondering
much, he mounts his steed, and rides through a land no longer waste,
while all the folk he meets bless and curse him; for, by asking concerning the Lance, has has brought the partial restoration of fruitfulness.
Had he also asked of the Grail, the curse would have been entirely
removed.

Now, there are certain points in this story which cannot fail to strike
those familiar with the Grail legend. Who are the two dead men of
the tale, the knight so mysteriously slain and the Body on the bier?
We never learn. Nor do we ever hear the nature of the quest—Was it
to avenge the dead knight of the castle? Was it to break the spell upon
the land? Manessier, who about fifty years later brought the *Perceval*
compilation to a final conclusion, gives, indeed, what purports to be
a continuation of the tale. Gawain is here besought by the sister of the
knight slain in his company to come to her aid against a foe, but the
story is *banale* to the last degree. There are points of contact with other
versions: the maiden's name is '*la sore pucele*', the name Chrétien gives
to the Grail King's niece; her foe is King Mangons, or Amangons, the
name of the oppressor of the maidens in the *Elucidation,* to which we
shall refer presently; but if there be any original connection with the
Bleheris version, that connection has become completely obscured.
Manessier, too, makes no attempt at solving the mystery of the Body
upon the bier: certain scholars have indeed identified the slain man
with Goon-Desert, or Gondefer, the brother of Manessier's Grail King,
whose death by treachery Perceval avenges. But this identification is
purely arbitrary; there is no bier in Manessier, it is, in fact, distinctively a feature of the *Gawain* version.

The connection of the wasting of the land with the death of the knight, if knight he were, is also uncertain; indeed this is a part of the story which appears to have been designedly left in obscurity—it is at this point that Gawain falls asleep. I am tempted to believe that those who told the tale were themselves at a loss here. Then the Grail is no Christian relic, it acts simply as a food-providing talisman, coming and going without visible agency. It is called the *rich*, not the *holy*, Grail. Nor does the explanation given of the Lance agree with the description; the stream of blood, which pours continuously from the weapon, and is carried out of the hall, whither, we are no told, can have no connection with the carefully-guarded relic of the *Saint Sang*. In truth, we may say without hesitation that the whole machinery of the story is definitely non-Christian, and that the explanation of its peculiarities must be sought outside the range of ecclesiastical tradition. At the same time certain of these features are repeated in a persistent fashion, even in the most definitely ecclesiasticized versions; a peculiarity which, I think, justifies the supposition that they form a part of the original Grail tradition.

Now it has seemed to me that an explanation of the most characteristic features of our story may be found in the suggestion that they are a survival, misunderstood and imperfectly remembered, of a form of Nature worship closely allied to, if not identical with, the Rites of Adonis so exhaustively studied by Dr Frazer in *The Golden Bough*. It will be remembered that the essence of these rites was the symbolic representation of the annual processes of Nature, the sequence and transition of the seasons. The god, Adonis, or Tammuz, or whatever he was called in the land where the rites were celebrated, typified the vivifying principle of vegetation; his death was mourned as the death of vegetation in winter, his restoration to life was hailed as its restoration in spring. An effigy representing the dead god was honoured with all the rites of mourning, and subsequently committed to the waves. Women especially played so large a part in these rites that an Arabic writer of the tenth century refers to the festival as El-Bugât, '*the festival of the Weeping Women*'.[6]

The central *motif* of the *Gawain* Grail-story is, I submit, identical with the central idea of the Adonis rites—a death, and failure of vegetation caused by that death. Both here and in the version given by the curious German poem of *Diû Crône*, where Gawain is again the Grail hero, we are told that the wasting of the land was brought about by the *Dolorous Stroke*. Thus the central figure, the Body on the bier, whose identity is never made clear, would in this view represent the dead god; the bleeding Lance, the weapon with which he was done to death (I think it more probable that the *Dolorous Stroke* was dealt by a Lance or Spear, as in the *Balin and Balan* story, than by a sword).

If we accept this view we can, I think, explain the origin of that mys-

terious figure of the Grail legend, the Maimed King. The fact that this
central figure was at the same time dead and alive must, when the real
meaning of the incidents had become obscured, and the story, imperfectly remembered, was told simply as a story, have been a source of
perplexity to the tellers. An easy way out of the difficulty—it was a very
real difficulty—would be to represent the king, or god, as desperately
wounded. That such an idea was in the minds of the romance writers
appears, I think, from the peculiar version of *Diû Crône*, where, when
Gawain has asked concerning the Grail, the Maimed King and his attendants vanish at daybreak; they were dead, but preserved a semblance
of life till the question was put. If the *Gawain* versions really represent
the older, and primary, group, it is possible that this particular rendering really preceded the Maimed King version, though in the form
preserved it is combined with it.

Again, in the very curious and unique *Merlin* MS, No. 337 of the
French MSS of the *Bibliothèque Nationale*, we find that Perceval is called
the son of the widow lady, while his father, the Maimed King, is yet
alive, and it is explained that, being desperately wounded, and only
to be healed when the quest is achieved, he is as good as dead, and
his wife may be reckoned a widow. These two instances will suffice to
shew that the transformation of the Body on the bier into the Maimed
King on the litter, is neither impossible nor unnatural. The two are really
one and the same.

Students of the Grail cycle will hardly need to be reminded that the
identity of the Maimed King is a hopeless puzzle. He may be the Fisher
King, or the Fisher King's father, or have no connection with either,
as in the Evalach-Mordrains story. He may have been wounded in battle, or accidentally, or wilfully, or by supernatural means, as the punish-
ment of too close an approach to spiritual mysteries. A proof of the
confusion which ultimately resulted from these conflicting versions is
to be found in the *Merlin* MS above referred to, where not only Perceval's father but two others are Maimed Kings, and all three sit at the
Table of the Grail. If such confusion existed in the mind of the writers,
no wonder that we, the readers, find the path of Grail criticism a rough
and intricate one! Probably the characters of the Maimed King and the
Fisher King were originally distinct, the Maimed King representing,
as we have suggested, the god, in whose honour the rites were performed; the Fisher King, who, whether maimed or not, invariably acts
as host, representing the Priest. It would be his office to preside at the
ritual feast, and at the initiation of the neophyte, offices which would
well fit in with the character of Host. Here, the name of Fisher King
is no given to him, but in certain texts which interpolate the history
of Joseph of Arimathea he is identified with that Monarch. It will readily
be understood that when the idea that the god was alive gained possession of the minds of those who told the story, there would be two

lords of the castle, and they would find some difficulty in distinguish-
ing the rôle of the one from that of the other. We may note that in this
(i.e. the Bleheris) version, in that of Wauchier de Denain at the conclusion of his section of the *Perceval*, in the Prose *Lancelot*, and in the
Queste, the Host is not maimed.

Again, this proposed origin would explain the wasting of the land,
the mysterious *Curse of Logres*, which is referred to alike in earlier and
later versions, and of which no explanation is ever given. As we saw
above, the essence of the Rites was the symbolic representation of the
processes of Nature. The festival of the death and revival of the god
took place at the Spring solstice; it was an objective parable, finding
its interpretation in the awakening of Nature from her winter sleep.
Here the wasting of the land is in some mysterious manner connected
with the death or wounding of the central figure; the successful accom-
plishment of the Grail quest brings about either the restoration of the
land to fruitfulness, or the healing of the King (Chrétien and Wolfram,
for example, have no Wasted Land). Thus the object of the Quest would
appear to be one with that of the Adonis-ritual.

This wasting of the land is found in three *Gawain* Grail-stories, but
by Bleheris, the version of *Chastel Merveilleus*, and *Diû Crône*; it is
found in one *Perceval* text, the Gerbert continuation. Thus, briefly, the
object of the Rites is the restoration of Vegetation, connected with the
revival of the god; the object of the Quest is the same, but connected
with the restoration to health of the King.[7]

I have before noted the fact that the role played by women in these
rites was of such importance that eventually it gave a name to the Festival. In the Notes to my translation of three visits paid by Gawain to
the Grail Castle, I remarked on the persistent recurrence in these stories of a weeping maiden or maidens, the cause of whose grief is never
made clear. In *Diû Crône*, where, as we have seen, the Maimed King
and his court have but the semblance of life and are in very truth dead,
the Grail-bearer and her companions are the only living beings in the
castle, and their grief is in a measure, comprehensible; they desire the
breaking of the spell which binds them to this uncanny company. In
what, in the *Perceval Studies*, I have designated as the *Chastel Merveilleus* version, a version midway between that of Bleheris and of Chrétien, there is but one weeping maiden, the Grail-bearer. In the curious
interpolation of the Heralds' College MS, when the broken sword is
restored to the Fisher King, he mentions among the results of the successful achievement of the quest, that the hero shall know why the
maiden weeps. I doubt very much whether the writer of the lines himself knew the reason! In the visit paid by Bohort to castle Corbenic,
it is Elaine, daughter of King Pelles, who weeps, because, being no longer
a maiden, she may no longer be Grail-bearer. As she is about to become
the mother of the Grail winner, and knows to what honour her son

Figure 7: 'She thought him a passing goodly knight on horse back' by
Ann Alexander.

is predestined, the explanation is not convincing; but there had to be
a weeping maiden in the story. The most curious instance of the persistence of this part of the original tradition is to be found in Gawain's
visit to Corbenic, in the prose *Lancelot,* where he sees no one, but twelve
maidens kneeling at the closed door of the Grail chamber, weeping
bitterly, and praying to be delivered from their torment. But the dwellers
in Castle Corbenic, so far from being in torment, have all that heart
can desire, and, moreover, the honour of being guardians of the (here)
sacred and most Christian relic, the Holy Grail.[8]

Now, in the light of the parallels already cited, is it not at least possible that these weeping maidens, who wail so mysteriously through the
Grail story, are a survival of, and witness to, the original source of that
story, that they are the mourning women of the Adonis ritual, the
'Women weeping for Tammuz'?

This interpretation would also explain the constant stress laid upon
the *general* mourning, even when the reason for this mourning appears
inadequate, as e.g. in the *Parzival.* Here we are told that the appearance of the bleeding Lance is the signal for such lamentation that 'The
folk of thirty kingdoms could scarce have bemoaned them more', Bk.
v. l. 130. Here certainly the Lance is that with which the king has been
wounded, but the *folk* of the castle are in no way affected, there is no
wasting of the land.

Again, in *Peredur,* at the appearance of the Lance all fell to wailing and lamentation, but here there seems to be no connection between the Lance and the wound of the king, which latter is the work of the sorceresses of Gloucester. If the original source of the story is to be found in the Adonis ritual, and if the mourning which is so marked a feature of that ritual be associated, as Drs Robertson Smyth and Farnell have suggested, rather with the death of the god than with the consequent failure of vegetation,[9] then we might expect to find the association of the mourning with the weapon which originally dealt the fatal blow to persist in versions which had dropped out the (originally) companion feature of the Wasted Land.

We have thus the following important points of contact between the Adonis ritual and the story of the Visit to the Grail Castle: the waste land; the slain king (or knight); the mourning, with special insistence on the part played by women; and the restoration of fertility; while certain minor points, such as the crimson covering of the bier, the incense, and the presence, in certain versions, of doves as agents in the mysterious ceremonies also find their parallel in the same ritual.[10]

To put the matter briefly, the scene enacted in the presence of the chance visitor to the Grail Castle involved the chief incidents of the Adonis rites. I would submit that whereas the presence of an isolated feature might be due to chance, that of a complete and harmonious group, embracing at once the ceremonies and the object of the cult, can scarcely be so explained.

To go a step further. Originally I entitled this paper *The Grail and the Mysteries of Adonis*. For the word *mysteries* I have now substituted *ritual*, in view of the perfectly well-grounded objection that, in classical times, the worship of Adonis was not carried on in secret. Nevertheless, I am disposed to believe that the word *mysteries* might, without impropriety, be used in connection with the celebration of these rites when in later ages Christianity had become the faith 'in possession', and the votaries of an older cult performed their rites under the ban of ecclesiastical disapproval. Much, of course, depends upon the character of the cult; the Adonis worship was in its essence a 'Life' cult, the life of the god ensuring the life of vegetation, and that in its turn the life of man; it is obvious that such a cult might possess an esoteric as well as an exoteric significance. To the ordinary worshipper the ritual would be an object-lesson, setting forth the actual processes of Nature, to the initiate it would be the means of imparting other, and less innocent, teaching as to the sources of life.

This much is certain: the Grail is perpetually treated as something strange, mysterious, awe-inspiring; its secrets are on no account to be rashly approached or lightly spoken of; he runs great danger who does so. Such terms could hardly be applied to the Adonis rites under ordinary conditions, and yet, as we have seen, the Grail story presents such a striking identity of incident with these rites that a connection between the two seems practically certain. We have to seek for some explanation which will preserve this connection while at the same time accounting for the presence of certain 'occult' features in the tale.

The explanation surely lies in the fact suggested above, that the Adonis cult was essentially a Life cult, and, as such, susceptible of strange developments. Dr Frazer has laid stress on the close connection which, in the minds of primitive worshippers, subsisted between the varying forms of life: 'They commonly believed that the tie between the animal and vegetable world was even closer than it really is—to them the principle of life and fertility, whether animal or vegetable, was one and indivisible'.[11] Dulaure, while assigning the same *origin* as does Dr Frazer to the ritual, definitely classes the worship of Adonis among those cults which 'assumed in process of time a distinctly "carnal" character'.[12]

The Lance and Cup which form the central features of the imagery of our story are also met with as 'Phallic' symbols, and I am strongly of opinion that many of the most perplexing features[13] of the legend are capable of explanation on the theory that behind the ordinary simple 'Vegetation' symbolism there lay something which justified so learned and acute a scholar as the late Professor Heinzel, whose works are a veritable mine of learning and ingenuity, in regarding our records of the Visit to the Grail Castle as records of an initiation *manquée*. Long since, in his study on the Old French Grail romances (*Die Alt-Französische Gral Romanen*, 1891) he suggested that the failure to put the question was equivalent to a refusal on the part of the neophyte to submit to the ordeal,[14] but, owing probably to the form in which he cast the results of his researches, much of their value has been obscured.

Let us note first, that whatever else changes in the story, the essential framework remains the same. Always the castle is found by chance; always the hero beholds marvels he does not comprehend; always he fails to fulfil the test which would have qualified him to receive the explanation of those marvels; always he recognizes his fault too late, when the opportunity has passed beyond recall; and only after long trial is it again granted to him. Let us clear our minds once and for all from the delusion that the Grail story is *primarily* the story of a quest; it is that *secondarily*. In its primary form it is the romance of a lost opportunity; for always, and in every instance, the first visit connotes failure; it is to redress that failure that the quest is undertaken. So esentially is this a part of the story that it survives even in the Galahad version; that immaculate and uninteresting hero does not fail, of course; but neither does he come to the Grail castle for the first time when he presides at the solemn and symbolic feast; he was brought up there, but has left it before the Quest begins; like his predecessors, Gawain and Perceval, he goes forth from the castle in order to return.

Now, let us accept for the nonce Professor Heinzel's suggestion, but for the word *refusal* substitute *failure,* and recognizing that the incidents related rest upon real objective facts, we may, perhaps, hazard a guess at the cause of this failure. In the Bleheris story we have seen that the hero was overcome by slumber at the critical moment of the King's recital, and only awoke to find himself alone upon the seashore, all trace of the castle having disappeared. This is again the cause of failure in the *Chastel Merveilleus* version. In the *Perlesvaus* three drops of blood fall from the lance on to the table, and Gawain, gazing upon them, falls into a trance, and can neither speak nor stir. In *Diû Crône* we have again the mysterious slumber, though here associated with the drinking of wine, the effect of which is to plunge Gawain's comrades, Lancelot and Calogreant, into a sleep which lasts till the question has been put, and the marvels explained. In this version also, we have the blood drops; but here, though they fall from the Lance, they are swallowed by the King, thus having no connection with the trance.

In the *Perceval* version, on the contrary, the blood drops are connected with a trance, but not with the Grail; and the hero's failure is accounted for on purely rational grounds, his too rigid adherence to the counsels of Gurnemanz.[15]

As we have seen, the *Gawain* versions certainly represent the older stage of tradition, and we may, therefore, fairly assume that, in the original form of the story, the failure to ask the necessary question was due to a mysterious slumber which overtook the hero at the crucial point of his test. But what caused this slumber? Is it too bold a suggestion that the blood drops, which are often so closely associated with the Grail, and are always found in connection with a trance, were the operating cause? that, in fact, they were employed to induce an hypnotic slumber on the part of the aspirant? We knew that in Mesmerism and kindred practices, the first step is to seize and fix the attention of the subject—I believe a glittering disc, or some such object, is often employed—in any case it is through the eye that the desired effect is produced upon the brain. In the case of Gawain, and of Perceval alike, we are told that it is the startling contrast of colour—the crimson blood on the white cloth, or snow—that fetters their attention. It is of course *possible* that the slumber was merely a literary device for winding up the story, but the introduction of the feature of restored vegetation shows that the tale was moulded by some one who understood its real significance; and slumbe hypnotically induced would be a very natural method of getting rid of an intruder who had stumbled upon rites not intended for general knowledge, and had failed to qualify for admission to their secrets. This much is certain, if the Grail stories have their root in the ritual of Adonis, we are dealing with a set of concrete facts, which must originally have admitted of a rational explanation. I would submit that if the slumber be really a part of the original tale, and there is every

reason to believe that it is, then it must be capable of a rational explanation, and I can, in no other way, account for its constant recurrence,
or for its connection with the blood drops, save on the hypothesis that
one of the trils to which the neophyte was exposed, and to which apparently he frequently succumbed, was the test of hypnotic suggestion.

But how shall we explain the Grail itself? Would it not be the vessel
of the common quasi-sacramental feast always connected with these
rites? It is interesting that the MS which gives us the best Bleheris text
also, in the same section of the work, offers us the only other instance
I know of the use of the word Grail. When Gawain enters the castle
of Brandelis, he finds a feast prepared, and boars' heads upon Grails
of silver. The other MSS have here substituted for *Grail* the word *Tailléor*.
It is thus practically certain that the writer of these tales, when he used
the word *Grail*, meant a Dish, and not a Cup. The magical features,
the automatic service, the feeding of the guests with all kinds of meat,
were probably later additions, borrowed by the story-tellers from the
numerous food-providing talismans of folklore. For we must ask ourselves how was the story told, from the inside or from the outside? That
is, was it intended to be a method of preserving, and handing on, the
tradition of these rites; or was it simply a story composed round this
ritual as a centre? The first hypothesis would appear to involve the
admission that the minstrels were the *conscious* guardians and trans-
mitters of an occult tradition; a view which, in face of the close connection now proved to exist between the minstrel guilds and the
monasteries, I do not feel able to accept. Also, we should then expect
to find one clear and consistent version; and I suspect that that version would have been less susceptible of Christianization. But if the
tale were told from the outside, if it were a story based upon, quite
possibly, the genuine experience of one who assisted by chance at the
celebration of these rites, ignorant of their nature and meaning, we can
understand how it would take and keep this particular form. One admitted to the full participation in this ritual might not talk about it, where
one possessed of but a partial and outside knowledge would be free
to speak. And as the story passed from one to the other, is it not probable that while the initiated might venture to add or correct a feature,
the uninitiated would introduce details which appeared to him suitable, but which were really foreign to the original trend of the tale? How,
except on the hypothesis of some such origin, explain the persistent
adherence to the framework of the story, or the hints as to the mysterious nature of the talisman, and the penalties to be incurred if its secrets
are revealed? Do not let us forget that it is precisely in this, the earliest
form of the tale, and in the confused version of the same offered by
the *Elucidation*, that the *secret* character of the Grail is insisted upon.
On any other hypothesis, what is this secret?

And now that I have had occasion to mention the *Elucidation*, I would ask, does not this theory of the Grail origins provide us, at last, with a possible solution of that most perplexing text? As is known to students of the subject, the *Elucidation* purports to be an introduction to the Grail story, and is found in three texts, the Mons MS of the *Perceval*, the Middle German translation of the continuation to that poem, and the (1530) printed edition of the work. It is extremely confused, and its connection with the other Grail texts has still recently been a complete puzzle. It starts with a warning from Master Blihis against revealing the secrets of the Grail. It then relates how at one time there were maidens dwelling in the hills, or wells, (the original word, *puys*, might be translated either way; I prefer the rendering of the German text, hills), who would offer food and drink to the passer by; but when King Amangons offered force to one, and took away her golden cup, they left the country; and, the writer goes on, 'the court of the Fisher King could no longer be found'. Nevertheless, Gawain found it; and we then have a summary of the Bleheris visit, given in terms often verbally identical with the text of Wauchier de Denain.

Some time ago, in the course of my *Perceval* studies, I came to the conclusion that the text at the root of the *Elucidation* was another, and apparently later, form of that used by Wauchier, and that in our English *Gawain* poems we had fragments of the same collection. Now, it appears to me, that we can suggest even a closer link. What if this text be really what it purports to be, the introduction to all the Grail stories? If it be the record of an insult[16] offered by a local chieftain to a priestess of these rites, in consequence of which they were no longer openly celebrated in that land, and, as the writer puts it, 'the court of the Fisher King (the Priest of this ritual) could no longer be found?' Would not that be the logical introduction to the tale of one who found, and knew not what he found? It may be that after all the *Elucidation* is not so badly named!

So far as the Christian aspect of the story is concerned, it is now beyond doubt that a legend, similar in all respects to that of the Grail, was widely current at a date long anterior to any of our extant Grail texts. The story, with Nicodemus instead of Joseph as protagonist, is told of two of the most famous of Continental relics, the *Saint Sang* of *Fescamp* and the *Volto Santo* of Lucca. The most complete MSS of the *Perceval* refer, as authority, to a book written at Fescamp. Who was the first to utilise the pseudo-Gospels as material for the history of mediaeval relics we cannot say, but, given the trend of popular thought, it was practically inevitable that if the Grail were to receive the Christian pedigree which in the natural process of development in a mediaeval atmosphere, given to edification, it was bound to receive, it was almost inevitable that it should be fathered upon either Joseph of Arimathea or Nicodemus; as a matter of fact both are called into the service of the romancers.[17]

Given these facts, on the one hand an exceedingly popular story, having for its central point of interest a vessel round which there hovered an atmosphere of mystery and dread—none dare speak of the secrets of the Grail—and connected in some unexplained manner with drops of blood and a bleeding lance: on the other hand, an equally popular legend connected with the Passion of Christ, and relics of that Passion; and does it not become easy to understand how on the common ground of the vessel of the ritual feast the two might meet, and eventually coalesce; the vessel of the Nature-worship being first connected with the Passion and finally identified with the chalice of the Eucharist. If I be correct in my suggestion as to the hidden meaning of this ritual, and that it was in truth a Life-cult, the Grail quest would be *the quest for life;* the Grail itself, under all its varying forms, the vessel in which the food necesary for life was presented to the worshippers.

I would earnestly ask all students of this fascinating subject to consider seriously whether the theory here sketched may not be found capable of providing that link between the conflicting versions which all previous hypotheses have failed to supply? On the theory of a purely Christian origin, how can we account for the obviously folkloric features of our tale? How could the vessel of the Christian Eucharist have become the self-acting, food-providing talisman, known not only to Bleheris, but also to the author of the *Queste?* How could Kiot, (the author of the lost French poem adapted by Wolfram von Eschenbach), have dared to turn it into a mere magical stone, a *Baetylus?* For if there be one thing certain, it is that the Grail had been Christianized before the day of Chrétien and Kiot. If, on the other hand, the vessel were a mere food-providing Pagan talisman, how, and why, did it become so suddenly Christianized? what was there about it, more than about the countless similar talismans, that would suggest such a development? But if the Grail were from the first connected with a form of religious worship, from the first surrounded with a halo of awe and reverence, we can understand that it would lend itself with admirable readiness to the process of Christianization. Even as we can undersand how Kiot, who was certainly a man of unusual learning, while he might shrink from Paganizing a fundamentally Christian relic, would have no scruple in substituting the object of one mysterious Pagan cult for that of another, and in replacing the vessel of the Adonis Rites by a Baetylus. One who knew so much may well have known what was the real character of the Grail. It seems to me that on this theory, and on this theory alone, can we account logically and harmoniously, alike for the development and the diversities of the Grail romances.

It is scarcely necessary to remind members of this Society that, in the interesting series of papers on the European Sky-God, contributed by Mr Cook to the pages of *Folk-Lore,* certain stories connected alike with Cuchullin and Gawain, are claimed as dependent on, and to be explained by, precisely the set of customs and beliefs with which I am here dealing. If the Green Knight be a survival of the Vegetation god, why not the Maimed King? I do not know how far Mr Cook's theories have met with the approval of folklore experts, but it does seem to me that when two enquirers, starting from different points, and travelling by different roads, reach precisely the same goal, there is at least an initial probability that the goal was once, very long ago, no doubt, the starting point of those diverging roads.

[1] See *The Arthurian Tarot* by John & Caitlin Matthews (The Aquarian Press, 1989).
[2] Cf. also *Zeitschrift für D. Alterthumskunde*, 1878; p. 84 *sqq*.
[3] Cf. M. J. Bédier's edition of the *Tristan*, and Dr Schofield's *English Literature*. For my notes on Bleheris, cf. *Romania*, xxxiii. p. 333, xxxiv. p. 100.
[4] B.N. 1453, fo. 113; *Elucidation*; B.M. Add. *Ib.* 614, fo. 138, etc.
[5] A translation of this, the *Diu Crône*, and Prose *Lancelot* versions will be found in No. vi. of *Arthurian Romances*, Nutt.
[6] Cf. *Legend of Sir Perceval*, pp. 330-36; *The Golden Bough*—under heading 'Adonis'. *Adonis, Attis, Osiris*, chap. viii.
[7] *Legend of Sir Perceval*, p.141. In the Didot MS of the prose *Perceval* we are told that as the result of the question the 'Roi Pesheor' will not only be healed but restored to youth, '*revenus en sa invence*'. This is also the result of the question in *Parzival*. According to Dr Frazer, it was an essential part of this Nature-cult that the god should be not merely living, but *young*.
[8] Cf. Notes to vol. vi. of *Arthurian Romances*.
[9] Cf. Farnell, *Cults of Greek States*, vol. ii., *Aphrodite*.
[10] Cf. Frazer, *Adonis, Attis, Osiris*, p. 7. The image of Tammuz was clothed in red, and incense was burnt before it. Doves were sacrificed to Adonis; *ib.*, p. 64. Doves appear both in the prose *Lancelot* Grail Visit and in *Parzival*.
[11] Cf. *Adonis, Attis, Osiris*, p. 5.
[12] Dulaure, *Divinités Génératrices*, pp. 69-70.
[13] E.g., the wounding of the Grail king. Cf. Dulaure, pp. 78, 81. The *Parzival* alone attributes the wound to his indulgence in unlawful love, but the injury is always the same.
[14] Prof. Heinzel's method was very confused, and references to the question are scattered throughout the long study.
[15] In the prose *Perceval*, however, there is a hint of the earlier form, as fatigue also plays a part in the hero's failure to ask the necessary question: 'e li sire le metoit en mainltes manieres de paroles por çou qu'il l'en demendast, mais il n'en fist riens, car il estoit anoies des 11 nuis devant qu'il avoit vellie, que por un poi qu'il ne chaoit sor la table'. Modena MS, fol. 59.
[16] If there be really Phallic symbolism in the tale, the wording of the affront is suggestive.
[17] For summaries of these legends, cf. *Legend of Sir Perceval*, chap. v. appendix.

Chapter 11.
Gawain at the Grail Castle

Of all the characters in the Arthurian cycle of stories, that of Sir Gawain is the least understood. In the earliest versions of the legends he is Arthur's greatest knight, Gwalchmai, the Hawk of May; by the time one gets to Malory and the flowering of the mediaeval romances, he has become a womanizer and a murderer, the exact opposite of the courtly, gentle knight and mighty warrior of his earlier self. The reasons for this are many and subtle; the change did not take place overnight. To the later Christian writers, Gawain had about him a taint of paganism—he carried the pentacle, the symbol of the Goddess, on his shield. For all that, in *Sir Gawain and the Green Knight*, the greatest poem of his adventures (see chapter 14), this becomes symbolic of the five wounds of Christ. Both sets of symbolism are of course applicable, but few recognized this at the time.[1]

Of all the knights who went in quest of the Grail, Gawain might once have been most expected to achieve some degree of success, but in keeping with the general decline in his character, he is represented in the majority of texts as failing. He is the first to volunteer to go forth on the quest, and one of the last to give up, but he never comes within sight of his goal—except in one text, Heinrich von den Tülin's *Diû Crone* (The Crown). This romance, written *c.*1230, is something of a rogue elephant among the corpus of poems and romances. Not only are the trappings of the Grail castle substantially different from those of the Perceval or Galahad stories, but the hero, unquestionably, is Gawain. This is refreshingly different, as indeed, is the whole text. The episode of *Gawain at the Grail Castle*, given here in the translation by J. L. Weston, bears all the hallmarks of an original mind; one who, unlike most mediaeval authors, did *not* chose to lean on earlier sources for his material. The result is strikingly different from most of the texts under review, and once again there is much here which will bear further meditation and work to unlock its deeper layers of meaning.

❧

Long and weary were the journeyings that good knight, Sir Gawain, made in search of the Grail; for he came even to a land wherein from the waxing to the waning of the moon there lacked not adventures stiff and stern. Yet his manhood stood him in good stead at need, otherwise had the toil and the strife weakened him overmuch. Howsoe'er it vexed him sorely. Yet the road led him at the last to a rich and goodly land, so well tilled that naught was lacking of the fruits of the earth, corn, and vines, and fair trees, all whereby man might live grew freely

on either hand. That was right pleasing to Sir Gawain, who was worn
with travel, for the land was like unto a garden, green, and in nowise
bare, and of right sweet odour; it might well be held for an earthly Paradise, since 'twas full of all delights that heart of man might desire.

But ere ever he came within its borders a strange adventure befell
him, for he saw a fiery sword, the breadth whereof he might not measure, which kept the entry to a fastness, within which stood a dwelling,
cunningly builded, but the walls whereof were clear and transparent
as glass; naught that passed therein might be held secret but 'twould
have been seen without. I wot not how it chanced, but 'twas void and
bare, and Sir Gawain deemed it strange and of ill omen; I think me
well 'twas of ill, for 'twas a wild land, but therewith he left it behind him.

So the knight journeyed through that fair country, where he found
all that heart desired, or that was needful to the body, so that his
strength came again unto him, and he was wholly recovered of the pains
which he had endured. And when he had ridden a twelve days' journey through the woodland he came again to an open country, and there
he did meet with his comrades, Sir Lancelot and Sir Calogreant, whereat
he was greatly rejoiced. The twain had wandered far astray, and save
for their arms he might scarce have known them. He found them sleeping under a tree, whither his road led him, for very joy he wakened
them. Then they greeted each other gladly, and told each to the other
the toils and the troubles that had befallen them as they rode singly
or in company on their quest.

No longer might they abide there, for it drew towards nightfall; and
as they went their way they beheld and saw how on the same track
a squire spurred swiftly towards them, nor would he slacken his pace
ere they met; right friendly was his mien as he bade Sir Gawain and
his comrades be welcome to God, and to his lord, and to himself, in
sooth he spoke truly and in no mockery, for good token he gave thereafter of his truth. He prayed them, in the name of his lord, that since
they were come into his land they would do him so much honour as
to turn aside unto his dwelling, for they were on the right road, and
'twas nigh at hand.

Sir Gawain made answer, 'I thank ye right heartily, ye and your lord,
know that we will gladly come unto your dwelling an' we be not forbidden by sword-thrust.' The squire spake again, 'This will I tell ye
surely, follow ye this road straight unto the Burg, 'tis here full nigh
at hand; I, having shown ye the road, will hasten thither, and ride ye
as softly as ye will.' With that he turned him again, and had swiftly
outridden them.

Know ye that the knights were not over-long upon the road, for the
twain, Sir Lancelot and Sir Calogreant, were sore a-hungered; sudden
they saw before them a castle, fair to look upon, and they deemed they
should find a goodly lodging therein. Without, on a meadow, was a

great company of knights, who vied with each other in skilful horse-
manship, as knights are wont to do. Without spear or shield, in courteous wise they rode hither and thither on the open field; but when the
three had come so near that they took knowledge of them, that noble
folk left their sport, and rode swift as flight over the meadow toward
the road, and received the guests with gentle greeting, as is love's custom, bidding them welcome to their lord's land. With that they took
them in safe-conduct, and led them even to the castle—I wot Sir Gawain
there found gladsome gain!

The Burg was fairly builded, and therein dwelt a great folk, knights
and ladies, who were right joyful as was fitting, that did Sir Gawain
mark right well, and drew comfort therefrom. So well did they receive
him that it grieved him naught that he was come unto their company;
they beheld him right gladly, and all that was needful to him they gave
him with full hand. So went he with the twain, Sir Lancelot and Sir
Calogreant, unto the lord of the castle, even as they showed him the
road.

'Twas the fairest palace ever builded, an the tale lie not no richer might
tongue of man describe, or heart of man conceive. Never might the
host be vexed through poverty, a courteous prince he was and good,
and wise withal I ween. For the summer's heat his hall was all bes-
trewn with roses, whereof of the perfume rejoiced him greatly. White
was his vesture, cunningly wrought and sewn with diaper work of gold,
'twas a skilful hand that wrought it! Before him sat two youths of noble
birth, whom he ever kept in his company; they jested lightly, the one
with the other, the while they played at chess before his couch, and
the lord leaned him over towards the board, for it gladdened him to
behold the game, and to hearken to their jesting.

When Sir Gawain entered the hall the host received them and his
two comrades well, and bade them be seated; Sir Gawain he made to
sit beside him on the couch, on a cushion of rose-coloured silk did they
sit together. In sooth there was pleasure enow of question and answer,
and of knightly talk betwixt the host and Sir Gawain; and they who
sat at the chessboard jested and made merry. Thus they made pastime
till nightfall, and then were the tables set that all might eat, nor was
any man forgotten, there was space for all.

Then the knights arose, and Sir Gawain also, but the host spake to
them all by name, for right well he knew them, and bade them sit by
him, which they were nothing loth to do. With that there came a great
company of knights and ladies, who saluted the host, as is the fashion
of women, and sat them all down. Long was the hall and wide, yet
'twas full in every part, and all the tables filled. After them came full
twenty chamberlains, young men of noble birth and courteous bearing, who bare napkins and basins, that did the knights mark well;
behind them were a great company, bearing candles and candlesticks

without number, with that was the hall so light 'twere hard to tell
whether 'twere day or night. And there followed thirty minstrels, and
others who sang full many a tuneful melody, all with one accord rejoiced
and sang praises.

The two knights and Sir Gawan sat beside their host, yet not on a
level, for Sir Gawain sat above, and they below, and the host 'twixt
the three. The others sat all around the hall, and ate each twain together,
a knight and his lady.

And when all were seated, and were fain to eat, then there came into
the hall a wondrous fair youth, of noble bearing, and in his hand he
held a sword, fair and broad, and laid it down before the host. With
that Sir Gawain 'gan to bethink him what this might betoken. After
the youth came cupbearers, who passed through the hall, serving wine
to all who were seated ere they might eat. Sir Gawain and his comrades did they serve first of all, the while the host sat beside them and
did neither eat nor drink. Nor would Sir Gawain drink, but for his comrades twain they were so sore vexed by thirst, that even though he bade
them refrain yet must they drink withal, and thereafter did they fall
into a deep slumber, and when Sir Gawain beheld this it vexed him
sorely.

Oft-times did the lord of the castle pray Sir Gawain to drink, as a
courteous host doth his guest, but otherwise was he minded, and well
on his guard, lest he too fall asleep.

At the last came in fair procession, as it were, four seneschals, and
as the last passed the door was the palace filled—nor were it fitting
that I say more. In the sight of all there paced into the hall two maidens
fair and graceful, bearing two candlesticks; behind each maid there
came a youth, and the twain held between them a sharp spear. After
these came other two maidens, fair in form and richly clad, who bare
a salver of gold and precious stones, upon a silken cloth; and behind
them, treading soft and slow, paced the fairest being whom since the
world began God had wrought in woman's wise, perfect was she in form
and feature, and richly clad withal. Before her she held on a rich cloth
of samite a jewel wrought of red gold, in form of a base, whereon there
stood another, of gold and gems, fashioned even as a reliquary that
standeth upon an altar. This maiden bare upon her head a crown of
gold, and behind her came another, wondrous fair, who wept and made
lament, but the others spake never a word, only drew nigh unto the
host, and bowed them low before him.

Sir Gawain might scarce trust his senses, for of a truth he knew the
crowned maiden well, and that 'twas she who aforetime had spoken
to him of the Grail, and bade him an he ever saw her again, with five
maidens in her company, to fail not to ask what they did there—and
thereof had he great desire.

As he mused thereon the four who bare spear and salver, the youths with the maidens, drew nigh and laid the spear upon the table, and the salver beneath it. Then before Sir Gawain's eyes there befell a great marvel, for the spear shed three great drops of blood into the salver that was beneath, and the old man, the host, took them straightway. Therewith came the maiden of whom I spake, and took the place of the other twain, and set the fair reliquary upon the table—that did Sir Gawain mark right well—he saw therein a bread, whereof the old man brake the third part, and ate.

With that might Sir Gawain no longer contain himself, but spake, saying, 'Mine host, I pray ye for the sake of God, and by His Majesty, that ye tell me what meaneth this great company, and these marvels I behold?' And even as he spake all the folk, knights and ladies alike, who sat there, sprang from their seats with a great cry, and the sound as of great rejoicing. Straightway the host bade them again be seated as before, and make no sound until he bade and this they did forthwith.

At the sound of the great cry the twain, Sir Lancelot and Sir Calogreant, wakened, for through the wine they had drunk they slept soundly, but even as they beheld the maidens who stood around the board, and the marvels that had chanced, they sank back into slumber, and so it was that for five hours sleep kept fast hold of them, the while the old man spake thus:

'Sir Gawain, this marvel which is of God may not be known unto all, but shall be held secret, yet since ye have asked thereof, sweet kinsman and dear guest, I may not withhold the truth. 'Tis the Grail which ye now behold. Herein have ye won the world's praise, for manhood and courage alike have ye right well shown, in that ye have achieved this toilsome quest. Of the Grail may I say no more save that ye have seen it, and that great gladness shall come of this your question. For now are many set free from the sorrow they long had borne, and small hope had they of deliverance. Great confidence and trust had we all in Perceval, that he would learn the secret things of the Grail, yet hence did he depart even as a coward who ventured naught, and asked naught. Thus did his quest miscarry, and he learned not that which of a surety he should have learned. So had he freed many a mother's son from sore travail, who live, and yet are dead. Through the strife of kinsmen did this woe befall, when one brother smote the other for his land: and for that treason was the wrath of God shown on him and on all his kin, that all were alike lost.

'That was a woeful chance, for the living they were driven out, but the dead must abide in the semblance of life, and suffer bitter woe withal. That must ye know—yet had they hope and comfort in God and His grace, that they should come even to the goal of their grief, in such fashion as I shall tell ye.

'Should there be a man of their race who should end this their sorrow, in that he should demand the truth of these marvels, that were the goal of their desire; so would their penance be fulfilled, and they should again enter into joy: alike they who lay dead and they who live, and now give thanks to God and to ye, for by ye are they now released. This spear and this food they nourish me and none other, for in that I was guiltless of the deed God condemned me not. Dead I am, though I bear not the semblance of death, and this my folk is dead with me. However that may be, yet though all knowledge be not ours, yet have we riches in plenty, and know no lack. But these maidens they be not dead, nor have they other penance save that they be even where I am. And this is by the command of God, that by his His mystery, which ye have here beheld, they shall nourish me once, and once alone, in the year. And know of a truth that the adventures ye have seen came of the Grail, and now is the penance perfected, and for ever done away, and your quest hath found its ending.'

Therewith he gave him the sword, and told him he were right well armed therewith, and however much he might bear it in strife never would it break, and be bade him wear it all his days. Thus did he end his tale, telling no more, save that he might now leave the quest he had undertaken, and that for the rest, on the morrow should his toil be ended. And in so far as concerned the maidens 'twas through their unstained purity, and through no misdoing, that God had thus laid on them the service of the Grail; but now was their task ended and they were sad at heart, for they knew well that never more should the Grail be so openly beheld of men, since that Sir Gawain had learned its secrets, for 'twas of the grace of God alone that mortal eyes might behold it, and its mysteries henceforth no tongue might tell.

With this speaking the night had passed, and the day began to dawn, and as his tale was done, lo! from before Sir Gawain's eyes the old man vanished, and with him the Grail, and all that goodly company, so that in the hall there abode none save the three knights and the maidens.

And Sir Gawain was somewhat sorry, when he saw his host no more, yet was he glad when the maiden spake, saying that his labour was now at an end, and he had in sooth done all that pertained unto the Quest of the Grail, for never elsewhere in any land, save in that Burg alone, might the Grail have been beheld. Yet had that land been waste, but God had hearkened to their prayer, and by his coming had folk and land alike been delivered, and for that were they joyful.

That day Sir Gawain abode there with his comrades, who rejoiced greatly when they heard the tale, and yet were sorrowful in that they had slumbered when the Grail passed before them, and so beheld it not. Good hostelry they found in that Burg, and when the morning dawned and they must needs depart then was many a blessing called down upon Sir Gawain by those maidens, that he might live many years in bliss and honour, this they prayed of a true heart, since he had set them free, and one blessing surely seeketh another. So the good knight departed from among them. Thus doth the Quest of Sir Gawain find an ending.

[1] See my *Gawain: Knight of the Goddess* (The Aquarian Press, 1990).

Chapter 12.

The Secret School of the Holy Grail

by A. E. Waite

Arthur Edward Waite (1857-1941) needs little introduction to anyone at all familiar with the beginning of the occult revival in the 19th and 20th centuries. He is among those whose influence, through his part in the founding of the esoteric Order of the Golden Dawn, has become almost legendary.

But Waite was much more than an occultist. He was a mystic whose studies led him far afield, into the writings of Christian theologians, Classical philosophers and the deep wisdom of the perennial philosophy. His autobiography, *Shadows of Life and Thought*, is one of the most remarkable documents of recent times, charting as it does the development of a mind ever restless for new knowledge and wider horizons.

Unfortunately, Waite's extremely dense style of writing has made a true assessment of his work difficult, and he has been called 'unreadable' by some critics. Yet his seminal study, *The Hidden Church of the Holy Grail* (1909) has been reprinted in recent years and has found many devotees)—it is still one of the most comprehensive accounts ever written. The chapter which follows, 'The Secret School', comes not from this book, but from a later version called simply *The Holy Grail*. It is far more straightforwardly written, altogether more readable, and, like all of Waite's writing, full of remarkable details, rare facts, and a deep sense of the numinous. Waite understood the varied polarities of the Grail cycle better than most who have written about it, and here he comes as close as any to finding a reason for the continuing power of the Grail symbology. It is remarkable piece of scholarship and inspiration, effortlessly combined; it should be read by any who are themselves on the quest.

Setting aside its sacramental past, the literature as literature is Celtic on the surface and Celtic also in atmosphere; but these are the vesture and the environment in which the spirit of its Mystery reposes. The Grail itself is in the root a Reliquary Legend. This Legend was taken over or invented and was connected with rumours of Secret Doctrine concerning the Eucharist and the Priesthood. It passed into Romance or was put forward therein, and it incorporated certain folk-lore elements which seemed adaptable to its purpose: they are naturally its hindrance. In the hands of the Northern French writers, it removed from the Celtic environment as it drew towards its term. We cannot explain therefore the French Cycles and much less the German Grail literature by means of the Celtic Church. On the external side it looks as if it came out of cells and stalls and scriptoria; but in the last resource

204 An Arthurian Reader

it cannot be explained by Rome. We have searched also the findings of qualified research on the Catharist Mystery; but it is not to be explained thereby. The Secret Doctrine reflected into the literature abode in a Secret School: it was a School of Christian Mystics and was of necessity Catholic at heart.[1] The Doctrine concerning it is that there were High Princes of the Spirit whose experiences surpass not only those of devout souls but of many of its great saints. Their time was not 'about half an hour' but an experience as if in perpetuity. The School would have said that the way of the Church, in thesis apart from practice, was a true way and not a good one only; but it would have added also that the heights are still the heights. It comes about therefore that any message of Secret Words and Super-Apostolical Succession can be only a shadow of reality until its life is attained within: yet that shadow is a sacred reflection. The claim concerning them is like a word written against the Churches, but those who are satisfied with the literal sense of sacred things are not defrauded thereby and can receive ministry therein. Yet the second sense remains, and it is brought from very far away, because it draws from the Sanctuary of the Soul. The Mystery which the School explored corresponded in figurative language to a Mass of the Beatific Vision. It is obvious that this was celebrated by the Hermit in the *Grand Saint Graal.* The Prologue to this Book is the nearest that we are likely to get on the pictured side of the Mystery. The Mass of the Grail is recoverable in the quest of consciousness; but it is understood that it takes place only in a Secret Church and that Church is within. When the Priest enters the Sanctuary he returns into himself by contemplation and approaches the Altar which is within. He says: *Introibo.* When he utters the words which are Spirit and Life, the Christ Mystical communicates to him in the heart; or, in alternative symbolism, he is raised into the Third Heaven and enjoys the dilucid contemplation. Like St Augustine, discoursing of the Holy Trinity, I do not put it in this way as one who is satisfied with the expression: only we must have some expression.[2]

As the Supreme Mystery of the Christian Church, the Eucharist is said to have been compared with the last Ceremony of Initiation, constituting the final enlightenment of the Neophyte. There may be some exaggeration in the statement; but those who were the original Stewards of the Christian Mystery had in many cases received the Mysteries of the Gentiles and may have adapted some of their procedure. The rumour which came into Romance—and this in the natural manner, because Official Religion, its variants and competitive substitutes permeated Romance everywhere—centred about the Eucharist, and in the minds of external piety was translated into memorials of the Divine Body and the Precious Blood. It would be idle to suggest that any Higher School of Religion was concerned with the veneration of Relics; but there would be a desire to behold behind the Eucharist that which was held in the

symbolism to abide and repose therein. Beyond all knowledge of the
outside world, founded on faith and teaching, there is another
knowledge; but it dwells in hidden places of the mind: it has, however,
its correspondences in Eucharistic terms, one of which is called the
Communication of Christ. In the deeper speculation behind the *Epiclesis* Clause, it is described otherwise as a Descent of the Comforter
within. He who has performed the one rigorously scientific experiment
and has opened the inward Holy Place does enter and that which takes
place answers to the Celebration of a Mass:[3] it is not as such the work
of an Official Priesthood, though it does not set it aside or compete
therewith. Herein is an experiment which I believe to be performed
even now in the world, because the great ventures of experience do
not pass into desuetude. The Grail Romances in their proper
understanding—but chiefly because of their implicits—recall this great
subject, testifying after many ways. The Grail is like a guide of the distressed in the Lesser Chronicles: they shadow forth that which is implied
inwardly by the Hidden Voice of Christ and the Holy Spirit. Their Secret
Words were Words of Power, because that which rules above rules also
below. As such the Lesser Chronicles did not derive from Fécamp, which
put forward only the wonder side of Transubstantiation. But the *Grand
Saint Graal*, which cuts short the discourse between Christ and Joseph
in the Tower and so suppresses all reference to the divulgation of Secret
Words, can derive no more than a reflection from this source and suffers
inevitably from the insufficiency of its doctrinal terms, above all on
the picture side. On the spiritual side there is no suggestion that
sacramentally the Arch-Natural Body of Christ is communicated to our
earthly part and the Divine Life to the human spiritual part. The *Perlesvaus* hints at a Secret of the Sacrament which was held in utter reserve,
telling us by inference that it was the revelation of Christ in His own
Person, behind which there is another Mystery. Curiously enough
perhaps, it is only in the texts of Transubstantiation that we find, approx-
imately or remotely, the suggestion of these deeper aspects.[4] The
Conte del Graal has not heard of them; the *Didot-Modena Perceval*
is aware of an undeclared Mystery, but has no licence to speak; the
German *Parzival* suggests an office of concealed mercy amidst suffering and hereof is Heinrich a shadow. Yet all of them, in their several
manners, are haunted from far away: Joseph II began in Priesthood and
the Perceval of Manessier ends therein, as if he too discerned that those
who attained the Great Mystery were made Priests thereby. I think also
that the Fish in the Metrical Joseph has curious sacramental intimations: it is a sign of spiritual sustenance, of Christ's Presence among
His faithful, and hence of the Eucharist. Recurring to the *Grand Saint
Graal*, it only duplicates one part of a canonical miracle. The Catholic
master-key is provided most surely by the Galahad Quest, where, long
after the Magical Marriage of High Art and Nature has taken place

in Transubstantiation, the Questing Knight bows his head, utters his
consummatum est, and is dissolved. I conclude that the Christian and
Grail Mystery of the Mass was a veil which at need could be parted
by warranted hands and that behind it there was found the Path which
leads to the Union. The knowledge of that Path arose within the Church
but led behind it, the Church remaining a gate by which man may enter
into attainment. The Quests of the Grail worked towards a knowledge
of the Path.

I speak of course as I find, and it is such a finding that it imposes
words of witness, not only in Hidden Temples when the Great Rites
are held but in the thoroughfares of life, or in books which all may
read and a few will cherish in their hearts. If I have said *Introibo* within
me through the days and the years; the *Vere dignum et justum;* and
the *Supplices rogamus ac petimus,* remembering *haec dona, haec
munera, haec sancta sacrificia illibata,* it is because of the *Galahad* and
the *Perlesvaus,* in part for what they are in themselves and in the greater
part for where they have led me, from Romance into Ritual and from
Ritual into that not undiscoverable realm which lies beyond and is called
the Mystery of the Faith.

But we have reached now a stage where it is necessary to glance at
other aspects which environed the Grail literatures, though in relation
to those which were considered previously.

It is wholesome to remember, among many other points that might
be enumerated:

1. That before AD 1000 Claudius, Archbishop of Turin, characterised
the censure pronounced on his anti-papal writings as the voice of the
members of Satan;

2. that Arnulph, Bishop of Orléans, at the Council of Rheims,[5]
pointed to the Roman Pontiff, saying: 'Who is that seated upon a high
throne and radiant with purple and gold?. . . If he thus follow uncharita-
bleness. . . he must be Antichrist sitting in the Temple of God';

3. that Everard, Bishop of Salzburg, said much later: 'He who is *servus
servorum Dei* desires to be Lord of lords; he profanes, he pillages, he
defrauds, he murders, and he is the lost man who is called Antichrist';

4. that Cardinal Benno, speaking of *Sylvester* II,[6] said that by God's
permission he rose from the abyss;

5. that the same Pope was described at the Council of Brixen as the
false monk and the prince of abomination.

These were the accusations of Prelates, and with them may be compared the opinion of Figueiras the Troubadour, who described Rome
as an immoral and faithless city, having its seat fixed in the depths of
hell; that of Petrarch, who called Avignon the Western Babylon, and—
like a comparison by way of antithesis to the Rich Fisherman—
exclaimed: 'Here reigns a proud race of Fishermen who are poor no
longer'; and that of the same poet, who described the Papal Court as

a people who follow the example of Judas Iscariot—in other words, selling God for money, like the King of Castle Mortal. So also St Bridget termed Rome the Whirlpool of Hell and the House of Mammon, wherein the devil barters the patrimony of Christ.[7]

These are the judgements on life and its conduct, on passion and policy, on the spirit of the world in the Holy Place and its centre: they are not impeachments of Doctrine and much less of that world of intimation and Experience which lies behind Doctrine. It is evident that on the side of government, apart or not from teaching, the yoke of Rome was no longer easy or its burden light. It is conceivable, from this point of view, and were other things equal, that the Grail symbolism of a bereft Castle or Temple might be an appeal against the Church as that which had become unfaithful to itself, a protest against the power of Lucifer which had invaded the Sanctuary. The admission of these facts does not derogate of necessity from the claim that the Church had all the means. Even in new definitions and altered practice there might by supposition be a guiding hand.

During the evolution of the Grail literature it will be remembered that two unhappy ferments were at work in the Western Branch: firstly, the denial of the Chalice to the laity; and secondly, the various doctrinal tendencies which resulted in the definition of Transubstantiation. From this point of view the wound of the Latin Church would be that it misconstrued the *Mysterium Fidei;* that it had in fact five wounds corresponding to the five changes of the Grail. Among these the last only seemed to be a Chalice, for it is said that there was none at that time, perhaps because *Dominus qui non pars est sed totum* is not contained in a Chalice, though the Lord is *Pars haereditatis meae et calicis mei.* Obviously the Latin Church cannot be accused of having failed to discern after its own manner the Body of the Lord, but that discernment was apart unfortunately from the life which its own Scriptures tell them is resident symbolically in the Blood. On the basis of Transubstantiation it might be difficult to reject the Roman plea, that he who receives the Body receives also the Blood, because that which is communicated *ex hypothesi* in the Eucharist is the Living Christ made flesh. On another basis, the implicit of such symbolism looks rather in the opposite sense, namely, that the Elements are twofold to shew how the flesh of itself profits nothing, while the Spirit and the Truth are the communication of Divine Life. By those who regard Transubstantiation as the burden of the Church which defined it, there is a disposition to condemn the Latin Eucharist as a dismembered Sacrament; by those who look upon the Observance as a mere memorial, all subtleties notwithstanding, there is a feeling that the remembrance is broken and that the isolated Sign does not signify fully. On the other hand, that view which belongs more especially to the Mystics, namely, that the Covenant of Christ to His followers concerns what I have called

so frequently the communication of Divine Substance does not of necessity affirm that the accidents of such communication are of vital consequence: if therefore transposition or substitution of external signs
need not occasion a shadow of vicissitude in the Mystery which is
imparted, it would follow that the Official Church was perhaps more
astute than otherwise when it denied the Chalice to the laity. For the
rest, and to extinguish these questions, those who speak of Christ's
Spiritual Presence say well, but the Mystery of Abiding Redemption
is the perpetuity of the Incarnation among those to whom Christ came
in flesh.

If it is not to be said that at the epoch of the Grail literature the highest
minds had grown weary of the Vatican and all its ways, it can be affirmed
at least that there were both competitive and uncompetitive streams
of tendency which pursued their paths openly and in secret towards
another term. I think that Southern France stands out obviously under
the first designation; but there were those also who raised no voice
of debate and pursued their secret way towards the realisation of Divine
Ends. They have had no remedies to offer on the practical side of things,
and they were too wise to denounce abuses which they were powerless
to rectify—even as I who write, supposing that I had attained the term
of the Great Experiment, should not for such reason be qualified to
purify the commercial houses of exchange. That term belongs to a region
about which it is idle to speak in connection with schemes of amelio-
ration or the raising of the masses. So far as those who have prosecuted
or do now follow it have led or lead to-day the life of the world, it is
implied in their calling that they should do what to do is given them;
yet in respect of the Experiment itself, if those who attain can lead others
in the way, they do not come with helping hands for the furtherance
and welfare of the body politic.

Some of them were Bishops and Priests in their days and generations,
some active in the world and some withdrawn in far-off priories or leading a Hermit's life. A few would not have passed muster as orthodox
in the clamour of doctrinal debate, supposing that they had frequented
the Schools. A few among these few were heard therein, some at earlier
and some at later dates than those of the Grail literature. Within the
limits of that period, there were those who left records behind them,
and they shew in a plenary sense that the writers were familiar alike
with Path and Term. They knew also the void in the heart of the age
and the deadly sickness of the outer Church. These old witnesses, whose
remains are with us, like golden sheaves of testimony, are indubitably
but signposts pointing to many others, their graduating pupils and their
silent followers, abiding in many places and helping to produce a still
but not ineffective spirit of the time. It is from out this stream of tendency that there came, as I believe, the voices of the Grail Books. They
were not of Bernard, him above all, of the impassioned Bonaventura,

Figure 8: 'Isolt and Palomydes' by Dora Curtis.

or of Victorines, any more than of Cistercians. They were of poets in
the stream and of a few who wrote in prose. They had heard the other
voices, and some may have lived among those who loved and honoured
them. Some of them spoke as from a great distance, amidst the dis-
traction of outward things and all the sorcery of sense. For others at
their best and highest, the efficacious Grail—that which is Life and
Grace—came not out of their literal or figurative fasts, their watches
and their prayers, but out of their hearts of ardour. They proposed Secret
Words and a Super-Apostolical Priesthood to body forth the accredited
fact of their Leaders' lonely state apart from all that raged about them,
shaping its own ends in the name of Religion. They knew that other
but not dissimilar Quests were pursued around them, many and strange.
They dreamed of Mysteries of Sanctity which as yet they had not
fathomed; it may even be that the story of Prester John expressed that
dream after a manner of parable in their yearning minds.[8] When they
left the House of Doctrine empty in respect of its chief Hallow, the Perlesvaus and the Queste testified only in their picture-form to the great
inhibition of the time. In other language, sounded on every side, the
dominant Church in arms had made void its claims and Sacraments.
This condemnation is written in great letters on many signposts of the
period and is heard in all its voices, those above all which rang through
Southern France. But the records of those who spoke otherwise than
in romance perished in the red Thermopylae of Toulouse and Montségur. There is only a vestige left to speak of the life-experiment behind
the white cord of all those lost legions. But it is just sufficient to indicate its analogies with that living catholic research which has been pursued everywhere and of that Mystery to which St Augustine alluded
when he said that Christianity had been always in the world, to which
the New Testament itself testified when speaking of the Lamb slain from
the foundation of the cosmic order. The Catharist may have connected
it only with primitive Christ Doctrine, as this was understood by him;
but it follows that those who look on the experiment as something which
became Christian at a certain date are in error over the elements of
the subject, to which there belongs in a superlative sense the locus com-
munis of the ecclesiastical test: quod semper, quod ubique, quod ab
omnibus. We should remember that things which concur with one
another do of necessity find one another at some point of their extension: so also the one Quest adopts many veils, but without diminu-
tion of identity. It has been disguised frequently under the old formula
concerning Words of Power; but though this is an obvious illustration
it carries a suggestion of fatality, because in no case did the sign sur-
vive the idea—and so lapse into superstition—more often or with greater
facility. In its proper understanding the term of Quest corresponds with
the conception of an union between the consciousness of the soul and
the Word of God, the verbum caro factum, declaring itself in the world

and in the heart of man. Robert de Borron, an emissary *ex hypothesi*, pictured it as Secret Words of Christ, leaving it seemingly an open question whether they were Eucharistic or not. Those or he who converted his work into prose knew otherwise or concluded that they could have no other office, and so allocated them accordingly, but hardly with an eye on the kind of Mass which was proffered to Simon de Montfort in Joinville's story, if only he came to see. The author of the *Grand Saint Graal*, having other intimations, including those which were incorporated in his Prologue, put forward his thesis in the guise of another Sacerdotal Mystery and followed those who had preceded him in developing a Conversion Legend. But the Companions whom he brought from Sarras, where the Evangelical Sodality received their titles in the Ordination of Joseph II, came over, it may be, in his dream, to convert the Papal Saracens of the twelfth century and not the Druids of old. Wolfram von Eschenbach represented the Secret Custodians as an autonomous Chivalry after the model of the Knights Templar, bringing into it materials from oriental sources and proclaiming that the Grail story, the oldest story of all, was written in the starry heavens, as no one doubts that it is who has contemplated the celestial sphere from a Darien peak of unity. Other Traditions had already presented Joseph of Arimathaea as the Grand Master of an Instituted Knighthood. The authors of the *Perlesvaus* and the Galahad *Queste* connected their whole subject with Eucharistic Transubstantiation as the most approximate gate through which they might draw others to follow those things which issue in mystery. But when this symbolism had served its purpose they were glad enough to present its dissolution, as I have shewn. They might have chosen other material; but it has been in no sense my design to suggest that they had overcome all burdens of their period by an excess of wisdom: the glass through which they looked was clouded and scoriated enough; their desk was difficult enough; and in leading towards their peculiar Doctrine as they did it may even be that the more intolerable aspect of Transubstantiation had not occurred to them. It is sufficient for our purpose that they discerned something of the secrets which lay beyond the Altar and the Sacrifice, and which had not been found by Rome. To do this they must have travelled far.

Did they know in the mind's contemplation—a few perchance—outreaching from afar, or—it may be—near at hand, something about a state of being which opens on the infinite? And because of that which in sacred hypothesis was communicated through the observance of the Eucharist, did they picture it as attained by the help of Secret Words used in Consecrating the Elements? Did certain others—who also knew—picture it as attained in ordination by Christ Himself? I question whether they would have dwelt upon an *Epiclesis* Clause, were there such in any Celtic literature; but I am certain in any case that they did not dream of a pan-Britannic Church. Nothing could be less

in correspondence with such an ambition than their conception of a
Mystery of Grace which could at no time have been expected to prevail in public. But seeing that the Mass went on for ever in the lands
and islands, had they found it by way of the Mass, as happened once,
it would seem to the Angel of the Schools? In a state apart and beyond
all declaration, did they dream of a Hidden Union and represent it to
themselves and others as something beheld inwardly by the help of
the Unspotted Sacrifice celebrated according to an Arch-Natural Mode?
In such case the Grail indeed is a Sacred Legend of the Eucharist, and
as behind its Castle of Souls there was a Hidden Paradise, so, like a
Grail which is behind the Holy Grail, there was conceived an inward
or transcendent sense of the entire Mystery.

Herein assuredly is the Quest for that which is real, wherein Enchantments dissolve and the Times of Adventure are also set over. The Enchantments are in the natural world and so again are the Adventures;
but the Unspelling Quest is in the world of soul. The witness of this
Doctrine, in one or other of its forms and under many veils, has been
always in the world. In its realisation the Shekinah is restored to the
Sanctuary: when it is overshadowed there is a Cloud upon the Sanctuary. It is the story of the individual man passing into the concealment
of the interior and secret life, but carrying with him his warrants and
his high insignia. In a word, it is that Doctrine the realisation of which
in the consciousness has been called, under all reserves and for want
of a better term, the Secret Church, even the Holy Assembly.[9]

The presence of this so-called Secret Church is like that of angels unawares. In the outer courts are those who are prepared for Regeneration and in the *Adyta* are those who have attained it: these are the Holy
Assembly. It is the place of those who, after the birth of flesh, which
is the birth of the will of man, have come to be born of God. It is in
the persons of those who are regenerate that the gates of hell cannot
prevail against this Church, or utterly against its working substitutes.
The place of the Holy Assembly is called Eden and Paradise: it is that
whence man came and whither he returns. It is also that unapparent
realm of being from which the Spirit and the Bride say 'Come'; or it
is the place of the Waters of Life, with power to take freely. It is like
the still, small voice: it is heard only in the midst of the heart's silence,
and there is no written word to tell us how its Rite is celebrated; but
it is like a Priesthood within the Priesthood and a Mass behind the
Mass. Its work upon things without is a work of harmony, wherein is
neither haste nor violence. There are no admissions—at least of the
ceremonial kind—to the Holy Assembly: it is as if in the last resource
a Candidate inducts himself. There is no Sodality, no Institution, no
Order which throughout the Christian centuries has worked in such
silence. It is for this reason that it remains an implicit in mystical literature rather than a formal revelation: it is not a revelation but an inher-

ence; when it is not an inherence, it is an attainment vaguely adumbrated. It is neither an interference nor a guidance actually: it is described better as an influence. It does not come down: more correctly it draws up; but it also inheres. It is the place of those who have become transmuted and tingeing stones.

The inspired poets and the great prose writers sat in their stalls and scriptoria during the High Adventurous Times, while the rumour of the Holy Grail moved through the world of literature. They dreamed of a Chivalry Spiritualised and a Church of the Holy Spirit. So came into being the *Perlesvaus,* the *Quest of Galahad,* perhaps even the *Parzival* of Wolfram. Whether in the normal consciousness I know not, or in the super-consciousness I know not—God knoweth—that dream of theirs was of a concealed Sanctuary behind the official Chancel and the visible Altar. This is the sense in which I understand my own and the other allusions to a Secret Church and its traces, wheresoever discovered. But, as before, I am not speaking of formal institutions, of esoteric brotherhoods, or incorporations of any kind: it is a question of inward realization, turned in a particular direction and of a growth therein. For the rest, a man need no leave the external Church if he enters that of the Spirit. It is not on record that Ruysbroeck ceased to say Mass because he had been in those heights and across those seas of which we hear in his *Adornment of the Spiritual Marriage*. At the same time his language is not exactly that of the Official Church in its earliest or latest Encyclical; it is not like that of St Irenaeus thundering forth against heresy or a modern Pope denouncing the spirit of Modernism. So also a lay member of any one among the Churches whose instruction has scarcely exceeded some Catechism of Christian Doctrine need not be less a Christian than he who has studied *Summa*. But again there are degrees of consciousness in the Mystery of Faith.[10]

The Secret Tradition in Christian Times is like the rumour of a Secret Sanctuary, and the Tradition has many voices. The voice at its highest of so-called Spiritual Alchemy, succeeding that of the Grail at a long distance, is like the voice of the Grail itself under another veil of symbolism; and it is witnessed that in those days many earnest persons beheld the Vessel of Singular Devotion. The voice of the Rosy Cross says that in places withdrawn He, being dead, yet testifieth. The voice of St John on Patmos says that he was given a book to eat and that in his mouth it was sweet but in his belly it was bitter, because thenceforward he was in travail with the Secret Doctrine. The voice of Masonry created a pregnant Legend to commemorate a great loss, and testified that the Quest would never end till the Speculative Masons recovered that which was once among them. The voice of the Rosy Cross said that, having found the body of the Master, the Brethren again closed the Sepulchre and set seals thereon, though they also looked for a great Resurrection. On these accounts and all others I have written this book

as the record of a Great Initiation. Meanwhile, the Churches are not
made void utterly, but they are in widowhood and desolation, holding the letter of the Word. We are not deceived by their distractions;
and yet it is certain also that Divine reflections abide with them. Chrétien may have drawn from an episodic Romance of Adventure in the
possession of a Count of Flanders. Master Blihis, great maker of fables,
may have recited things with or without consequence concerning Quests
and Findings. Neither theirs nor others that could be cited are Books
containing the Secret Words of the Eucharist or texts of the Secret Ordination. The Legends of Welsh Saints may tell us of Sacred Hosts coming down from Heaven; but the *Epiclesis* Clause—again, if the Welsh
had it in their Mass—is not the Lost Word which we seek like the Mason.
Other stories, for all that I know, may recount Consecrations by Christ,
and the inventions may be famous indeed, but they are likely to want
that atmosphere which fills the Chronicles-in-Chief of the Holy Grail
with meanings and suggestions of meaning. Therefore I hear and listen
with all my ears while the voices of many Traditions say the same things
differently. The Holy Sepulchre is empty; the Tomb of Christian Rosy
Cross is hidden in the House of the Holy Spirit; the Word of Masonry
is lost more desperately the more often it is found in the Arch and the
High Grades; the Zelator of Alchemy looks in vain for a Master. The
Traditional Book of the Grail, by whatever name of convention we may
choose to term it—*Liber Gradalis* or *Sanctum Graal*—remains beyond
external finding, like the Grail itself. But beyond this world of loss there
lies a world of attainment and the Grail is found therein, perchance—
as well it may be—by some among you who listen and—not, as I pray,
impossibly—by me who bears this witness, but assuredly by many to
come, as there were many in the past behind us, who raise their lamps
and lanterns to light our clouded ways.

Within the Christian centuries, the first witness of the unity, of the
state beyond the Vision, which is that of *anima transformata in Deo*
was he who is called Hierotheos, on the hypthesis that the text which
passes under this name is antecedent to pseudo-Dionysius and was or
may have been the work of that master to whom the latter appealed.
He testifies concerning the Second Birth of the Soul, to its experience
of Mystical Death, the Resurrection therefrom and in fine the Soul's
Ascension, when the Mind of Soul is united with the Universal
Essence.[11] It is notable and pregnant that at such an early date—
whatever the date was, fourth or fifth century—the epochs of the Christ
Life in Nazareth were adapted thus to the story of the Christ Life in
the individual soul. The self-styled Areopagite follows—or precedes as
the case may be—and does no adopt the formulary of this symbolism.
Dionysius is he for whom an all-perfect *Agnosia* 'is a knowledge of Him
Who is above all known things'.[12] He is the expositor of a Secret and
Mystical Theology which is to be distinguished from another that is

evident and known. The *Agnosia* which knows is of course a contradiction in terms, and the Dionysian Jacob's Ladder is an ascent into attainment on the rungs of paradox. God is not so much light as darkness, were it lawful to conceive Him as either; but the kind of darkness is greater light than any light of earth or mind. He is approached by the way of negation rather than an affirmative way, and His quest is in a cloud of unknowing. We are not concerned, however, with portents on the Path of Attainment but with the Term itself. It is an union in the highest part of soul with That Which is unknown by mind, but above the mind is known.[13] The Latin Church, which could not dispense with Dionysius because of his *Ecclesiastical Hierarchy,* has put up as it could with his *Mystical Theology,* and being in that position has had to maintain its orthodoxy. He himself, who knew that the path which he proposed to travel was in pure theism, set off by invoking the Holy Trinity, which Christianity might never have dreamed of, so far as his text itself is concerned. He who borrowed from Proclus knew well where his source was. In the seventh century there is St Maximus, who wrote Greek *Scholia* on Dionysius and affirmed that the soul is united with the Unknown Divinity by the suspension of all cognition.[14] John the Scots follows in the ninth century. I have shewn elsewhere that as regards the return of man's spirit to God it is for Erigena a path of seven stages, the last of which is the absorption of the soul in Deity.[15] He was not a witness of experience, his great dedications being those of realisation in the logical mind. We are brought to the threshold of the Grail period when we glance at Hugh of St Victor and his successor Richard of the same monastic house, for they belong to the twelfth century. The first tells us that to ascend unto God is to enter into oneself and to transcend oneself. Richard says of the soul: *Ascendat per semetipsum super semetipsum,* being the clearest intimation possible that the knowledge of God is attained in exploration of the world within us.

At once by necessity and purpose, this is a bald sketch and passes through a field which I have travelled already in the past. It would demand a special study to exibit the influence of Dionysius on later Christian Mysticism, through the translation into Latin of his writings by John the Scot, and that of Erigena Johannes in many directions. There arose in this manner an unincorporated school of experience which was with the Church and was of it in the deeper sense, but was following indubitably a course in which the Church and its Offices had the least possible part, always excepting the great symbolical sacrifice and living memorial of the Holy Mass. Its chief developments were subsequent to the Grail period, towards the close of which St Bernard, St Francis of Assisi and St Bonaventura are illustrious signposts but are not of the School itself, though the Franciscan movement had later developments which were in an occasional proximity thereto, while later still the so-called *Book of the Man from Frankfurt,* Nicholas of Basle and Rulman Merswin were of its spirit at the root thereof. There is an excellent estimate of Erigena By Dr F. W. Bussell,[16] which exhibits the kind of influence that he would exercise, his Theophany in respect of the universe, his unbending monism, his deification—*Theosis*—of the soul, its absolute resumption into God. At the Grail period itself the New Apocalypse of Joachim and his followers is a pregnant sign of the times; but to this I have referred elsewhere. My position is that the Latin Church has tolerated its Mystics as it best could when they were of the Dionysian type, and when there was no excuse or opportunity for dealing with them in a summary fashion; that it condemned and persecuted them when it might and dared; but that it had no use for any, or if any, for those only who were characterised by dreams and visions, who suffered from stigmatic and other pathological conditions, who had marriages with the personal Christ, more especially when the nuptials were made evident—so to speak—psychically by rings or crowns and by choirs of angels for witnesses. The pseudo-miraculous side was the side which appealed and that only, because Rome was dedicated above all to the phenomenal aspect of things; and (1) to rigid and literal dogma, literally and rigidly understood in the teeth of St Augustine on the Trinity and in the teeth of the Apostles' Creed in its titular designation as *Symbolum;* (2) to the multiplication of dogma, as if the Mystery of Faith could be exhibited more intelligibly by ever increasing broidery on the veils thereof. How should Rome take into its heart the *Agnosia* of Dionysius and the *Theosis* of John the Scot? But the one is a plain statement on the bankruptcy of the logical understanding when confronted by the issues of Reality, from which it follows that the Way to Reality is in another mode of mind; and the other is that to which the Mysteries of valid experience have borne their witness in all ages, and without break or interruption through all the Christian centuries. In the face of the rack and the faggot it may have camouflaged its authentic findings, but ever are the findings there: the *Theosis* of experience is as much in Ruysbroeck, all his concessions notwithstanding to the regnant dogmatism which affirms separation for ever; and it is almost as much in Gerson, who accuses Ruysbroeck of Pantheism. It does not come into mythical records as a favoured point of view, but because the faithful annals of experience could bear no other witness.

Robert de Borron may have written already his *Joseph*—thus starting Grail literature on its historicity side—when Clement III encouraged the Calabrian Abbot Joachim to continue his apocalyptic writings, in AD 1188, and Frederic II was his patron when Joachim died in 1200. A few years later the *Queste* crowned the French annals of the Grail. Here is one of the spiritual aspects in which the Legend grew up and flourished, and about it also surged the material terror and unrest of the times. The year 1198 ushered in the consolidation of Papal Monarchy, as it is called, under the auspices of Innocent III.

And now to move one step forward, being the last point to which I can take the subject: the place of the Cup in this extension of the symbolism under the light of all its analogies, corresponds to the place of Spiritual Life; to the rest of knowledge; to the receptacle of the Graces which are above and to the channel of their communication to things which are below; but this is the equivalent *ex hypothesi* of the Arch-Natural Eucharist. In a word, it is the world not manifested, and this is the world of Adeptship, attained by Sanctity. In so far therefore as it can be said in the open day, hereof is the message of the Secret Tradition in Christian Times on the subject of the Grail Mystery. So also, under a certain transfiguration, does the Grail still appear in the Hidden Sanctuaries.

But it was an Empire more than a Monarchy in the dream of theory and less or more substantially in the world of fact. 'The temporal sword of St Peter stretched far beyond Italy and Germany to the limits of Christendom, and the spiritual relationship in its political interpretation implied the vassalage of Europe to the See of Rome.'[17] But it happened that the policy of Innocent in his relations with England and his duel with King John 'alienated the heart of a nation for ever from its allegiance to the Papacy'.[18] It was the days of Interdict; but no sentence pronounced in Rome and no Kingly submission was destined to make England a fief of the Papacy. The Interdict passed in fine, and *Magna Charta* followed when 'the Pope stood side by side with John and his tyranny'.[19] So was there sown successfully and ineradicably the seed of an 'antipapal spirit preceding the Reformation'. And the Tree of the Grail Legend was putting forth branches and flowers. Was the spirit not rife already in England during the reign of Henry II? And if in England, at that distance from the centre, we have only to look at Rome during the pontificate of Innocent III, at France and Germany. The story repeats itself in many places and times. Very often also it was the spirit of Christ, as understood by earnest Christians, which was set against the spirit of Rome. It was of those who believed in the doctrine so much and so well that they denounced the lives and ambitions which gave the lie to doctrine. It was of those who resented doctrinal accretions. It was of those who chose the peace and recollection of the inward way, who 'let the legions thunder past and plunged in thought again'. It was of those who adored Masses and bowed to sacred Relics. It was of those who compared the pattern of the gospel with the pattern of Rome. It was of those who led the life that they might know the true doctrine. It was of those who by leading the life had passed behind the doctrine. Not least of all and possibly more than all, it was of those who said unto themselves: 'The end is everywhere'; that the Spirit of God has left the Church because of the evil therein.

So it came about that the Grail was taken away. But before it ascended to Heaven, he who wrote the *Queste* saw to it that the real meaning should emerge. In the authentic state of attainment, and with a valid sign of the union in the Sacred Host between his lips, the Grail went up with Galahad. And it is thus in other stories, even in the medley of the *Conte.* It is with the Perceval of the Didot-Modena text in a most secret place of the Hiddenness; it is with him of the *Perlesvaus,* who went over a great sea. In other words, it is still in the heart of the elect, of those who have led the life and found the Doctrine in the Path of Union. This is the Secret of the Grail.

[1] Catholic in the sense of Rome at the highest point of Roman Catholic experience in the way of the Mystic Life; but Catholic also in a sense unacknowledged by Rome and officially beyond its purview.

[2] Remember Schiller in his *Wallenstein*: 'But still the heart needs a language.'

[3] Because the experiment is on the subject of that communication which has been mentioned above in the text. The Christ is personal only in the sense of Indwelling Divinity.

[4] Possibly because the Master who said that 'He who eateth my Flesh and drinketh my Blood', etc., said also that 'the Flesh profiteth nothing', and thus opened a world of possibility concerning Spirit and Life in the Word.

[5] Such a Council was held in 1119, under Calixtus II.

[6] He reigned from AD 999 to 1003. I am not quoting chronologically.

[7] St Bridget died in 1373.

[8] It is meant only that the derision of that great hoax had possibly a purpose behind it.

[9] In so far as it has passed into expression, the idea of the Communion of Saints in the Sanctuary of the Secret Church is that of an union in still consciousness fixed on the abiding God, realised within. It is not the union one with another in psychic consciousness of *Frater Ex Millibus Electus* and *Frater Vix Unus Ex Millibus* under seals of the Rosy Cross in a state of absorbed contemplation, and remembering the Golden Doctrine that *Immanuel*, God is with Us. The reason is that we meet at the figurative and mystical centre by a participation in God-consciousness and not otherwise. The deep inward state in which such realisation takes place alone is not a travelling in the so-called spirit vision, when Z∴Y∴X∴ and W∴V∴ may haply encounter each other in a mutual psychic act. The mystical centre is not, in other terminology, a dream-medium which is and has been a realm of meeting from time immemorial, all the wide world over. Experiences of this kind would lead nowhere, even if prolonged for ever. The true meetings are not in time and place and not in the external personalities. When those who have dwelt at the centre return therefrom to take up their part in manifestation, it is then that they know one another in the authentic sense, wherever they meet abroad.

[10] And the Mass of an Angel of the Schools is something more in the spirit thereof than that of an average Parish Priest, who has no eyes beyond the letter.

[11] It will economise space if I refer at this point to my *Way of Divine Union*, 1915, pp. 170-172.

[12] Letter I to Gaius Therapeutes.

[13] *Tract on Mystical Theology*, Cap. I.

[14] Migne's edition of Dionysius, Vol. II, col. 422.

[15] *Way of Divine Union*, p. 166.

[16] *Religious Thought and Heresy in the Middle Ages*, 1918, pp. 672-679.

[17] Mary I. M. Bull: *A Short History of the Papacy*, 1921, p. 161.

[18] Ibid, p. 162.

[19] Ibid, Cf. Matthew Paris. 'The Sovereign Pontiff who ought to be the source of sanctity, the mirror of piety, the guardian of Justice, the defender of truth, protects such a man. Why does he take his part? To engulf the riches of England in the coffers of Rome's avarice.'

PART THREE: THE REALM OF THE IMAGINATION

Chapter 13.

The Life of Sir Aglovale de Galis

by Clemence Houseman

Clemence Houseman was the sister of the well-known poet A. E. Houseman. She is one of several writers who have taken up the enigmatic hints scattered throughout the *Morte D'Arthur* and set themselves to supply the missing elements of the story.

Malory does not tell us much about Aglovale, save that he is one of the sons of King Pellinore, himself one of the first and greatest heroes of the Round Table, that he was a brave and strong knight and that he was accidently killed by Lancelot during his rescue of Queen Guinevere from the stake. However, Aglovale must have lived through most of the great adventures of the Round Table, including the Quest for the Grail, in which his own brother Perceval was one of the successful seekers.

Clemence Houseman's remarkable book, which has not been reprinted since it first appeared in 1905, puts together, from clues scattered through various Arthurian texts, a convincing story which would not have shamed Malory himself. Her grasp of the mediaeval mind and the stuff of the romances makes for exciting reading—though she is never consciously over-archaic in her use of the so-called 'high' style.

The three chapters excerpted here set the scene for a life which is full of drama, tragedy and triumph. It is the portrait of a deeply private man forced to live too much in the world, to which he is ill-suited. It is memorable long after a first reading, as is the picture of a decaying Arthurian world, already overshadowed by the dark and destructive impulses which were to destroy it from within.

The quotation from the mediaeval spiritual text of the *Theologia Germanica*, with which the author prefaces her book, sets the scene as well as anything could:

> 'When a man truly perceiveth and considereth himself who and what he is, and findeth himself utterly vile and wicked and unworthy, he falleth into such a deep abasement that it seemeth to him reasonable that all creatures in heaven and earth should rise up against him. And therefore he will not and dare not desire any consolation and release, but he is willing to be unconsoled and unreleased; and he doth not grieve over his sufferings, for they are right in his eyes, and he hath nothing to say against them.'

CHAPTER 1

The first record of Aglovale shows him in boyhood tilting among others with his younger brother Lamorak. Under conduct of old squires the boys trained on the castle green, watched from above by fair, kind critics, damsels and dames, one a queen. Aglovale, then in early teens, held his own with sufficient address among his fellows to take the lead that was fitting his birth. Young Lamorak in due time hurled against him; and Aglovale, the elder by a year, the taller by a head, went shocked over his horse's tail. Loud sprang cheers from the rest, and on high white hands fluttered applause.

When later the boys ranked for the mellay, King Pellinore, with an honoured guest, young King Arthur, came out to watch, and the Queen, descending, stood with them under the gateway. Throughout the tough game the names of the rival brothers were calling. 'Lamorak, Lamorak,' rang like the beat of steel; less strong for a rallying cry tossed the name of Aglovale.

Behind his leader, little Durnor rollicked along heedless of danger, was rescued by Aglovale, was spared by Lamorak, till he and his cob tumbled perilously, and he was led away perforce, despite his valiant laughter and tears.

Fortune went with Lamorak, for his emulation was a contagious ardour; while Aglovale, nervous and dour, did little to stay defeat.

Then the Queen, proud of her dearest son Lamorak, told how he had forejusted his elder; thereupon King Pellinore well pleased also, called the pair out to run a course before King Arthur.

'You are fit enough, boys?'

'Yes, yes, sire!' shouted Lamorak, passing fain and eager.

Aglovale said nothing; he was badly bruised, but he would not plead. So matched with his younger brother he could get no credit, Lamorak could get no shame. Deep, then, bit the snake that poisoned his life thereafter. He set his teeth and wheeled for position. 'Lamorak, Lamorak,' hammered heavy on his heart, and his own name scarcely could he hear as their young fellows shouted.

Down went Lamorak. No fault was his, for his girths were rotten and broke. He rose fierce and clamorous, and sprang to the first horse that offered, eager to dispute his brother's nominal advantage. Aglovale claimed none. 'Though a back should break,' swore Lamorak, ''tis not I shall quit the saddle.' Again they ran; and Aglovale, the elder by a year, the taller by a head, went shocked over his horse's tail. How 'Lamorak, Lamorak' rang!

Away pranced the gallant boy; he saluted the Kings, the Queen; he flung off and sprang up to the mother, bareheaded for her kiss.

Aglovale stood up mute as death, came on foot, leading his horse, saluted, and passed. Arthur spoke kindly, commending both. The Queen looked after her son with tardy compunction, and when she saw him standing apart, stepped down and crossed to him over the green, pacing slow with folded arms; for in those days she went heavily with a double burden that proved to be Percivale and his sister Saint.

'Are you hurt, my son?'

He lied, saying, 'No'.

Her kind, grave eyes questioned his sombre countenance.

'By this is a noble knight shown: that he rises with no rancour from a fair overthrow; that he admires the force that can bring him down; that he knows no base envy.'

Aglovale breathed patiently. He dared not out with another word lest the shame of weeping should attend. In his heart he cried, 'Does he love you more than I, that you should love him more than me?'

'Ah, Aglovale,' said the Queen, wistfully, 'a degree of excellence you might have brought from the ground, though Lamorak from the selle brought more. Then had I been a happier mother and proud of both my sons.'

Aglovale quivered and hung his head silent; and she turned away sighing over his evil temper. From the incoherent conscience of youth he could not declare how the intolerable bitterness of overthrow lay in her balancing his loss so lightly against Lamorak's gain.

Yet then and afterwards, for all the Devil did with Aglovale, never could he kindle in him the least spark of hatred against his brother Lamorak.

On a day not long after, the Queen sent for Aglovale to her chamber, and showed him, pacing the court below, King Pellinore and a stranger, whose hand rested on his shoulder, whose face was addressed to him as the moon's to her earth, whose voice and laughter rang the tune of close and familiar friendship.

'That is Sir Griflet le Fise de Dieu, a good knight that I would you should love and honour.'

Then with her arm round the boy's neck she told how that friendship sprang: young Sir Griflet, on the first day of knighthood, sought to win worship of King Pellinore, who first refused him, warning him of his might; and when he would not be stayed, lightly smote him down; and then the King took him up nigh slain, gave him wind, and set him on his horse again, commending him for his great heart. And thereafter, she said, Sir Griflet loved and worshipped him greatly.

Aglovale sighed against her heart. He understood; and he willed to love and worship Sir Griflet.

That good queen did not herself fail to be gracious and generous when within her woman's sphere she was tried. From the wedding of Arthur and Guenever, King Pellinore returned with a goodly young knight, his new-found son Tor, the love-child he to a peasant girl had given, and she to her man Aries the cowherd, eighteen years before. Here may not enter the full tale of how noble blood sent Tor from the low estate of his mother with a bold request straight to the presence of his unguessed father; and how Arthur gave him knighthood before his own

nephew Gawaine, and was justified straightway by his noble deeds, while
Gawaine fell to disgrace. All this is written in the books of my most
dear Master whom I love so much.

The Queen, large-hearted, greeted her lord's son sweetly, fairly,
without misgiving for his peasant mother. She found for him room in
her good grace next her own sons, aye, in the end above one, and he
her firstborn; for Tor had touches of his father, was gentle, courteous,
of good parts, passing true of his promise; and he never did outrage.

Aglovale's likeness to his father was but in strong hawk features and
swarthy skin. The stately build inherited by Tor was not to be his; manhood could hardly redeem the lank and awkward sprouting of his youth.
Lamorak, in the bloom of boyish grace, preluded the man of perfect
strength and beauty, whose fine force and prowess ranked him equal
with great Launcelot, and Tristram biggest of Arthur's knights.

Still, as the boys grew Lamorak gained over Aglovale; and Tor—the
strong, admirable Tor himself—freely owned that the day would soon
come when he, too, would be bettered of his brother; and Pellinore
of himself said the same in his heart.

From their blunt play the boys went early to the sharp work of battle. When Danes and Irish landed in hosts against Arthur and ravaged
from North Wales, Pellinore, staying for larger levies, sent on Tor with
a troop of his best knights; and Aglovale and Lamorak, as young squires,
attended on their bastard brother.

A horrid foretaste they had when by night the active Irish rushed the
unwary camp where in the midst lay Guenever withal. From shrouds
of destruction Tor cut them out, and with him they headed a desperate stand to bar the way that the Queen had gone, with but four to
defend her: Arthur, Kay the foster brother, Gawaine, and Griflet.

Step by step, stubborn Tor and his poor few gave back before heavy
odds, till the night went blind, and broken and dispersed through the
forest they fought or fled. Aglovale and Lamorak held together, swept
away from Tor's voice by a surge of rattling steel. Joining in breathless
rallies that scattered again with loss, wounded, horsed, and unhorsed,
spent with the weight of harness, through that dreadful night they
endured a dark, inglorious struggle.

About dawn as they fell into a broad greenway, a foul knight came
by who spurred upon Aglovale. His weary arm beat down the spear;
it missed his side, pierced his thigh clean through, bore him to earth
and broke. Then Lamorak, savage, houghed the horse without scruple, and stood before his brother in stout defence. Aglovale on his knees
fought too. Down the greenway came the tramp of riders whose call
was 'Stranggore', and some spurred forward to the boys at bay. Aglovale
called for rescue, but Lamorak cried, 'Let be, let be! I will deal in full
payment.' And even as he spoke, with a stroke deep through the gorget, he ended his work.

Figure 9: 'He drew his sword and set his shield before him, and gave the serpent a deadly buffet' by H. J. Ford.

Fresh come at need here rode King Bagdemagus and his knights of Stranggore, with news of Pellinore following up from the south; with news of Tor whose driven foes they circled to head; but of Guenever and her four without news. By him the sons of Pellinore were not left horseless to foul murderers of the wounded; though scarcely might Aglovale ride for his hurt wherein the truncheon stack. To stay him from a fall a young squire of his age came to ride on the one side, as Lamorak rode on the other; this was Meliagraunce, son to King Bagdemagus.

On they rode under sky-dawn for the edge of the forest. And as the broad Humber opened ahead, flashing to the tide's uprush, helms golden in the first sun moved forward down a silver glade. Here shone lost Arthur and his fellows with a gathering troop; he, Gawaine, and Griflet each bore token of a king he had slain, while Kay bore two.

Forth into the open swung the joint force, and lo! on Humber's tide far out steered a dark blot, where Guenever went safe on a ferry barge; and on Humber's bank glittered the thousands of the Danes and their allies, rank on rank, well ordered, pricking forward.

'Can our hundreds face these?' said Bagdemagus.

'Aye,' answered Arthur, 'for see, now they find their dead.'

Even Guenever, far off, must have heard and shuddered at the dreadful cry of rage and lamentation that went up from the desolated hosts; and close after may have heard, too, the first great crash of battle; for while yet the foe reeled and surged and thronged, Arthur bore down upon them and began to slay.

In that battle Aglovale had no part. Lamorak shot away to the charge, and he was following insanely when Griflet saw him, reeling, loose-reined, clinging to the saddle peak. He cursed him roundly for a fool, guided him clear of the rush, brought him to a stand, and bade him go back. Where Griflet left him he stayed, nor went back nor forward.

The heart of Denmark was broken for its king; and Tor drove in on the rear the shattered strength of Ireland; and the allies, men of the Vale and of Soleise, between the Humber and backward pressure, turned frantic and fought friend and foe alike. That day there was fearful slaughter of the dense hosts of the invaders.

After the field was won, Tor found his brother fainting on his horse's neck. Weeping for joy, he lifted him down and cared for him; from the stiffened wound he drew out the spear head, and staunched the fresh blood that sprang free, comforting, praising, regarding naught else, refusing to leave him until Arthur summoned.

Then Aglovale, looking after, saw not far off King Arthur and his knights gathered red from the field; and Queen Guenever was come again and stood near between Kay and Gawaine. Fair gold was her hair. Fair gold was the hair of his mother, Pellinore's queen.

The King stood there with his sword bare in his hand to give knight-

hood. Aglovale sprang to his feet: the first to come and kneel was young
Lamorak. More he could not stand to see. His wound broke out stream-
ing afresh; for pure envy also his nostrils gushed blood; so fierce, then,
was the stress of the master passion of his youth.

After Lamorak came Gawaine's two brothers, Gaheris and Agravaine,
and many another; among the rest, Meliagraunce. And when the last
stood up a knight, Arthur questioned after one more. Tor answered
him; Lamorak, Bagdemagus, Griflet answered him.

Across the greensward ran Tor; in all his harness he ran. He lifted
Aglovale.

'I cannot stand or go,' said the boy, feebly.

'You shall! Aglovale, it is for knighthood of King Arthur!'

He drew his young brother's arm round his neck and lifted him along.
Lamorak came too, and between them they took him and helped him
to his knees before Arthur. Excalibur touched his shoulder, and his
famishing spirit was satisfied.

Tor set him on his feet. 'Keep up,' said Lamorak, low, 'for we go before
Queen Guenever.'

'Keep up,' said Tor, low, 'for we pass by Sir Gawaine and his brethren.'

Sweet salutation the fairest of women gave, and gracious thanks to
each, and praise namely to Sir Tor. Fair gold was her hair. On Lamorak
her eyes rested, because of his boyish grace and beauty. She said in
her heart, and afterwards to Arthur, 'An angel, a man, and a devil.'

'A man indeed,' said Arthur, 'but no devil, and on my faith no angel.
Good knights all they will prove.'

Gawaine and his brethren eyed hard the sons of Pellinore, for blood
feud was unfinished, and these sons of Lot were passing good haters.
Gawaine and Tor saluted coldly. Yet sooth that day had cancelled an
old misdeed recorded in the books of him I love so much, restoring
to Gawaine the fair place long withheld him in Queen Guenever's
regard. Let it be said of him that then, and always, faithful and blameless was his worship of Arthur's queen; and for the oath she had
imposed on him in his day of disgrace ever was he gentle and courteous to all ladies, and to all men who asked he showed mercy. The blood
of Pellinore would ask none of him; nor would Dinadan, nor Bagdemagus.

One envied Aglovale. Said Meliagraunce, 'For your night of defence,
Sir Aglovale, would I give my day of onslaught; for to me dearer than
knighthood were such fair and particular greeting from Queen
Guenever.'

Aglovale wondered, and liked the youth, nor thought ill of the words.
Alas! he so speaking was at first dawn of a passion that afterwards drove
him to rape and treason, and brought him to so evil an end that
Guenever denied him life and Arthur begrudged him burial.

Fuller reward awaited Sir Tor at Camelot; he, Gawaine, Griflet, and

Kay were chosen in place of knights of the Round Table fallen by the Humber. My most dear Master has told at length how the vacant sieges were filled; and also of the strict fairness of Pellinore, and of the resentment of King Bagdemagus. Of Aglovale in boyhood there is no more to tell.

CHAPTER II

Tor, the firstborn of King Pellinore, came to be the best beloved of all his sons. Sown in the waste, left to grow untended, he, in the flower of youth, approved the father generously, nor brought him any reproach for long neglect. Well might joy and pride in the heart of Pellinore rise up to claim him, and love swell stronger by delay. So, too, in other fathers sprang a like devotion at sight of their stranger sons: in Bors when he took White Helin; in Launcelot when Galahad came. The names of three other sons stand in dark contrast, three who forfeited their father's love, and carried curses: Aglovale, son to King Pellinore; Meliagraunce, son to King Bagdemagus; Mordred, son and nephew to King Arthur.

Yet even in early blameless years Aglovale, the heir, came to know that his father for Tor's sake, and his mother for Lamorak's sake, begrudged him his birthright. He knew, too, that Tor felt with the Queen, Lamorak with the King. As for Durnor, he held Durnor of slight account—Durnor!

Howbeit at that time all four brethren were named for high promise, approved of tried knights, well esteemed of their young fellows. And later, spite of all defect, three houses won to matchless fame in Logris: Arthur with his nephews, Launcelot with his brethren, Pellinore with his sons.

Rot at the core showed suddenly in Aglovale. Great justs were held at Cardiff in the presence of Arthur and his Queen, what time he bestowed an earldom upon Sir Tor, then of full age. There Tor won the degree on the first day; and on the second day Lamorak won it; and on the third day a strange knight came in, who smote down Aglovale and Durnor and many more and won the degree: his name, Sir Bagdemagus, King of Stranggore. Then Aglovale plucked up his horse and rode straight away north. Darkness covers here the ways he went.

Days went by, and weeks, and months, without any tidings, good or ill. With the new year came King Bagdemagus again, seeking after his lost son Meliagraunce. Sir Aglovale, he said, had come into Stranggore when justs were holding, and there he had smitten down Sir Agravaine and many others; and so brim and merry was he, that his son Meliagraunce would fellowship with him, and had gone in his company leaving no trace.

More days, weeks, months, went by. Lamorak and Durnor went and came, Tor came and went and came again, but Aglovale did not come.

From the Marches of Northgalis blew rumour of evil deeds: of lands harried, travellers and pilgrims robbed, knights murdered, and ladies misused. My most dear Master tells how there, at a later date, foul love and foul war prevailed, until Sir Launcelot came to make an end of Sir Turquine the murdered, and Sir Peris the ravisher.

A riding damsel came through Cardiff, a fair, fierce, reckless creature, who, though young she was, had led an adventurous life, with easy love and deadly hate, revel and hardship, quick laughter and desperate cries, some soft memory enshrined, and some hot malice unspent. Out of such a store she could weave many marvellous tales of adventure, never two alike. She, too, spoke ill of the Marches, and told of the infamous practice of two whom she named the Savage and the Sinister; how unfairly and barbarously they had slain a noble young knight; and how unfairly and barbarously they would have used his damsel, but that she wisely and wittily feigned and played to set them one against the other, till they fell to fighting, and she by good fortune escaped them both.

With touches of art she embellished her tale, yet her voice and eye showed that for once something was suppressed, and that this adventure was more near herself than others of which she feigned.

When she departed Durnor ran after. 'Why called you that one Sinister?'

'He fought left-handed,' she answered.

It was a trick that Aglovale practised.

Durnor went back, armed, and took horse. As he rode out Tor and Lamorak met him and questioned.

'I go to look up brother Sir Aglovale,' he said carelessly, and passed.

The two looked at each other.

'I shall follow,' said Tor.

'I also,' said Lamorak.

So they armed quickly, took horse, and went after Durnor.

Northward the three rode together. And many days they spent questing through the Waste Lands, and the Marches of Northgalis and Gore, at that time the most lawless wilds in Logris, for there two wanton queens fostered misrule out of hatred and treason to King Arthur. Some robber knights they fought and slew by the way, but neither Sir Peris nor Sir Turquine did they chance to meet.

They came at last upon one who was pitilessly robbing a gentlewoman of her fair young daughter. Lightly he set down his prize at Lamorak's challenge, rode against him full knightly, broke a spear and got a fall. Up he rose, pulled out his sword, and caught it in the left hand. He saw that the three bore the arms of Galis, and turned to flee. They hemmed him in, all but sure of him.

Lamorak sprang down. 'I require you of your knighthood to tell me your name?' He would not, and struck. 'Stay your hand,' said Lamorak, 'till I be better appointed.' His shield he cast aside; he plucked off also gorget and helm and cast them down. With naught to defend his head but his sword he advanced, and struck, and struck again.

So like St George he looked that a very stranger might have faltered, loth to strike upon that bright head. Aglovale sobbed, flung away his sword, and to Lamorak's distress kneeled and held him by the knees weeping. They wept together all four—even Durnor.

King Pellinore never questioned close as to how and where Aglovale had been found, for he was willing to know no worse than he could guess; and each brother guessed alone in his own heart; even Durnor bared none of his conjectures. But certain knowledge of misdoing came afterwards by means of Meliagraunce. He came by Cardiff with one Sir Gawdelin, such an one as himself, whose life was marred by the folly of an unlawful and unrequited passion. These two at the supper talked upon dangerous ground, for both were loose-tongued and had little discretion in their cups. Aglovale with them drank hard, but for his part said little. Suddenly he was aware that he was detected and betrayed; for as Meliagraunce was weaving a tale more graceless than merry, he saw King Pellinore smite down his head, and Durnor grow red and curse under his breath, and Lamorak lift and stiffen. Under their dreadful silence he assented steadily when Meliagraunce demanded confirmation. Durnor came to him afterwards and blurted out all: some small and peculiar detail mentioned by Sir Meliagraunce had been given also by the riding damsel, so serving to link his story with hers. Meliagraunce himself never knew what mischief he had done.

Not to Aglovale alone was this discovery bitter shame. King Pellinore had to own in his heart that his son, so like him in feature, revealed also dark traits of character he deemed all dead and gone with his own youth. Lately he had come to think better of him, seeing him back among his brothers, valiant and eager as Lamorak, prudent and serviceable as Tor, tough and staunch as Durnor; and mainly was he gratified to perceive ripening in him something of his own stern temper, just sense, and keen brain, meet for the son and heir who should rule wild Galis after him. Now, because of those dead sins yet living, King Pellinore smote down his head and went heavily.

Aglovale held on resolutely, determined to blot out the past with fair fame. Yet all the while his heart held its old bane, that would coil and sting, spite of the true love he bore his brother Lamorak; and though no word nor sign escaped to betray it, the evil within was working his countenance to express a nature marred and unlovely.

By joust and field Lamorak blazed on his way of resplendent valour, the most insatiable fighter that ever lifted sword. He was still but a youth when called to the Table Round, where, according to Merlin's writing, he sat at his father's side hard by the Siège Perilous.

Then Aglovale failed again. Since Lamorak he could not hate, wild

envy set him in loathing against himself and his own barren life. So
virulent was this moral distemper that he was smitten with physical
sickness; sleep went from him, and old wounds in his body ached,
opened, and bled afresh. Madness was hovering. He took horse and
reeled away into night.

For over a year his record stands well-nigh blank. Only his own evidence tells that he left the realm of Logris and tried for solace new ways
of abuse, ranging the seas, one of a notorious crew whose sail became
a curse and a terror to the trader and his town.

He rallied when war came: the great war with Rome, when Arthur
and his host passed over to Flanders, and went on kingdom by kingdom to the conquest of Christendom. To Barflete came Pellinore and
his three sons, Tor, Lamorak, and Durnor, each in a great galley stuffed
with fighting men well appointed. Came Aglovale by night, landing
alone from a poor cog-boat, sans horse or the price of one, with naught
but the harness on his back, red-rusted with brine. A very just estimate of him lay heavy on his welcome; no account of his doings was
required of him, and he tendered none. Durnor alone, the while he
served like a squire to the tarnished heir, hit at him with hard times
of derision. But to Durnor indifference gave licence.

In that great campaign Aglovale showed at his best, for he had gifts
for marshalling hosts of war such as were rare to find in those emulous
days of personal valour. King Pellinore gave him full scope, setting him
in command above his brothers, and Tor and Lamorak were as right
hand and left to him in their loyal support, gladly admitting his right
and worth. His was not brilliant work and fortunate, like Sir Gawaine's,
whose star ascendant at that time outshone all others; but what he did
King Arthur marked well and approved, for he, the great leader, could
best of all appraise the young knight's sound instinct in methods of
war. So when the year closed on him victorious at Rome, crowned
Emperor by the Pope, when he summoned his Round Table there and
filled up the sieges, Sir Aglovale de Galis was duly called and placed.

Knights of highest worship sat hard by the Siege Perilous that awaited
the coming of the best knight in the world. To the right of it sat King
Pellinore, then Sir Lamorak, then Sir Marhaus, the best knight of Ireland;
to the left sat Sir Bors the Good, with Sir Launcelot and his brother
Sir Ector; Sir Tor was not far, with Sir Gawaine for his opposite. Distant by many degrees from that zenith, Sir Aglovale had his place, for
dearer to Arthur was the stout heart and arm than the good head. And
the mind of Aglovale inclined the same way; he would gladly abandon
all the credit won in command, but once to have in his ears such a
roar of welcome and acclaim as rose from fighting ranks when Lamorak
rode in.

On that high day Durnor, riding behind his brothers, saw a hard-
featured man thrust through the crowd and catch at Sir Aglovale's knee,

calling him by a strange name. Aglovale struck his hand aside, tossed
him a piece of gold, and passed. The man, a seafarer by his dress, fell
back and plucked at a Welshman with a question; Aglovale, with a stony
countenance, rode on ignoring salutations. His day was darkly overcast. Durnor was ashamed to watch or to question; he went on wondering.

At the day's end the same stranger entered as a suitor before King
Pellinore and his sons, and got leave to speak.

'My lord sir Aglovale,' he said, 'is it sooth that to-day, for the honour
of the Round Table, you will grant any man his suit except it be
unreasonable?'

Aglovale eyed him sternly and answered, 'Aye.'

'Then, my lord, I desire and pray that you take me to serve you.'

An angry red mounted to Aglovale's brow. The stranger spoke on hur-
riedly.

'I ask to be no more than your groom, your henchman, your valet,
albeit I am not more meanly born than some who are squires. And
I will promise you very faithful service for the sake of one I shall never
meet again, because, my lord Sir Aglovale, of the resemblance you bear
him.'

Said Durnor, whose tongue was more ready than his wits, 'Hey,
brother, you knew him not, and he mistook you!'

Said the stranger quickly, with his eyes still on Sir Aglovale, 'Before
to-day never has my lord your brother set eyes on me.'

Aglovale strode forward and struck him on the mouth. 'Brose, you
lie!' he said.

Confounded stood the suitor, savage but cowed. He got his voice,
and said thickly, 'My Lord, if I live you shall repent of this.'

Said Aglovale, wickedly, 'Get you gone, would you go to hell in your
own time.'

Said Brose, 'At your heels, my lord, will be time enough for me.'

King Pellinore spoke, seeing Aglovale finger at his sword. 'Fair son,
he stands a suitor on your honour to-day.' And at that his son ground
his teeth and laughed harshly.

Said the King to Brose, 'By my counsel you and your suit withdraw.'

The man spoke up resolutely, though his hard-favoured countenance
twitched.

'Truly sir, my lord your son may hold my suit unreasonable, since
he does not please to forget that when he saw me before, for my sins
I was a galley-slave.'

Still, as he spoke he kept his eyes upon Sir Aglovale, who turned his
to watch his father's face. Both drew the breath of hard conflict.

'And yet is my suit not unreasonable, since who would serve him more
truly and faithfully than one he delivered out of that hell.'

'Here, you dog!' cried Aglovale, in a black rage, 'for the honour of the day and because of my word you shall have your asking. But by God!' he added through his teeth, 'you shall sweat for it hereafter.'

Again King Pellinore warned Brose off his dangerous ground, guessing heavily at ugly concerns behind his son's truculence.

'His man am I,' came the answer, 'at what service and what wage he wills. He knows I am able enough. I was the first he made free. Me he set to loose Christians while he went killing Saracens; and not one was left alive; and it was a great galley; and we, slaves with our chains, were all my lord Sir Aglovale had to back him. Moreover, he stood to fight unarmed, and so fought and won.'

Aglovale cursed and flung out his sword, beside himself with rage. His brothers by force stayed him, and got Brose away and stowed safe till that madness should be past.

Be it known forthwith that master and man kept each his word. Aglovale stinted not by harsh and brutal usage to tempt the man to his worst; and Brose endured, steadily and patiently biding his time to be approved, until his master recognized with wonder that this dog was the faithfullest of his kind, following him out of real devotion. Straight he acknowledged, 'Brose, I do repent', and never thenceforth had a doubt of him till came the time of double parting when broke the unhappy heart of Aglovale. Brose, in an after day, when, as shall be told, he followed Percivale, professed what secret virtue in his master had drawn him to allegiance. 'Never have I heard him complain,' he said. No man, save Nacien the Hermit, did ever so truly as Brose read the worth of that distorted nature at its worst.

Now, as to the conclusion of this passage, had Aglovale chosen to hold his peace, the truth might not have come to light, for Brose told no more, refusing to answer any question but in his mater's presence; and drunk or sober, he never let loose his tongue till the end came. But Aglovale, when his brothers turned to him with new worship, and his father with kind reproach, because he had despised the approval of their love, felt this load more heavy to bear than any deserved disgrace. So as they would not cease and let him go, 'I was one of them,' he said; 'I, too, was a galley-slave.'

That was not enough, though his voice and his face were frightful. So gross an outrage to him but moved their common blood with indignation.

Said Lamorak under his breath, 'I rather would have died.'

Aglovale heard. 'I, too,' he said, 'even as due by a halter.'

Durnor gaped and gasped, 'As due!' Aghast stared King Pellinore and Tor and Lamorak. His few words were enough to set their guesses; and he watched the leap and run, the pause and flow of apprehension in their looks. Now they knew why he at one time, before they came to Rome, had avoided the coast; there at Genoa their eyes had seen rotten bodies dangling above the tide-mark; they had heard tell of a well-

dreaded corsair barque, decoyed and betrayed there by means of a Sara-
cen emir. Yes, they knew; only Durnor did not understand. Durnor
was a dense fool.

King Pellinore broke silence. 'And yet you live!'

His unworthy son came to him, followed after him, kneeled to him,
and held his knees in mute entreaty.

'You felon proclaimed! Why had you not your dues?'

'Pardon, sire, because there is that in me that is due to you.'

King Pellinore cut him short with a heavy curse, and in his passion
turned and struck the woeful mask that was his living disgrace.

'Oh, you lie—you lie!' he cried.

At that Aglovale stood up and pulled out his sword; taking it by the
point, he presented the hilts to King Pellinore.

'Prove that upon my body, sire, an you please,' he said desperately.

The King gripped with a will.

'Stand aside, Sir Tor,' cried Aglovale; 'as for this matter you shall not
come between me and my father.'

But Tor said, 'Ah sire, are all the good strokes of that sword clean
gone from remembrance?'

'Answer! Why had you not your dues?'

He writhed and faltered. 'I was not so well worth a halter as some
others; and—and I was valued to ransom as a king's son.'

'Ah, wretched blabber!'

Again Tor came between. 'Speak again, brother—say you never
acknowledged your birth!'

'Yes, bastard, I did. I acknowledged my birth, unawares, even as you
did among your mother-brethren. Ah, sire, pardon me that at least!'

'What more have you to tell, felon?'

'Sire,' said Aglovale, 'boots it to know more of what I did, or what
others did with this sinful body of mine, since my name and my lineage went not with it?'

'Unhappy fool! Does not your rascal fellow know you?'

Aglovale answered knightly, 'My fellows now are knights of the Round
Table; and excepting you, sire, and my fair brothers, and my lord King
Arthur, none of them that bear life shall charge disworship against my
name and lineage but I will prove upon his body that he lies.'

King Pellinore went up and down thinking a great while. Then he
put back Aglovale's sword into his hands and said heavily, 'See you
fail not. When your gallows deeds be known, or keep you body alive
in the Devil's name—or God have mercy on your soul!'

In this he reckoned amiss, for Brose proved close and sure, and
Aglovale lived longer than the devil in him, and died the last of his
mother's sons.

Now, it is recorded that after these wars with Rome, Pellinore set his
son Aglovale as warden at Cardigan. Maybe this in a manner was

banishment till he should have earned full forgiveness, although later
the lordship of Cardigan is called his appanage. Here Aglovale sped
ill; for, after a turn of staid and strict government, he fell to ways of
misrule. For a brief space he made a fine show of it, merry and brim
in living and fighting. He lured Durnor to him, and despised him that
he came. Many drew to him at that time; and any who had earned the
King's displeasure could find with him countenance and welcome. So,
though riot and misrule were doubtless all his sins, he gave large cause
for the count of treason.

After remonstrance and a threat, King Pellinore made short work.
He rode in on surprise with a great plump of spears, and Aglovale, sur-
rendering without a stroke, was deprived of land and rule, and imprisoned with undue rigour.

He never complained, for, indeed, the odd good in him lent him a
patience and submission rare to find among wrongdoers. The inter-
cession of his mother and his brethren, and namely of Sir Tor, restored
him to freedom and grace.

But too soon his better self went to the winds as before. This time
Lamorak was partly to blame. The words he used enter here not indeed
in time and place as recorded by my most dear Master, who for his
part kept not strictly to the order of events, as can be shown on his
telling of the jousts at Avilion and at Kinkenadon by the Sands.

Jousts were called beside the isle of Avilion for the proving of Arthur's
young nephew Gareth, then newly sprung from the scullery into sudden fame and well-earned love of his lady Liones. Thither came his
mother, Morgause, Queen of Orkney, still with her fatal beauty as keen
as when Arthur, her unknown brother, wooed her to guilty love. On
Lamorak she looked, and Lamorak looked on her, and for their bane
love sprang.

Marvellous deeds of arms Lamorak did that day, out of measure fain
to win worship before her. Fighting was like a revel to him, till in the
midst of his ecstasy he chanced to see his two brothers, Aglovale and
Durnor, overthrown. That turned him to rage; four knights went down
to his spear; more to his sword; others fled. Aglovale and Durnor he
horsed again, but in his heat he did not spare them words.

Shame on them! cried Lamorak, to fall so off their horses. Knights
that were knights indeed, he said, should fight on horseback; fighting
afoot, he said, was but meant for spoilers and felons. So he spoke heedless in his heat. 'Sit fast upon your horses,' he cried at parting, 'or else
fight never more afore me.'

Durnor emptied language and protest after him; but as for Aglovale
his blood rose and broke forth, so that it ran from the ventails of his
helm and he had to lift the vizard.

'How, brother,' said Durnor, 'fell you so hard?' But when he viewed
a face pallid and hard-set, even he could read and understand.

'Nay, nay,' he said in clumsy kindness, 'Aglovale, he never meant it so! Oh, he had clean forgot all that, or never had he spoken so!'

'By your leave, fair brother,' returned Aglovale, 'I can hear as I list; and, if I list, gainsay.'

Durnor looked after him as starkly he rode into the fray. 'When he goes to work with his lips white, he kills. Now God have mercy on some man's soul.'

His cast was true enough. Aglovale that day was curst and forebore none. After that he was lost again for many a day, and with him Brose.

Tidings came of him returned and dwelling at Cardigan. Thither rode Tor and Durnor, and bore back good report of him, as they found him, sober, just, wise, and knightly in all ways. But Tor owned to King Pellinore that their welcome had not been brotherly, Sir Aglovale, cold and reserved, showing with a manner of precise courtesy a mind inclined to quarrel. Durnor laughed and made excuse, in that he was assotted on a passing fair wench, and an exigent. So had he mistaken sweet Gilleis, Aglovale's last and only true love.

When King Pellinore afterwards passed to Cardigan, Aglovale had flown, none knew thither, and sweet Gilleis lay in the tomb.

CHAPTER III

Nacien the Hermit, gathering worts high up on Wenlock Edge, saw a knight come riding below, followed far behind by one afoot, running, stooping, shunning the open. Over rough and smooth rode the knight spurring hard. The jaded horse stumbling on broken ground, fell and did not rise; whereat suddenly he pulled out his sword, and rove that good beast through the body. Forward on his feet he started in a hasty aimless fashion; his shield he flung away, then his helm; piece by piece he stripped off his harness, and cast it from him.

'Now see I,' said Nacien, 'that a fiend rides him.' And he went down to meet him till the sound of groaning came to his ears and words of blasphemy. The secret follower came nearer, saw the old man ahead, and stood up with a gesture of warning. Right so the knight caught sight of him.

Brose turned to flee, for Aglovale made fiercely after him with his sword drawn. Brief was the chase: Brose missed footing, fell, rose up lamed, faced round on his master, and held up entreating hands. In vain: deep into his side bit the relentless sword. For a moment Aglovale looked on the fallen man, then his reddened blade he flung afar, and kneeling he tried to staunch the bleeding life.

'It was foully done,' said Nacien. 'Go you, murderer, and bring water.' And Aglovale went like a bidden child.

Even with that first look on the two men Nacien knew that his work lay rather with the soul of the one than the body of the other.

But for Aglovale he could do nothing till Brose had taken good hold of life. Neither day nor night would that unhappy master quit his man; scarcely would he speak or eat, and sleep he did not till on the third night Nacien beguiled him with a drink.

Then said Brose weakly, 'For the love of God help my master lest he die of his shut heart.' And when Nacien commended his devotion so evilly rewarded: 'Nay,' said Brose, 'he had threatened and I had promised. In following I broke my word; his my master kept.'

But of counsel and consolation Aglovale took as little heed as of admonition and rebuke, till the day came when Nacien told him Brose was sure of recovery. Then he was moved to blessings and thankings and promises for gratitude, and the good man, seeing his time, with grave authority called on him to confess his sins.

Aglovale looked at him darkly. 'I want no absolution,' he said.

'My son,' said Nacien, 'I bid you to penance in confession.'

'Yea, that I want,' said Aglovale, after long silence.

'In the name of God!' said Nacien.

Aglovale did not kneel. He stood up and bore the light of day and Nacien's eyes through all. His tongue failed him at first. 'Gilleis!' he said, and stopped dumb, struggling.

'In the name of God!' repeated Nacien.

Once more the wretched man said 'Gilleis!' And further, 'Her I did not ravish.

'Two men knocked at midnight and asked her pity on one sore wounded; and she being a lone maid feared to unbar. Yet because of their need and the bitter frost, and because they swore steadily her maidenhood should get no hurt, her pity was so wrought upon that she gave them entrance. And she did also all service she could for him wounded; for he asked her to ransack his wounds in knee and breast. So first she unbound his knee and salved and dressed it, and greatly he complained the while of the wound in his breast. So very softly she handled the bindings; but as she drew off the last fold there was no blood, and on the breast uncovered there was no wound. Whole he was but for a prick in the knee. Like a bird she went to the door as Brose shot in the outside bolts. She stood and put her hands over her face, and I watched her and never stirred. And after a while she said, Why had I done so? I said, for want of her pity on the great wound in my breast, and greatly I complained.

'She had eyes like a heifer's that could not show anger. Her hair was wheat-brown. Her skin was like lime blossom, and as sweet was the scent she gave. God never made woman-flesh more quick and tender to the influence of man. Though I never touched her I troubled her, and she writhed and drew her mantle around.

'She put me in mind of my oaths, and I said until they were broken I was not forsworn. Yet she lamented for her good name; and then I reached out my sword to her, and bade her make it good on me if she chose. Yet I played with her then, knowing that she could not. And when she put the pommel between her feet and felt the point with her hands, I laughed, knowing this also she could not do. And at that she wept, and her tears—Gilleis—even for her tears I never stirred. But she had to hear, and she could not hide.

'So I told her how, lying hurt, I had looked down from a window, and had seen her kiss given to a tall squire, as never had a kiss been given to me. And I told her how I would have had her by force, had I loved her but as I had loved others. She answered that her squire was now a knight; and was I so base, she said, as to shun knightly contest, when she doubted not he would prove upon me that he was the better man of his hands. I said I had done enough with woman on the grave of lord or lover to know that not so ever would sweet kindness freely given touch my lips; that way came only light love or heavy curses. I said I could not boast to be better of my hands than he, as I had not tried him. Yea, he had good looks for her eye, a good name for her ear, while I was swart and halt, and I was he called Sinister. But he had no force to love her as I loved; and I would for one night so possess her eye and her ear that she could not choose but know I loved her better than he. And that was true. She looked at me and covered her face and held her peace. Though by falsity I won her, that was true.

'She had to hear, and she could not hide. But in the end I grew ashamed and repented; and before dawn I confessed all: how her solitude that night had been contrived by force and fraud; and how by means of Brose I had ensured that my going should be spied to defame her; and how I hoped after to carry on the game. But I told her that now the bolts had been long withdrawn, and while dawn was far I would take myself away to prevent my own mischief. ''God amend all,'' said Gilleis, as I went.

'Now when I issued to the night all the world was white with snow. Then I hardened my heart as I left my tracks upon it. And the skies had no ruth. At dawn a boatman found me fallen, and lifted me down to the river; and I left amends to God and went with the stream.

'Her knight, Sir Berel, lay in Ireland held at ransom. A poor man he was, and Gilleis la Orpheline, in ward of an old knight his father, had been living meanly to buy him free. Now when after many days Brose traced me out, he brought word how my footprints had undone her, for her tale was incredible to the old man, and he cursed her for his son and departed. And soon after he died. I turned again, and vowed to her I would do anything she should require. She was so gentle I never heard a hard word, but then she did require a hard penance. For slander she cared little, except at the ears of the two most dear to her, of whom one was now dead; and her request was that I should pass to Ireland, and acknowledge my treason to her knight under oath, and abide by his ruling. I said this was not according to the course of knightly usage. She urged no further and asked no more, so I swore to it and went.

'Methought as I went I heard devils laughing at what should come; but lo! when I had told him all, he believed me! Knowing my name and my ill-fame, yet he believed me! A good knight he was and courteous; but I came away sore and angry because he would not promise so much as to break a spear on me when he might dispose of his body; for he said as I had made amends in better sort than by way of arms, he declined to require it otherwise. So I left him unransomed and came again to this land.

'Then I went to tell Gilleis how I had sped. But I lied. I had told him all truly, I said; and no, I said, he did not believe me. I kissed her in her swoon to seal the lie.

'It came to pass before the year was out, Brose laid me again at her gate, wounded in deep earnest. I cried out when I saw her that I would not keep those terms, that rather than burn through such another night I would take the frost. Yet when I opened my eyes to life, Gilleis was there tending me; and for many days Gilleis. And before I had strength to take—she gave.

'Her most sweet affection once mine, grew passing well, and was the dearer under peril of instant bitter ending. Before long Brose brought me word of that knight Sir Berel; by the good offices of the first of Irish knights Sir Marhaus, he was at liberty and returning. Then I took horse and rode down to the Marches to await him at the Forest Cross-roads. For two days I watched there till he came. He came bound hand and foot, laid across the saddle. In like manner two followed behind. I knew him, for his beaver was broken away; me he knew by my arms. In God's name he called on me to remember my offers, and to help them from a foul knight and a murderous, who had overcome them. He besought me to turn from ado and rather carry warning of their case to Sir Marhaus, who followed nigh, for this knight was so big of his hands that few might match him. I knew well who drove them so: that was Sir Turquine, brother to Sir Carados, whom Launcelot met and slew as so he drove Sir Gaheris. He smote foully at the bound man as he rode past him to come at me. Then I turned and fled, and laughed as I rode. And in a little while I escaped from Sir Turquine and came to the open. Then I lamed my horse, and rode on again at a soft pace till I met a big knight, no other than Sir Marhaus. We saluted, and he asked me of three knights who were of his fellowship. I told him that beyond the river I had seen one knight, driving three before him, bound across their horses; and I taught him the way contrary, and excused myself from him because my horse was lame. So misguided he departed. And I deemed I should keep the love of sweet Gilleis, for I knew more than a little of the ways of Sir Turquine, and that knights who fell into his hands were seen no more.

'Though by frauds I won her and kept her, I would not have her fastened to me by any bond but her free love, and spite of her woman's wish we never came to wedlock. Then came promise of another bond. I carried her to Cardigan, and there the summer months ran over with such bounty of love no word can tell, and half I thought no bolt would ever strike me for my sins.

'On a windy day, looking out, I saw Sir Marhaus ride past to take the sea for Ireland. The one I feared to see was not among his company. So I turned and kissed Gilleis with a glad heart. I kissed her never again living or dead. Then I took horse, and I saw, as I rode the heights, the ship labour out to sea and dwindle away. I rode far that day, and fought and slew because I was light of heart.

'But meanwhile the winds were so strong and contrary that the ship put back for Galis, and about sundown fell to wreck on the bar. All this Gilleis spied from her tower, and she sent down her barge and a messenger, praying all to return to take lodging. And when Sir Marhaus was come, spent with sickness and the sea, Gilleis herself in her kindness came into the hall to ask how he did. I came homing, and from without I saw her bright head pass, and being glad I called to her by name; and she looked out smiling. Now when Sir Marhaus heard her name he considered her well, and asked her of her grace to tell him if she were Gilleis la Orpheline; and she said, "Aye." And seeing how she was girdled high, he deemed all was well and asked eagerly after his friend Sir Berel, and how he had sped out of peril in the Marches. Her eyes filled at his name, and she said she knew naught of that. Then he held her in blame, letting her know of her knight's good faith, and lamented for him, supposing him to have been shamefully slain. I entered and stood at gaze, and Gilleis stood and looked at me. He knew me by my arms, and saluted; and as I made no return, he put me in mind of our meeting, and what had passed between us. All white she was. She stood looking into my face. She put her hands to her girdle. "Lie still, lie still!" she said, and fell down.

'Afterwards she sent for me, and meekly prayed me to tell her the whole truth. Yet of her own wit she knew it already. So I kneeled by her and told her all, as it had been an old dream. She turned her head and lay quiet and never spoke to me more. And before long, having put from her untimely the burden she had of me, she died. And I have buried her.

'She loved me best. Had she loved him so, I deem she surely could have lived. She loved me best, and therefore has she died.

'Curse me! You, Sir Nacien, if you have the gift to draw curses, speed now on me the worst curses you know.'

Nacien the Hermit spoke for consolation: 'Doubt not,' he said, 'but that God shall reward you for your sins.'

'The right avenger is dead,' said Aglovale, heavily. 'While I buried her he died. Sir Marhaus turned back on a quest through the Marches, and there shortly he met with Sir Turquine, and fared no better than others before him: overcome, stripped naked, beaten with thorns, prisoned underground. There in prison he found his friend, whose two fellows were dead, who was then near death, who died that same night. On the morrow Sir Turquine was slain by Sir Launcelot.

'I also went and sought the Marches for Sir Turquine or any there appointed to slay me. I found my brother Sir Durnor. Sir Turquine had dealt with him. He told me how Sir Berel was dead, but he could not tell me where Sir Marhaus had gone. So I left him complaining that I would not stay.

'Sir Marhaus, when he stood and told me how he had spoken with Gilleis, looked as my father King Pellinore looked when once he struck me. And he excused himself from my roof and went out straight. He did not put me to any question. He left me untouched. He was not quite ready to slay me then; but surely now he should be ready. Yet Sir Marhaus and I have not met again.'

Suddenly Aglovale writhed, waved out his sword, and fell to raving blasphemously that he would not take his death of any man of less worship than Sir Lamorak, his brother; and rushing out like one possessed, he went shouting for Sir Marhaus over the hillside, and Nacien saw him no more till another morn.

So began the healing of Aglovale. Day by day the holy man handled him to ransack all his life and discover his bane; gentle and severe, compassionate and unsparing, he found the way to win of that perverse nature trust and reverence. Before Brose was whole the Hermit was ware of the meekest penitent that ever he ordered, who followed him in prayer and fasting and hearing Mass daily. Nacien also gave him a cilice for wear that he put off neither by day nor night. Brose fretted seeing his master go so lean, and warned him he was in no case to win worship.

'Hold your peace,' said Aglovale, 'nor tempt me.'

Then Nacien called him, seeing him fit to be instructed of the spiritual knighthood. He declared the virtue of perfect faith and a pure spirit that should achieve more than strength and hardihood; while every blow given should yield praise to God, and every blow taken should yield prayer; when overthrow could touch no shame, and excellence no vainglory. He said also that those of this holy knighthood should slay no man unhappily by misadventure, nor should any of a good life get wound of them, for the grace of God should be in their hands, because they should be maidens clean of life and heart.

'Alas, alas!' said Aglovale.

Further, Nacien spoke by prophecy of the best knight of the world, who should do marvels without fail; and of the visitation of the Holy Grail, that all should follow and none should see, save he and his fellows, the pure and the chaste. And while Aglovale bowed down his

An Arthurian Reader

head and wept to hear, there entered his heart vision of his young
brother Percivale, with a giving of love and worship for the boy's innocence and truth. He vowed then that never should Percivale learn any
harm by him.

All this Nacien gave him to know to confirm him in humility against
his old lust for earthly worship and his envy. He warned him in chief
against envy of his brother Sir Lamorak. Aglovale withstood him.

'My brother Sir Lamorak I do and ever shall above all men love and
worship. Is this envy?'

His old passion took him hard suddenly. 'Ah, Lamorak, Lamorak!'
he cried, 'but little love have you for me and no worship. Ah, Lamorak!'
And tears and blood sprang from him.

He was brought to sounder conditions by the day of departure, for
Nacien, seeing his danger, not only showed him how envy had sent
him upon evil courses, but also how his natural affections were disor-
dered and mischievous.

Said Aglovale, 'Yet God made me so.'

'Nay,' said Nacien, 'you are not made, but making. One only came
made from the womb. Not before the day of your death will God have
made you.'

'Pray for me,' said Aglovale at the last, on his knees asking blessing.
'Pray to the high Father that He hold me in His service. While I am
alive pray for me, and when I am dead, pray some prayers more or less
for my soul.'

The holy man blessed him, and promised him then, that if he
amended his life well, God should grant him his death by the hand
of a right noble knight, and so sent him from the peaceful height down
to be proved of the world.

Chapter 14.

Sir Gawain and the Green Knight

Probaly the most famous individual Arthurian text, apart from Malory's *Le Morte d'Arthur*, is the 13th Century poem, *Sir Gawain and the Green Knight*. It is a work of remarkable richness, boldly and brilliantly written in an unforgettable style. Along with Chaucer's *Canterbury Tales*, it is the most studied mediaeval text of all.

It is also an exciting, moving and colourful story, which has been interpreted several times as an opera,[1] as a film,[2] and many times as a play or retelling. Few will ever forget, once they have read it, the first appearance of the terrifying Green Knight in the hall at Camelot, or the outcome of the 'Christmas game' which he offers to play with one of Arthur's knights.

Here also we find the finest portrayal of Gawain, a knight famed for courtesy and chivalric behaviour—a far cry from the rather unpleasant character he becomes in the late romances (see p. 196). Above all, he is a human being, not some vague abstraction of knightly excellence; Gawain succeeds by failure of a kind, and by accepting, in a moment of very human fear, the help of magic against magic.

The two episodes presented here are from the beginning and end of the poem. In between these there are a number of adventures—though never taking us far from the central plot, another unusual aspect of the Gawain-poet's craft. Three times Gawain is tempted by his host's beautiful wife, while her husband is out hunting—incidentally described with such detail as to be wholly unforgettable. Three times Gawain comes close to giving in to temptation. Finally he accepts a gift that he believes will save his life—but this is only the latest of the twists and turns of this extraordinary story.

We do not know who wrote *Sir Gawain and the Green Knight*. That he is one of the finest poets of his time—perhaps of any time—is beyond dispute. Unfortunately he wrote in a northern dialect of Middle English, not easily read by most people; so that we have had to opt for a translation, not into verse but into a mixture of prose and poetry which none the less captures much of the original flavour. It was made by the Revd Ernest Kirtlan in 1912 and is still one of the best renditions to be found.

❦

This King Arthur was at Camelot at Christmas with many a lovely lord, and they were all princely brethren of the Round Table, and they made rich revel and mirth, and were free from care. And betimes these gentle knights held full many a tournament, and jousted in jolly fashion, and then returned they to the court to sing the Christmas carols. And

the feasting was for fifteen days, and it was with all the meat and mirth
that men could devise. And glorious to hear was the noisy glee by day
and the dancing by night, and all was joyous in hall and chamber,
among the lords and ladies as it pleased them, and they were the most
renowned knights under Christ and the loveliest ladies that ever lived;
for all these fair folk were in their first age, and great were they

> in mirth,
> The gayest in the land,
> The king was of great worth,
> I could not name a band
> So hardy upon earth.

And when the New Year was come, on that day the nobles on the daïs
were double served, when the king came with his knights into the great
hall and the chanting in the chapel was ended. And clerks and others
set up a loud cry, and they kept the Feast of Christmas anew, and they
gave and received New Year's gifts, and much talking was there about
the gifts. And ladies laughed full loudly, though they had lost in the
exchange, and he that won was not wroth, as ye will well trow, and
they made all this mirth together as was fitting for the season. When
they had washed, they worthily went to their seats, each according to
his rank, as was seemly. And Queen Guinevere was full gaily attired
as she took her seat on the daïs, and on fair silks under a canopy of
costly Tarsian tapestry, embroidered with the finest of gems that money
could buy on

> a day
> The comeliest lady, I ween,
> She glanced from eyes that were grey,
> Her like that he had seen
> Truly could no man say.

But Arthur would not eat until all were served, for he was so jolly, and
almost like a child. Little recked he of his life; and so restless was he
that he could not sit or recline for long, so active was his young blood
and his brain. And there was another strange thing about him because
of his noble birth, that he would not eat on these high days until he
had heard some eerie tale of marvellous adventures, of his forbears or
arms, or else that some knight joined with another in jousting, life for
life as hap would have it. This was the custom of the King when he
was in court at each feast as it came amongst his noble household

> in hall,
> Therefore so bold of face
> He sat there, strong in stall,
> In that new year of grace
> Much mirth he made with all.

Thus was the King in the high seat talking before the high table of courteous trifles and good. Sir Gawain was sitting beside Guinevere. Agravayn of the hard hand sat on the other side, and both were sons of the king's sister and very strong and faithful knights. Bishop Bawdewyn was at the head of the table, and Ywain, son of Urien, was eating by himself. And they were all on the daïs, and well were they served, and afterwards many a true man at the sideboards. With the crashing of trumpets came the first course, and with banners and beating of drums and piping loud, so that many a heart heaved full high at the sound, and there were many dear and full dainty meats. And there were so many dishes and such great plenty that it was hard to find room to set before the folk the silver service that held the courses

> on cloth,
> Each man as he loved himself
> There laughed he without loath,
> Each two had dishes twelve,
> Good beer and bright wine both.

Now will I tell you no more of the serving, for ye may wot well no want was there. Another and a full new wonder was drawing near. Scarcely had the noise ceased and the first course been served in the court, when there came in at the hall door an ugly fellow and tallest of all men upon earth. From his neck to his loins so square set was he, and so long and stalwart of limb, that I trow he was half a giant. And yet he was a man, and the merriest that might ride. His body in back and breast was strong, his belly and waist were they small, and all his features

> full clean.
> Great wonder of the knight
> Folk had in hall, I ween,
> Full fierce he was to sight,
> And over all bright green.

And he was all clad in green garments, and fitting close to his sides was a straight coat with a simple mantle above it and well lined with gay and bright furs, as was also his hood hanging about his locks and round his shoulders; and he had hosen of that same green on his calves, and bright spurs of gold, that hung down his legs upon silk borders, richly striped, where his foot rested in the stirrup.

And verily all his vesture was of pure green, both the stripings of his belt, and the stones that shone brightly in his gorgeous apparel, upon silk work, on his person and saddle; and it would be too tedious to tell you even the half of such trifles as were thereon embroidered with birds and flies in gaudy greens, and ever gold in the midst. The pendants of the hores's neck-gear, the proud crupper, the ornaments, and all the metal thereof, were enamelled of green; the stirrups that he stood

in of the same colour, and his saddle-bow also; and they were all glim-
mering and shining with green stones; and the foal on which he rode
was of that same hue

> certain
> A green horse great and thick,
> A steed full strong to strain,
> In broidered bridle thick,
> To the man he was full gain.

Thus gaily was this man dressed out in green, and the hair of the horse's
head was of green, and his fair, flowing locks clung about his shoulders; and a great beard like a bush hung over his breast, and with his
noble hair was cut evenly all round above his elbows, and the lower
part of his sleeves was fastened like a king's mantle. The horse's mane
was crisped and gemmed with many a knot, and folded in with gold
thread about the fair green with ever a fillet of hair and one of gold,
and his tail and head were intertwisted with gold in the same manner,
and bound with a band of bright green, and decked with costly stones
and tied with a tight knot above; and about them were ringing many
full bright bells of burnished gold. Such a horse or his rider were never
seen in that hall before or

> with eye.
> 'He looks like flashing light.'
> Say they that him descry,
> 'It seemed that no man might
> His dintings e'er defy.'

He had no helmet or hauberk, nor was he armour-plated, nor had he
spear or shield with which to smite; but in one hand he held a holly
branch, that is most green when the groves are all bare, and in the other
he held an axe, huge and uncanny, and a sharp weapon was it to
describe whoso might wish. And the head thereof measured an ell,
and its grain was of green steel and of hewn gold, and the broad edge
of it was burnished brightly, and as well shaped for cutting as a razor.
And the sturdy knight gripped the steel of the stiff staff that was wound
round with iron right along its length, and engraven in green with many
noble deeds; and lace lapped it about and was fastened on the head,
and looped about the handle full oft with many tassels tied thereto
and broidered full richly on buttons of bright green. And the man haled
into the hall, and pushed forward to the high daïs, fearful of nothing,
and saluted no one, but looked scornfully over them all. The first word
that he uttered was 'Where is the chief of this company? Gladly would
I see that man in the body, and speak with him seasonably

in town.'
The knight cast round his eye,
And reelèd up and down,
He stopped and 'gan to spy
Who was of best renown.

When they all looked at him, and every man marvelled much what it
might mean that a man and his horse should be of such a colour of
green, green as the grass and greener, as it seemed, than green enamel
upon gold shining brightly. All studied him carefully, and came nearer
to him, for they had seen many wonders, but nothing like unto this;
therefore the folk deemed it to be a phantom or some faery. And many
of them were afraid to answer him; astounded at his voice, stone still
they sat. And there was a solemn silence through that rich hall, as
though they had all fallen asleep

speedily;
Not all, I trow, for fear
But some for courtesy:
Let him whom all hold dear
Unto him make reply.

When Arthur on the high daïs beheld that adventure, and royally did
reverence unto him, for nothing could affright him, and he said, 'Sir,
welcome art thou to this hall. I am Arthur, the head of this hostel. Alight
from they horse, and linger with us, I pray thee, and afterwards we will
come to know what thy will is.' 'Nay,' quoth that fellow, 'As He that
sitteth on high shall help me, it is not mine errand to dwell any while
in this place, but I am come because the fame of thy knights is so highly
praised, and thy burgesses and thy town are held to be the best in the
world, and the strongest riders on horses in steel armour, and the bravest
and the worthiest of all mankind, and proof in playing in all joustings;
and here, too, courtesy is well known, as I have heard say; and it is
for these reasons that I am come hither at this time. Thou mayest rest
assured by this holly token I hold in my hand that I am come in peaceful wise, and seek no quarrel; for had I come in company, in fighting
wise, I have both a helm and a hauberk at home, and a shield, and
a sharp and brightly shining spear, and other weapons I wield there
as I ween; but because I wage no warfare, my weeds are of softer sort.
But if thou art so bold as all men say, thou wilt grant me in goodly
wise the games I ask

by right.'
Then Arthur he did swear,
And said, 'Sir courteous knight,
If thou cravest battle bare
Thou shalt not fail to fight.'

'May I tell thee in good faith, I seek not to fight, for the men on this bench are but beardless children, and if I were hasped in arms on a high steed there is no man here to match with me. I only crave of this court a Christmas game, as this is the feast of Yule and New Year, and many here are brave. And if any in this house holds himself so hardy and is so bold-blooded and so utterly mad that he dare strike one stroke for another in return, I will give to him this costly axe, that is heavy enough, and he shall handle it if he likes, and I will bide the first blow as bare as I sit here. If any fellow here be so brave as to do what I say, let him come forward quickly and take hold of the weapon, and I will quit claim upon it for ever. It shall be his very own. And I will stand strongly on this floor to abide his stroke if thou wilt doom him to receive another stroke in return from me; yet will I grant

delay.
I'll give to him the blow,
In a twelvemonth and a day.
Now think and let me know
Dare any herein aught say.'

Now, if this man astonished them at the first, even still more were they astonished at this word, both high and low. The man rode firm in the saddle, and rolled his red eyes about, and bent his rough, green shining eyebrows, and stroked his beard, waiting for some one to rise. And when no one would answer him, he coughed loudly and scornfully, and said, 'What! is this Arthur's house that all men are talking of? Where are now your pride and your valour, your wrath and fury and great words? for now is the revel and renown of the Round Table ovecome by one word, for all of you are terrified though no blow has been struck.' Then he laughed so loudly that King Arthur was grieved thereat, and the blood, for shame, shot upwards into his bright face

so dear.
He waxed as wroth as wind,
So did all that were there,
The king was bravely kind,
And stood that strong man near.

And he said, 'By heaven, fellow, thy asking is strange, and since thou dost seek after foolishness, it behoves thee to find it. I know of no single man among us that is aghast at thy great words. Give me thy axe, for God's sake, and I will grant thee the boon thou cravest.' Arthur leapt forward towards him and caught him by the hand. Then fiercely alighted that other fellow from his horse. Arthur seized the axe, gripping it by the handle, and strongly brandished it about. The strong man stood towering before him, higher than any in the house, by his head and more. Stern of mien, he stood there and stroked his beard, and with face unmoved he drew down his coat, no more dismayed for the dints he was to receive than if any man upon the bench had brought him to drink

of wine.
Gawain sat by the queen,
To the king he did incline,
'I tell thee truth I ween,
This mêlée must be mine.'

If thou wilt allow me to come down form this bench and without fault leave this table and stand by thee there, and if my liege lady likes it not ill, I will come to thine aid before all this noble court; for methinks it is not seemly that when such a thing as this is asked in this great hall, that thou shouldest deal with it thyself, though thou be eager to do so, when there are so many brave men about thee, on the benches, that, as I hope, under heaven, are not more precious than thou art, nor are they more able-bodied on the field, when there is any fighting. I am the weakest and most feeble of wit; and who seeketh truth knows that the loss of my life would be a small matter. I have no praise except that thou art mine uncle, and no goodness in my body have I except thy blood that flows in my veins. Since this affair is none of thine and I have first made demand for it, it falls to me; and if I acquit not myself comely, let all this noble court

me blame.'
The knights whispered that day,
And all agreed the same—
The king must yield the fray,
And give Gawain the game.

Then the king commanded the knight to rise up, which he readily did, and set himself fairly and knelt down again before the king and received from him the weapon, and the king lifted up his hand and gave him God's blessing, and prayed that both his heart and hand might be hardy and strong. 'Take care, cousin, that thou set one blow upon him, and if thou doest it well, then shalt thou bide the blow that he shall give thee afterwards.' Gawain went forward to the man with the axe in his hand, and the Green Knight boldly bided his coming and flinched not at all. Then said the Green Knight to Sir Gawain, 'Let us make well our covenant ere we go further. First, I want to know thy name—tell my truly.' 'In good faith,' said the knight, 'my name is Gawain, and it is Gawain that offers to give thee this blow, whatsoever befall him afterwards; and in a twelvemonth and a day thou shalt take back the blow with any weapon thou likest, if I shall be

alive.'
That other answered again,
'Gawain, so may I thrive,
For I am fiercly fain
Of the blow that thou wilt drive.'

Then said the Green Knight, 'Well it pleases me that I shall take at thy hand that which I sought in this hall. And thou hast truly rehearsed all the covenant I asked of the king; save that thou shalt pledge me to seek me thyself wheresoever thou dost hope to find me on the earth, and to fetch thee such wages a thou wilt deal me to-day in the presence of this noble company.' 'Oh tell me,' quoth Gawain, 'where must I seek thee? Where is thy place? By Him that made me, I wot not where thou dwellest, nor do I know thee, Sir Knight, nor thy court, nor thy name. But tell me that truly, and what is thy name, and I will use all my wit that I may win thither, and that I swear by my sooth.' 'It will suffice in the new year,' quoth the Green Knight to Gawain the gentle, 'if I tell thee truly when I have received the blow at thy hand. Then it is that I will quickly tell thee of my house, my home, and my name. Then mayest thou ask my faring, and hold the covenant, and if I say nothing at all, then will it speed thee better, for you mayest linger in thy land and seek to fare no farther in search of such

a sight.
Take now the weapon grim,
Let us see how thou canst smite.'
'Gladly,' said he to him;
Then stroked the axe that knight.

The Green Knight then prepared himself, bowed down a little, and discovered his face, and his long and lovely locks fell flowing about his head and he bared his neck for the business in hand. Gawain gripped the axe and held it up aloft. He put his left foot forward, then he let the axe fall lightly down on the naked neck so that it sundered the bones, pierced through the flesh, so that the point of the steel bit into the ground, and the head of the Green Knight fell to the earth. And many kicked it with their feet as it rolled there, and blood rushed forth from the body and shone red on the green garments. Yet not a whit did the Green Knight falter nor fall, but started strongly forward on stiff shanks where the men were standing, and caught hold of his head and lifted it up. Then he went to his horse, seized the bridle, stepped into the saddle, and striding aloft, he held his head by the hair, and as gravely he sat in the saddle as though no evil had befallen him and he were not headless

in that stead.
He swayed his trunk about,

The ugly body that bled;
Many of him had doubt
By the time his reasons were said.

He held up the head in his hands, and addressed him to the dearest
of those on the bench, to wit, Sir Gawain; and the eyelids were lifted
up and looked forth, and the lips moved and said, 'Take heed, Sir
Gawain, that thou art ready to go and seek me till thou find me as
thou hast promised in this hall with these knights as witnesses. To the
green chapel thou shalt come to receive such a blow as thou hast given,
on New Year's morning. And many know me as the Knight of the Green
Chapel. Fail not, then, to seek me until thou findest me; therefore come
thou, or recreant shalt thou be called.' Then roughly he turned his reins,
haled out of the hall door, with his head in his hand, and the horse's
hoofs struck fire from the flinty stones. No one there knew of what
kith or kin he was, or whence he came.

Straightway
Of the Green Knight they made light,
Yet it was thought that day,
A marvel, a wondrous sight,
Though, laughing, they were gay.

Now, though Arthur the Gentle at this had great wonder, he let no
semblance thereof be seen, but spake with gentle speed to the comely
Queen Guinevere: 'Dear lady, let not this day's doings dismay thee
at all. Such craft well becomes the Feast of Christmas; gamings and
interludes and laughing and singing and carollings of knights and ladies.
And now can I dress myself for meat, for a wondrous adventure have
I seen.' He glanced at Sir Gawain and said, 'Now, sir, hang up thine
axe; hewing enough has it done for to-day.' Then they hung it up over
the daïs at the back of the high seat, that all men might look upon
the marvel of it and truly tell the wonder of it. Then went these two,
the king and the good knight, to the table, and brave men served them,
double of all dainties, with all manner of meat and minstrelsy. In good
weal they passed the day, but it came to an end, and night

was near.
'Now, Sir Gawain, be sure,
turn not away for fear
From this grim adventure
That thou hast promised here.'

'Now,' said Sir Gawain, 'this is a desert place, I trow. This oratory is
loathsome, overgrown as it is with weeds, and well it befitteth that fellow clad in green, for his devotion to the devil. Now in my five wits
I ween it is the very devil himself who has made this tryst with me,

Figure 10: 'Now passed Sir Gawain in God's behalf through the realms of logres' by Frederic Lawrence.

that he may destroy me. This is a chapel of ill-luck, and the most accursed kirk that I have ever seen, and may ill luck befall it.' With his helmet high on his head and lance in hand, he wandered up to that rocky dwelling. Then came there from a rock in that high hill beyond the brook a wondrous strange noise, and it clattered among the cliffs as though it would cleave them asunder, as though one were grinding a scythe upon a grindstone, and it made a whirring sound like water in a mill, and rushed and sang out and was terrible to hear. 'By God Himself,' said Gawain, 'that is the noise of armour which is being made ready for that fellow wherewith he may come forth to meet me

> by rote.
> Let God work me woe.
> It helpeth me not a mote,
> My life though I forgo,
> No noise shall make me dote.'

Then in a loud voice the knight 'gan call, 'Who dwells in this place and would hold parley with me? For now is good Sir Gawain in the right way at last, and if any man would have aught with him let him come hither quickly; nor or never is his chance.' 'Tarry a moment,' quoth a voice on the hill above his head, 'and thou shalt receive all that I promised thee in right good time.' Thereupon he rushed forward at a great speed till he arrived near a crag and came whirling out of a hole in a corner of it with a fell weapon in his hand; and it was a new Danish axe with which to give the blow, with a huge piece of steel bent at the handle, and it was four feet long and filed at the grindstone, and it gleamed full brightly. It was the Green Knight, dressed as at their first meeting, the same in face and legs, looks, and beard, save that he went on foot. When he reached the water he would not wade therein, but hopped over on his axe and strode boldly forward over

> the snow.
> Sir Gawain the knight 'gan meet,
> To him he bowed not low;
> The other said, 'Now, my sweet,
> The tryst thou keepest, I trow?'

'Gawain,' quoth the Green Knight, 'may God protect thee. I wis thou art welcome to my place, and thou hast kept thy promise as befitteth a true man. Thou knowest the covenant between us made—how a twelvemonth ago thou didst take that which befell thee and I was to be quits with thee on this New Year's Day. We are alone verily in this valley; there are no knights here to separate us. Doff thy helmet and take thy pay, and make no more ado than I did when thou didst whip off

Figure 11: 'He struck at him mightily' by Frederic Lawrence.

my head at one blow.' 'Nay, by the most high God,' said Gawain, 'so
I have spirit I grudge thee not thy will for any mischief that may befall
me; but I stand here for thy stroke, and do not deny thee thy will

anywhere.'
Down he bent his head.
And showed his neck all bare.
There was no sign of dread,
Or that he would not dare.

Then the Green Knight gat himself ready quickly, and gathered up his
grim weapon with which to smite Sir Gawain, and with all the strength
of his body he raised it aloft and made a feint of destroying him and
drove it downwards as though he were right angry with him, so that
the doughty knight would have been killed by that blow. But Gawain
started aside a little from the axe as it came gliding downwards to destroy him on that hillside, and shrank a little from that sharp iron with
his shoulders. And the other withheld somewhat the shining weapon,
and then reproved the princely knight with many a proud word. 'Thou
art not Gawain,' said he, 'that is holden to be so brave that never winced
a hair by hill or valley, for now thou dost flee for fear, ere thou art hurt
at all. Never heard I of such cowardice of that knight, neither did I
shrink or flee when thou didst strike me, nor did I cavil at all in King
Arthur's house. My head flew down to my foot, yet I fled not, and thou,
ere any harm befell thee, waxest timid in heart. The better man of the
two it behoves me to be called

therefore.'
Quoth Gawain, 'I shrank once,
But so will I no more,
Yet though my head fell on the stones
I cannot it restore.'

'But hasten thou, and let us come to the point. Deal me my destiny,
and do it out of hand, for I will stand thee a stroke, and start aside
no more till thine axe hath smitten me: have here my troth.' 'Have at
thee then,' quoth that other, and he heaved the axe aloft and looked
so angry that he might have been a madman. He struck at him mightily, but withheld his hand suddenly ere it could hurt him. Gawain
promptly abided it and shrank in no limb of his body, but stood still
as a stone or a tree stock that is rooted in the rocky ground with a
hundred roots. Then merrily 'gan he speak, the man in green, 'So now
thou hast thy heart whole and while it behoves me to smite. Hold high
thy hood that Arthur gave thee, and keep thy neck to thy body lest
it get in the way again.' Gawain then answered him full fiercely, and
with heart sorrow, 'Strike then, thou bold man; thou dost threaten too
long. I hope that thy heart may wax timid.' 'Forsooth,' quoth that other,

'so fiercely thou dost speak, I will no longer hinder thee of thine errand

right now.'
Then took he a stride to strike,
And wrinkled lips and brow,
No marvel it did him mislike,
Who hoped for no rescue now.

He raised lightly his axe and let it fall with the barb on his bare neck;
and though he hotly hammered he did not hurt him much, but cut
his skin a little. The sharp sword pierced through the flesh, so that the
bright blood spurted over his shoulders to the ground; and when he
saw the blood on the snow he started forward more than a spear length,
hastily seized his helmet and put it on his head, and adjusted his shield;
then brandishing forth a glittering sword, he spake fierce words, and
never since his mother bare him was he half so merry. 'Cease now from
thy strokes. Offer me no more. I have taken a blow in this place without
striving; if thou givest me any more I will readily return them, be ye
of that well assured,

my foe.
But one stroke shall on me fall,
The covenant was right so
Made by us in Arthur's hall,
And therefore, knight, now ho!'

The man held back and rested upon his axe, set the shaft on the ground,
and leaned on the point, looked at Sir Gawain, and saw how bravely
he stood there, doughty and dreadless and fully armed, and in his heart
he was well pleased. Then spake he merrily and loudly, with a rushing
sound, and said, 'Bold man, on this hill be not thou so angry, for no
man has done thee wrong, unmannerly nor in any wise, except as was
agreed in the court of King Arthur. I promised thee a stroke—thou hast
it; hold thyself well payed. I hereby release thee of the remnant and
of all other rights. Had I so liked, I could have dealt thee a worse blow;
but first I menaced thee in playful wise, and cut thee not at all, though
with right I proffered it to thee for the covenant made between us the
first night when thou faithfully didst keep thy troth and gavest me all
thy gain as a true man should. The second blow I gave thee for the
morning when thou didst kiss my beautiful wife, and gavest me the
kisses, and for the two kisses I gave here but two blows without scathe

or tear.
A true man keeps his sooth,
And no scathe need he fear;
Thou didst flinch at the third, in truth,
So that stroke I gave thee here.

'For in truth thou art wearing my weed in that same woven girdle which my wife gave to thee, as I wot well. And I know all about thy kisses and thy virtues also, and it was I myself who brought about the wooing of my wife. I sent her to assail thee, and I found thee to be the most faultless man on earth; as pearl is of more price than white pease, so is Gawain, in good faith, than all other gay knights. But, good sir, in this thou wast lacking a little in loyalty, not in any amorous working or wooing; but that thou didst love thy life the less I blame thee.' Then Sir Gawain stood thoughtful for a long time, and he trembled with rage, and all the blood of his body rushed to his face, and he shrank for shame all the time the Green Knight was talking. And the first words he uttered were, 'A curse on both cowardice and covetousness! In them are both villany and vice, that destroy virtue.' Then he caught hold of the girdle and violently flung it at the knight. 'Lo, there is the false thing, and may evil befall it. For fear of thy stroke cowardice seized me, and for covetousness I was false to my nature, which is loyal and true as befitteth a knight. Now am I faulty and false and fearful. May sorrow betide Treachery and Untruth

and Care.
I know thee knight here still.
All faulty is my fare,
Let me but thwart thy will,
And after I will be ware.'

Then the other laughed and said, 'I reck nought of the harm I had of thee, for thou hast made such clean confession of thy misdeeds, and hast done such penance at the point of my sword that I hold thee free from thy fault and as innocent as if thou hadst never forfeited innocence since thou wast born. And here I give to thee again the girdle, that is gold hemmed and green as my gown. And thou shalt think on this chiding when thou goest forth among princes of price, and this shall be a pure token of thy chance at the Green Chapel, to chivalrous knights. Thou shalt come in this New Year and turn again to my dwelling, and we will spend the remnant of this noble feast in revellings as shall

be seen.'
Thus invited Sir Gawain the lord,
And quoth he 'My lady, I ween,
She shall thee well accord,
Though she was thine enemy keen.'

'Nay, forsooth,' quoth Gawain, and he seized his helmet, gracefully doffed it, and thanked the Green Knight. 'Sadly have I sojourned, and may joy betide thee from Him who hath all men in His keeping. Commend me to that courteous one thy noble lady, and to the ancient dame,

my honoured ladies who have so cunningly beguiled me. It is no wonder
if a fool go mad in loving, and through the wiles of a woman he brought
sorrow, for so was Adam beguiled by one woman and Solomon by many;
and to Samson, Delilah dealt him his weird, and David was beguiled
by Barsabe, through whom he suffered great loss. All these were troubled by the wiles of women. Great joy it would be to love them well,
and believe them not, if a man could do it. For of those under heaven

> have mused,
> All of them were beguiled
> By women that they used;
> Though I be now be-wiled
> I think I am excused.'

'But for thy girdle;' quoth Gawain, 'God reward thee for it, and I will
wield it with good will, not for the gold, nor the samite, nor the silk,
nor for its pendants, nor for weal nor worship, nor for its fair work-
ings, but as a sign of my surfeit oft shall I look upon it; and when I
ride in renown I shall feel remorse for the fault and cowardice of the
crabbed flesh, and how easy it is to be smirched by filth, and thus,
when pride shall prick me through prowess of arms, the sight of this
lovely lace shall moderate the beating of my heart. But one thing I pray
thee, and may it not displease thee, since thou art lord of that land
where I have sojourned with thee in worship—and may the Lord reward
thee that sitteth on high and upholds the heavens—tell me thy name,
and no more do I ask thee.' 'That shall I tell thee truly,' quoth that
other. 'Bernlak de Haudesert I am called in this land; and through might
of Morgan le Fay, who lodges in my house, and the cunning of the clergy,
I am well learned in crafts. She was the mistress of Merlin, and many
has she taken captive by her wiles. For she has made love for a long
time to that famous clerk that knows all your knights

> at home.
> Morgan the goddess
> Therefore is her name;
> There is no haughtiness
> She cannot make full tame.'

'It was she who brought me in this wise to your joyous hall, to assay
the pride thereof if it were truly spoken of, and to put to the test the
great renown of the Round Table. She it was who made me do this marvel to put you all out of your wits, in order to vex and pain Guinevere
and to cause her death, together with all that ghostly game and the
knight with his head in his hand before the high table. It was the work
of Morgan, who is that ancient dame thou didst see in my house. And
she is thine aunt, and half-sister to Arthur, the daughter of the Duchess

of Tintagel, who afterwards married Uther and gave birth to Arthur, who is now king. Therefore I implore thee, come and see thy aunt. Make merry in my house, for my servants all love thee, and I wish thee well, by my faith, as any man under heaven because of thy great truth.' But Sir Gawain denied with a nay, and said he would not in any wise. Then they embraced and kissed and commended each other to the King of Paradise, and they parted right there

> on the wold.
> Gawain mounts horses, I ween,
> To the king's town hastes him, bold.
> The knights, in weeds of green,
> Went o'er the moorland cold.

Gawain rode over wild ways of the world. Sometimes he found rest in houses, and sometimes in the open air, and had many adventures in the valleys, and oft he overcame, and I will not try to tell it all. The hurt was healed that he had in his neck, and he still carried the glittering belt at his side; under his left arm was the lace, tied with a knot, in token that he was taken in a fault. Thus he came to court, a knight in all unhurt. There was joy in that hall when the great ones knew that Sir Gawain was come back, and great gain they thought it. The king kissed the knight, and the queen also, and many a faithful knight sought to embrace him, and they asked him of his faring, and he told them all the wonders thereof and all the labours he had endured, the chance of the chapel, the doings of the Green Knight, the love-making of the lady, and of the lace last of all. Then he showed them the cut in his neck which for his disloyalty he received at the hand of the Green Knight

> for blame.
> He moaned as he did it tell,
> The blood to his face then came,
> As he groaned for grief as well,
> When he showed it to them for shame.

'O, my lord,' quoth the knight as he handled the lace, 'this is the bond and sign of my shame, this is the loss and hurt that I have suffered through cowardice and covetousness. It is the token of untruth, and I must needs wear it while life shall last, for none may hide it, for when it is once fixed upon any one never will it pass from him.' The king comforted the knight, as did all the court; and they laughed loudly, and it was agreed that all the lords and ladies of the Round Table, each member of the brotherhood, should have a lace belt, a band of bright green, and wear it for the sake of Sir Gawain as long as they lived. And this was the renown of the Round Table, and he that had it was held in great honour for evermore, as I have seen it written in the best book of romance.

Thus in King Arthur's day did this adventure betide. The Brutus books bear witness to it, since the bold Knight Brutus came hither first after the siege and the assault ceased at Troy, as

I wis.
Many adventures herebeofre
Have befallen such ere this.
Now He that thorn-crown for us bore
Bring us to His bliss. Amen.

HONY SOYT QUI MAL PENCE

[1] *Gawain and the Green Knight* by Richard Blackford (1982) and *Gawain and the Green Knight* by Harrison Birtwistle (forthcoming).
[2] *Gawain and the Green Knight* (1973) and *Sword of the Valiant* (1983).

Chapter 15.

Medraut and Gwenhwyvar

by Edward Frankland

Edward Percy Frankland, who died in 1958 aged 74, came from two generations of scientists. He himself trained as a chemist and held a Ph.D. from the
University of Würzburg, where he also studied history. When ill-health forced
him to abandon his academic career, he took up farming in Westmoreland.
He was an excellent shot, a skilled forester and a pioneer of skiing in Britain.

All of these remarkable abilities equipped Frankland to write a series of excellent novels about the Vikings, a whole number of thrillers set in and around
the landscape he knew, and a brilliant early novel of Arthur (*The Bear of Britain*, Macdonald, 1944) which is still one of the best of its kind.

In an additional note to The Times obituary in 1958, Dr Arnold Toynbee
wrote:

> 'If a Norseman, or a wolf, or King Arthur had suddenly appeared he
> would not have been taken aback, and he would have faced any of them
> calmly. To see the country under his guidance and to hear him talk
> about its past were rare pleasures.'

This is what makes Frankland's Arthurian writing so satisfactory and believ-
able; he had a firm grasp of early British history, and above all he loved the
land. *The Bear of Britain* was one of the first serious attempts to place Arthur
into a fully realized historical background.

Apart from this, Frankland also wrote a panoramic novel called *England
Growing*, which traced the history of the land in a series of sketches dating
from Roman times to the present. The second episode, set in the year 515,
is called '*Medraut and Gwenhwyvar*'; it is reprinted here for the first time
since its original appearance in 1945. It paints a small-scale, rather grim picture which demonstrates not only the depths of Frankland's knowledge, but
also his sense of style and abilities of characterization.

⌁⌁⌁

OCTOBER, 515

More than four hundred years had gone by, but in general aspect there
was little change on that gentle hillside where Celsus and Varro had
sat watching the sunset. It was an autumn evening; the wooded heights
across the valley showed a tapestry of russet oak, lemon-yellow birch,
fiery rowan; innumerable trees lifting their rounded heads into the waning sunshine, each revealed for a little while as an individual in that
vast community by a glittering fringe of light on wet foliage.

The seedling oak that Varro had brushed with his foot was now grown

to a giant overshadowing the whole glade with its mighty limbs, and
this was perhaps a symptom of a decline in human achievement, not
only in the Vale of Lune but throughout the old Roman province of
Britannia. The village was still there, but with only a score of peaked
roofs rising above a wall nearly buried in nettle brakes and ragwort.
The road, laid out with ruthless precision through scrub and bog, a
monument to the engineering skill of Celsus and his associates, was
now a smooth green track, narrowed to little more than a footpath by
advancing tides of bracken. The trees arched over it, making a dark
tunnel where the forest grew thick; the curbed and cambered surface,
the deep side trenches, were almost imperceptible undulations on the
sea of ling that covered the high hills. Wild beasts made more use of
the old road than men did in these days; wolves and deer roamed along
it, blackcock found it a pleasant ground for their tournaments, but this
evening the forest rang with the tramp of an army coming from the
North—a thudding on hard turf, a snapping of sticks, a scraping and
rustling among out-thrust branches and briars. It might have been the
ghost of an old Roman army that emerged on to the pastured glades
that surrounded the village, a much battered and dishevelled ghost.
At its head loped a huge man, barefoot and bareheaded, carrying a
standard, carved not with the Eagle of Rome but with the Red Dragon
of the Cymry. Behind him on a white stallion rode a soldier cloaked
and helmeted much after the fashion of Publius Valens, a bearded man
with golden curls, broad and sinewy, his bare knees dark with dirt and
sunburn, and scarred with old wounds, his face grimly handsome, his
gaze remote and yet watchful, like that of a seaman or a shepherd. There
followed about a thousand men shouting and singing vaingloriously,
yet moving with some attempt at discipline; most of them had rusty
helmets and loricas such as legionaries might have worn, a few carried
the curving rectangular shield and the short stabbing sword, but for
all that they were more akin in their looks to the old enemies of Rome,
the black curly-headed Silures, the skulking Brigantian tribesmen, the
ferocious savages from the foothills of Caledonia. For this was the army
of Arthur, the son of Uther Pendragon, the spearhead of the British
race in its desperate struggle for life after the Roman had relaxed his
grip on the land, men gathered from the combes of Dyvnaint, the plains
of Gwent, the forest valleys of Reged and Strathclyde, men prepared
to shed their blood in the cause of a nation and not with the fatal facility of the Celt, in the private quarrels of princes. The raiders from Hiber-
nia had come and gone, leaving every town and villa of western Britain
a heap of ruins, the Caledonians had swarmed southwards to the very
walls of Londonium, the Saxons had got a footing on the eastern coast
and were settling wholesale on deserted territory far inland. Arthur
was the response of Britain to these disasters. Eleven great victories
in the North had banished the Saxon raiders from the shores of Ber-

neich and driven the Pictish king to take shelter in his mountains; now the army was returning to fling itself against an immense host of Saxons pressing towards the Severn. In the tramp of Arthur's legionaries Britain heard an echo of the mighty blows struck for her deliverance in past centuries by the Emperors Severus and Theodosius; the Red Dragon of the Cymry seemed the lineal descendant of the Eagles, and Arthur was hailed with reverence by the common people and with jealous fear by the local tyrants as 'Yr Amherawdyr', the Imperator.

Beneath Varro's oak Arthur drew rein and Kai, the bare-headed giant, planted the standard in the turf. The men halted, leaning on their spears, and through their ranks two riders pressed forward to join Arthur; a young man, dark-eyed, with an almost girlish beauty, a harp on his back and a subtle smile on his clean-shaven face, and a woman with long golden hair, lovely of feature but overcast by a shadow of sullenness and brooding desire. For a moment the two men and the woman sat motionless on their tired horses that drooped their heads to the flowery grass, three glorious figures towering above a host of wild and evil faces, caught in the radiance of the setting sun, still unaware that their lives were interwoven by a fatal passion, a passion that would make their names famous for many a thousand years: Arthur, his nephew Medraut, and his wife Gwenhwyvar; three great landmarks standing up in the fog of doom that was descending on Celtic Britain.

'Sound the trumpet!' said Arthur.

A man stepped out of the ranks and tilted a long brazen trumpet towards the dark hills. An echoing blast rang through the forest glades, and in answer to it came a hurrying procession of men, women and children from the village. They dropped on their knees and gave a wavering shout: 'Hail, Arthur yr Amherawdyr!'

'What place is this?' Arthur fixed his gaze on a grey-haired man who knelt foremost among the village folk.

'This is Cair Coit Lon, and I am Rhyderch, lord of all this land that lies between the sea in the west and the high hills in the east,' said the old man, rising to his feet.

'Here shall we overnight, Rhyderch, and tomorrow we march on against the foes of Britain.'

'Little we have for our own use, Arthur, a little meat, a little milk, a little mead, but all of it is yours.'

'Men we must have too. The utmost strength we must draw from the land to save it from the Saxons.'

'Men have gone already from Cair Coit Lon to march under the Red Dragon, but none has come back. What news do you give me, Arthur, of my youngest son, Owen map Rhyderch?'

'Gloriously he fought at Abergleinwy and at Traeth Treuroit, and he fell before the Broch of Guinion, but not till he had hewn down the Saxon standard.'

Figure 12: 'He shall receive the high order of knighthood tomorrow' by
A. G. Walker

The old man bowed his head for a moment. 'Five other sons I had,' he said, 'and they all died in battle, not with the foes of our race, but with war bands from Elmet, from Reged, and from Gwyneth. Sharper are the teeth of our own countrymen than those of the Pictish wolves from Celidon or the Saxons from the plains of Deivr.'

'We are the Cymry,' said Arthur, with a gesture towards his host thronging more and more thickly into openings of the wood, and overflowing the dykes into the tiny stubble fields that lay about the village. 'We shall trample down the hatred that leaps up like fire among the rulers of Britain. Under this standard we shall gather the spearmen of Gwyneth, the axe-bearers of Powys, the archers of Gwent. Like a band of brothers pledged to conquer or die, there come to meet me Maelgwn, Vortipore, Conan, and Cuneglas. Together we shall drive the Saxons into the sea as we have driven the Picts to their mountains.' He unsheathed his great sword Caledwlch and waved it aloft, the magic sword that had brought him victory in all those desperate battles between the glassy reaches of Cluyd and the storm-beaten coast of Berneich. A great roar of exultant voices answered him, a forest of spears shot up and sank back at the slant as the army plunged forward, the white stallion reared, with wild eyes and lashing tail he clattered over the stream and carried Arthur through the gateway of Cair Coit Lon. Only Medraut and Gwenhwyvar drew aside under the oak and watched the rush of hungry wolf-like men go by, raising a chant in fierce yet musical voices: 'Cymry in victory, Cymry in woe...'

The woman stirred impatiently in the saddle, her eyes gleamed at the young man under lowering brows.

'Can he do as he says? Is there a man who can master all Britain and ride it with bridle and spur, making princes and people yield to his will as Emperors did in the old days?'

'There may be such a man.' Medraut gazed at her, baring his teeth in stealthy excitement.

'But not Arthur?'

'He is the soldier, the hero, the man of principle, wading deeper and deeper in seas of blood, his eyes ever turning towards the fading glory of a sunset.' Medraut made a quick gesture towards the clear greenish sky overhung by purple-bellied clouds in the west. 'But ahead of him there is a dawn that he cannot see. Night comes first, and all that Arthur stands for shall perish.'

'Night comes,' she repeated, almost in a whisper. 'The night is ours. Medraut. Too many are the eyes of day, and deadly is Caledwlch; friendly to us are the great dark trees, the high bracken, the glades where wolves bay at the moon, while Arthur sits in council with his champions, by the firelight in Cair Coit Lon.'

With a sudden movement of rein and heel he pressed his horse up to hers, his arm went round her, his hand cupped her breasts, slid over her thigh and felt her body yearn towards him as a cat thrusts itself against the hand that caresses it.

'Sin,' he said mockingly. He set his teeth and drove his fingers into her flesh. 'Deadly sin, so say the priests of God; but what power over us have they, now that night falls on Britain? It is evil that shall triumph in the time that comes; our pride shall be in cruelty and lust, and treachery shall go unashamed. A new Britain will rise out of the smoke of burning huts; out of the screams of raped women and children tossed from spear to spear, and my task it shall be to build it afresh. I shall wield the Saxon and the Pict like two sharp-edged weapons to undo the work of Arthur, to fell the lazy tyrants that snarl at each other among the western hills. It is I that shall open the dykes and breach the walls so that a wave will wash over all that is left of Rome and bear me to power in Britain, in Celidon, in Eire.'

A chill of foreboding passed over Gwenhwyvar.

'Have you the second sight, Medraut, that you can foretell glory for yourself!' she said, looking uneasily at the gnarled trunks of the trees, black against the sunset, as though they in their strength and silence, in their centuries of knowledge, could see what was as yet dim to her and Medraut, the outcome of this supreme treachery in a world where all were false and fickle save only Arthur.

'Visions come to me when I lay my fingers on the harp,' he answered, and passed his hand over his eyes as though to banish something he feared to see.

'Do visions come when you play with my body, does it kindle nothing in you but lust?'

'Well I know that you carry Arthur's child, that our play is barren, pleasure for the sake of pleasure only, evil for the sake of evil; yet a time will come when you shall give me children and their seed shall shake the world.'

'Let us go now!' she said urgently, gathering up her reins with sudden violence. 'Let us ride away through these woods far from the sound of Arthur's trumpets ... This torment that we endure, cloaking our desire amid the ranks of the Cymry, let us end it and begin the work you have in mind. Eastward, behind these shaggy hills, the Saxon halls are thick on the plain about Cair Ebrauc; there are the men who will help you to power.'

'To me it is no torment, to draw my sword for the Cymry, to sing them songs as they go from fight to fight, while in my mind's eye I see them lying dead, the Red Dragon fallen before the White, a grave for March, a grave for Gwythyr, a grave for Gwgawn of the Ruddy Sword ...'

'A grave for Arthur?' she said, staring at him in horror and yet in love.

'The time is not yet ... blood must flow and yet more blood, British and Saxon, before the hour comes when Britain shall see me for what

I am . . .' His voice died away in a hoarse whisper as the vision swam slowly before his drugged senses, the vision that followed like some faint echo from the tumult of his thoughts down the corridors of time; a fading sunset, a watery plain, a low hill with black, writhing thorn trees under which lay the tumbled corpses of Arthur's champions, and then a monstrous figure, rent with wounds, staggering to meet him; a sword whirling against the yellow sky like the flight of a bat . . .

Chapter 16.

The Dream of Rhonabwy

Breuddwyd Rhonabwy or the *Dream of Rhonabwy* is a Welsh mediaeval story written in the 13th century. It first appeared in the English language in the collection of ancient British stories entitled *The Mabinogion*, translated by Lady Charlotte Guest (1812-1895) between 1838-1849.

The Arthur who appears in this story is not the mediaeval King of Camelot but the battle-leader of the Heroic Age of post-Roman Britain. The hero of the story, Rhonabwy, lives in mediaeval times when Wales was still struggling under the Norman yoke. He dreams of the past glories of his race while he is wrapped up in a yellow ox hide. Little does he know about the druidic tradition of dreaming or prophesying while wrapped in a bullshide.

His dream reveals Arthur in the timeless dimension of the Otherworld where battles are refought and where mysterious and magical events take place. The incident of Owain and the ravens is bewildering for the reader—are the Ravens birds or are they Owain's troops called 'Ravens' just as Achilles had his Myrmidons(ants) in the *Iliad*?[1] Arthur and Owain play at *gwyddbwyll*, which was a form of chess in which a central king with a handful of supporters strove to outwit a greater number of opposing warrior-pieces.

Once the reader understands that the dream is happening in the Otherworld, and not in historical time, it will be clear how Arthur and his men can fight again the Battle of Badon, and how it is that Rhonabwy can be met by Iddawg the Churn of Britain, he who provoked the Battle of Camlan at which Arthur and many of his warriors died or departed.

Most interesting in this text is the role call of Arthur's followers which very much follows the ancient British tradition and which can be compared with a similar list in *Culhwch and Olwen*, another story from the *Mabinogion*.[2]

This story is interesting in another respect since it shows clearly the transition from oral tradition to written tradition:

> 'because of the various colours that were upon the horses, and the many
> wondrous colours of the arms and of the panoply, and of the precious
> scarfs, and of the virtue-bearing stones',

no-one is able to tell this story without a book, says the text. Readers might also note the regalia of Arthur, including the ring with its precious stone: Iddawg tells Rhonabwy that because this ring has special properties, he will be able to remember everything that he sees in his dream. Would that we all might have the ability to not only dream such dreams, but to remember them so clearly!

Madawc the son of Maredudd possessed Powys within its boundaries, from Porfoed to Gwauan in the uplands of Arwystli. And at that time he had a brother, Iorwerth the son of Maredudd, in rank not equal to himself. And Iorwerth had great sorrow and heaviness because of the honour and power that his brother enjoyed, which he shared not. And he sought his fellows and his foster-brothers, and took counsel with them what he should do in this matter. And they resolved to dispatch some of their number to go and seek a maintenance for him. Then Madawc offered him to become Master of the Household and to have horses, and arms, and honour, and to fare like as himself. But Iorwerth refused this.

And Iorwerth made an inroad into Loegria, slaying the inhabitants, and burning houses, and carrying away prisoners. And Madawc took counsel with the men of Powys, and they determined to place an hundred men in each of the three Commots of Powys to seek for him. And thus did they in the plains of Powys from Aber Ceirawc, and in Allictwn Ver, and in Rhyd Wilure, on the Vyrnwy, the three best Commots of Powys. So he was none the better, he nor his household, in Powys, nor in the plains thereof. And they spread these men over the plains as far as Nillystwn Trevan.

Now one of the men who was upon this quest was called Rhonabwy. And Rhonabwy and Kynwrig Vrychgoch, a man of Mawddwy, and Cadwgan Vras, a man of Moelvre in Kynlleith, came together to the house of Heilyn Goch the son of Cadwgan the son of Iddon. And when they came near to the house, they saw an old hall, very black and having an upright gable, whence issued a great smoke; and on entering, they found the floor full of puddles and mounds; and it was difficult to stand thereon, so slippery was it with the mire of cattle. And where the puddles were, a man might go up to his ankles in water and dirt. And there were boughs of holly spread over the floor, whereof the cattle had browsed the sprigs. When they came to the hall of the house, they beheld cells full of dust, and very gloomy, and on one side an old hag making a fire. And whenever she felt cold, she cast a lapful of chaff upon the fire, and raised such a smoke, that it was scarcely to be borne, as it rose up the nostrils. And on the other side was a yellow calf-skin on the floor; a main privilege was it to any one who should get upon that hide.

And when they had sat down, they asked the hag where were the people of the house. And the hag spoke not, but muttered. Thereupon behold the people of the house entered; a ruddy, clownish, curly-headed man, with a burthen of faggots on his back, and a pale slender woman, also carrying a bundle under her arm. And they barely welcomed the men, and kindled a fire with the boughs. And the woman cooked something, and gave them to eat, barley bread, and cheese, and milk and water.

And there arose a storm of wind and rain, so that it was hardly possible to go forth with safety. And being weary with their journey, they
laid themselves down and sought to sleep. And when they looked at
the couch, it seemed to be made but of a little coarse straw full of dust
and vermin, with the stems of boughs sticking up therethrough, for
the cattle had eaten all the straw that was placed at the head and the
foot. And upon it was stretched an old russet-coloured rug, thread-
bare and ragged; and a coarse sheet, full of slits, was upon the rug,
and an ill-stuffed pillow, and a worn-out cover upon the sheet. And
after much suffering from the vermin, and from the discomfort of their
couch, a heavy sleep fell on Rhonabwy's companions. But Rhonabwy,
not being able either to sleep or to rest, thought he should suffer less
if he went to lie upon the yellow calf-skin that was stretched out on
the floor. And there he slept.

As soon as sleep had come upon his eyes, it seemed to him that he
was journeying with his companions across the plain of Argyngroeg,
and he thought that he went towards Rhyd y Groes on the Severn. As
he journeyed, he heard a mighty noise, the like whereof heard he never
before; and looking behind him, he beheld a youth with yellow curling
hair, and with his beard newly trimmed, mounted on a chestnut horse,
whereof the legs were grey from the top of the forelegs, and from the
bend of the hindlegs downwards. And the rider wore a coat of yellow
satin sewn with green silk, and on his thigh was a gold-hilted sword,
with a scabbar of new leather of Cordova, belted with the skin of the
deer, and clasped with gold. And over this was a scarf of yellow satin
wrought with green silk, the borders whereof were likewise green. And
the green of the caparison of the horse, and of his rider, was as green
as the leaves of the fir-tree, and the yellow was as yellow as the blossom of the broom. So fierce was the aspect of the knight, that fear seized
upon them, and they began to flee. And the knight pursued them. And
when the horse breathed forth, the men became distant from him, and
when he drew in his breath, they were drawn near to him, even to the
horse's chest. And when he had overtaken them, they besought his
mercy. 'You have it gladly,' said he, 'fear nought.' 'Ha, chieftain, since
thou hast mercy upon me, tell me also who thou art,' said Rhonabwy.
'I will not conceal my lineage from thee. I am Iddawc the son of Mynyo,
yet not by my name, but by my nickname am I best known.' 'And wilt
thou tell us what thy nickname is?' 'I will tell you; it is Iddawc Cordd
Prydain.' 'Ha, chieftain,' said Rhonabwy, 'why art thou called thus?'
'I will tell thee. I was one of the messengers between Arthur and
Medrawd his nephew, at the battle of Camlan; and I was then a reckless youth, and through my desire for battle, I kindled strife between
them, and stirred up wrath, when I was sent by Arthur the Emperor
to reason with Medrawd, and to show him, that he was his foster-father
and his uncle, and to seek for peace, lest the sons of the Kings of the

Figure 13: 'The coming of Sir Gareth' by A. G. Walker.

Island of Britain, and of the nobles, should be slain. And whereas Arthur charged me with the fairest sayings he could think of, I uttered unto Medrawd the harshest I could devise. And therefore am I called Iddawc Cordd Prydain, for from this did the battle of Camlan ensue. And three nights before the end of the battle of Camlan I left them, and went to the Llech Las in North Britain to do penance. And there I remained doing penance seven years, and after that I gained pardon.'

Then lo! they heard a mighty sound which was much louder than that which they had heard before, and when they looked round towards the sound, they beheld a ruddy youth, without beard or whiskers, noble of mien, and mounted on a stately courser. And from the shoulders and the front of the knees downwards the horse was bay. And upon the man was a dress of red satin wrought with yellow silk, and yellow were the borders of his scarf. And such parts of his apparel and of the trappings of his horse as were yellow, as yellow were they as the blossom of the broom, and such as were red, were as ruddy as the ruddiest blood in the world.

Then, behold the horseman overtook them, and he asked of Iddawc a share of the little men that were with him. 'That which is fitting for me to grant I will grant, and thou shalt be a companion to them as I have been.' And the horseman went away. 'Iddawc,' inquired Rhonabwy, 'who was that horseman?' 'Rhuvawn Pebyr the son of Prince Deorthach.'

And they journeyed over the plain of Argyngroeg as far as the ford of Rhyd y Groes on the Severn. And for a mile around the ford on both sides of the road, they saw tents and encampments, and there was the clamour of a mighty host. And they came to the edge of the ford, and there they beheld Arthur sitting on a flat island below the ford, having Bedwini the Bishop on one side of him, and Gwarthegyd the son of Kaw on the other. And a tall, auburn-haired youth stood before him, with his sheathed sword in his hand, and clad in a coat and cap of jet-black satin. And his face was white as ivory, and his eyebrows black as jet, and such part of his wrist as could be seen between his glove and his sleeve, was whiter than the lily, and thicker than a warrior's ankle.

Then came Iddawc and they that were with him, and stood before Arthur and saluted him. 'Heaven grant thee good,' said Arthur. 'And where, Iddawc, didst thou find these little men?' 'I found them, lord, up yonder on the road?' Then the Emperor smiled. 'Lord,' said Iddawc, 'wherefore dost thou laugh?' 'Iddawc,' replied Arthur, 'I laugh not; but it pitieth me that men of such stature as these should have this island in their keeping, after the men that guarded it of yore.' Then said Iddawc, 'Rhonabwy, dost thou see the ring with a stone set in it, that is upon the Emperor's hand?' 'I see it,' he answered. 'It is one of the properties of that stone to enable thee to remember that thou seest here to-night, and hadst thou not seen the stone, thou wouldest never have been able to remember aught thereof.'

After this they saw a troop coming towards the ford. 'Iddawc,' inquired Rhonabwy, 'to whom does yonder troop belong?' 'They are the fellows of Rhuvawn Pebyr the son of Prince Deorthach. And these men are honourably served with mead and bragget, and are freely beloved by the daughters of the kings of the Island of Britain. And this they merit, for they were ever in the front and the rear in every peril.' And he saw but one hue upon the men and the horses of this troop, for they were all as red as blood. And when one of the knights rode forth from the troop, he looked like a pillar of fire glancing athwart the sky. And this troop encamped above the ford.

Then they beheld another troop coming towards the ford, and these from their horses' chests upwards were whiter than the lily, and below blacker than jet. And they saw one of these knights go before the rest, and spur his horse into the ford in such a manner that the water dashed over Arthur and the Bishop, and those holding counsel with them, so that they were as wet as if they had been drenched in the river. And as he turned the head of his horse, the youth who stood before Arthur struck the horse over the nostrils with his sheathed sword, so that, had it been with the bare blade, it would have been a marvel if the bone had not been wounded as well as the flesh. And the knight drew his sword half out of the scabbard, and asked of him. 'Wherefore didst thou strike my horse? Whether was it in insult or in counsel unto me?' 'Thou dost indeed lack counsel. What madness caused thee to ride so furiously as to dash the water of the ford over Arthur, and the consecrated Bishop, and their counsellors, so that they were as wet as if they had been dragged out of the river?' 'As counsel then will I take it.' So he turned his horse's head round towards his army.

'Iddawc,' said Rhonabwy, 'who was yonder knight?' 'The most eloquent and the wisest youth that is in this island; Adaon, the son of Taliesin.' 'Who was the man that struck his horse?' 'A youth of forward nature; Elphin, the son of Gwyddno.'

Then spake a tall and stately man, of noble and flowing speech, saying that it was a marvel that so vast a host should be assembled in so narrow a space, and that it was still greater marvel that those should be there at that time who had promised to be by mid-day in the battle of Badon, fighting with Osla Gyllellvawr. 'Whether thou mayest choose to proceed or not, I will proceed.' 'Thou sayest well,' said Arthur, 'and we will go altogether.' 'Iddawc,' said Rhonabwy, 'who was the man who spoke so marvellously unto Arthur erewhile?' 'A man who may speak as boldly as he listeth, Caradawc Vreichvras, the son of Llyr Marini, his chief counsellor and his cousin.'

Then Iddawc took Rhonabwy behind him on his horse, and that mighty host moved forward, each troop in its order, towards Cevndigoll.

And when they came to the middle of the ford of the Severn, Iddawc turned his horse's head, and Rhonabwy looked along the valley of the Severn. And he beheld two fair troops coming towards the ford. One troop there came of brilliant white, whereof every one of the men had a scarf of white satin with jet-black borders. And the knees and the tops of the shoulders of their horses were jet-black, though they were of a pure white in every other part. And their banners were pure white, with black points to them all.

'Iddawc,' said Rhonabwy, 'who are yonder pure white troop?' 'They are the men of Norway, and March the son of Meirchion is their prince. And he is cousin unto Arthur.' And further on he saw a troop, whereof each man wore garments of jet-black, with borders of pure white to every scarf; and the tops of the shoulders and the knees of their horses were pure white. And their banners were jet-black with pure white at the point of each.

'Iddawc,' said Rhonabwy, 'who are the jet-black troop yonder?' 'They are the men of Denmark, and Edeyrn the son of Nudd is their prince.'

And when they had overtaken the host, Arthur and his army of mighty ones dismounted below Caer Badou, and he perceived that he and Iddawc journeyed the same road as Arthur. And after they had dismounted he heard a great tumult and confusion amongst the host, and such as were then at the flanks turned to the centre, and such as had been in the centre moved to the flanks. And then, behold, he saw a knight coming, clad, both he and his horse, in mail, of which the rings were whiter than the whitest lily, and the rivets redder than the ruddiest blood. And he rode amongst the host.

'Iddawc,' said Rhonabwy, 'will yonder host flee?' 'King Arthur never fled, and if this discourse of thine were heard, thou wert a lost man. But as to the knight whom thou seest yonder, it is Kai. The fairest horseman is Kai in all Arthur's Court; and the men who are at the front of the army hasten to the rear to see Kai ride, and the men who are in the centre flee to the side, from the shock of his horse. And this is the cause of the confusion of the host.'

Thereupon they heard a call made for Kadwr, Earl of Cornwall, and behold he arose with the sword of Artur in his hand. And the similitude of two serpents was upon the sword in gold. And when the sword was drawn from its scabbard, it seemed as if two flames of fire burst forth from the jaws of the serpents, and then, so wonderful was the sword, that it was hard for any one to look upon it. And the host became still, and the tumult ceased, and the Earl returned to the tent.

'Iddawc,' said Rhonabwy, 'who is the man who bore the sword of Arthur?' 'Kadwr, the Earl of Cornwall, whose duty it is to arm the King on the days of battle and warfare.'

And they heard a call made for Eirynwych Amheibyn, Arthur's servant, a red, rough, ill-favoured man, having red whiskers with bristly hairs. And behold he came upon a tall red horse with the mane parted on each side, and he brought with him a large and beautiful sumpter pack. And the huge red youth dismounted before Arthur, and he drew a golden chair out of the pack, and a carpet of diapered satin. And he spread the carpet before Arthur, and there was an apple of ruddy gold at each corner thereof, and he placed the chair upon the carpet. And so large was the chair that three armed warriors might have sat therein. Gwenn was the name of the carpet, and it was one of its properties that whoever was upon it no one could see him, and he could see every one. And it would retain no colour but its own.

And Arthur sat within the carpet, and Owain the son of Urien was standing before him. 'Owain,' said Arthur, 'wilt thou play chess?' 'I will, Lord,' said Owain. And the red youth brought the chess for Arthur and Owain; golden pieces and a board of silver. And they began to play.

And while they were thus, and when they were best amused with their game, behold they saw a white tent with a red canopy, and the figure of a jet-black serpent on the top of the tent, and red glaring venomous eyes in the head of the serpent, and a red flaming tongue. And there came a young page with yellow curling hair, and blue eyes, and a newly-springing beard, wearing a coat and a surcoat of yellow satin, and hose of thin greenish-yellow cloth upon his feet, and over his hose shoes of parti-coloured leather, fastened at the insteps with golden clasps. And he bore a heavy three-edged sword with a golden hilt, in a scabbard of black leather tipped with fine gold. And he came to the place where the Emperor and Owain were playing at chess.

And the youth saluted Owain. And Owain marvelled that the youth should salute him and should not have saluted the Emperor Arthur. And Arthur knew what was in Owain's thought. And he said to Owain, 'Marvel not that the youth salutes thee now, for he saluted me erewhile; and it is unto thee that his errand is.' Then said the youth unto Owain, 'Lord, is it with thy leave that the young pages and attendants of the Emperor harass and torment and worry thy Ravens? And if it be not with thy leave, cause the Emperor to forbid them.' 'Lord,' said Owain, 'thou hearest what the youth says; if it seem good to thee, forbid them from my Ravens.' 'Play thy game,' said he. Then the youth returned to the tent.

That game did they finish, and another they began, and when they were in the midst of the game, behold, a ruddy young man with auburn curling hair and large eyes, well-grown, and having his beard new-shorn, came forth from a bright yellow tent, upon the summit of which was the figure of a bright red lion. And he was clad in a coat of yellow satin, falling as low as the small of his leg, and embroidered with threads of red silk. And on his feet were hose of fine white buckram, and buskins of black leather were over his hose, whereon were golden clasps. And in his hand a huge, heavy, three-edged sword, with a scabbard of red

deer-hide, tipped with gold. And he came to the place where Arthur
and Owain were playing at chess. And he saluted him. And Owain was
troubled at his salutation, but Arthur minded it no more than before.
And the youth said unto Owain, 'Is it not against thy will that the attendants of the Emperor harass thy Ravens, killing some and worrying
others? If against thy will it be, beseech him to forbid them.' 'Lord,'
said Owain, 'forbid thy men, if it seem good to thee.' 'Play thy game,'
said the Emperor. And the youth returned to the tent.

And that game was ended and another begun. And as they were
beginning the first move of the game, they beheld at a small distance
from them a tent speckled yellow, the largest ever seen, and the figure
of an eagle of gold upon it, and a precious stone on the eagle's head.
And coming out of the tent, they saw a youth with thick yellow hair
upon his head, fair and comely, and a scarf of blue satin upon him,
and a brooch of gold in the scarf upon his right shoulder as large as
a warrior's middle finger. And upon his feet were hose of fine Totness,
and shoes of parti-coloured leather, clasped with gold, and the youth
was of noble bearing, fair of face, with ruddy cheeks and large hawk's
eyes. In the hand of the youth was a mighty lance, speckled yellow,
with a newly-sharpened head; and upon the lance a banner displayed.

Fiercely angry, and with rapid pace, came the youth to the place where
Arthur was playing at chess with Owain. And they perceived that he
was wroth. And thereupon he saluted Owain, and told him that his
Ravens had been killed, the chief part of them, and that such of them
as were not slain were so wounded and bruised that not one of them
could raise its wings a single fathom above the earth. 'Lord,' said Owain,
'forbid thy men.' 'Play,' said he, 'if it please thee.' Then said Owain
to the youth, 'Go back, and wherever thou findest the strife at the thickest, there lift up the banner, and let come what pleases Heaven.'

So the youth returned back to the place whre the strife bore hardest
upon the Ravens, and he lifted up the banner; and as he did so they
all rose up in the air, wrathful and fierce and high of spirit, clapping
their wings in the wind, and shaking off the weariness that was upon
them. And recovering their energy and courage, furiously and with exul-
tation did they, with one sweep, descend upon the heads of the men,
who had erewhile caused them anger and pain and damage, and they
seized some by the heads and others by the eyes, and some by the ears,
and others by the arms, and carried them up into the air; and in the
air there was a mighty tumult with the flapping of the wings of the
triumphant Ravens, and with their croaking; and there was another
mighty tumult with the groaning of the men, that were being torn and
wounded, and some of whom were slain.

And Arthur and Owain marvelled at the tumult as they played at
chess; and, looking, they perceived a knight upon a dun-coloured horse
coming towards them. And marvellous was the hue of the dun horse.

Bright red was his right shoulder, and from the top of his legs to the centre of his hoof was bright yellow. Both the knight and his horse were fully equipped with heavy foreign armour. The clothing of the horse from the front opening upwards was of bright red sendal, and from thence opening downwards was of bright yellow sendal. A large gold-hilted one-edged sword had the youth upon his thigh, in a scabbard of light blue, and tipped with Spanish laton. The belt of the sword was of dark green leather with golden slides and a clasp of ivory upon it, and a buckle of jet-black upon the clasp. A helmet of gold was on the head of the knight, set with precious stones of great virtue, and at the top of the helmet was the image of a flame-coloured leopard with two ruby-red stones in its head, so that it was astounding for a warrior, however stout his heart, to look at the face of the leopard, much more at the face of the knight. He had in his hand a blue-shafted lance, but from the haft to the point it was stained crimson-red with the blood of the Ravens and their plumage.

The knight came to the place where Arthur and Owain were seated at chess. And they perceived that he was harassed and vexed and weary as he came towards them. And the youth saluted Arthur, and told him that the Ravens of Owain were slaying his young men and attendants. And Arthur looked at Owain and said, 'Forbid thy Ravens.' 'Lord,' answered Owain, 'play thy game.' And they played. And the knight returned back towards the strife and the Ravens were not forbidden any more than before.

And when they had played awhile, they heard a mighty tumult, and a wailing of men, and a croaking of Ravens, as they carried the men in their strength into the air, and, tearing them betwixt them, let them fall piecemeal to the earth. And during the tumult they saw a knight coming towards them, on a light grey horse, and the left foreleg of the horse was jet-black to the centre of his hoof. And the knight and the horse were fully accoutred with huge heavy blue armour. And a robe of honour of yellow diapered satin was upon the knight, and the borders of the robe were blue. And the housings of the horse were jet-black, with borders of bright yellow. And on the thigh of the youth was a sword, long, and three-edged, and heavy. And the scabbard was of red cut leather, and the belt of new red deer-skin, having upon it many golden slides and a buckle of the bone of the seahorse, the tongue of which was jet-black. A golden helmet was upon the head of the knight, wherein were set sapphire-stones of great virtue. And at the top of the helmet was the figure of flame-coloured lion, with a fiery-red tongue, issuing above a foot from his mouth, and with venomous eyes, crimson-red, in his head. And the knight came, bearing in his hand a thick ashen lance, the head whereof, which had been newly steeped in blood, was overlaid with silver.

And the youth saluted the Emperor: 'Lord,' said he, 'carest thou not for the slaying of thy pages, and thy young men, and the sons of the nobles of the Island of Britain, whereby it will be difficult to defend this island from henceforward for ever?' 'Owain,' said Arthur, 'forbid thy Ravens.' 'Play this game, Lord,' said Owain.

So they finished the game and began another; and as they were finishing that game, lo, they heard a great tumult and a clamour of armed men, and a croaking of Ravens, and a flapping of wings in the air, as they flung down the armour entire to the ground, and the men and the horses piecemeal. Then they saw coming a knight on a lofty-headed piebald horse. And the left shoulder of the horse was of bright red, and its right leg from the chest to the hollow of the hoof was pure white. And the knight and horse were equipped with arms of speckled yellow, variegated with Spanish laton. And there was a robe of honour upon him, and upon his horse, divided in two parts, white and black, and the borders of the robe of honour were of golden purple. And above the robe he wore a sword three-edged and bright, with a golden hilt. And the belt of the sword was of yellow goldwork, having a clasp upon it of the eyelid of a black sea-horse, and a tongue of yellow gold to the clasp. Upon the head of the knight was a bright helmet of yellow laton, with sparkling stones of crystal in it, and at the crest of the helmet was the figure of a griffin, with a stone of many virtues in its head. And he had an ashen spear in his hand, with a round shaft, coloured with azure blue. And the head of the spear was newly stained with blood, and was overlaid with fine silver.

Wrathfully came the knight to the place where Arthur was, and he told him that the Ravens had slain his household and the sons of the chief men of this island, and he besought him to cause Owain to forbid his Ravens. And Arthur besought Owain to forbid them. Then Arthur took the golden chessmen that were upon the board, and crushed them until they became as dust. Then Owain ordered Gwres the son of Rheged to lower his banner. So it was lowered, and all was peace.

Then Rhonabwy inquired of Iddawc who were the first three men that came to Owain, to tell him his Ravens were being slain. Said Iddaws, 'They were men who grieved that Owain should sudffer loss, his fellow-chieftains and companions, Selyv the son of Kynan Garwyn of Powys, and Gwgawn Gleddyvrudd, and Gwres the son of Rheged, he who bears the banner in the day of battle and strife.' 'Who,' said Rhonabwy, 'were the last three men who came to Arthur, and told him that the Ravens were slaughtering his men?' 'The best of men,' said Iddawc, 'and the bravest, and who would grieve exceedingly that Arthur should have damage in aught; Blathaon the son of Mawrheth, and Rhuvawn Pebyr the son of Prince Deorthach, and Hyveidd Unllenn.'

And with that behold four-and-twenty knights came from Osla Gyllellvawr, to crave a truce of Arthur for a fortnight and a month. And Arthur rose and went to take counsel. And he came to where a tall, auburn, curly-headed man was a little way off, and there he assembled his counsellors. Bedwini, the Bishop, and Gwarthegyd the son of Kaw, and March the son of Meirchawn and Caradawc Vreichvras, and Gwalchmai the son of Gwyar, and Edeyrn the son of Nudd, and Rhuvawn Pebyr the son of Prince Deorthach, and Rhiogan the son of the King of Ireland, and Gwenwynwyn the son of Nav, Howel the son of Emyr Llydaw, Gwilym the son of Rhwyf Freinc, and Daned the son of Ath, and Goreu Custennin, and Mabon the son of Modron, and Peredur Paladyr Hir, and Hyveidd Unllenn, and Twrch the son of Perif, and Nerth the son of Kadarn, and Gobrwy the son of Echel Vorddwyttwll, Gwair the son of Gwestyl, and Gadwy the son of Geraint, Trystan the son of Tallwch, Moryen Manawc, Granwen the son of Llyr, and Llacheu the son of Arthur, and Llawvrodedd Varvawc, and Kadwr Earl of Cornwall, Morvran the son of Tegid, and Rhyawd the son of Morgant, and Dyvyr the son of Alun Dyved, Gwrhyr Gwalstawd Ieithoedd, Adaon the son of Taliesin, Llary the son of Kasnar Wledig, and Fflewddur Fflam, and Greidawl Galldovydd, Gilbert the son of Kadgyffro, Menw the son of Teirgwaedd, Gwrthmwl Wledig, Cawrdav the son of Caradawc Vreichvras, Gildas the son of Kaw, Kadyriaith the son of Saidi, and many of the man of Norway and Denmark, and many of the men of Greece, and a crowd of the men of the host came to that council.

'Iddawc,' said Rhonabwy, 'who was the auburn haired man to whom they came just now?' 'Rhun the son of Maelgwn Gwynedd, a man whose prerogative it is, that he may join in counsel with all.' 'And wherefore did they admit into counsel with men of such dignity as are yonder a stripling so young as Kadyriaith the son of Saidi?' 'Because there is not throughout Britain a man better skilled in counsel than he.'

Thereupon, behold, bards came and recited verses before Arthur, and no man understood those verses but Kadyriaith only, save that they were in Arthur's praise.

And lo, there came four-and-twenty asses with their burdens of gold and of silver, and a tired way-worn man with each of them, bringing tribute to Arthur from the Islands of Greece. Then Kadyriaith the son of Saidi besought that a truce might be granted to Osla Gyllellvawr for the space of a fortnight and a month, and that the asses and the burdens they carried might be given to the bards, to be to them as the reward for their stay and that their verse might be recompensed during the time of the truce. And thus it was settled.

'Rhonabwy,' said Iddawc, 'would it not be wrong to forbid a youth who can give counsel so liberal as this from coming to the councils of his Lord?'

Then Kai arose, and he said, 'Whosoever will follow Arthur, let him be with him to-night in Cornwall, and whosoever will not, let him be opposed to Arthur even during this truce.' And through the greatness

of the tumult that ensued, Rhonabwy awoke. And when he awoke he
was upon the yellow calf-skin, having slept three nights and three days.

And this tale is called the Dream of Rhonabwy. And this is the reason that no one knows the dream without a book, neither bard nor
gifted seer; because of the various colours that were upon the horses,
and the many wondrous colours of the arms and of the panoply, and
of the precious scarfs, and of the virtue-bearing stones.

---

[1] This and other mysteries are discussed in *Arthur and the Sovereignty of Britain:
King and Goddess in the Mabinogion* by Caitlín Matthews (Arkana, 1989).
[2] See: *The Warriors of Arthur* by John Matthews & Bob Stewart (Blandford Press,
1987).

Chapter 17.

Guinevere and Lancelot

by Arthur Machen

Arthur Machen (1863-1947) was one of the best of the early esoteric novelists. Like A. E. Waite (see Chapter 12) he was for a time a member of the Order of the Golden Dawn, and there is an underlying sense of realism in all his descriptions of magic which has only been surpassed by Charles Williams in books such as *War in Heaven* and *The Place of the Lion*.

Machen's best books are probably *The Great Return* (1923) and *The Hill of Dreams* (1907), both of which deal with the impinging of the Otherworld upon the lives of 'ordinary' people. He also wrote a number of excellent short stories and essays, of which the following, *Guinevere and Lancelot*, was originally published in 1908.

Born at Caerleon-upon-Us (Arthur's headquarters, according to early British tradition), Machen was first and foremost a Celt who recognized the magical qualities inherent in the ancient myths and legends of Britain, particularly those which pertained to Arthur. In an essay on the Grail, he praised Waite's *Hidden Church of the Holy Grail* for its recognition of the secret school which carried the mystery of the sacred vessel throughout time.

Wherever possible, Machen brought these ancient mysteries into the present, giving them a contemporary slants, as Charles Williams was later to do. In the work which follows, however, we are firmly in the time of Arthur, but this story of the most famous lovers of all time is given a new, almost cosmic dimension through Machen's knowledge of the inner mysteries and the hints he makes about Otherworldly influences.

Upon a morning in May a man kept his master's sheep on the hills that are above the Forest of Dendreath, in the midst of the Isle of Britain. It was very early in the morning when the man came out of the shelter that he had made between two rocks, and the dew was thick upon the short grass, and at the sun rising all the land glittered as if it had been the Shining Isle beyond the waves of ocean, and an odour of sweetness rose up from the region of the leaves. Then the sun ascended in his splendour, and the mists in the forests vanished away, and the shepherd saw before him all the wonders of the Forest of Dendreath. In the west he beheld the Road of the Eagle that issues from the waste land of Cameliard; and suddenly he was amazed, for far away he saw a red flame and a white flame advancing side by side along the alley of the wood.

Now, these flames were indeed nothing but that famous knight of

high worship, Sir Lancelot, the principal warrior of the Order of the
Round Table, and beside him Guinevere, that was to be Arthur's queen.
When the shepherd far on the wild hill had seen them they had but
come forth from a shade of beechen leaves, and as they appeared suddenly in the open glade the sunbeams smote upon them, and so bright
was Lancelot's armour made that it was as if it spouted white fire, and
Guinevere was as the burning of vehement flames. Upon her head she
bore a cap of golden cloth, curiously adorned with jewels such as rubies
and carbuncles and chrysoprases, and her cotehardie was of red samite.
And about her she held a cloak of flame-coloured satin, and her belt
was of gold and crystals. Golden was the glory of her hair. So they rode
through the alleys of the forest in the sweetness of the May morning,
amidst the glittering of many leaves stirred by the wind of heaven. And
at their passing by all the choir of the birds of the wood exulted. Deep
from the shade in the heart of the forest Eos the nightingale chanted
the melody of lovers with unwearied antiphons; to him gladly replied
the blackbird, a master of song; the blackcap was of their chorus; from
the throats of smaller birds there rose a sweet sound like that of pipes
of faerie. So journeyed Sir Lancelot and the lady by the ways of the happy
forest, one glancing gently on the other as they rode at a merry pace.

Now, when Sir Lancelot brought Guinevere from her father's castle
in Cameliard, they rode for a day and found no adventure. But as night
fell, and the sun went down, and it grew dark, they heard a noise as
of crackling flames, and the sky grew red; and they saw a high hill before
them, and on the height of it a fair castle was built, with lofty walls
and many springing towers and pinnacles. But a black smoke swelled
up from it, and great flames encompassed it, and as they looked there
was a roaring and a riving as of thunder; and then that fair and goodly
place fell apart, and was dashed down into the dust, being consumed
with fire. 'Alas, fair lord,' 'said Guinevere, 'what castle was this, and
who was the lord of it? What evil chance hath so piteously destroyed
it all?' 'Lady,' replied Sir Lancelot, 'that I may scarcely tell. Let be awhile,
and it may be that we shall fall in with some man who shall advise
us.' And then they pressed a little forward, and Sir Lancelot found a
poor man hidden amongst the thorns and bushes by the way, and he
asked the man what enemy had come upon the castle, and for what
cause it had thus been burned and ruined. 'Sir,' said the poor man,
'ye are to understand that this castle was the castle of Sir Sagramour
of the Fair Mourne, that was a knight of great worship, and a noble
warrior, and the lord of all these lands. And it fell out by evil chance
that he saw Eglaise, the daughter of King Ryon of the Rugged Island,
as she went forth from her chamber to hear mass, and the hearts of
these two became inflamed with love, and so they fled away together
and dwelt happily at that castle for a year and a day. Then cometh King
Ryon against Sir Sagramour and taketh his castle and burneth it as ye

have seen, and Sir Sagramour is slain, and his wife with him, and no living man is left therein.' Then Sir Lancelot and Guinevere, the queen that was to be, marvelled, and went on their way; and said Guinevere: 'I see very well that this love is both piteous and cruel, since by it husband and wife are slain, and a fair hold has its portion with ashes and destruction.' 'Will ye say so, lady?' answered Lancelot. 'Consider well that by this same love is all the round earth ordered, with the shining of the stars at night, and with all the spheres of the heavens, and with the perpetual choirs of Paradise. And without this love ye are to understand right as the doctors teach us, that there were no brightness of the sun at all, nor any light of the moon, nor should there be any green thing upon the earth, nor any bird of the wood, nor beast of the rocks, nor fishes in ocean; nay, when love shall pass, then passeth man also. And ye shall not say that this knight and his sweetheart were unhappy nor of an ill end, for to our lord Love they did great worship and great honour, and were well rewarded of him, so that they dwelt for a year and a day in the estate of gladness, and now praise God in Paradise, in the bliss that is perdurable and everlasting.' 'Oh, knight,' said then Guinevere, 'I see well that ye are a great lover and a high master—yea, a very doctor of love; and well I wit that in the King's court at Camelot ye have the love of many ladies, and bear the palm of all amorous knights.' 'Lady, ye judge falsely, since never yet have I loved maid nor wife.' 'Is this as ye say, of very truth?' 'It is as I have said, lady, and ye must know that I am none of the knights of the bower, but of the stricken field, where I do battle for my lord, King Arthur, against his enemies, and against the foes of all the land.' 'Nevertheless, sir knight, of love ye speak very honestly and fairly, and ye hold love in great worship, as is plain to see, and so at last ye shall doubtless receive the high guerdon and reward of that lord Love whose lauds and offices ye so well recite.' And then that fair lady looked on Sir Lancelot with right good liking. And as they passed on their way they came to a lake, and all about it there were yew-trees set as a high hedge, and from the shadow of these trees they heard issuing a noise of lamentation. 'What is this?' said Guinevere. 'Let us delay and listen.' And there was a sound of a man who wept, and after his weeping they saw him take a lute, and he sang this melody:

> I make an incantation against the brightness of the sky:
> I make an incantation against the shining of the sun:
> I make an incantation against the wind of heaven.
>
> I utter a spell against the boughs of the oak,
> Against the aspen and the alder, the willow and the birch,
> Against the budding of every tree that is in the wood.
>
> I bind a charm against the rose that it blossom not:
> May my magic bring darkness on the generation of the flowers:
> May blackness consume the grass of the fields.

Let there be a mighty spell upon the melody of the birds,
Let the green perpetual choir be silent,
Let the song of fairyland be heard no more.

For in Gwenllian was the brightness of the sky,
She was the splendour of the heavenly sun,
She imparted sweetness to the breeze from on high.

In her were contained the delight of the woods,
The sweetness of the rose, the pleasure of the flowers.
Her voice gave rapture to the song of the birds.
The joys of the world have departed with her to Paradise.

And Guinevere and Sir Lancelot went on their way, considering the
sad estate of this desolate lover, and again the lady spoke and said:
'What say ye, sir knight? Will ye still be so hardy as to praise this love
that bringeth men into so piteous a case? Heard ye not how he spoke,
saying that all joys had departed with the lady that death has taken
from him?' 'Lady,' said he, 'there shall come a day when ye shall understand well that, albeit lovers may die and perish, yet love remaineth
ever immortal, since no pangs of death may ever assail him.' And a
second time Guinevere looked gently on Sir Lancelot, and in her heart
she had him in right good liking.

After this fashion Sir Lancelot and Queen Guinevere passed through
the regions of Britain, till they drew near to Camelot, where King Arthur
held his court with his Knights of the Round Table. And as they paced
through the Forest of Dendreath they could see through the boughs
of the trees the open country shining before them, and Sir Lancelot
said: 'Lady, in a day's journey we shall come to Camelot, and there
shall we find King Arthur and all his Knights of the Round Table, and
the ladies of his court, and the saint that shall make you King Arthur's
queen.' And she knew not what she should have said to this, and her
heart grew sad; and then she bethought her of an old tale and matter
of wizardry, or so men say. And she gazed at the trees of the wood,
searching for a tree that she knew of; and as they came to the wood's
verge she saw her desire, and broke off a little bough from a wych-elm
that grew by the way. Then she has broken this bough in twain, and
one she has hidden about her, and the other she has given to the knight,
saying: 'I wit well that all of my lord's knights are men of truth and
gentle dealing, and I think that of them all ye be not the least. Wherefore, whatsoever ye swear to me, sure am I that ye will perform your
oath and keep it, and never gainsay it not so long as ye live.' 'Ye say
rightly, lady. What will ye that I swear to you?' 'I will have you swear
that evermore while ye be quick and in this life ye keep this bough that
I give you, for to be a token of this wayfaring and of my wedding of
my lord, King Arthur.' 'So shall it be, very willingly,' and Lancelot swore
this by holy rood. Then at the end of their way they came to high
Camelot, the golden and glorious city of King Arthur, and by the

Figure 14: 'Queen Guenevere' by Dora Curtis.

high saint were King Arthur and the Lady Guinevere made man and
wife.

There was a day when Queen Guinevere, that now is married to King
Arthur, sat with her ladies in her bower, and they were at sport, devising of certain flowers, that were their lovers, and of their divers properties. Said one damosel: 'I know a rose-tree that rises not too tall, and
it grows in a low garden, and four shining waters are about this garden,
and five lions keep watch over this garden, and six thorns there be on
this rose-tree, and one blossom only. Tell me where my rose is hidden.'
Then, by computing of numbers, the other ladies made out the name
of a knight and spoke it, and they all laughed with glee; and so sped
their sport very merrily. But all the while the Queen sat silent, and she
looked out of the window of the high tower, and saw far away the green
trees in the wood, and the road by which she had passed from
Cameliard to Camelot. And whereas her ladies spoke of flowers and
of the knights their lovers, so her thoughts fell on the bough of the
wych-elm which she had broken with Lancelot; and fervently did she
desire the love of this knight in her heart. Then did she wholly burn,
then did her heart become as a coal of fire, and forthwith she went
apart and wrote a scroll, and sent the writing to one that dwelt in Camelot, being a man reputed a sorcerer and a great clerk in art magic. So
it fell out that Guinevere stole away in the night-time, and came to a
hidden place in a wood that was near to Camelot, and there the wizard had already his cauldron of sorcery and incantation. And he had
made set about this cauldron a ring of fires, and a shining smoke went
up from the vessel as it were quick glass, and within the ring you might
see divers puppets and images in wax and in wood, shamefully devised
and foully wrought, having on their foreheads and their breasts the
signs and marks of the devils of hell and of the cursed gods and goddesses of heathen men. And with the wizard there was a lad that all
the while made the fires to burn with spices and gums of Satan, and
a black smoke rose up from these flames. Then came the Queen into
the ring, and at the wizard's bidding she doffed all her clothes and
stood naked by the cauldron, and so she dipped the elm wand into
the bubbling of the cauldron, right as the wizard commanded her.
Forthwith ye might hear a noise and a rushing sound amongst the black
branches and thickets of the wood, the great boughs of the trees tossed
one on other, and said the wizard: 'Now, madam, the Hosts of the
Air draw near; now is at hand the Army of Tzabaoth.' Then, in the
shimmering and in the shining of the glassy smoke that rose from the
cauldron there showed the shapes of the Mighty Ones, and to the Mightiest did Guinevere there make offering of herself; and, this done, 'Now,'
said the wizard, 'is the time come.' Then drew forth Queen Guinevere
the wych-bough from its place and again dipped it down three times
into the cauldron of incantation and drew it forth, saying—

One was one in the wood,
On the tree of old enchantment;
One was made twain in the wood,
A word of wisdom was uttered.
Now, one calleth to one,
One tree cannot be dissevered.
By the sign of union
Let the parted be joined together.

Then, with the great word of incantation, the lady made the sign, and forth came flying in the air Sir Lancelot, in his ghostly body. And from that night Sir Lancelot, that was the flower and crown of all King Arthur's warriors, durst not deny the Queen Guinevere in anything, but loved her from that time forth.

Now at that time it is to be understood that Camelot was the wonder and prize of all the cities in the Isle of Britain, nay, of the whole world. For, like that city of Syon, it was set on a high hill, and encompassed on every side by rich gardens and bowers of delight and orchards and pleasure places. And on high were the palaces of the warriors and the choirs and altars of the saints, and the most lordly palace of the Emperor Arthur, as it were a mountain on a mountain. And here were assembled all the rarities and precious things of the whole world, and all the instruments of wisdom, and all the books in which the secret things were written, which Merlin had gathered together from all the coasts of the world. In this city did Sir Lancelot and the Queen have their pleasure and delight and dalliance, and by art magic no eye could discern their pleasures, while they lived in wantonness. And ever Sir Lancelot, that was a loyal knight in his heart, must grieve and mourn for his piteous transgression against his lord, and ever must he weep and lament in his chamber for this mortal sin, and ever must he strive that it be put from him. Yet, by virtue of the spell and by the cauldron of incantation, he was without succour and relief, and what the Queen would that must he do. And it fell out that one night he strove against the word of incantation and magic, and it was as if his heart was bursten within him, and down fell he on the floor of his chamber, as though he were stark dead. Then came his squire, and to him it seemed that the spirit was departed from Sir Lancelot, and he made a lamentable crying, and still Sir Lancelot lay there like a dead man. And when the life returned to him he that was the mightiest of all King Arthur's Knights of the Round Table was, as it were, a little child, and no strength nor virtue was there left in his body. And while he lay there, there came without his window one of Guinevere's damsels, taught by the Queen, and thus she sang to him:

All through the nightertale I longed for thee,
In loneliness, and harkened for the door
To open, or a footstep on the floor.

O lief sweetheart, I pray thee pity me,
I hunger for thy kisses evermore;
All through the nightertale I longed for thee.

Delight is turned to woe, and misery
Is my solace, certes, my heart is sore,
Yet these poor lips a smile at morning bore,
Though all the nightertale I longed for thee.

Wherefore henceforth Sir Lancelot strove no more, but lived deliciously
in the golden meshes of the Queen's desires. And so to them twain
the fruits of the orchards of Camelot were as apples of Avalon and
golden delights, and the gardens were as walks of Paradise, and the
feasts in King Arthur's hall were like the perpetual entertainment of
the Blessed and Venerable Head of Bran Vendigeid, and the singing
of the birds was as the song of the Three Fairy Birds of Rhiannon.

And one year King Arthur kept the feast of Pentecost at Camelot,
as his custom was for the most part, and thirteen churches were set
apart wherein King Arthur and his court heard mass. And afterwards,
when they were in hall, suddenly there fell a silence, and each man
looked on other and was afraid. Then there was a noise like thunder,
and the roof was all afire; and then they heard in that place a melody
as of the choirs of Paradise and the rejoicing of the angels, and ye would
have said that there was an odour in that hall as of all the spicery of
the world. And all the knights fell down on their knees together, and
they saw as it were a hand pass from one end of the hall to the other
and go forth; and the hand bore up the holy and blessed Vessel of the
Sangraal, wrapt about in veils of red samite, and there was a shining
of light that made the sun darkness; and to Sir Lancelot, because of
his deadly sin, it was as if a sword had pierced his body, for his flesh
began to tremble when he beheld the spiritual things. Yet he might not
put his sin from him, but ever again returned to his dalliance with the
Queen, for the spell that she had set upon him could not yet be broken.

Now, with the passing of the years, it happened that the bough of
wych-elm that Queen Guinevere had severed in the wood withered and
shrank, and, though the Queen and Sir Lancelot might keep each their
portion never so well, the leaves that were on the boughs fell off. And
when a leaf fell off then it vanished away, and as it vanished there flew
forth a great bird, black as coal; and these birds perched on the trees
of the wood, and cried out as men passed by, 'Guinevere is the leman
of Sir Lancelot'. And so this sin could no longer be covered, and all
the court of King Arthur had knowledge of these birds and of what
their message was, and some believed it and some not, but all looked
strangely on Sir Lancelot and Queen Guinevere. And it fell out at last
that Guinevere took out her portion of the bough and set it before her,
counting the leaves that remained; and suddenly she must go forth
from her chamber to sit in hall; and by ill chance she had forgotten

the bough, so that one of her damsels cometh in, and seeing it, casteth
it into the fire. And in that moment was Sir Lancelot set free from the
virtue of the enchantment and the wizardry that had been done upon
him; and in that moment came the lad that had prepared the fires of
the sorcery, and confessed all to the King, and the report of this was
made known to all the city of Camelot. Then the anger of King Arthur
was like to burning of fire, and he sent ten knights, that were the mightiest that he had, to waylay Sir Lancelot, that they might slay him forthwith and hew his body in pieces. So these knights went forth, and they
came upon Sir Lancelot as he walked in his garden, and he had no arms,
but only a short sword, upon him. Then they cried: 'Now shall ye surely die, thou foul and disloyal knight, for the deep dishonour that ye
have done our lord the King', and they ran at him to kill him. But,
for all their mail, five of them did he leave for dead in that garden,
since he was the most valorous and most mightiest of all knights that
ever have been in this world; and so the five knights that were left in
life fled away from before Sir Lancelot. Then would Sir Lancelot
endeavour to bring forth the Queen harmless, but he might not, she
was so closely kept; and so Sir Lancelot fled forth from Camelot, and
gathered his kinsfolk about him, if haply he might deliver the Queen
from prison. For Arthur swore that for wizardry and disloyalty she
should be burnt. But afterward King Arthur repented of his oath, and
Guinevere dwelt, as all men know, in an abbey of nuns at Amesbury,
and in due time was Sir Lancelot hallowed Bishop of Canterbury. And
so, having repented of their sins, they both departed from this life: on
whose souls may God have pity.

Chapter 18.
Arthur of Little Britain

The following extract comes from a little known late romance which has been unjustly neglected by students of the Arthurian myths.[1] It is a richly embroidered story of enchantment and adventure, in which the young Arthur proves himself a mighty warrior in his own right and courts the beautiful Florence. Many of the adventures, like the one given here, are clearly of an Otherworldly provenance. In particular, the Perilous Bed episode, which is known from other texts, speaks of an Otherworldly setting.

Arthur, undaunted, performs feats of astounding bravery and wins for himself the Sword Clarence (or Clariens)—another name for the more famous Excalibur. It is awarded to him by no lesser person than Persephone, Queen of Faery, who is herself an earlier version of the Lady of the Lake.

The exact date of composition is not known, though it may be conjectured that it was written between the middle of the 15th and the first third of the 16th centuries. The edition from which the present text comes was published in 1609, in an English translation by Lord Berners (famous as the first translator of Froissart's *Chronicles*). Once again, as with the *Merlin and Grisandole*, I have chosen to retain the original spelling and orthography rather than spoil the flavour of the text. Glosses will be found in the footnotes for unfamiliar words or phrases.

How that Arthur conquered the Castell of the Porte Noyre by his prowes, and slewe all them that kepte it: and how after that he entered into the halles of the palays, wher he was assayled of two grete and horryble lyons, and of a grete gyaunt, & how he ouercame them all wyth grete payne, and acheued all the meruayllous aduentures of the Castel, the which are right wonderous to reherse.

Whan that Arthur was departed fro Gouernar, he toke the waye on the ryghte hande, and so rode forth .iii. dayes, without findinge of ony aduenture, or ony maner of hous or place: how be it, by the counseyle of his hoost, he toke with hym sustenaunce for hym selfe and for his horse, for the space of thre or foure dayes; and thus he passed by many valeys and mountaynes, so that he and his horse were right wery; & on ye fourth daye he founde an hydeous ryuer, depe & perfound; the bankes were so hye fro the water, y^t he coulde not se it ren,[1] ye whiche water rored and brayed, & ran so swyftely, that none myghte passe w^toute drowning; and in certayne places it was full of grete and

Arthur of Little Britain

myghty rockes, the whiche were of suche heyght, that fro the valey bynethe, the toppe of them myght vnnethes[2] be sene: the whiche rockes were soo full of vermyn, that all the ryuer thereby stanke abhomynably. At the last, Arthur found a lytle way alonge by the ryuers syde on the lyfte hande, in the whyche he rode so long tyl it was hye none, & than he espyed a lytel streyght waye bytwene two mountaynes, the whiche were of a meruaylous heyght; than he founde a lytell narowe brydge ouer this ryuer, the whiche w^t moche payne he passed ouer; than he entred in to a streyght causy[3] made of stone, wherin he rode forth, and on euery hāde of hym all was but grete maresses[4] and foule stynkynge waters, the whiche waye brought hym streyght vnto the Porte Noyre, the whiche was the strongest castell of all the worlde; and so whan he came to the brydge & gate therof, there he founde .xii. knyghtes all armed on horsbacke, .vi. at the one ende of the brydge, and .vi. at the other ende; and at the gate there were .xii. other knyghtes on fote, holdyng hatches and mases of stele in theyr handes, to the entent to kepe that none sholde entre in to the castell; & aboue, on the barbycans & bowlewerkes,[5] there stode men of warre with crosbowes and other wepens to defend the place. And al this season, in the Moūt Peryllous, was mayster Steuen, clerke to the fayre Florence, doughter vnto the myghty kynge of Soroloys, Emendus; who had lien there nye the space of a yere, to abyde the comynge of that knyght, that sholde acheue al the aduentures of that castel; and in his company was the cōstable y^t kepte the palayses & halles w^{t}out the castell of the Porte Noyre: & than mayster Steuen knewe by his bokes & connynge of astronomy, that ye knyght sholde come the same daye; therfore he & his company mounted on the walles of the palays, to se how the knyghte sholde do, that was as thā come to ye gate of the castel of the Porte Noyre.

And whan the fyrst .vi. knyghtes sawe Arthur, they toke theyr sheldes & speres. Than Arthur sayd to Bawdewyn: Frende, I haue nede now to take good hede, therfore tari you here without, & let me alone with them. Than these .vi. knightes ran all at ones on Arthur on the brydge, and strake him with speres & swerdes; but for all that he felte no hurte: but he encountred soo with the firste, that his spere dyd glyde thrugh his body, & so he fell downe dead, and the spere breake, and with the tronchon thereof he strake the seconde so curteisly, that he ouerthrewe both horse and man, & fell besyde the brydge into the water; and whan he had though to haue releued him self agayne out of the water, than Bawdwyn cast him downe agayne into the riuer, & so there he was drowned: thā Bawdewyn toke his spere and brought to Arthur, wherwith he strake an other knyght so rudely, that the heade of the spere perced his herte, and so fell downe dead; & whan the .iii. other knights saw y^t theyr .iii. felowes were slayne, they fledde backe agayne ouer the brydge, and went to theyr felawes at the bridge fote: & Arthur folowed them, his swerde in his hāde, & strake one of them, that he claue hym to the sholdres; than al the remenaūt ran at ones at him, but he defended hym selfe valyauntly, as he that noo thynge fered, for suche was his manner, the more he hadde to do, the greater grewe his strength and courage; & so he put hym selfe betwene them and the gate, because of them that were on the walles, for they dyd hym muche trouble and assayled hym on all sydes: & euer ryght noblye he defended hym selfe, and gaue such strokes, that he made to flye into the felde, heades, armes, and handes; & who so euer he felled to the erth, neuer rose agayne, for Bawdwyn toke them by the legges, & dyd caste them ouer the brydge downe into the ryuer, wherin they were drowned: than Arthur begane to chafe and waxe angry, and layde on soo faste rounde about hym, that finally he slewe them all, saue two, who fledde in at the gate, and thought so for to haue escaped: but Arthur hasted hym soo faste after theym, that he stroke of one of theyr heades, and as the other stouped to haue entred in at the gate, Arthur strake hym so fyerslye[6] on the backe, that he claue hym nye asonder; than they that were on the bowlewerkes & on the walles, dyd caste at hym many grete stones and other wepens, but they coulde do hym none hurte, bycause that he was so nere to the gate. Than whā the other .xii. knights, whiche were on fote within the gate, sawe the dyscomfyture of theyr .xii. felowes that were on horsbacke, done al onely by one man, they were ryght sorowful, and so ran out all at ones at hym with grete hatches in theyr handes: & whan Arthur sawe them, he fered gretly Assyle his good horse, therefore he alyghted & delyuered hym to Bawdewyn, & badde hym to go tye hym wythout the brige fote; than Arthur encoūtred so with the fyrst, that he made his head to flye in to the fyeld, and the seconde he gaue suche a stroke, that he claue his head nye to the tethe. And whan mayster Steuē, who was on the walles of the palays, sawe the noble prowes of Arthur & the great strokes that he gaue, sayd to his company: Verely, behold yonder is the noblest knyght of the worlde; it is he that shall acheue the aduentures of this place; it is the same knyghte that we haue taryed here for so longe; & euer Arthur fyersly fought amonge this people, and bette them downe one after an other: and among them there were was one so grete & byg as thoughe he had bene a gyaunt, who ran at Arthur, & or he was ware toke hym by the legges, and pulled hym so fyersly, that they fell downe both togyder to the erth; but Arthur fel vnderneth the grete churle; and than one of yᵉ other knights, whā he sawe Arthur lye on the erth, he lyfte vp his axe & thoughte to haue striken Arthur on the hed: but in their hurteling togider the stroke lyght on the grete deuyll, soo that hys hugged[7] and foule heed flewe to the earth. Than Arthur lepte on his fete, and sayde: Syr, I thanke thee, for thou haste delyuered me from muche payne and jeopardye; and syth thou hast delyuered me of thys gret foule deuyll, I shal paye the anone thy wages; and therwith lyfte vppe hys swerde and gaue him such a stroke, that he claue his head asonder; than Arthur abandoned hym selfe amonge the remenaunt so fyersly, that he made great plente of hedes and armes to fal to the groūd; and, to make shorte processe, he dydde soo moche, that none of the .xii. were lefte on liue, but al were slayne, and christened in the water by Bawdewyn, for he was to theym a good god fader. Than Arthur stepte in at the wycket of the gate: than al those that were on the walles did shote and caste at him, & euer he bare of wyth his shelde as well as he myght, tyl at the laste he came to them, and the fyrste that he mette wyth loste his lyfe, & there dyde such meruayles, that it was wounder to thynke thereof: for some he threwe ouer the walles, and some lept into the water, so that fynally they were slayne & drowned, & none lefte on lyue in all the castell that he coude find or here: & Bawdewin was right sore trauayled wyth castynge of them in to the water that were slayne. Than Arthur sayde to Bawdwyn: Frende, I wyll go entre into the grete palays of Aduentures, the which he sawe before hym in the castel; therfore, Bawdewyn, I wyll y^t ye abyde me here in this court, & kepe well my horse Assyle tyll I come agayne to you. Syr, said Bawdewyn, for Goddes sake put not youre selfe noo more in ony place where as ye thynke is ony greate peryll. Well, said Arthur, care not for y^t, but I praye you do as I say, & loke in no wyse ye come to me wythout I cal you: thā Arthur moūted vp certane greces[8] to entre into the hall of the palays, ye which was ye way to ye Mount Peryllous: and there he found the moost fayre hous that euer was sene, sette all aboute with ymages of fyne golde, & the wyndowes were all of fyne ambre, wyth many hye clere wyndowes; and out of this hall he entred in to a chambre the moste rychest that euer was seen; for syth God first made mankynde, there was no maner of hystorie nor bataile, but in that chambre it was portrayed with golde and asure, & other fresshe coloures, so quyckely adurned,[9] that it was wonder to behold: there was portrayed how God dyde create the sonne and the mone, & in the rofe were all the vii. planettes wrought with fyne golde and syluer, and all the sytuacyons of the heuens, wherin were pyght many carbuncles & other precyous stones, the whiche dyde cast grete clerens bothe by daye and by nyght. To saye the trouthe, it was the most rychest chambre and the wonderfullest, that euer was seen in all the worlde; Proserpyne, quene of the fayry, caused it thus to be made. Also there were dyuerse beddes wonderfull ryche, but specyally one, the whiche stode in the myddes of the chambre, surmounted in beaute all other: for ye vtterbrasses[10] therof were of grene jasper, wyth grete barres of golde set full of precyous stones, and the crāpons were of fyne syluer enbordered wyth golde, the postes of yuery,[11] with pomelles of corall, and the staues closed in bokeram couere dwyth crymesyn satyn, & shetes of sylke with a ryche couerynge of ermyns, and other clothes of cloth of golde, and foure square pyllowes wrought amonge the sarasyns: the

curtaynes were of grene sendall vyroned with golde & asure, and rounde
aboute this bedde there laye on the flour carpettes of sylke poynted
& enbrowdred with ymages of golde: & at the foure corners of this bedde
there were foure condytes meruaylously-wrought by subtyll entayle, out
of the whiche there yssued so swet an odour & so delectable, y^t al
other swetenesse of the world were as no thynge to the regarde therof;
& at the head of thys bedde there stode an ymage of golde, and had
in hys lyfte hande a bowe of yuery, and in his right hande an arowe
of fyne syluer: in the myddes of his brest there were lettres that sayd
thus: Whan thys ymage shoteth, than all this palais shall tourne like
a whele, & than who so euer lyeth in this bedde shall dye, without it
be that knyghte to whome this bedde is destenyed vnto.

And whan Arthur saw the noblenesse of thys chambre, and specyally of this bedde, he had great pleasure to behold it, and sayd to him
selfe, how that at all aduentures that he wold lye downe on the bedde,
and not to ferre for anye drede of death; & as he was lyeng downe on
this bedde, he espyed in euerye corner of the chambre a gret ymage
of fine golde standynge, eche of theym holdynge in theyr handes a great
horne of syluer, &, by theyr countenance, redy to blow. Than Arthur
herde a great voyce, whyche was so loude and horryble, that master
Steuē, who was in the playes w^{t}out the castell, myght ryght wel here
it: the which voyce sayd: Behold now the ende! Than mayster Steuen
sayd to hys company: I am sure ye knyght is entred into ye palays w^{t}in
the castel; God defend hym from all yll encōbraunce![12] Than al the
palays begā to tremble & shake wondersly; so moche, that at the last
one of the iiii. ymages begā to blow his horne so loud, that it might
wel be herde the space of a myle; than the palays trembled so sore,
y^t all shold haue fallen to peces: the dores & windowes oftē tymes dyd
open & close agayne by theyre owne accord: than Arthur hearde aboute
him gret noyse of people, as though there had bene a thousande men
togyder, but he coulde se no creature: at the last he perceyued greate
lyghte of torches, & euer he herde styll the noyse of people comynge
and goynge aboute ye bedde, & also herde the brayenge of an hydeous ryuer, so y^t it semed to hym that it had ben the roringe of the
wylde see; ther with he felte such a terryble wynde, that he had moche
payne to sustayne hym on his fete.

Than Arthur assayed agayne to haue layne downe on the bedde: than
the voyce began to crye agayne, & sayd: Beholde now the ende! Than
the seconde ymage began to blowe; than came there in to the chambre
suche noyse & tourment, that Arthur was nye defe wyth ye terryble
dynne, & the palays than began sorer to tremble than it dyde before,
so that Arthur thought surely y^t all ye palays sholde haue fallen: than
Arthur drewe hym towarde the bedde, & as he wold haue layne hym
downe, he sawe on hys ryght hande a grete lyon, fyers & fell,[13] comynge to hymwarde, gapīge and rampynge to deuour hym, & so assa-

syled hym ryght rudely, & wyth hys pawes toke Arthur so by the sholder, that his harneys coulde not kepe him, but y^t his sharpe clawes entred in to his fleshe: and as the lyon wolde haue taken hī by ye heed, he cast his shelde before hym, & the lyon dasht it wyth his pawes all to peces, and nye had ouerthrowen hym to ye erth: but than Arthur toke his strength to hym, & as the lyon was rampīge before hym, he put his sworde clene thrugh his body, & so the lyon fell downe deed to the erthe; & Arthur was ryght sore hurte in the sholder, and bledde faste. Than he approached agayne to the bedde to haue layde hym downe: than ye thyrde ymage fyersly dyd blowe his horne, & out of the ende therof, by semynge to Arthur, there yssued out an other lyon, greter & stronger than the other was.

Whan Arthur sawe hym, he cryed to God & to our blesed Lady, to helpe & socour hym from yll deth and foule encombraūce: & so the lyon dressed hym towarde Arthur, & strake at hym wyth hys brode pawes, & Arthur helde before hym the remenaūt that was left of his shelde, but the lyon shortly brake it all to peces, as though it had bene but glasse; & with one of his fete he toke Arthur by ye lyfte syde, and rased fro him a gret parte of his harneys, & his doublet and shert, and a gret pece of his flessh to the bare rybbes; & if God had not there helped hī, he had rendred his mortall lyfe: than Arthur wyth his swerde strake of the lions fote that was vnder his syde, & therwith the lyon fell to the erth, &, or he rose agayne, Arthur recouered another stroke, and strake of his heade by the shuldres: than Arthur toke a fayre cloth of sendall that laye on the bedde, & therwyth wrapped his woūdes & staunched them frome bledynge. Than he approched agayne to the bedde to lye downe to rest hym: and than sodenly the fourth ymage began terrybly to blowe his horne: therwith Arthur loked behind hī, & espyed a great giaunt comyng to hī warde, who was .xv. fote of length, betynge togeder his tethe as though they had bene hamers strikinge on a stythy, who had in his hand a great axe, wherof the blade was wel thre fote longe; the whiche was so longe & sharpe, that it would cutte clene asonder euery thynge that it touched. And whan thys gyaunt sawe these lyons dede, he was so sore dyspleased, that he was all in a rage, and so rowled vp his eyen, and dashte togyder his tethe, and ran fyerseley at Arthur, thynkynge to haue stryken of hys head: but Arthur feared moche the stroke and lepte asyde, wherby ye stroke wente besyde hym, and dasht into the pauement so rudely, y^t the blade of the weapon entred therin juste to the heade: & than Arthur strake him with his swerde, but the stroke mounted vp agayne, and wold in no wyse enter, for he was harneysed with the skynne of a ser-pent, the whiche was so hard, that no wepen could empoyre it. And whan Arthur saw y^t, he was ryght sore displeased, and lyfte vp his swerde agayne, & strake the giaunt on the heade more rudely than he didde before; but all that aualed not, for it semed to him that he strake on a stethy of stele. Than Arthur fered him selfe gretely: than the gyant strake many strokes at Arthur, but alwayes he watched so the strokes, that he dydde let theim passe by hym without ony hurte or domage; for he perceyued ryght well, that if the gyaunte dyd light on him with a full stroke, there was none other way with him but death.

Thus this gyant euer pursued Arthur to haue striken him, but alwayes Arthur watched the strokes and voyded them wysely, and oftentymes strake the gyaunt agayne, but he coulde doo hym no hurte. Thus they fought a grete space, not ferre fro the ryche bedde in the myddes of the chambre: than the giaunt with grete yre lyfte vp his fauchon[14] to haue stryken Arthur vpon the head, and the stroke came brayeng, & dasht into the erth lyke thonder, for Arthur auoyded craftely the stroke, the which entred and cut asonder a greate brase of a benche, that stode before the bedde, of white yuery: & so the stroke descēded downe into the erth thrughout all the pauement, for the gyaunt was so sore dyspleased, that his weapon entred thrugh bothe wode & stone, and into the erth to the hard head, and therwith the blade of his fauchon brast clene asonder in the myddes: & whan the giaunt sawe that, he fared lyke a fende of hell, and so toke the handlynge therof and cast it at Arthur, but wysely he dyde auoyde it, & so it lyghted on the wall of the chambre, wherin the stroke entred well a fote and an halfe: than the gyaunte lepte to the brase of the benche that he had cut asonder before, and wold haue tasshed it out of the benche, but it was so sore bounde with crampons of stele to yᵉ benche, that he coude not remeue it; & as he stouped to pull therat. Arthur espyed hym, & how the serpentes skynne was but shorte behynde his backe, & so vnder the skynne he dasht his swerde in to his bely to the crosse; than the gyaunt fell downe & made a terryble braynge, the whiche myght well be herde a grete waye of: than Arthur recouered on hym an other stroke, & so dasht his swerde in to his herte; than he made a greter crye than he did before, and ther with his soule passed awaie to the deuill of hell. Than yᵉ noyse was hearde agayne that sayde, Beholde thende!

Than was Arthur so wery, & so sore trauayled, and is woūdes bledde so fast, yᵗ he had much payne to sustaine himselfe on his fete: how be it, as wel as he might he repayred downe to the ryche bed, & alwayes his swerde in his hand, & therwith layd him down on the bed: than the ymage of gold at the beddes head with his bow & arowe dyd shote, & hytte one of the wyndowes so sore, yᵗ it flewe wide open with the stoke, out of whiche window there yssued suche a smoke & fume so blacke, yᵗ it made al the hous so darke that Arthur coude se nothing; the which fume stāke so abominably, that Arthur therby was nye dead; than there rose such a wynde so grete & feruent, that it brast the glasse windowes & latesses, so that the tyles & stones flew all about the hous lyke hayle; and it thōdred so terrybly, that al the erth shoke, and the paleys trembled like to haue gone all to peces; and at the last he per-

ceyued a brēnynge[15] spere al of fyre, the whiche was comynge to hymwarde; therwith he lepte fro the bedde & fledde fro the stroke, and
sawe where yt wente in at an other lytell chambre by, & fell on a knyght
as he lay a bedde, and so brente hym clene thrugh: and the fyre
descēded thrughout bedde and chambre and al & sanke depe in to the
erth: then sodeynly brast asonder two pyllers whiche susteyned the
couerynge our the bedde, and than al the hole palays began to tourne
aboute lyke a whele: than Arthur ranne to the ymage of golde that stode
at the beddes heed, & enbraced it in his armes, for the ymage remoued
noo thinge: and this tourneng of the palays endured a grete space. And
Bawdewyn, Arthurs squyer, who was wythout in the courte, pyteously
wepte & demened ryght grete sorow for ye fere that he had of his
mayster, for he thought veryly how that he was but deed, and sayd:
A! my lorde Arthur! the best knight, the moost noble and hardy, the
moost sage and curteyse creature that euer was fourmed by Nature,
alas! why dyde ye entre in to this vnhappy castell, for I thynke surely
ye are but deed!

    And so than at ye last ye tournynge of thys palays began to sece, and
the derkenes began to auoyde & to waxe fayre and clere, and the ayre
peasyble:[16] than Arthur sate hym downe vpon the ryche beddes syde,
ryght feble & faynte, bycause of the grete troble that he had endured,
and for the ferefull horryblenes y^t he had seen and herde. Than whan
it was thus waxed fayre & clere, than the voyce sayd agayne twyse: It
ys ended! it ys ended! & whā mayster Steuen herde that voyce, he sayd
vnto his compani: Veryly the aduentures of the palays in ye castell of
the Porte Noyre are acheued; therefore I am sure it can be none other
wyse that that ye knight is there, eyther he is dead or elles ryght sore
wounded: & than he wēt & gadred herbes, suche as he knewe were
ryght precyous for all maner of woūdes, and made of theim to gyue
vnto Arthur, if it were his fortune to fynde hym alyue: & Baudewyn,
who also had herde the voyce, thoughte verely than that Arthur had
ben dead, and sayde to him selfe, that neyther for ye dyspleasure of
his lorde, nor yet for feare of ony other thyne, he wolde abyde no longer;
but y^t he wold mount vp into the palays to se if he coude knowe howe
his lorde dydde; & so wēt vp ye stayres w^t his swearde in his hande,
and passed thrugh the hall, and entred in to the chambre where as
Arthur was sittynge on the beddes side: than was Bawdewyn glad whan
he sawe his mayster alyue, and demaunded him howe he didde. And
Arthur answered, and said, how that he was ryght wery, and sore
wounded.

    Than Bawdewyn was ryght sorowfull at his herte, for he fered gretly
leste that he had some mortall wounde, and sayde: Syr, may it please
you to shew me your woūdes? It pleaseth me right well, sayd Arthur.
Than Bawdewyn vnarmed hī, and serched all his woundes, for he was
a ryght good surgyne and wasshed and staunched his woundes, and

softly dyd anoynt them, the whiche did him righte grete ease. Than
Arthur armed hym agayne, and sayd, that he wolde go serche ferder
ouer all the palays, to know yf there were ony mo aduentures: & therwith there entred in to yᵉ chambre a yonge varlet, who accustomably
before apparayled the mete and drīke that serued for the knightes that
were dead at the gate of the castel: & whan he came before Arthur,
he kneled downe, & sayde: A! gentyll knight, I crye you mercy! for
Goddes sake saue my lyfe, for I am a pore verlet, that serued, for my
lyuing, the knightes that ye haue slayne. Thou shalte haue noo hurte,
sayde Arthur, on the condycyon that thou wylte tell me the trouthe,
whether there be in this castell any moo men or women? Syr, sayd the
verlet, here in this place there be noo moo creatures, but all onelye
two prysoners, who were delyuered to my maysters, whome ye haue
slayne, to be kepte here in prison, to the entente that it shoulde neuer
be knowen where as they were become; & they were sente hyther by
the cōmmaundement of the Duke of Bygor. Well, good frende, sayd
Arthur, brynge me to them.

Than the varlet conuayed him streyght to the prison where as they
were closed in, and the varlet didde vnlocke al the dores, which were
meruaylously wrought; and at the laste they came to a grete cofer all
of yren,[17] whiche was surely made fast to the wall wᵗ gret bondes &
barres of stele: than Arthur did so muche by his strength, that he brast

Figure 15: 'The Damosel of the Lake' by Ann Alexander.

open the cofer, & toke out the prysoners with much payne, for they
were sore charged with boltes of yren, so that they coude stere no maner
of waye. And whā they were loused, one of them sayde: A! dere lorde,
I wote not what ye be, nor whether ye haue taken vs out of prison for
our welthe or for our hurte: but, for Goddes sake, rather than ye shold
put vs agayne into this cofer, fyrst strike of our hedes. Certaynly, sayde
Arthur, we haue non entent to do you any maner of hurt; therefore
tel me of whens ye be, & where ye were borne! A! syr, sayde they, we
are so nye ouercome for lack of mete, and so sore brused withal, yᵗ
we can scant speake ony worde: therfore, syr, for Goddes sake gyue
vs some mete! Frēdes, sayd Arthur, I can not tel whether there be ony
mete & drinke in this hous or no. Yes, syr, sayd the varlet, here in this
hous is suffycyent, and it were to receyue the myght Emendus, Kynge
of Soroloys. Well, sayd Arthur, than go fetche theym some parte thereof.
Than the varlet set vp the tables, & dyd set on them brede and wyne,
and other mete sufficient, and than they all dyd eate and drynke as
muche as dyd please them: and whan they had done, the varlet
demaūded of the prysoners if they wolde be shauen; & they answered:
Yes, with a right good wyl. Than the varlet apparayled all thinge redy,
for he was a good barbour. And whan they were shauen, than the varlet
brought thē gownes of the knyghts that were slayne; & whā they were
apparayled, they semed wel to be extraught of a noble lygnage: and
so thee were in dede, as ye shall here after.

> How Arthur, after yᵗ he had acheued yᵉ aduentures of the palays &
> delyuered the prysoners, & after how yᵗ he acheued the aduenture yᵗ was
> in the galary goyng in to the gardin of the Mount Perillous, & by his might
> with a grete barre bet downe ii messyue ymages of coper, eche of them
> holding a flayle, yᵗ was of such wyght yᵗ x men myght scant lyfte one of
> them fro the erth, wherwith they were euer beting wyth greate strokes made
> by enchauntment, to thentent that none sholde passe in to the gardyns
> of the Mount Peryllous; & so than fayled & ended all the enchauntementes
> of that place.

After that Arthur had delyuered these prysoners and acheued the fore-
sayd aduentures, than the varlet came to hym, and sayd: Syr, it is of
trouth that ye haue fordone & ouercome all the aduentures of this place
sauynge one, & that is in yᵉ galery goynge in to yᵉ gardyn; and, syr,
yf that were fordone, than euery body myght goo & come in to this
castell as surely as in to ony other place. Well, good frende, quod Arthur,
I praie you bryng me thyder. Syr, with a ryght good wyll, sayd yᵉ
varlet; but, syr, we must haue fyrst some fyre with vs, for yᵉ galery is
so derke that we can se no thynge there.

And so than they lyghted torches, & wente forth so ferre, that at the
laste in a lytell strayte way, Arthur foūde two ymages of coper, one on
the one syde, & an other on yᵉ other syde, & they had eche of them
a grete flayle in theyr handes, wherwith they contynually bete downe

ryght, yᵉ whiche was made by enchauntement, so that no creature coude passe by them without deth: and whan Arthur sawe them, he toke his swerde in his hande, & layde on with all his myght on these mahomettes,[18] in such wyse that his stroke might wel be herd of a great waye; but for all that he coude not enpayre them: thā he perceyued wel that hys swerde coude do hym but lytel helpe, wherfore he toke in his hād a gret bar of a dore that he foūde there, & therewith he laid on so fast, that finally he bet downe both these mahomettes: than all the enchaūtmēt began to faile, for than he myght se clerely al about them: & wyth strayning of him selfe in this bataile, his woundes braste out agayne on bledyng; wherfore he was fayne to vnarme hī in the same place, & than Bawdewin dyde staūch al his woūds againe, and dressed them newly with swete and soft oyntementes. Than he wold haue armed hym agayne; but than the varlet sayde: Syr, your harneys shall but hurt your woūdes, hardely leue it here styll, and arme you no more; for surely, syr, ye be nowe in as good sauegarde as though ye wer by your fader that engendred you. Frende, sayd Arthur, loke that here be no treson. Syr, I waraūt you on payne of my heed: syr, boldly now ye may enter into the gardyn, & there ye shall fynde a noble clerke, who is son to a king, who is pertayning to a ryghte hye and mighty pryncesse, the noble Florence, doughter and eyre to the puyssant King Emēdus, who hath bene there more than this halfe yere to abyde for your cominge. For me? sayde Arthur; thou wotest not what thou saist, for how shold he haue ony knowledge of me? Syr, sayd yᵉ varlet, I can not tell you, but surely it is as I saye, therfore let vs go thyder.

So they wente forth & entred in the gardyn, wherin was all the plesure that coud be thought: and as they went forth therin playenge, there came to Arthur a fayre yonge varlet, & goodly dyd salute hum, and sayd: Syr, ye be ryght herteley welcome into the londe of Soroloys, as the moost desyred knyght that euer was gyrde wᵗ swerde. Why, good frende, sayde Arthur, where is that place that I am so sore desyred in? Syr, sayd he, in all the lōde of Argence. Fayre frende, sayd he, & why am I so sore there desyred? Syr, yᵗ cā the prysoners, that ye haue delyuered, shewe you full well. Why, quod Arthur, how know they what I am? Syr, as God helpe me, ye are better knowen here thā ye are ware of: for here is in this gardyn a noble clerke, son to a kyng, who hath taryed here a grete season, who knoweth you wel. . .

In the name of god, sayd Arthur, I haue great meruayle howe ye can tel me all this. And as they were thus talkynge, there came to them a grete flocke of knyghtes: than yᵉ varlet sayd: Syr, yonder is my sayde lorde, who is coming to you. Nay, said Arthur, I shall vnto him; at whiche tyme, this sayd maister Stēuen was apparayled in a mātell of vyolet chamlet, & in a sircote of grene satyn furred with ermyns; & as soone as he sawe Arthur, he auayled[19] hys bonet & dyd salute hym. Than Arthur sayd: A! gentyll mayster, it is to me a grete rebuke, that

so noble a man as ye be, sholde do to me so greate reuerence. Than
the mayster dyde smyle, and toke hym by the hande, and sayd: Syr,
we haue longe trusted for the welth & honour that is nowe come to
you: therfore, nowe ye be welcome as the chefe souerayne knyght of
all the wyde worlde: syr, now I thinke to go se this palays, in to the
which neuer man entred before, saue onelye you, for ye are the fyrste
that euer entered therto, & that is by your noble valure. Syr, I know
wel ye be sore woūded, therfore I haue made for you a lytle drynke;
and than he sente for it incontynent; & whan it was come, he sayd:
Syr, drynke therof hardelye, feare for nothyng, in the name of God,
for I desyre more youre health and honor, thā of ony other creature
liuying. Than Arthur toke it and dranke wel thereof; and as soone as
it was spredde abrode in his vaynes, he was thereby sodeynly all hole
& more lustyer than euer he was before, for than he thought y^t his
strength was doubled; & truelye in a maner so it was, for by the vertue
of these herbes he had ye grace, y^t fro thens forth there was neuer man
y^t coude drawe out of his body only blode, but onely the foule monster of the Brosse, w^t whome he fought at great jeopardye, as ye shall
here afterwarde. . .

*[Arthur spends the day at the castle, in the wonderous gardens attached to
it. He is richly entertained by Master Steven and the knights who were imprisoned there, and he hears much of Master Steven's lady, Florence, and is much
intrigued thereby. . .]*

> Howe Proserpyne, Quene of the Fayrye, aboute mydnyght appered to
> Arthur w^t grete lyght of torches, and howe that she shewed him that
> wythin the Mounte Peryllous there was the whyte shyeld, and the good
> swerde, enchaunted, called Clarence; and howe that he shuld haue them
> w^t moche honour yf his herte durst serue hym. And howe the nexte daye
> Mayster Steuen led Arthur into the herber where as the white shelde was,
> the which coud neuer be remeued fro the tree whereon it hanged, and
> how that Arthur toke it at his ease, and Clarence the swerd also, the whiche
> coude neuer, before that tyme, be drawen out of the sheth, nor it wold
> helpe no body but all onely Arthur, who drew it out lyghtly, and after
> that it did him moche helpe, as ye shall here after.

Whan the mayster Steuen was departed, than Arthur layde hym downe
in the ryal ryche bedde, and slepte well all his fyrst slepe tyll it was
about mydnyght; than he awoke and saw grete clerenes of torche lyght
afore hym, and perceyued, stonding before his bedde, a quene crowned
w^t gold, who was the most fayre creature y^t euer was sene; and he
thought she spake to him, & sayde: Arthur, frend, here is in this place
the whyte shelde, & Clarence the goode swerde of the fayry, therfore
thou shalt haue moche honour yf thy herte be good. And therwith she
vanisshed away; whereof Arthur had grete meruayle, both of her beaute,
& also of there sodayne departing: thus remayned Arthur tyll it was
clere day, than he rose, & mayster Steuen came to hym, and they went

and herd masse; & after masse Arthur sayde to the mayster: Syr, I cā
not tel what quene it was, y^t this nyght was with me in the chambre
where as I laye, but it was the goodlyest fygure of a woman that euer
I sawe: & she sayde to me, how y^t ther was in this place the whyte
sheld and the good swerde Clarence. And whan mayster Steuen herd
that, he smyled, and sayd: Syr, I see well it is you to whome the swerde
and sheld is destenied vnto: dyuerse knights hath assayed to take them,
but they could neuer remeue them fro the place where as they be, therfore now I thīke they haue founde theyr mayster. Syr, let vs goe thyder,
& see what wyll fortune.

Than they yssued out of ye palays and went into the gardyn, where
as was the ryche pauylyon. . . the which was of the rychest werke of
the world, of grene satyn & crimsē, bordred w^t golde & asure, & the
post that bare it was of fyne yuery, and the cordes of grene sylke, and
in the toppe therof stode an egle of borned golde, and at the two corners
there stode two grete gryffons shining agenst the sonne. Than Arthur
remembred his vysion that he had or he departed out of his owne
countre, & so he behelde the egle a grete ceason, and at the last he
came to the pauylion. Than Arthur sawe before hym in the front therof,
the personage of a quene crowed with gold, the whiche crowne hadde
vi. braunches, the whyche signified vi. realmes, and in eueri braunche
there were wrytten letters: and in ye fyrst was wryten Emendus the
myghty Kynge of Soroloys; & this braunch was chefe and highest of
all other; and in ye seconde was wryten Florēce, Quene of the realme
of Blaūche Toure; & in the thirde was giuē the Kīg of Orqueny; and
in the fourth was wryten Piuthens, Kyng of Valefounde, father to mayster
Steuene: and in the v. King of Normall; & in the vi. Ismaelite the Geant.
This crown was set ful of precius stones, and ths image was fayre and
gentil to behold, with her forehead playne and whyte, and her heer
like the colour of gold, her browes small and propre, and somwhat
drawynge to the browne colour, and her visage playn, neyther to longe
nor to rounde, coloure lyke as roses and lilies togider had ben medled,
her nose long and streyght, and her ruddy mouth somwhat smylynge,
her eyen lowly, and al her body and other mēbres made without ony
reprehencion by the ordynaunce of Nature, who had set in all her
beaute; and she was vestured wyth a samyte of grene, streyte gyrde
to her w^t a lace of golde, so that somwhat her lytel rounde and lyly
whyte brestes might be sene, the whiche became her wonderslye wel,
and ouer al this she had on a sircote of crymsen lined w^t vyolet sendall, & her wide sleues were of grene embordred w^t floures of golde
and with ryche pearles. And this ymage helde bytwene her handes a
chaplet of sylke wrought subtylly full of freshe floures, and aboute the
border therof were letters wrought of precyous stones that sayd: He
shal kepe me for his owne that shall haue this chaplet. And when Arthur
had red wel at length these letters, and sawe the freshe beaute of this

ymage, than his herte opened for grete loue, & wit grete and feruent desyre he loued the presentacyon of that ymage, and therwith stode before it in a grete study.

Than mayster Steuē sayd: Syr, I ensure you my lady is suche as this ymage representeth. Syr, sayde Arthur, than in her is all the beaute of the world. Ye, syr, sayde the mayster, there be two persones y^t resēbleth this ymage: first, the quene y^t ye saw tis last nigth appere to you, who is called Proserpyne, quene of the fayry, who dyd gyue to my lady Florēs this castell & this pauilion, & destenyed on her, how y^t she sholde neuer be maried but to the best knyght of the worlde, & to hym this ymage sholde gyue her chaplet y^t she holdeth in her hands; &, syr, I trust it be you. Secōdly, also my lady Florēs in all thinges resembleth to this ymage; and so the Quene Proserpyne, & my lady Florence, & this ymage, are in al poyntes so like, y^t ye can not know the one fro the other; & the hye braūche y^t is in the crown of this ymage, betokenet ye mighti King Emendus, fader to my lade Florens; and the seconde sygnifieth my ladies realme, and the other iiii. represente iiii. other kīges, who are subiectes to my lady Flores & to her fader; therefore, syr, & it please you let vs enter into is pauylyon, & se wheder ye may haue the sheld and swerd that all other haue fayled of.

And so they entred into the pauilion; and in the myddes therof Artur sawe where there hanged on a perche the shelde and the swerd. Than Arthur wente thereto boldly, and toke it as easely as thoughe it had bene his owned before: than he sette his hande to the swerde, and so drewe it out of the shethe, and the blade therof was so clere, that it dyd cast meruayllously grete clerenese, and therfore it was called Clarēce; and before that tyme it was neuer drawen out of the shethe nor sene with mānes eye; and Arthur delte as easely therwith as he dyd w^t his owne. And whan mayster Steuen sawe this, he had grete joye, and sayd: Syr, I se well ye are the same knyght that it was deliuered vnto, therfore nowe I haue grete joye, and I trust that God shall cause you to attayne to muche honour and noblenesse. . .

---

[1] In fact the hero is not Arthur Pendragon, King of Britain, at all, but a later Arthur, descended from Lancelot du Lac; but for all that, his adventures betray all the usual form and style of the Arthurian genre.

[2] *Ren* = run.

[3] *Vnnethes* = underneath.

[4] *Causy* = causeway.

[5] *Maresses* = morasse.

[6] *Bowelwerkes* = bulwarks (i.e. battlements).

[7] *Fyersley* = furiously.

[8] *Hugged* = huge.

[9] *Greces* = egresses (i.e. stairs).

[10] *Adurned* = adorned.

[11] *Vtterbrasses* = vallances.
[12] Yvery = ivory.
[13] *Yll encōbraunce* = ill encumberence (i.e. difficulty).
[14] *Fyers & fell* = furious & evil.
[15] *Fauchon* = a one-edged sword.
[16] *Brēnynge* = burning.
[17] *Peasyble* = peaceable.
[18] *Yren* = iron.
[19] *Mahomettes* = autometons (i.e. works of the devil).
[20] *Auayled* = took off.

Chapter 19.

Merlin and Vortigern

by Katherine Buck

The extract which follows comes from a remarkable epic poem, *The Wayland-Dietrich Saga* which runs to some nine large volumes and several thousand lines. Its author, K. M. Buck, spent many years of her life in its composition, covering a huge range of time and material in the creation of what would be, had it been completed, nothing less than the recreation of an English mythology, a kind of poetic Geoffrey of Monmouth; this daunting task was later undertaken by another great mythographer, J. R. R. Tolkien.[1] Unfortunately, Miss Buck died before the work could be brought to a conclusion and what we have is only a portion—albeit a vast one—of an even larger work.

Beginning with a fragmentary Norse poem, concerning the smith-god Wayland and his quest for his swan-wife, the work grew in its making to encompass the Dietrich Saga and, subsquently, the entire early history of Britain—including the years of Roman occupation and their aftermath—the Age of Arthur. Drawing on Geoffrey of Monmouth's *History of the British Kings* and Layamon's *Brut*, the author created a veritable epic.

The section quoted here deals with the famous story of Merlin and Vortigern's Tower, and the prophecies made there. The verse is tough and sinewy, moving along with a swing. It is not 'great' poetry, whatever one may mean by that, but it has many admirable qualities, not least of which are the author's imaginative scope, her understanding of the variety of this country's inner landscape, from which she has drawn this heroic poem. It is hoped that this extract may urge readers to investigate further the rich treasury of material contained in the *The Wayland-Dietrich Saga*.

❧⚜❧

How Vortigern fled before Hengest, and would build a Castle—The Prophecy of Merlin.

Thus did the heathen ravish all the land
Of Middle Britain at their wicked will;
But Vortigern, as though a naked man,
Defenceless fled within the heart of Wales
Far beyond Severn, with a scanty train;
And they were poor, but yet the wily King
Had kept in secret hoard the stolen gain
That he had ta'en from Constant, the Boy-Monk.
This he now used and spent it craftily.
He bade his men ride through the Western Lands

To summon all of every sort or kind
Willing to earn his fee. Some Britons came...
The Scots flocked in; and many well-born Thanes,
Eager for gold and strife, rode in to him.
Then summoned he his elders and wise men;
Wizards in whom he trusted he called there,
Clerks and philosophers, to ask their rede,
How he should act, how best maintain his right
Were he assailed by mighter men than be...
'Good Masters, give me counsel, there is need.
What shall I do if there come over-sea
Dead Constant's brethren, who for little cause...
Did I not ever cherish Conan's Line?...
Hate me so sore? And how shall I defend
Myself against the treacherous Saxon fiends?
Shall I not build me in this waste a Burgh
Wherein my folk and I may live at ease,
And hold it against Hengest with great strength?
Then will I win again my towns to me,
And take revenge upon my cruel foes
Who have slain my dear friends and wrested thus
The Kingdom from my hands ... God curse them all!
But where and how shall I now build this Burgh?'
Quoth then a wise man used to giving rede,
'Wilt hearken, my Lord King, and I will shew
A good thing to thee ... I would now advise
That on the mount of Eryr thou shalt build
A castle with stone walls, a mighty burgh,
For there thou mightest dwell in peace and joy.
Still hast thou silver in thy hand and gold
To keep the folk who help thee, so thy life
May yet be happy and more fortunate.'
So Magan spake, a very learned man,
Who was that time the King's Chancellor.
Said then the King, 'Let it be known in haste
Amongst my people that I go to seek
The Mount of Eryr there to rear a burgh.'
So came he to that mountain that was called
By Romans Mons Heriri, but is now
Snowdon in Saxon tongue, and this he found
Indeed a place most fitting to his mind.
Now 'neath his hand he set all Northern Wales,
For his armed host he bade o'errun the land.
Masons he summoned from the country round,
The best he could, and set them straight to work...

Horns he had blown, whereby he quickened them...
Some delved a dyke, some tended great machines
That hewed apace, others prepared the lime.
When they had dug the dyke and deepened well,
O'er all they reared a wall, nor had they lack
Of engines for the work, more than five score
Were busily employed. The lime and stone
They laid together and with mortar fixed,
Making all fast. So toiled they every day,
Yet to their sorrow every night that passed
Their work was all undone and fell to ground.
The solid mountain quaked beneath their feet,
And some there said the very earth did sink.
The more they toiled and moiled and higher built,
The greater was the fall... So sped the days;
A sen'night passed, and what each day they raised
Was every night o'er thrown, till not one stock
Or stone remained of all their laboured pile.
But all was swallowed up as by the soil,
Though none knew how it vanished. In great fear
The masons told the King, who was adread,
Grieved and most sorrowful; while all his host
Were terribly afraid, for every man
Looked to see Hengest fall upon their rear.
When Vortigern asked counsel of his Lords,
They said in haste, 'None of us know the cause.
Here is art-magic... Sire, send for wise clerks,
Magicians who know ghostly things withal
By force of study, wherein they are skilled...
We are not masons or philosophers,
We are thy fighting-men, trained but to war.'
Quoth Vortigern, 'Methinks, Sirs, ye say sooth,
Ye are no good in counsel, by my troth.'
Then sent he for his sages, world-wise men,
Wizards and sorcerers. 'By my faith,' he said,
'I marvel greatly what may be amiss
With this fair tower of mine that it doth fall,
Nor will the earth sustain it. Search ye, Sirs,
Enquire into this thing and find out how
My burgh's foundations may be firmer set,
Else shall ye rue this day!' They bowed in fear,
'My Lord, we wit not, but we will enquire...
The stars may tell us much and we will seek
The truth by science of Astronomy;
For here are seven of us who are skilled

In reading from the Lights of Heaven that
Which shall befall unto the sons of men.
Thou shalt know all; of that, King, be thou sure'.
Quoth then the King, 'In three days tell me all'.
But said their leader, 'Nay, not so, O King,
What thou dost ask is surely a great thing,
We must have respite for at least eight days'.
The doubtful King a surly nod vouchsafed;
'Go,' said he, 'take th' appointed time and seek
The very truth... Fail, and ye lose your heads.'
They set to work and lots they gan to cast,
Tried divinations, incantations made...
Into two bands they did divide themselves;
Some hurried to the woods, some to cross-ways;
Then each sat down alone to weave his spells.
It was about the summer solstice when
The elves are busy amidst mortal men.
One of the sages went at dead o' night
To gather fern-seed, thinking thus he might
Make himself vanish ere worse evil came...
But he found none, and groaned in blank despair.
Another, Teirgwoedd named, went far afield
To find selago, the fair golden moss
That grows in marshy soil. He sought it long,
For he was fain to crush beneath his feet
The spongy moss, whereby he thought to learn
The speech of birds and beasts... Oh, long he sought
The cloth o' gold, the club-moss, everywhere,
But found none to his will... Then in its stead
He sought the savine, devil's tree well-named,
The cypress of the heath, dwarf juniper,
That witches love, and wizards... First he laved
His body and his feet in water fair,
Bathing in running brook; then clad in white
He offered sacrifice of bread and wine
Unto Toranis, Mother of the Earth;
So took in hand a brazen hook to cut
The yellow catkins; for with iron must not
The precious shrub be touched, or ill would come
And wars on all the world... He found at last
That which he sought, the savine that grows wild,
In a lone valley far from haunt of man,
Close to a rippling brook that wound its way
Across the marshy meadows, reed o'ergrown.
He traced a circle, mutt'ring secret runes,

And covered o'er his hand with a white cloth
Of linen freshly spun and never used;
Then with right hand thrust through left tunic sleeve,
With little finger's tip well crooked and curved,
Till like unto the crescent moon it shewed,
He rooted up the sacred plant with awe,
And so returned. Yet he, for all his toil,
Gat no response nor solace for his care,
Nor heard he aught in speech of beast or bird
Save mocking jangling talk that vexed him sore.
Another man of dreams and fantasies,
Mathonwy named, at least so I have heard...
Not he who was the sire of Math, but one
Who was his kinsman, sib to Gwydion...
Went forth alone and came to a wide heath
Where hawthorns grew, and sloes, and junipers,
With service-trees that the Gauls know as sorbs,
Whereof they make good wine for thirsty men.
Quoth Wayland, 'Drink, man... Pledge me in the same...
Bathilda, fill the cup for our good guest...
Witga, go bear it to him courteously.'
Cried Witga, 'Tell us more... I want to know
What Hengest did and Ochta in this hour.'
He drew nigh to the minstrel. In his hand
Gave the gold goblet filled with sparkling wine,
Then looked up in his face confidingly.
With friendly smile Guest spake unto the child,
Set arm about him, drew him on his knee,
'Listen then, Lordling, listen heedfully.'
Mathonwy sought a tall crab-apple tree
And cut therefrom a rod whereby he thought
He might divine strange things, I know not what...
Another went by light o' the full moon
To cut a hazel-wand, and others plucked
The four-leaved clover, knapweed, honesty...
The plant whose pods shew lustrous in the dark
With such a brightness that men lunary
Do call its silvery disks... and other herbs;
Valerian, and periwinkle blue,
With egremaine, the wily sages culled;
And vervain, Odin's blood, that to the sun
Is consecrate, they each one cut and smeared
The juice thereof upon them, for thus they
Thought to obtain the object of their quest,
And learn the secret of the crumbling wall...

But this herb plucked they at the dead o' night
Ere moon was risen, when the sun was set,
For mystery doth shroud its solemn rite;
And honey poured they from fresh honey-combs
Unto Toranis; and great Artio,[2]
Akin unto that goddess of the earth
Whom we call Hertha in our Northern tongue;
Lest they should be offended at the theft
Of their most precious herb... One sage was there,
A master of illusion whose true name,
So I have heard, was Collfrewi the Wise,
Whom some call Tregetour,[3] for his great skill
In making things seem other than they are.
He took with him a lean black whelp on chain,
And went with stealthy steps to a lone moor
Where stood the Justice-tree of Vortigern.
Thence dangled in the rising whining wind
The bodies of three thieves hung lately there.
The soft breeze stirred their long locks to and fro,
And swayed their lifeless forms in mockery;
Till rising, gaining force, it rocked them so
They seemed to leap in sport from off the ground...
Yet ne'er again would they their footing find,
Their dance had end but in eternity...
Behind their backs their arms were ruthlessly
Strapped very tight... Their bodies naked were,
Save for the scanty clouts that wound them round,
Exposed to wind and weather, sun and rain,
Defenceless 'gainst the sharp nebs of the crows,
The greedy ravens' cruel beaks and claws,
That had fed well... Yet were these hapless three
Once merry boys who laughing leapt in play,
Once babes loved by their mothers tenderly,
Who loved them still and mourned them bitterly...
Little recked Collfrew of their grievous woe,
Who stood beneath that ghastly gallows tree,
And in the dim light of the waning moon
Searched carefully and long and patiently...
Till near the old oak's root he saw at last
A light as of a candle shining out,
Though fitfully, and often it was quenched
By shadows of the corpses overhead.
It was the mandrake, nourished by men's blood
Who have died a hard death, not peacefully.
Then Collfrewi with savage joy drew near,

Unsheathed the sword he had slung at his side
Wherewith he made three circles round the tree.
He stood a moment, wind against his back,
Facing due west, then knelt and made well fast
The plant to the whelp's tail, which whining crouched,
Licking his hands, until with a sharp kick
He drave it off. The frightened beast wild plunged
And dragged from out the muddy dew-damp earth
The ugly root of the black bryony.[4]
Yet not with ease came forth its fleshy stem,
But hoarsely shrieking with a horrid cry,
Like to a man in mortal agony,
As though it felt its dissolution nigh;
And the black whelp with loud discordant howl,
Foaming in madness, yelled in sympathy,
Then leapt into the air convulsed, so died...
But with a cautious step and furtive eye
Collfrewi crept to where the great root lay
Which seemed to quiver, and he heard it groan.
He picked it up, though somewhat gingerly,
Detaching it from the dead whelp's long tail...
Almost he dropped it, for it seemed to him
Like to a swarthy-bearded goblin grim,
Yet grasping it he placed it in his breast,
And so slunk home by creeping dread possessed,
Nor gained he what he wanted, for in vain
He made his incantations... The black root
Would not divulge the secret of the wall.
But it appeared the Chief of the Wise Men,
Whose name was Joram, so I have been told,
Had better fortune than the other seers,
For he took mistletoe from the great oak
That stood before the ruined temple, where
The trees grew thickest in the hidden dell...
There did the Druids once make sacrifice...
Around his neck a sprig of mistletoe
He twined with secret rites and fervent prayers,
Then gathered other herbs... the garlic rare
That is called wizard's garlic and that plant,
The creeping periwinkle, hundred-eyed,
That is the sorcerer's violet well named;
And many other plants he culled ere morn,
Then went apart unto a place forlorn,
Where four roads met upon a barren moor.
Now Joram held in his right hand a ring,

A triple cincture of thick massy gold,
Set with a single gem of wondrous worth.
It was not diamond nor sapphire stone,
Nor yet a ruby nor an emerald;
But from its facets gleamed ten thousand eyes
That shone with radiance as of light divine,
To which the lurid lightning of the skies
In fierces blackest storm were but as gleam
Of will o' wisp that dances in a bog...
'Twas like an opal, strangest of all stones
And most imbued with magic. 'Twas inscribed
With curious runes and figures mystical,
Well known to wizards' eyes. This ring he set
On his left hand's third finger, and he took,
Standing within the cross ways, a bronze knife,
Cutting the sods till round his feet he carved
A circle full complete. Therein he stood,
Making his Incantation, chanting low
Strange spells and terrible... Muttering he spake
The Word of Power and called on unknown Names...
'In the name of the Father of Evil I bind ye,[5]
Ye Gods of my fathers, I seek ye, I find ye...
Come Nodens, Nuada and Lud of the Ocean,
Come Oengus Mac Oc, whose Father is Mider,[6]
King of the Faeries. Come Mider, come Etain,
The Goddess of Sunrise. Great Dagda, come hither!
O Camulos, Cumall and Nwyvre! I praise ye,
Where art thou, Gwydion? Where is fair Cairbre?
Aitherne I call, Lleu Llawgyffes, I greet thee,
O God of the Daylight, and thou too, Lugh Lamhfada.
Lilita Mahita, the Strangler of Children,
Thou who hast many Names. Miduch and Zarduch,
Come thou with Her who giveth the Victory,
Andrasté, who heard once the prayer of Boudicca...
Come ancient Sirona, and thou fierce Bodb Catha,
The Wager of Warfare, and thou great Toranis,
The Lady of Thunder!... O come Ye all hither
Your servant implores you, who ever adores you!...
Reveal to me, shew me... Hide not, I conjure ye,
The Source of this Trouble... What stirs the foundations
Of Vortigern's Castle? O hear, I beseech ye,
The Voice of the Wizard, of Joram your Servant!
Am I not wise in the lore of our Fathers?
And then your ears stopped that ye will not hear me?
O Baäl, O Jupiter Ammon, I praise ye...

By the hand of Nuada, the Right Hand of Silver,
By the Ladder of Jacob, the Cloak of Elijah,
The Rod of Mar-Aaron, the Ark of Mar-Noah,
By the Cauldron of Plenty, by Bran's Head I bind ye...
I bind the Black Serpent, the Red Snake, the Grey One,
The Dumb Snakes, Sea-Monsters, the Brood of Zargigin...
Zerizin, I bind her; Edilta, I chain her;
I hold fast Pegogha, I loosen not Geós...
Martlos I fetter, set gyves on Apíton;
Dirba escapes not... What was it crawled by me?
Was that a Viper?... I meant not to call it...
Though the charm be compelling, I would not these creatures
Were here in the flesh... I call but their phantoms...
In the name of Mar-Harshal, avoid thee, base serpent!
In the name of Tumaïl, make dumb the opponent!
Turn Vortigern's heart that he slay me not helpless!
All savage revenge, abominable actions,
The wiles of Shaitan who is doomed to destruction,
Do I bind and expel from my life; and I curse them,
Anathematize them, by all I hold Holy...
Great Caddis, Strong Tarsi, and most Mighty Makbi!
O Bacchus and Jonadab, Shamuni the Martyr,
Phoebe and Tabitha, Mary and Martha,
Mar-Aha, Mar-Abdisho! Keep me, preserve me!...
I'll turn my steps homeward, for my heart doth much fail me.'
For seven nights the Wizards wove their spells,
And practised their Black Arts with careful toil,
Yet might they not discover by their skill,
For all they did, on what account it were
That the strong wall of Vortigern's high tower
Should fall each night and all the toil be lost.
Then were they grievously perturbed in mind,
Until at last that Sage, their Leader wise,
Whose name was Joram, cried he had the cause
Discovered by his Art and potent Spells...
At least he said so, though it well may be
He lied to gain more time. But thus spake he
To wondering Vortigern with solemn words,
'O King, know thou if men may ever find
In any land a male child born on earth,
Without a father amongst sons of men,
Let but his breast be opened while he breathe,
And take therefrom his blood and mix with lime,
So slake the mortar and well temper it,
Then lay it on the wall, and thus make sure

The deep foundations of thy mighty Tower...
Then, by my life, I swear to thee, O King,
Thy Burgh shall stand... Aye! While the world endure.'
When Vortigern had heard his words he sent
His chosen envoys riding through the land
To seek out such a child, or man maybe,
Who never had a father. Two and two
The messenges rode out as they were bid.
Wide o'er the land they fared, and two of them
Went over westwards, seeking earnestly.
Due west they rode until at last they came
With weary limbs to where a city lies,
That then was called Aelecti,[7] in the March
Of Glevesing, a district near the Usk.
Now later this Caer Myrddin had for name;
And long years after old Caer Vyrddin too,
A fortress strong that Maxen Wledig built,
Was called Caermarthen; but Aelecti still
Maes Aleg had and shall have for its name,
Therewith the honour of the Wizard's birth.
Before the Burgh in a broad pleasant way
The town lads gathered were in merry play...
Weary the Knights, and very sorrowful,
In heart exceeding heavy; they sat down
To rest them on the green where the lads played,
And watched the sport with half-unseeing eyes,
Holding their horses' bridles listlessly,
Nor had they hope to find here that they sought.
Now was the day far spent, though still the sun
Shot flickering rays of light through linden leaves
Upon the green... The children's voices rang
In merry chorus, clear their laughter flowed
As rippling water to the Knights' tired ears...
But, as it often chances amongst bairns,
After a while the boys' play turned to strife,
And they began to wrangle noisily.
One of the elder lads smote a hard blow,
Chiding his fellow, who with swollen face,
Bruised and tear-stained, did cower back in fright,
Holding his arm to shield him, and in spite
Reproached his comrade very bitterly;
For he was wroth to be thus struck and shamed.
Cried Dinabus, the lad who had the blow,
'Merlin, thou wicked boy, what hast thou done?
Misgotten wretch and fatherless art thou,

And hast thou dared to smite me? 'Tis a shame
And thou shalt suffer for it... Hold they peace!
Nor think to make it up... I'll not forget...
I am a King's son, thou art come of naught...
For all thy mother calls thee Emrys... Ah!
How dar'st thou strive with me the better born?
Hadst best be heedful... It were well for thee
Thou shouldst not vex me overmuch lest I
Were tempted to reveal the ill I know...
Speak not against my lineage, saucy cur,
Am I not come from noble Earls and Kings?
But thou, O wretch, if thou wouldst now set forth
Thy kindred, why thou dost not even know
Thy father's name... How couldst thou know it? Say!
Who never knew thy sire nor had one... Ah!
Thou hast no right to walk amongst us free...
A fool thou art to think thou art my peer,
Keep not thy distance, prithee! Here am I,
Born of Blood-Royal on both sides... thou, forsooth,
Hast for a mother one of evil fame,
Who loved a fiend, may be... Who knows the truth
As to thy kin and what or who thou art?
The Devil is thy father or else none!'
At which the Knights quick lifted up ther heads,
Hearing the noisy talk and bitter gibes
Of weeping Dinabus... They, rising up,
Drew night unto the lads and looked on them,
Asking their neighbours what this thing might mean.
Said Keredig, the elder of the Knights,
Unto his fellow, 'Hark ye, Madoc, now...
What if our quest be done?' Then turning, he
Asked of the bystanders yet more earnestly
To tell him of this boy; who made reply
That no man knew his father in the town,
But that his mother was a Princess born,
Daughter was she unto a well-known King
Who ruled Demetia, lately gone from Wales
On a far journey into Eastern Lands.
This lady now was nun, lived holy life,
Lodged in St Peter's Abbey in the town.
Quoth Keredig, 'Lead me unto your Reeve,
The Provost of this city, I am come
On the King's business.' So they came within
Unto the Warden, who was Eli called.
Said Keredig, 'Sir, we are Vort'gern's Knights,

And have found here amongst you a young lad,
Called Merlin Emrys, if we hear aright;
We know not who his kin. Sir, on thy head,
If thou wouldst keep in safety life and limbs,
Hear thou the King's Command, and tarry not!
Take him in haste and with his mother send
By us, the Royal Messengers, the lad
Unto King Vortigern. If thou willst not,
Shortly shalt thou be hung, this city burnt,
And all its folk destroyed... 'Tis the King's word!'
Quoth Eli, bowing low, 'Sir, well I wot
That all this land doth lie in Vort'gern's hand,
And we are all his men, then who am I
That I should disobey... More power to him...
Sirs, very gladly will we do his will.'
Forth went the Reeve and the chief citizens,
And found the boy called Merlin playing still
Amongst his fellows. Him they forthwith took,
Gripping him by the arm. His comrades laughed,
And Dinabus was glad to see the boy
Thus led away. For Dinabus now thought
That he was in disgrace and would be slain,
Or at the least was like to lose his limbs...
But therein thought he wrong... Far otherwise
The fate of Merlin ere his life was done.
Then Merlin also laughed and said to them
Who held his arms, 'I am the one ye seek
Whose blood is wanting to King Vortigern'...
Whereat they marvelled, saying 'How knowst thou
What we are wanting of thee? Come along,
The King would see thee, boy.' Said he, ' I come,
Yet harm not my sweet Mother, gentle Knights,
And I will tell ye why your strong tower falls'...
Whereat they wondered more... Sir Madoc said,
'A marvellous boy, i' faith, and bold enow...
'Tis pity he must die at the King's will'...
But Keredig reproved him for that speech.
'The King is our good Lord, his Will is Law.
What matter if a hundred boys he slay?
The deed is his, not ours... We are his men,
We do our duty, our Liege Lord obey...
Madoc, thou art but a soft-hearted fool!'
So came they to that minster where there lay
The Lady who was mother to this boy,
A hooded nun; and with them went with grief

The good clerk Blaise, who was the Master wise
Of Merlin and his mother... So they took
The Lady and her son with Eli's leave,
Aelecti's Warden, and rode to the King...
But first young Merlin called his Master dear,
And bade him if he loved him have good cheer.
'For I must go,' said he, 'with these King's men,
Yet fear not, Master, I shall fend me well
And come in favour; but do thou go north
Unto Northumberland where are great woods
And forest country wild... Abide me there...
Thou wottest well thou hast begun a Book
Wherein thou hast writ down full many things
That are most strange and passing marvellous...
Now salt thou have more leisure... Write then all
The wondrous things that happen in this land,
And I will come and bring thee tidings soon.
As long as the world lasts, good Master mine,
Folk shall be glad to read within thy book.'
Thus Merlin spake as though he Master were
And Blaise the child his pupil... For my part
I saw this Blaise and heard all from his lips
Concerning Merlin, who was Emrys called,
And therefore ye may know I speak the truth...
As for the book, Blaise wrote as he was told,
And it was called the Book of the Saint Graal,
Which later told of many marvellous things,
Of Uther and of Arthur, noble Kings,
And of their Knights and of the Sacred Quest
That hath no end... Of all this that Book tells[8]...

Then came the Reeve Sir Eli and the Knights
Unto the foot of Snowdon, where the King
Lay in his Camp uneasily. Word came
That two Knights were returned and brought him that
He had commanded. Blithe was Vortigern,
And greeted well Sir Eli and his Knights...
'Be welcome, Provost, we will speak anon,
Welcome, my men... Say on, say on! What's done?'
Quoth then Sir Keredig, 'My Lord, we bring
Merlin Ambrosius here... a wondrous child...
And verily unless he wished to come
We had not found him, Sire... It seems to me'...
Cried Vortigern in angry wise, 'What now?
What mean ye, Sirs? Who is this Merlin then

Of whom ye speak?... Have he not found for me
The child without a father? Have ye not
Brought me his blood, as I desired of ye?'
'Sire,' said the Knight, 'this is the very child,
This Merlin, whom ye seek... Yet of good will
We pray thee slay him not... 'Tis a brave boy...
Wilt thou not see first, Sire? Here have we
Brought him and his fair mother, nobly born,
Who now is nun and lives a holy life.'
Quoth Vortigern, 'Fetch ye this Lady in,
For I would speak with her'... Then gave he word
Twelve trusty Knights should have the boy in charge
And guard him with all honour heedfully.
The Lady he received full kindly then
With honour as beseemed her noble birth.
With fair looks spake he very courteously,
'Dear Lady, say to me of thy good will...
Nay, be it well with thee, have thou no fear...
Where wert thou born, whose daughter mayst thou be?'
The nun made answer in low voice but clear,
'The third part of this country in the hand
Of Kynan lay, Kynan the Lord of Knights,[9]
He was my sire'... Quoth Vortigern, 'Come now,
Sit thou beside me, Lady'... Sweetly he
Spake to the nun as though she were his kin...
'Wilt tell me now?... It shall be well with thee...
This boy of thine, Merlin, thy son, who then
Was father to him? Who amongst the folk
Was deemed in truth his sire? Wilt tell me, Dame?'
The nun, her drooping head bowed on her breast,
Sat silent by the King and thought awhile.

After a time she spake, with head hung low
And flushing greatly... 'Lord, it is a tale
Of wondrous strangeness'... Mildly quoth the King,
Crafty was he and full of evil guile,
'Answer me truly, Lady, for by none
Save thou alone can I know what has chanced.
If thou wouldst save the life of thy dear son
Tell me his father's name'... Said she at last,
'So God have me in keeping if I know,
For I ne'er saw him save once in a dream,
A vision of the night... I cannot tell
If he were man or ghost who came to me...
This is the truth, I pledge it on mine oath...

My father Kynan loved me passing well
Who was his only daughter... I was fair,
And well-grown for mine age, but just fifteen;
and as I lay soft slumbering in my bower
Amongst my maidens sleeping peacefully,
There came before me each night in my dreams
The fairest thing that ever I had seen;
As 'twere a Knight arrayed in shining gold,
Who glided near, and glistening the gleam
Of that bright vision to my dazzled eyes.
Oft it drew near me, oft it came full nigh,
Oft it embraced me and oft softly kissed,
And none saw it save I... By night and day
This presence sought me ever when alone...
In truth it haunted me, a moment there,
Then in an instant gone I knew not where...
But as a man he spake soft words to me
Within mine ear, and as a man indeed
He dealt with me... But though these many times
He had speech with me, ever he kept close
After that first fair vision that I had,
So that I saw him not... Nor can I say
If he were man indeed... But at the last
I found the world had changed and all things seemed
Distasteful to me, everything was strange,
The presence came no more, I missed it much,
I cared no more for dance or merry play...
My light and graceful limbs seemed heavy grown...
My meat I loathed... My maids looked oft at me
And whispered 'mongst themselves... I wept alone...
I knew not what came on me, much I feared...
Until at length I knew the truth at last,
And when my time was come I bare this boy...
I know no more... I know not in this world
Of what strange creature was this child begotten,
Be it evil thing, or sent by God to me...
Alas! Lord King, I cannot tell thee more...
As I do hope for mercy I know not
What else to tell thee of my little son
How he came in this world... I know no more...
And more I will not say'... She bowed her head,
In her white hood she hid her flushed hot face...
The King said naught, but sat long pondering,
Then bade the nun withdraw, who weeping went.
He had the boy brought there and gazed on him,

Then sent for his good Councillors to come,
And told them all... They gave him cunning rede
That he should send for Malgan, a wise man;
Wondrous in learning, who knew many crafts,
Well he could counsel, far he could direct;
He knew the Lore and Wisdom of the sky,
With every language he was well acquaint.
He came to Court and greeted fair the King,
'Hail to thee, Lord! Long life, O Vortigern!
I am come to thee, shew to me thy will.'
Then the King told those things that he had heard
And asked his counsel... 'Give me rede, good Sage,
And thou shalt have a passing rich reward.
Is this child him I seek or has he sire?'
Quoth Malgan musing... 'I know well hereof,
For I have read in ancient histories
That in unearthly wise are some men born...
Wise Apuleius herein makes report
That in the air are certain beings found
Betwixt the moon and earth, who there shall range
Till Doomsday come... If, King, thou seekst to learn
As to the nature of these spirits, know
They do partake of men and angels both,
And some are harmless, others evil work.
Their home and region rightly is the air,
Yet sometimes they will seek this world of ours.
They are called *Incubi Daemones;* though
They have not power to do folk mickle harm,
Yet mortals they deceive, trick and annoy.
'Fore men in dreams they fitful come and go,
And oft delude them by Arts Magical;
Their nature to this lends itself full well,
And many a maiden has had cause to rue
Their knavery in this wise thus deceived.
It may well be that thus was Merlin brought
Into this world, begotten of a fiend,
For of no earthly father has he come.'
Cried Merlin suddenly that all did start,
'King! Thou bidst thy men seize me, drag me here...
My Mother thou has reft from convent cell...
Tell me thy will... What has thou sent for me?
For I would learn wherefore thou wantest me.'
Quickly said Vortigern, and he was wroth,
For never heard he child so boldly speak,
'Merlin, know it thou shalt. Now, mark me well,

Thou son of no man born... Dar'st thou thus speak
Unto thy King? Boy! Thou art malapert...
And wouldst thou know the cause I sent for thee?
This must thou hear, and quicker than thou choose,
Thou forward lad!... I have begun to build
A mighty tower... Much money hath it cost...
Five thousand masons work each day for me
Laying the stones with mortar tempered well...
No workmen in the land so skilled; no stones,
No lime in all the world can better be...
But all their work is wasted... What by day
They raise, by night is swift destroyed... And lo!
The day has not so many hours to work
But that the night hath equal to destroy.
O much my substance thus has wasted been
In vain endeavours... I know not, O boy,
Whether thou hast heard news of this, but learn,
My Wise Men and my Wizards say to me
That never shall my tall tower stand secure
Unless the stone and lime shall well slaked be
With blood of one who is known fatherless...
And that art thou... They have said unto me
That if I drain the blood from out thy breast
As thou standst living there, and work my will,
Putting it to my lime, then shall my Tower
Stand firm to the world's end... Now knowst thou well
How it shall be with thee... Forthwith prepare!
Guards! Bare his breast... Bring ye the blunt bronze knife
That once the Druids used for sacrifices.'
Merlin heard all but shewed no signs of fear.
Frowning he faced the guards as they drew near,
Till much astonished they fell back a pace.
Angered he seemed and spake as though in wrath,
'Now God Himself, the Lord of all, forbid
That by my heart's blood thy tall castle stand!
Or thy stone wall keep steady! Think not, King,
That my spilt blood shall bind they castle wall...
Liars are thy wise men, deceitful all...
They lie before they face and mock at thee...
That will I shew thee ere this day be out.
'Twas Joram said this, he who is my foe,
For he hath by his secret arts discerned
That I am likely one day to displace
Him and his fellows from their lofty seats.
I can but laugh at his poor malice, Sire,

His want of reason and his lack of wit,
I will confess I was shaped for his bane.
Bid now thy Sages come before me here
Who prophesy so glibly of my blood...
Liars are they, liars I'll prove them, Lord...
And if I say thee truth anent thy wall,
Why it downfalleth, and do prove my words,
Shewing that they speak leasing, then, Lord King,
If I shall mend thy wall give me their heads!'
Said the King quickly, 'By my hand I swear,
And I will keep that oath, their heads are thine!'
Then, much astonished, Vortigern bade send
For Joram and his compeers, who came there
And at his bidding stood before the boy,
Though right unwillingly, uneasily,
They stood as man appointed soon to die.
They looked at Merlin and he gazed on them
Very intently, marking every man,
Then burst out laughing... 'Masters,' said he then,
'Mighty Magicians, who read in the Stars
All hidden things, divining them with ease,
Tell us, I pray, why the King's work doth fail?'
Then angry grew his voice, and fierce his air,
'Say to me, Joram, traitor... Vile art thou
And loathsome to my heart... Why falls the wall?
Say to me why it happens that the tower
Should not stand firm? Say to me what doth lie
At the dyke's bottom? Answer, thou Wise Man!'...
But Joram said no word as he were dumb...
'Make plain, ye Wizards all, what troubles now
The deep foundations, causing all to fall.
When ye have certified the cause thereof,
Tell us the cure. But if ye cannot shew
Why the earth nightly doth devour this tower,
How can ye then divine my blood shall bind
The stones together that it may endure?
If ye are thus unwilling to declare
Who labours secretly to make it fall,
How can ye think it shall be credible
That my blood shall avail to make it sure?
Point out the cause of trouble to the King,
Then cry aloud the cure and the remedy'...
Their heads sank low, in truth they could not tell...
With dull lack-lustre eyes they looked on him
Trembling in terror... bowed down to the ground...

The King's guards closer drew and ringed them round...
Quoth Merlin, 'King, hold Covenant, cause thou
This dyke to be digged deeper seven feet;
Then shall ye find a stone that is most fair
And wondrous broad and long for all to see'...
At Vortigern's command all issued forth
And stood before the site where was the tower...
The dyke was delved as Merlin did direct,
And there the stone was seen as he had said.
Quoth Merlin, 'King, hold Covenant! Say now,
Joram the Master, whom my soul doth hate...
Unto the King and me, what kind of thing
Lies hid beneath the stone and bides his time?'
Joram was still, he knew he could not tell...
He cringed in fear, his face grew deathly pale...
The others shook in terror, dreading death...
Said Merlin, seeing the wise men abashed,
Smiling a little, 'Sire, give ear to me.
Beneath the deep foundations of your tower,
Below this stone there lieth a great pool
Both wide and deep... Dig ye away the stone,
The water ye shall find anon... Dig deep...
Then shall the King see why his tower doth fall.'
The King bade men should dig and it was done;
The pool revealed even as Merlin said.
'Masters and great Magicians!' cried he then,
'Hearken once more... Ye who would mix my blood
To make your mortar, tell us now the truth...
What is it that lies hid in this same pool?'
Daunted the sages stood and spake no word
For good or ill... And they were sore adread.
Cried Merlin, 'King, hold thou thy Covenant!
Ask me now Joram, who is my fell foe,
What lieth at the bottom of this pool,
Winter and summer, keeping watch and ward...
But give him time, King... He will answer thee'...
Then in deep wrath turned Vortigern to the Sage,
'Answer, thou fool! Or thou shalt surely die!
Dost thou not hear? Art dumb? Come, answer me!'
Then Joram sullenly replied, 'Nay, Lord,
I know naught of the matter... This mad child
Doth mean my death... I am thy faithful Seer...
I prophesied as I thought sooth, my Lord...
Our Omens shewed'... 'Silence!' roared Vortigern,
'Prate not of lying omens... Stand ye there

And wait the upshot.... Hold his arms, ye Guards!
And see the other sages go not hence...
I'll deal with them anon'... Said Merlin, then
Looking at Joram, laughter in his eye,
'King, keep thy Covenant! Let your men dig
Trenches and gutters... Drain the water off...
Yet there is need to do all this with care...
Aye! Take ye heed!... For 'neath this water sleep
Two dragons strong and grim, one north, one south...
The first of milk-white hue, its like ne'er seen,
The other red as blood, no beast so bold.
And every midnight these two creatures meet
To fight together, through which contest fierce
Thy walls fall down, the earth begins to sink
And thy tower tumbles... Nor shall by my blood
Thy work be made to stand, it seems to me...
Though blood perchance shall flow ere all is done.'
The King, who greatly marvelled at his words,
Bade his men drain the pool, which being done,
From out the shining depths the dragons rose
Making great din, and met together there,
Down in the dyke fighting most fiercely then...
Never saw any a more loathely fight...
Flames of fire flew from each great monster's throat,
With teeth and claws and sting-armed tails they fought,
The venomed foam fell from their clashing jaws.
The monarch saw the battle, and the beasts
With their grim gestures marked. He felt adread,
Astonished at the wonder that he saw;
And all his men fell back, nor dared come near.
Upon the bank above the pool he sat,
And watched beneath his hand what should ensue.
First was the white worm uppermost, the red
Crushed underneath; but afterwards the white
Fell under the red dragon wounded sore...
There gat he mortal sting. Each slunk away
Into his hole that no man saw them more.

The King's men were full glad, great was their bliss,
Ye not long after they were full of woe...
Their doomsday tarried not, e'en now its dawn
Rose red upon them, though they did not know...
They all cheered Merlin, greatly loving him,
But Joram and the Wizards hating sore,
Cursing them roundly for their lying lips...

Said then the King where he sat on the brink
Of the now empty pool, 'Come hither, boy!
Expound these things to me, thou Wondrous Child...
Yet first be justice done'... He made a sign...
His Captain of the Guard gave then the word
Unto the lictors who stood ready there,
Their fasces on their shoulders, who unbound
Their gleaming sharp-edged axes... Instantly
The seven Sages, Joram and his friends,
Were swiftly seized, thrown down, their necks laid bare,
Close stretched athwart a block of building-stone;
Thus were beheaded ere they had had time
To scream out more than one brief useless prayer
For mercy to the King, who only smiled.
Merlin looked gravely on, but when the guards
Would have seized Malgan, who stood calmy there,
Watching his fellows die, yet shewed no fear,
The lad cried out, 'Nay, spare him, my Lord King!
For he willed not my death, nor told thee lies...
King Vortigern, keep Covenant with me!'
The King said, 'Let him go... Boy, he is thine'
So Malgan 'scaped with life in that dread hour.
Merlin went quickly unto the dead men
Who lay there still enough, their sorceries done.
He took from Joram's finger the strange ring
Wherein the opal glowed... It now appeared
A dull and lifeless thing... He slipped it on,
And lo! It flashed in thousand rays of fire.

> How Vortigern asked Merlin of the Future, but found no Comfort in
> his Prophecies—How Saint Germanus and Saint Patrick, trusting in his
> 'Breast-plate,' reproved Vortigern—How the Sons of Constantine landed
> at Totnes, marched against Vortigern and besieged him in his Castle
> of Genoure—The Burning of the Castle and the Fate of Vortigern and
> Rowena.[10]

The King went to his tent and by the hand
Led the lad with him, lovingly he spake:
'Merlin, thou art most welcome in my Camp,
All that thy heart desires is freely thine...
Of silver, gold, and goods, take what thou wilt'...
For in his heart he deemed through this strange boy
To win him back his Realm; but otherwise
This thing fell out ere many days had end...
Then asked the King of his dear new-found friend,
'Tell me now, Merlin, dearest lad to me

Figure 16: 'It was the mandrake, nourished by men's blood/Who have died
a hard death, not peacefully.' by Elizabeth Goodwin.

That ever I have found, what tokeneth then
Those fiery dragons that made such a din....
The stone... the water... and that wondrous fight?
Tell me of thy good will and what all this means?
Thereafter thou shalt tell me other things...
How I shall guide me best, how I may win
My Realm once more from Hengest, who hath done
Such mickle harm to me? How shall I guard
Against my foes, the sons of Constantine?
When comes my death on me and by what means?
Can I avert it? Tell me that, dear child'...
He shuddered as he spake, and turned away,
A sudden horror in his flickering eyes,
For Vortigern of death had a great dread
By reason of the wrongs he wrought alway.
Then Merlin told him much I will not say
Concerning those fell dragons... I fear me
To say o'er much of Merlin's prophecies,
The meaning thereof being hid from me,
And we would think I lied if aught fell out
Other than I should say... But this he said:
That the Red Dragon signified fair Wales,
How in the end she should have victory
And triumph o'er her former foes and live...
And this he said concerning Vort'gern's fate,
So Blaise hath told me who from Malgan's lips
Did hear the same, a prudent man and wise,
Nor do I think that both these men have lied...
'King, thou art rash, in counsel most unwise,
To ask of things best hid from mortal eyes...
Thou wouldst hear of the dragons and their fight,
Their fierce assaults thou fain wouldst understand?
Know then these dragons do betoken things
That yet shall come, their wars, their ventures bold,
Their fated folk... Now hadst thou wiser been,
Prudent in thought as doth become a King,
Hadst thou first asked how thou mightst 'scape the hour
When sorrow falls on thee and grievous care...
Then had I told thee surely'... Said the King,
Humble his mien, abased his haughty mood,
'Merlin, dear friend, tell me what I shall do,
What cometh on me?' 'Blithely will I say,'
Said Merlin boldly, 'what thou askest now,
Yet ever will it grieve thee... Hearken then!
King! King! Beware! From kin of Constantine

Cometh great dole upon thee... By his sons
Shalt thou taste death... Already with high hearts
Armorica they leave... Already they
Sail o'er the sea... To-morrow come to land
At Dartmouth in Totnes... I see their sails...
Fourteen great galleys... A fair well-found fleet...
Much evil hast thou done these Princes, King,
Much evil will they do to thee... Revenge
Their brother's wretched fate... In an ill hour
Thou didst betray young Constant to his death...
In an ill hour set Crown upon thy head...
In an ill hour to thy most bitter loss
Thou calledst to thy help the Saxon hounds...
Unto thy bane thou tookst as Bodyguard
Those who were Pagans, thou, a Christian man...
Now will they prove thy doomsmen, so beware!
Now art thou caught between two raging fires.
Thou art as man beset by arrow-storms
Before, behind... I know not if thy shield
Should be raised right or left... On one road comes
The Saxon Band eager to work thee harm;
Along the other soon will march the host
Of those the rightful heirs of Constantine,
Ready to pluck the Crown from off thy head,
The Realm from out thy hand, and to exact
The price due to them for their brother's blood.
Flee as from fire!... Escape, King Vortigern!
Quickly if so thou mayst... For lo! they come
Swiftly upon thee... Wheresoe'er thou goest
They will pursue thee'... Vortigern shrank down;
He listened 'gainst his will, trembling he heard,
And muttered, 'Must it be? Is there no way
To 'scape my dreaded fate, O Merlin, say!
I am not ready, I would first prepare...
My sins are heavy, they do irk me sore;
Time would I have, time only to repent'...
Merlin's hard voice rang in his throbbing ears,
'Nay, King! There is no way... thy doom is sure.
Upon the bed thou madest thou must lie...
What time had Constant when he came to die?
Short is the day and swift the fate of Kings...
I see the Saxons' faces red with blood,
Hengest shall perish, Horsa lieth slain,
Yet of the White Horse shall some colts remain
Who shall feed on the pastures of this land...

First shall Aurelius Emrys reign, then die,
By poison murdered. After, cometh one,
Uther Pendragon... He too poisoned dies,
But first shall wage grim war... His son shall reign,[11]
Who out of Cornwall comes, a savage Boar,
Bristled with steel, a Boar that burns the Burghs...
All traitors shall he slay, thy wealthy kin
He shall destroy... A noble King shall be,
Even in Rome shall he be held in awe...
He fells his foes... yet at the last shall fall
By treason of his dearest... Sooth I say,
But soft are not the tidings unto thee...
Fly with thy men, thy foes draw nigh thy Court...
God's Priests approach... I hear their solemn Hymns...
Escape, O King, while yet thou hast the time...
Yet seek not burgh nor castellated tower,
Dwell rather in the greenwood, though God's Ire
Maybe shall find thee there... I have no power
To help thee further... Thou has heard my rede...
Hard is the death of those who die by fire'...
Then Merlin ceased from speaking, and went forth,
Taking his Mother with him... But the King
Sat there till morn brake, dolefully, alone.
Then rousing, he bade thirteen trumpets blow
And marched forth with his host in close array
Toward the South Lands making hasty way...

[1] *The Lord of the Rings* and other works.
[2] Rhys, *Hibbert Lectures*, p. 73.
[3] Triad 90. Cf. Chaucer 'House of Fame', Bk. III. *Tregetour*, i.e. Juggler.
[4] Sometimes called Mandrake. Folkard, pp. 427-8.
[5] The Invocation of Joram. Cf. The Book of Protection (Syriac Charms) ed. H. Gollancz; Rhys, *Celt. Heath.*, pp. 199-200, Dion Cassius, *Hist. Romana*, LXII, *Nero* 6 (6).
[6] Cf. Rhys, pp. 144, *seq. In Mac Oc* = 'the Young Son', or *Mac ind Oc*, son of the (two) Young Ones.
[7] i.e. *Campus Electi* = the Field of the Chosen One. Probably Bassaleg *(Maes Aleg)* in Glewysing, Monmouthshire. Cf. Nennius, *Hist. Brit.* 41; Irish Nennius, ed. Todd and Herbert, XVIII. p. 93 *(Magh Eillite)*, and *App.* XV., p. xxv., G. of Monmouth, Wace and Layamon gave Carmarthen in its place. G. of M. VI., *cap.* 17 (Kaermerdin).
[8] Cf. *Merlin*, Part I. ed. II. B. Wheatley, E. E. T. S. *No.* 10, pp. 22-3.
[9] Or Conan. Not Conan Meriado, but perhaps Kynan, brother of Helen (wife of Maxen Wledi). Cf. Vol. III, p. 191, VI. p. 347, etc.
[10] Layamon, ed. Madden, II. pp. 245-55, Wace, *Brut*, I. 7726-7848, G. of Monmouth, Bk. VIII. ch. 1-2.
[11] King Arthur.

Chapter 20.
Morte Arthure

The *Morte Arthure*, an alliterative poem written *c*.1340-1360, from which the following extract comes, was attributed to Robert of Thornton whose name appears at the end. However, this ascription is now believed to be that of the scribe or copyist who made the version of the manuscript from which this translation was made.

Whoever the author was, he had a fresh and original style and used language like a master. Malory, whose own *Morte d'Arthur* was written sometime after, (*c*.1485) almost certainly drew upon it for the final chapters of his book.

The *Morte Arthure* also contains one of the most extraordinary symbolic passages in the whole of Arthurian literature. This is the famous *Dream of Arthur*, where the king, shortly before the final battle in which the flower of the Round Table will perish, dreams of Fortune's Wheel and is shown how the deeds of kings and men are subject to mightier laws than those of their own devising. This was a favourite theme with mediaeval writers who saw all life as mutable and lost no opportunity to say so. The *Morte Arthure* says it rather better than most however, and stretches the concept to cosmic limits. The final scene tells of the death of Arthur, starkly and simply and with no hint of the King's return in time of his people's need. It makes grim reading, but it is very much the stuff of heroic narrative as is all the Matter of Britain. The translation quoted here is that of Andrew Boyle.

KING ARTHUR'S DREAM

Then the noble king spake these words: 'Now we may revel and rest for Rome is our own: set our hostages at ease—the handsome children: and see that ye give them everything that is in my camp. The Emperor of Germany and all the east marches, we shall be the overlord of all that is on earth. Ere the Cross[1] days we shall take over these lands and on Christmas day be crowned: and I shall reign in all our royalty and hold my Round Table with the rents of Rome as I well please: then-after shall I go across the great sea with good men-at-arms to revenge the Man that died on the Cross.' Then this comely king, as the chroniclers tell us, goes blythely to bed with a light heart: he flings off his clothes speedily and slackens his girdle, and for want of slumber falls asleep speedily. But by one after midnight his whole manner has changed, on that morning he met with full wondrous dreams. And when his dreadful dream has reached its end the king trembles with fear, as though he would die, and sends for his magicians and tells them his fears.

'Since I was born, i' faith, so frightened I was never! Wherefore investigate it thoroughly and tell me the meaning of my dream and I shall readily tell you the whole truth. Methought I was in a wood astray by myself so that I knew not which way I should go, for wolves and wild boars and wicked beasts walked in that desert to seek their prey. These lions full dreadful to behold licked their teeth after lapping up the blood of my faithful knights. Through that forest I fled where the flowers grew high to hide me for fear from those foul creatures. I came to a meadow enclosed by mountains the most beautiful that men might behold on this middle region.[2] The space was round and grown over with clover and grasses: the vale was even round with silver vines with golden grapes, greater ones than which were never seen: edged with shrubs and all manner of trees—avenues of trees and shepherds thereunder. All fruit was produced that flourishes on earth fairly bedecking the branches of the trees in the enclosure: there was no dripping of dew to injure aught, with the heat of the day all the flowers were quite dry. Then came down into the vale from the clouds a duchess fairly clad in diapered garments, in a bodice of silk of a very rich hue all overlaid to the hems with embroidery and with lady-like lappets the length of a yard: and all delightfully adorned with golden ribbons, with gems and besaunts[3], and other bright stones her back and breast were bedecked all over, with a caul and crown she was fairly bedight, and anything so comely of colour was never known. She whirled a wheel about with her white hands and turned it over artfully whenever she chose. The wheel was of red gold with noble jewels in it covered with ornaments and many rubies, the spokes were bedecked all over with silver bars, and stretched out full fair for the space of a spear-length: thereon was a chair of chalk-white silver bedecked with carbuncles changing in hues: upon the outer circle there clung kings in a row with crowns of bright gold that burst asunder: six from that seat full suddenly fell each man by himself and said these words:

' ''That ever I reigned on that rocking wheel I rue for ever! There was never so rich a king that reigned on this earth! When I rode with my company I wrought nothing else but hunting and revelling and taxing the people, and thus I spent my days as long as I lasted and therefore I am grievously damned for ever.'' The first was a little man who was laid beneath, his loins were all lean and repulsive to see, his hair grey and long the length of a yard, his flesh and his body lamed full sore: one eye of this man was brighter than silver, the other was more yellow than the yoke of an egg. ''I was lord,'' quoth the man, ''of many lands and all men praised me who lived on this earth, and now I am

left no covering to heal my body, but now I am lost for ever; believe
ye the truth.''

'The second man in truth that follow after them was more trusty in
my mind and more powerful in arms: oft he sighed softly and said these
words: ''On yon seat have I sat as sovereign and lord and ladies loved
to fold me in their arms; and now my lordships are lost and laid aside
for ever.'

'The third man truly was fierce and broad of shoulders—a fierce man
to threaten though thirty were gathered against him: his diadem was
dropped down—all decked with stones and set with diamonds and
adorned for the nonce. ''I was dreaded in my days,'' he said, ''in many
realms and now am damned to be dead, the greater my grief therefore.''

'The fourth was a fair man and powerful at arms—the fairest of figure
that ever was formed. ''I was strong in my faith,'' he said, ''while I
reigned on the earth—famous in far lands and the flower of all kings;
now my face is faded and it hath foully befallen me, for I am fallen
from afar and am surely friendless.''

'The fifth was a fairer man than many of these others, a powerful
man and fierce with foaming lips: he clung fast to the rim of the wheel
and held with his arm, but yet he failed and fell full fifty feet: and he
sprang and leapt and spread out his arms, and at the distance of a spear-
length he spake these words: ''I was a knight in Assyria and set by myself
as sovereign and seigneur of many kings' lands: now from my security
I am suddenly fallen and by reason of my sin yon seat hath caused me
to repent.''

'The sixth had a psalter fairly bound with a surplice of silk sewn right
beautifully—a harp and a handsling with hard flint stones: what harm
he hath received he tells full soon. ''I was deemed in my days,'' he said,
''one of the doughtiest in deeds of arms that dwelt on this earth: but
I was marred on earth in my greatest strength by this maiden so mild
that moves us all.''

'Two kings were climbing and scrambling so high, the top of the wheel
they were anxious to reach: ''This carbuncle chair we claim,'' said they,
''as two of the most principal men on earth.'' These nobles were chalk
white—their cheeks and all their body, but the chair above they never
reached. The furthermost was beautiful with a large forehead, the fairest
in feature that ever was formed, and he was dressed in robe of a noble
blue with *fleurs de lys* of gold spread all over it: the other was clad
in a coat of bright silver with a fair cross carved of fine gold; four crafty
little crosses by the great cross are seen, and thereby I knew the king
who seemed anointed.

'Then I went to that fair lady and greeted her pleasantly, and she
said, ''Welcome truly, thou art well met: thou shouldest honour my
will—didst thou know all truly—above all the valiant men on this earth:
for all they honour in war thou hast won by me, I have been friendly

to thee, and unkind to all others: this thou hast found, i' faith, and full many of thy knights, for I felled down Sir Trolle with fierce knights: wherefore the fruits of France are freely thy own: thou shalt reach the chair, I choose thee myself before all the best chieftains of this earth''. She lifted me up lightly with her slender hands and set me softly in the seat and gave me the sceptre. Skilfully with a comb she combed my hair so that the crisping crook reached my crown: she set on my head a diadem that was bedecked full fair-enamelled with blue and the earth painted thereupon encircled with the salt sea and on many sides in sign that I was indeed sovereign of the earth.

'Then she brought me a sword with a full bright hilt and bade me brandish the blade. ''The sword is thy own: many a swain had spilt his life-blood with a blow from that sword, for while thou wieldest that weapon it shall never betray thee.'' Then she goes to take rest and rests where she likes to the trees of the wood—fairer than ever. There was no orchard so fair among those of the princes of the earth nor adornment so proud save Paradise alone. She bade the boughs to bow down and bring to her hands the best of the fruit that they bore on the high branches. Then they did according to her behest all together at one time—the highest trees of each copse, I promise thee forsooth. She bade me spare not the fruit but eat as I chose. ''Eat of the finest, thou fair man, and reach out for the ripest and enjoy thyself: rest, thou royal king, for Rome is thy own, and I shall readily give thee rest at the earliest moment and hand thee rich wine in rinsed cups.'' Then she went to the well by the edge of the wood that was full of wine and ran wonderfully: she caught up a cupful and covered it fairly: she bade me take a deep draught and drink to herself, and thus she led me for about the space of an hour with all affection and love that any man could wish for: but at mid-day then all her manner changed and she threatened me greatly with wondrous words. When I cried upon her she cast down her brows. ''King, thou speakest in vain, by Christ that made me! for thou shalt lose this game and thy life afterwards, thou hast lived enough in luxury and lordship.''

'About she whirled the wheel and whirled me under till all parts of my body was smashed to pieces, and by that chair my chin was chopped asunder, and I have shivered with fear since this happened. Then I awakened in truth after that dreadful dream, and now I await my fate, say what thou wilt.'

'Man,' said the magician, 'thy fortune is passed, for thou shalt find here thy foe, ask whom thou wilt. Thou art at the highest, I promise thee forsooth; attempt what thou wilt, thou shalt gain no more! thou hast shed much blood and destroyed many guiltless folk in thy pride in many kings' lands: repent thee of thy wrong doing and prepare thee for death. Thou hast had a vision, Sir King, take heed if thou wilt, for thou shalt fiercely fall within five winters. Found abbeys in France, the fruits are thy own, for Froill and for Ferawnt and for the fierce knights that thou hast boldly left for dead in France. Take heed yet of the other kings and consider in thy heart, for they were renowned conquerors and crowned on earth. The eldest was Alexander whom all the earth praised: the next was Hector of Troy—that chivalrous man; the third Julius Caesar, who was held a giant, in each gentle journey adjudged by knights. The fourth was Sir Judas, a full noble jouster, the masterful Maccabeus, the mightiest in strength: the fifth was Josua—that bold man-at-arms whom in eastern Jerusalem occasioned much joy. The sixth was David the good—deemed among kings one of the doughtiest that ever was dubbed, for he slew with a sling by the skill of his hands Goliath the great giant the grimmest on earth: who afterwards composed all the great psalms that are set in the psalter with beautiful words.

'The two climbing kings, I know it in truth, shall be called Carolus the son of the King of France: he shall be cruel and keen and held a conqueror and shall gain by conquest full many kingdoms, he shall obtain the crown that Christ bore himself and the real lance that struck his heart when he was crucified on the cross, and all the keen nails, knightly he shall conquer it for Christian men's hands.

'The other shall be Godfrey who shall revenge God on the Good Friday with gallant knights: he shall be Lord of Lorraine, with the permission of his father, and after in Jerusalem there shall be great joy, for he shall recover the cross by craft of arms and shall be crowned king anointed with chrism: to no duke in his day shall such good fortune befall, nor such evil endure when the truth shall be made known. For they bring thee to make up the number of the nine noblest men named on earth: this shall be read in romance by noble knights, accounted and made known to revelling kings, and deemed on doomsday for deeds of arms to be the doughtiest that ever dwelled on this earth: so many clerks and kings shall speak of your deeds and help account of your conquest in chronicles for ever. But the wolves in the wood and the wild beasts are some wicked men that attack your realms, who have entered thy kingdom during thy absence to annoy thy people—foreigners and enemies from unknown lands. Thou shalt have tidings, I trow, within ten days that some trouble has arisen since thou departedst from home. I warn thee to repent and confess thy wicked deeds! Man, mend thy ways, ere mishap befall thee, and meekly ask for mercy for thy soul's sake.'

Then rises the noble king and put on his garments, a red jerkin—rose coloured—the fairest of flowers, a gorget and pawnce and a rich girdle: and over all he wears a hood of full rich scarlet and a pillion hat that was adorned full fair with stones from the east, right precious stones; his gloves were gaily gilt and embroidered at the hems with small ruby stones full gracious to see; his beddy greyhound, and his sword, and no man else, and he hurries over a broad meadow with heavy breathing in his heart: then he follows a path along the edge of the wood, becomes troubled in spirit at a high road, musing by himself. At the rising of the sun he sees coming towards him by the shortest route to Rome a man in a great cloak with wide garments, with a hat and high shoes homely and round. With flat farthings the man was adorned all over: many shreds and tatters hung at the edge of his skirt, with scrip and pilgrim's cloak and many scallops, both pike and palm, all that a pilgrim should have. The man straightway greets him and bade him good-morning; the king lordly himself in the language of Rome—Latin all corrupt—full fairly speaks to him.

'Whither goest thou, man, walking thus alone while these parts are at war?—I hold it full risky: here is an enemy with a host under yon vines; an they see thee, forsooth, sorrow betideth thee; save thou hast a safe-conduct to the king's self, knaves will kill thee and take all thou hast: and if thou keepest the high way they will also seize thee, save thou have speedy help from his noble knights.'

Then spake Sir Cradock to the king's self, 'I shall forgive him my death, as God is my salvation—any man under God that walks on this earth—let the keenest come that belongs to the king's army, I shall encounter him as a knight—as Christ will have my soul. For thou mayest not take me nor stop me thyself, though thou be richly arrayed in fine garments, I shall not stop or hesitate by reason of this war to go where I will—not for any man of this world who was made on earth. But I will pass on in pilgrimage to Rome to purchase the pardon of the pope himself: and of the pains of Purgatory to be fully absolved. Then shall I surely seek my sovereign lord, Sir Arthur of England, that illustrious man, for he is in this empire, as noble men tell me—warring to the east with awful knights.'

'From whom comest thou, bold man,' quoth the king then, 'who knowest King Arthur and his knights also? Wert thou ever in his court while he was in his own country? Thou speakest so kindly, it comforts my heart: for well art thou come and wisely dost thou seek him, for thou art a British knight as I know by thy broad speech.'

'I ought to know the king, he is my noble lord, and I am called in his court a knight of his chamber: Sir Cradock was I called in his fair court, keeper of Carleon under the king himself. Now I am driven out of the kingdom, with sorrow in my heart, and that castle hath been taken by foul men.' Then the noble king caught him in his arms, brushed off his helmet and kissed him full soon, and said, 'Welcome, Sir Cradock, as Christ is my help: my dear cousin by birth, thou chillest my heart, how fares it in Britain with all my bold men? Are they destroying or destroyed or altogether killed? Tell thou me kindly all that hath befallen, I have no need to doubt thee, for I know thee to be true.' 'Sir, thy warden is wicked and wild in his deeds, for he hath wrought much sorrow since thou passed out of the country. He hath taken castles and

crowned himself, and seized all the rents of the Round Table: he hath
divided the realm and dealt it out as he liked, he hath dubbed the Danes
dukes and earls, and spread them over all parts, and hath destroyed
cities: Saracens and Saxons on all parts he hath assembled a court of
strange men, sovereigns of Surgenale, and many soldiers of the Picts
and Pagans and proved knights of Ireland and Orgaile, outlawed men:
all those men are knights that lived in the mountains and have leading
and lordship as they like best. And Sir Childrike is held a chieftain
there; that same chivalrous man oppresses thy people: he robs thy
monks and ravishes thy nuns and ever rides with his host to tax the
poor people. From the Humber to Hawick he holds his own and all
the county of Kent is his by treaty: the fair castles that belong to the
crown, the woods and fair forests and the sea shores—all that Hengist
and Horsa held in their time. At Southampton on the sea there are seven
score ships, filled with fierce folk out of far lands, to fight with thy men
when thou assailest them. But yet another word truly, as yet thou
knowest not the worst: he hath wedded Gaynor and holds her his wife
and dwells in the wild bounds of the west marches and hath wrought
her with child as witnesses tell. Of all the men of this earth, he was
most unworthy as a guardian to keep women! Thus hath Sir Mordrede
marred us all! Wherefore have I come over these mountains to tell thee
the truth.'

Then the valiant king for sorrow in his heart and for the cureless woe
became pale. 'By the rod,' said the king, 'I shall revenge it; he shall
repent full swiftly for all his foul deeds.' All weeping for woe he went
to his tent: then sadly the wise king awakened his men, called together
with the trumpet kings and others, calls them to council and told them
of what had befallen:

'I am betrayed by treason, for all my true deed, and all my work is
overthrown; it chances no better. He shall misfortune meet who wrought
this treason an I may surely take him—as I am a true lord. This is
Modrede the man that I most trusted; he hath taken my castles and
crowned himself with the rents and riches of the Round Table: he hath
made all his retinue of renegade wretches and divided up my realm
to various lords—to soldiers and Saracens from far lands. He hath wedded Gaynor and holdeth her to wife, and a child is conceived—so my
misfortune will have it. They have gathered on the sea shore seven score
ships full of fierce folk to fight with me. Wherefore to Great Britain
we must set out to destroy the man that hath caused us this evil. No
bold men shall go save those on fresh horses and well tested in battle,
the flower of my knights: Sir Howell and Sir Hardolfe shall here remain
to be lords of the men that belong to me here: to take charge of Lom-
bardy that no man rise against me, and to take heed of Tuscany carefully as I bid them: to receive the rents of Rome when they are counted
out: to note the day when they were assigned to be brought, or else

all the hostages without—the walls shall be hung straightway all together on high.'

THE DEATH OF ARTHUR

Sir Mordrede the Malebranche with all his folk now comes on the field the more to our danger, for he had him himself behind within the edge of the wood. He had seen the encounter right through to the end how our chivalrous men had fared in the chance of arms, he knew that our folk were overcome and left for dead, to encounter the king he soon found his way. But the craven wretch had changed his arms: he had truly abandoned the saltier engrailed and taken up three lions all of bright silver passant on purple with rich precious stones so that the king should not recognise the cowardly cur: by reason of his cowardice he cast off his attire: but the goodly king knew him full soon and speaks to Sir Cador these kindly words—

'I see the traitor coming yonder full eagerly: yon fellow with the lions is like to himself. Evil shall betide him if I may reach him for all his treason and treachery as I am a true lord! To-day Clarente and Caliburne shall meet together to test which is keener in cutting or harder of edge: we shall test fine steel upon fine armour. That Clarente was my daintiest darling sword and held full dear, kept for the coronations of anointed kings: on days when I dubbed dukes and earls, it was boldly carried by its bright hilt: I never durst soil it in deeds of arms, but ever kept it clean for my own use. But I see Clarente unsheathed—the crown of all swords—my wardrobe at Wallingford, I wot, is destroyed: for no man knew of it save Gaynor herself, and she had the keeping of that noble weapon and of the closed coffers with the crown jewels, the rings and the relics and the regalia of France which was found on Sir Froll when he lay dead.' Then Sir Marrate in anger meets Sir Mordrede with an armoured mace, he strikes at him mightily: the border of his headpiece he burst asunder so that the bright red blood runs over his coat of mail. The man flinches at the blow and turns pale, but yet he waits like a bear and grimly strikes at him. He draws out a sword that is brighter than silver: it was Sir Arthur's own and Uter his father's; in the wardrobe at Wallingford it used to be kept: therewith the vile dog reaches him such a blow that the other withdrew afar off and durst do nought else; for Sir Marrate was a man marred by age and Sir Mordrede was mighty and in his greatrest strength: no man, in knight or other, might come within the reach of that sword but would lose his life-blood. Our prince perceives this and strikes his way through the crowd by force of his arm, meets with Sir Mordrede and cries out fiercely—

'Turn, false traitor: thou deservest no better: by great God thou shalt die by the force of my hands! No man nor riches of this world shall rescue thee.' The king strikes him knightly with Caliburn, the corner of the bright shield he cuts asunder and into the man's shoulder the width of a span so that the bright red blood could be seen on the mail. He shudders and shrinks but retreats but little and rushes forward quickly in his bright garments: then the felon with his fine sword strikes out sharply and cuts asunder the loins on the far side through the tunic and splint armour of the fair coat of mail; he pierces through Arthur's flesh half a foot long: that dread blow was his death, the greater the pity that ever such a doughty man should die save at God's will. Yet with Caliburn his sword full knightly he strikes, thrusts forward his bright shield and covers himself: then he sweeps off the sword hand of Mordrede as he glances by, an inch from the elbow, he hacks it asunder so that he swoons on the grass and falls in a faint. Through the arm covering and bright mail he was so cut that the sword hilt and the hand lie on the grass. Then speedily our man pulls off his front armour and thrusts him through with his sword to its bright hilt so that he sprawls on the ground and sinks down to die.

'In truth,' said the dying king, 'it seemeth wrong to me that such a false thief should have so fair an end.' When they had finished this fight, then was the field won and the false folk are left for death upon the grass: to the forest some of them fled and hid in the groves and our fierce fighting folk follow after them: they hunt and hew down these heathen dogs and slay in the mountains Sir Mordrede's knights: there escaped no Childe nor chieftain nor other, but they are all chopped down in the chase without pity.

But when Sir Arthur anon finds Sir Ewayne and noble Sir Errate and other great lords, he takes up Sir Cador with sorrow in his heart, Sir Clegis, Sir Cleremonde those fair men-at-arms, Sir Lothe and Sir Lyonell, Sir Lancelot and Lowes, Marrake and Meneduke that were every mighty; with sorrow he lays them together on the ground and looks at their bodies, and with a loud voice as one that wished to die and has lost his joy, then is distracted as one made and all his strength fails: he looks up aloft and all his face turns pale: down he falls full soon and sinks in a swoon, but he rises on his knees and cries full often—

'Fair king with thy crown, I am left in sorrow: for all my lords in the land have been slain! They who did me honour by grace of God and upheld my manhood by the might of their arms, made me great in the world and master in earth: in a direful time the mishap took place, that I, for a traitor, have lost all my true lords. Here rests the rich blood of the Round Table, overthrown by a rebel, the greater the pity! I may now helpless rest on this heath like a woeful widow that hath lost her lord. I may sorrow and weep and wring my hands for my wisdom and honour is past for ever. Of all lords now I take leave till my death: here is the blood of Britons loosely killed, and now on this day my joy is ended for ever.'

Then gather together all the men of the Round Table, to that noble king they all ride: then assemble together full seven score knights in the sight of their sovereign that was left wounded. Then kneels the crowned king and cries aloud—

'I thank thee, God, for thy grace, with a good will that thou gavest us strength and wisdom to conquer those men and hast granted us the victory over those great lords! He never sent us shame nor any ignominy on this earth, but ever gave us the upper hand over all other kings: we have no time now to follow up these lords for yon bold man hath wounded me full sore. Let us go to Glastonbury; nothing else will be of use to us. There we may rest in peace and see to our wounds. For this good day's work may God be praised for he hath thus destined and decreed that we should die among our own men.' Then they carry out his commands at once and go to Glastonbury by the shortest road: they reach the Isle of Aveloyne and Arthur alights there: he goes to a manor for he could go no further. A surgeon of Salerno examines his wounds and the king sees by the examination that he can never be whole again, and soon to his faithful men he says these words—'Do ye call me a confessor with Christ in his hands: I shall receive the sacrament in haste whatever betides: Constantine my cousin shall bear the crown as it falls to him by kinship if Christ will allow him. Man, for my blessing, bury those knights that in battle were killed with swords: and thereafter go straight to Mordrede's children and see that they be slain privily and cast into the water: let no wicked weed wax nor flourish on this earth: I warn thee for thy honour do as I bid thee! I forgive all wrongs for the love of Christ in Heaven: if Gaynor hath wrought well, may it well betide her!' He said *In Manus* boldly on the place where he lay and thus passed away his spirit and he spake no more. The baronage of Britain then, bishops and others go to Glastonbury with sorrowful hearts to bury their bold king and put him in the earth with all the honour and profusion that was due to him. Fiercely rang the bells and toiled his *Requiem*, they sang masses and matins with mournful notes: holy men dressed in their rich robes, pontificates and prelates in their precious garments, dukes and knights in their mourning clothes, countesses kneeling and clasping their hands, ladies languishing and downcast to see: all were arrayed in black, women and others that were seen at the burial with flowing tears: never was so pitiful a scene in their time! Thus died King Arthur, as authors allege, who was of Hector's blood the king's son of Troy and of Sir Priamus the Prince praised on earth; from thence all his bold ancestors brought the Britons into Great Britain as the *Brut* tells us.

etc. explicit.

Here lies Arthur a king that was and will be.
Here endes 'Morte Arthure' written by
Robert of Thornton.

R. Thornton aforesaid who wrote this, may he be blessed of God. Amen!

Chapter 21.
Beyond the Blue Septentrions
by Fiona MacLeod

Fiona MacLeod was the pseudonym adopted by writer William Sharp (1855-1905). This choice of a female persona gave him the freedom he sought to reach the into the deepest levels of his subconscious, where he found a 'dream-self' who taught him the mysteries of the Celtic folk-soul and enabled him to write a series of strange and wonderful books. They are filled with the spirit of the Western Highlands where he had spent much of his childhood among Gaelic-speaking fishermen and shepherds, and with something more—a strange, mysterious sense of the Otherworldly which seems always to imbue his writing, whether it be of the inner history of the island of Iona, or the haunting tales, spun from the world of the imagination, of which 'Beyond the Blue Septentrions' is one of the finest.

It makes a fitting conclusion to this selection in being a 'new' legend of Arthur which yet contains the seeds of all the most ancient tales and myths which surround him. Of the star-lore hidden within the Arthurian mythos little has yet been written; yet there is much to be discovered still, which once it is known will throw much light upon the ultimate mysteries of the Matter of Britain. Perhaps indeed someone who reads this story will find therein clues to their own search which will lead them to see further. There will always be those who add to the legends, as long as there are those who wish to hear the stories of Arthur and his times.

❦

A LEGEND OF THE POLAR STARS

The Star Septentrion is, for the peoples of the North and above all for the shepherd, the seaman and the wayfarer, the star of stars. A hundred legends embody its mystery, its steadfast incalculable service, its unswerving isolation over the Pole. Polaris, the North Star, the Pole Star, the Lodestar, the Seaman's Star, the Star of the Sea, the Gate of Heaven, Phoenice, Cynosure, how many names, in all languages, at all times. The Mongolian nomad called it the Imperial Ruler of Heaven: the Himalayan shepherd, Grahadāra, the Pivot of the Planets: the Arab knows it as the Torch of Prayer, burning for ever at the portal of the heavenly Mecca. It shines through all literature, since (and indeed long before) Euripides wrote his superb verse of how the two great North-ern constellations which encircle Polaris, Ursa Major and Ursa Minor, the two 'swift-wandering' Bears, 'guard the Atlantean Pole', till a poet of our own time wrote the less majestic but not less lovely line relating to these constellations which gives the title to this paper. In all ages, too, the dreaming mind of man has imagined here the Throne of the Gods, the Seat of the Mighty, the last Portal of the Unknown. It is the Flatheansas of our Gaelic ancestors, the ultimate goal of the heroic spirit: the Himinbiorg, or Hill of Heaven, of the Norsemen of old, and the abode of Heimdallr, the guardian of the bridge Bifröst (the Rainbow) which unites Asgard the Everlasting with that brief whirling phantom, the Earth. It is Albordy, 'the dazzling mountain on which was held the Assembly of the Gods' of the ancient Teutonic peoples: the mysterious Mount Mēru, the seat of the gods, of the Aryan dreamers of old, and the Hindu sages of later time: 'the holy mountain of God' alluded to in Ezekiel—so, at least, it has been surmised.

'The blue Septentrions'. . . Boötes with Arcturus, the Great Bear, the Lesser Bear, the Pointers or the Northern Hounds, the North Star. . . what legend, what poetry, what romance, what wonder belongs to these stars and constellations which guard the marches of the Arctic North. To the mass of what is already extant, what need to add further matter? And yet there is ever new justification in that continual need of the soul to hear over and over again, and in ever-varying ways, even the most fragmentary runes or sagas of this unfathomably mysterious stellar universe which encloses us with Silence and Beauty and Wonder, the three Veils of God—as the Hebridean isleman, the Irish Gael of the dreaming west, and the Arab of the Desert alike have it.

I have elsewhere spoken of the legendary association of Arthur (the Celtic-British King and the earlier mythical Arthur, semi-divine, and at last remote and celestial) with Arcturus, that lovely Lamp of the North, the glory of Boötes. But now, I may add what there I had to omit.

In all European lands, and above all in the country of the West, there is none without its legend of King Arthur. The Bretons claim him as theirs, and the places of his passage and exploit are familiar, though only the echo, only the phantom of a great fame ever reached Arvôr. In the Channel and Scilly Isles the story runs that there is Lyonesse, and that Arthur sleeps in a cavern of the seas. The Cornish folk and their kindred of Somerset and Devon believe there is not a rood of ground between Camelot and Tintagel where the great King has not dwelt or passed. Wales calls him her son, and his chivalry her children, and the Cymric poets of a thousand mabinogion have sung his heroic fame. Clydesdale, that more ancient home of the Cymri, has dim memories older than what Taliesin sang: Arthur's Seat hangs above Edinburgh, a city so old that a thousand years go its earlier name was forgotten; and from the Sidlaw to the Ochil, from blue Demyat to grey Schiehallion, old names and broken tradition preserve the obscure trails of a memory fallen into oblivion, but not so fallen that the names of Arthur and Queen Guinevere and wild-eyed Merlin of the Woods have ceased to stir the minds of the few who still care for the things that moved our fathers from generation to generation. The snows of the Grampians have not stayed the wandering tale: and there are still a few old people who recall at times, in the winter story-telling before farm-kitchen fires, how the fierce Modred, King of the North, made Queen Gwannolê his own, and how later, in a savage revenge, Arthur condemned her to be torn asunder by wild horses. Lancelot passes from the tale before it crosses the Border, and as it goes north (or is it not that as it comes south?) Merlin is no more a courtier but a wild sooth-sayer of the woods, Queen Wanders or Gwannolê or Guinevere is tame-less as a hawk, and Arthur himself, though a hero and great among his kind, is of the lineage of fire and sword.

Where is Joyeuse Gard? Some say it is in the isle Avillion off the Bre-ton shore: some that it is in Avalon, under the sacred hill of Glaston-bury: some that it is wet with the foam of Cornish Seas: others aver that it lies in fathomless silence under the sundown wandering wave and plunging tide. Another legend tells that it leaned once upon the sea from lost haven under Berwick Law, perhaps where North Berwick now is, or where Dirleton looks across to Fidra, or where the seamews on ruined Tantallon scream to the Bass.

Arthur himself has a sleeping-place (for nowhere is he dead, but sleeps, awaiting a trumpet-call) in 'a lost land' in Provence, in Spain, under the waters of the Rhine. Today one may hear from Calabrian shepherd, or Sicilian fisherman, that the Great King sleeps in a deep hollow underneath the Straits of Messina. And strangest of all (if not a new myth of the dreaming imagination, for I have not been able to trace the legend beyond a modern Slavonic ballad) among the Car-pathian Highlands is a nameless ancient tomb lost in a pine-forest, where at mid-winter a bear has been seen to rise, walking erect like a man, crowned with a crown of iron and gold holding a single shin-ing stone magnificent as the Pole Star, and crying in a deep voice, '*I am Arthur of the West, who shall yet be king of the World.*'

Strange indeed, for here among the débris of the lost history of Arthur—that vast shadowy kingly figure whose only kingdom may have been the soul of primitive races, and whose sword may have been none other than the imagination that is for ever on its beautiful and perilous quest—here among that débris of legend scattered backward from the realms of the north across Europe is one, remote as it is, which brings us back to the early astronomical myth that identifies the great Celtic champion with the chief constellation of the north.

But as I have heard this fragment of our old lost mythology related in a way I have not seen in any book, I will give it here altered but slightly if at all from one of the countless legends told to me in my childhood.

At sunset the young son of the great King Pendragon came over the brow of a hill that stepped forward from a dark company of moun-

tains and leaned over the shoreless sea which fills the west and drowns
the north. All day he had been wandering alone, his mind heavy with
wonder over many things. He had heard strange tales of late, tales about
his heroic father and the royal clan, and how they were not as other
men, but half divine. They were not gods, he knew, for they could be
slain in battle or could die with the crowding upon them of many years:
but they were more terrible in battle than were the greatest of men,
and they had vision and knowledge beyond the vision and knowledge
of the druids, and were lordly beyond all men in mien and the beauty
of courtesy, and lived beyond the common span of years, and had secret
communion with the noble and invisible company. He had heard, too,
of his destiny: that he, too, was to be a great king, as much greater
than Pendragon, than Pendragon was above all the kings of the world.
What was Destiny, he wondered. Then, again, he turned over and over
in his mind all the names he could think of that he might choose for
his own: for the time was come for him to put away the name of his
childhood and to take on that by which he should be known among
men.

He came over the brow of the hill, and out of the way of the mountain-
wind, and, being tired, lay down among the heather and stared across
the grey wilderness of the sea. The sun set, and the invisible throwers
of the nets trailed darkness across the waves and up the wild shores
and over the faces of the cliffs. Stars climbed out of shadowy abysses,
and the great chariots of the constellations rode from the west to the
east and from the north to the south. His eyes closed, but when he
opened them again to see if a star quivering on the verge of the horizon
had in that brief moment sprung like a deer above the drowning wave
or had sunk like a white seabird passing out of sight, he saw a great
and kingly figure standing beside him. So great in stature, so splendid
in kingly beauty was the mysterious one who had so silently joined
him, that the thought this must be one of the gods.

'Do you know me, my son?' said the kingly stranger.

The boy looked at him in awe and wonder, but unrecognizingly.

'Do you not know me, my son?' he heard again... 'for I am your
father Pendragon. But my home is yonder, and there I go before long,
and that is why I have come to you as a vision in a dream...' and,
as he spoke, he pointed to the constellation of the *Arth*, or Bear, which
nightly prowls through the vast abysses of the polar sky.

When the boy turned his gaze from the great constellation which hung
in the dark wilderness overhead, he saw that he was alone again. While
he yet wondered in great awe at what he had seen and heard, he felt
himself float like a mist and become like a cloud, and, as a cloud, rise
beyond the brows of the hills, and ascend the invisible stairways of the
sky.

When for minutes that were as hours he had moved thus mysteri-

346 An Arthurian Reader

ously into the pathless and unvisited realms of the air, he saw that he had left the highest clouds like dust on a valley-road after one has climbed to the summit of a mountain; nor could he see the earth save as a blind and obscure thing that moved between the twilights of night and dawn.

It seemed to him thereafter that a swoon came over him, in which he passed beyond the far-off blazing fires of strange stars. At last, suddenly, he stood on the verge of Arth, or Arth Uthyr, the Great Bear. There he saw, with the vision of immortal not of mortal eyes, a company of most noble and majestic figures seated at what he thought a circular abyss but which had the semblance of a vast table. Each of these seven great knights or lordly kings had a star upon his forehead, and these were the stars of the mighty constellation of the Bear which the boy had seen night after night from his home among the mountains by the sea.

It was with a burning throb at his heart that he recognized in the King of all these kings no other than himself.

While he looked, in amazement so great that he could hear the pulse of his heart, as in the silence of a wood one hears the tapping of a woodpecker, he saw this mighty phantom-self rise till he stood towering over all there, and heard a voice as though an ocean rose and fell through the eternal silences.

'Comrades in God,' it said, 'the time is come when that which is great shall become small.'

And when the voice was ended, the mighty figure faded into the blue darkness, and only a great star shone where the uplifted dragonhelm had brushed the roof of heaven. One by one the white lords of the sky followed in his mysterious way, till once more were to be seen only the stars of the Bear.

The boy-king dreamed that he fell as a falling meteor, and then that he floated over land and sea as a cloud, and then that he sank as mist upon the hills of his own land.

A noise of wind stirred in his ears, and he felt the chill drew creep over his hands like the stealthy cold lip of the tide. He rose stumblingly, and stood, staring around him. He was on the same spot, under the brow of the hill that looked over the dim shoreless seas, now obscure with the dusk. He glanced upward and saw the stars of the Great Bear in their slow majestic march round the Pole. Then he remembered.

He went slowly down the hillside, his mind heavy with thought. When he was come to the place of the King his father, lo, Pendragon and all his fierce chivalry came out to meet him, for the archdruid had foretold that the great King to be had received his mystic initiation among the holy silence of the hills.

'I am no more Snowbird the child,' the boy said, looking at them fearlessly, and as though already King. 'Henceforth I am Arth-Urthyr.[1] for my place is in the great Bear which we see yonder in the north.'

So all there acclaimed him as Arthur, the wondrous one of the stars, the Great Bear.

'I am old,' said Pendragon, 'and soon you shall be King, Arthur, my son. So ask now a great boon of me and it shall be granted to you.'

Then Arthur remembered his dream.

'Father and King,' he said, 'when I am King after you I shall make a new order of knights, who shall be strong and pure as the Immortal Ones, and be tender as women, and simple as little children. But first I ask of you seven flawless virgin knights to be of my chosen company. To-morrow let the woodwrights make for me a round daïs or table such as that where we eat our roasted meats and drink from the ale-horns, but round and of a size whereat I and my chosen knights may sit at ease.'

The King listened, and all there.

'So be it,' said the King.

Then Arthur chose the seven flawless virgin knights, and called them to him.

'Ye are now Children of the Great Bear,' he said, 'and comrades and liegemen to me, Arthur, who shall be King of the West. And ye shall be known as the Knights of the Round Table. But no man shall make a mock of that name and live: and in the end that name shall be so great in the mouths and minds of men that they shall consider no glory of the world to be so great as to be the youngest and frailest of that knighthood.'

And that is how Arthur, the son of Pendragon, who three years later became King of the West, read the Rune of the Stars that are called

Figure 17: 'The Shadow of Coegfran' by Fred Richards.

the Great Bear and took their name upon him, and from the strongest and purest and noblest of the land made Knighthood, such as the world had not seen, such as the world since has not known.

---

[1] Pronounced *Arth-Uir*, or *Arth-Ur*. In ancient British *Arth* means Bear, and *Utyr* great, wondrous.

Bibliography

Source books

Karr, Phyllis Ann, *The King Arthur Companion*, New York, Chaosium Inc., 1983.

Lacy, Norris, J. (ed.), *The Arthurian Encyclopedia*, New York, Garland Press, 1986.

Pickford, C. E. & Last, R. W., *The Arthurian Bibliography* vols. 1-3, Cambridge, Boydell and Brewer, 1981-88.

Reiss, E., Reiss, L. H. & Taylor, B. (eds.), *Arthurian Legend and Literature: An Annotated Bibliography*, New York, Garland Press, 1984.

Texts

The Alliterative Morte Arthure, trans. V. Krishna, University Press of America, 1983.

Didot Perceval, trans. Dell Skeels, Washington University Press, 1966.

The English Merlin, ed. H. B. Wheatley (2 vols), reprinted Greenwood Press, 1969.

Historia Regnum Brittaniae, Geoffrey of Monmouth, trans. S. Evans, Dent, 1912.

Lais of Marie de France, trans. G. S. Burford & K. Busby, Harmondsworth, Penguin, 1987.

The Mabinogion, trans. Lady Charlotte Guest, John Jones, 1977.

Morte d'Arthur, Sir Thomas Malory, University Books, New York, 1966.

Parzival, Wolfram von Eschenbach, trans. A. T. Hatto, Harmondsworth, Penguin, 1980.

Perceval, Chrétien de Troyes, trans. N. Bryant, Cambridge, Boydell & Brewer, 1982.

Perlesvaus (The High History of the Holy Grail), trans. N. Bryant, Cambridge, Boydell and Brewer, 1983.

The Quest for the Grail, trans. P. Matarasso, Harmondsworth, Penguin, 1969.

The Rise of Gawain, Nephew of Arthur, trans. Mildred Leake Day, New York, Garland Press, 1986.

Y Seint Greal, ed. & trans. R. Williams, Jones(Wales) Ltd, 1986.

Sir Gawain and the Green Knight, trans. J. R. R. Tolkien, London, Allen & Unwin, 1975.

Vita Merlini, Geoffrey of Monmouth, trans. B. Clarke, Cardiff, University of Wales Press, 1976.

Works by contributors to this volume

Closs, Hannah, *Deep are the Valleys*, Vanguard Press, 1963.
——*High are the Mountains*, Vanguard Press, 1963.
——'The Meeting of the Waters' in *At the Table of the Grail*, ed. John Matthews, London, Arkana, 1987.
——*The Silent Tarn*, Vanguard Press, 1963.
——*Tristan*, Vanguard Press, 1976.
Frankland, Edward, *The Bear of Britain*, London, Macdonald, 1940.
Machen, Arthur, *The Hills of Dreams*, A. Barker, 1968.
Macleod, Fiona, *The Dominian of Dreams*, London, Heinemann, 1912.
——*Iona*, Edinburgh, Floris Classics, 1982.
——*Pharias*, London, Heinemann, 1927.
——*The Washer of the Ford*, London, Heinemann, 1927.
Rolt-Wheeler, Francis, *Mystic Gleams from the Holy Grail*, London, Rider, (n.d.).
Stein, Walter, Weltgeschichte im Lichte Des Heiligen Gral (The Grail in the 8th century) J. C. Mellinger, 1986.
Waite, A. E.., *The Hidden Church of the Holy Grail*, Rebman, 1909.
Weston, J. L., *From Ritual to Romance*, New York, Doubleday, 1957.
——*Legends of Sir Lancelot du Lac*, David Nutt, 1901.
——*The Legend of Sir Perceval* (2 vols), David Nutt, 1906.
——The *Quest of the Holy Grail*, Bell, 1913.

Further Reading

Anderson, Flavia, *The Ancient Secret*, Thorsons/R.I.L.K.O., 1987.
Heywood, Thomas, *The Life of Merlin*, Jones(Wales) Ltd, 1987.
Jung, Emma, & Von Franz, M. L. *The Grail Legend*, Element Books, 1987.
Knight, Stephen, *Arthurian Literature and Society*, Macmillan.
Loomis, R. S. (ed.) *Arthurian Literature in the Middle Ages*, Oxford University Press, 1969.
——*Development of Arthurian Romance*, New York, W. W. Naughton, 1963.
Massingham, H., *Downland Man*, J. Cape, 1926.
Markale, Jean, *King Arthur, King of Kings*, Gordon Cremonesi, 1977.
Matthews, Caitlín, *Arthur and the Sovereignty of Britain: King and Goddess in the Mabinogion*, London, Arkana, 1989.
——*Mabon and the Mysteries of Britain: an Exploration of the Mabinogion*, London, Arkana, 1987.
Matthews, John, *The Grail: Quest for the Eternal*, London, Thames & Hudson, 1981.

——(ed.) *At the Table of the Grail*, London, Arkana, 1987.

——, & Matthews, Caitlín, *The Aquarian Guide to British Myth and Legend*, Wellingborough, Aquarian Press, 1988.

——, & Green, Marian, *The Grail-Seeker's Companion*, Wellingborough, Aquarian Press, 1986.

——, & Stewart, Bob, *Warriors of Arthur*, Poole, Blandford Press, 1987.

Senior, Michael, *Myths of Britain*, Orbis, 1979.

Stewart, R. J. *The Mystic Life of Merlin*, London, Arakana, 1986.

——*The Prophetic Vision of Merlin*, London, Arkana, 1986.

A Celtic Reader
Selections from Celtic Legend, Scholarship and Story
Compiled and edited by John Matthews
Foreword by P.L. Travers

From the rich array of history, religion, myth and story that makes up the Celtic tradition, John Matthews brings together here a selection of writings which takes the reader on a fascinating journey through distant realms.

As in *An Arthurian Reader*, he has sought out lesser-known and unusual sources rather than presenting those more generally available. This collection of lore, life and literature sets forth the Celtic world, from the Druidic priesthood and rites to the bardic heritage, from the distant origins of the Celtic peoples to the colour and drama of their culture. Tales of adventure, magic, mystery and wonder from pre-Christian Ireland and Arthurian Britain interweave with ancient fables, Taliesin's poetry, excerpts from *The Mabinogion*, historical investigations into the ancient past and modern adaptations of ancient themes. Combining the talents of authors like Iolo Morgannwg, Thomas Samuel Jones, Ross Nichols and 'A.E.', the result is a glowing tapestry of Celtic life.

Through this carefully-selected anthology, the reader is taken back to the ages of myth and legend and drawn into the remarkable and mysterious Celtic culture which gave rise to unforgettable art, intricate jewel-like myth and stories of gods, heroes and monsters. Fine drawings and engravings from a variety of artists are interspersed throughout, illustrating every aspect of the Celtic heritage.